Writing That Works
How to Write Effectively on the Job

Writing That Works
How to Write Effectively on the Job

Walter E. Oliu
U.S. Nuclear Regulatory Commission

Charles T. Brusaw
NCR Corporation

Gerald J. Alred
University of Wisconsin—Milwaukee

St. Martin's Press
New York

Acknowledgments

BIOSPHERICS, INC., for business letters on pp. 227–228.

POPULAR SCIENCE for passage on windmills, p. 29. Reprinted from *Popular Science* with permission © 1979 Times Mirror Magazines, Inc.

RANDOM HOUSE, INC., for sample dictionary entry, p. 146. Reproduced by permission from *The Random House College Dictionary,* Revised Edition. Copyright © 1975, 1979 by Random House, Inc.

READERS' GUIDE TO PERIODICAL LITERATURE for sample entry, p. 239. Copyright © 1976, 1977 by The H. W. Wilson Company. Material reproduced by permission of the publisher.

Preface

Writing That Works is designed for students of varied academic backgrounds and occupational interests whose jobs will, or already do, require writing skills. The approach taken here to strengthening those skills is as practical as the tasks to which the skills will be applied. Each chapter provides abundant and realistic examples drawn from a wide range of occupations, as well as carefully structured exercises and writing assignments. The text is unusually comprehensive, and probably few instructors will wish to assign every chapter. We have built into the book sufficient flexibility to enable instructors to choose the sections they consider most important for any particular class. At the same time, we feel that a text such as this should be made inclusive enough to serve as a reference tool for the student long after the course is over, since no course can possibly cover all the writing concerns students will encounter once they are actually on the job.

An important feature of the text is that it allows the student to write complete assignments at the outset, when motivation is highest. Three brief chapters at the beginning guide the student through all the steps in the writing process—planning, writing, and revising—with special emphasis on the questions writers must ask as they approach any writing task: What is my purpose in writing? For whom is the writing intended? How much information must I include? By page 27 the student is familiar with the principles of effective paragraph writing, including transition between paragraphs and successful openings and closings. And by page 47 the student has been introduced to the essentials of revision—the objective evaluation of one's own writing for its accuracy, completeness, grammatical correctness, and physical appearance.

Chapters 4 and 5 go on to present the range of rhetorical strategies that should be a part of every writer's basic equipment. Chapter 4 considers techniques for arranging information and ideas into a meaningful whole—by steps, by time or space, by order of importance, and by degree of specificity. Each approach is illustrated with an example taken from an occupational context. The importance of establishing one's purpose is reinforced in Chapter 5, which presents various methods of development: process explanation, description, comparison, division and classification, definition, and cause and effect. The chapter concludes with a discussion of persuasiveness. Again, each rhetorical method is illustrated by one or more job-related examples.

Chapters 6 and 7 focus on the writer's choices in constructing effective sentences and on ways of achieving precision and conciseness, especially by the careful selection of words and the avoidance of inappropriate jargon. Chapters 8 and 9, on spelling and vocabulary building, are designed for either classroom use or independent study. Both chapters are broken into segments that can serve as the basis for periodic assignments throughout the course. Thus, as the term progresses, students can gain increased competence in fundamental language skills that should enhance the composition skills they are also developing.

These first nine chapters, then, may be thought of as dealing with the skills and strategies basic to all writing, regardless of the particular documentary form it may take in the context of a specific job and writing situation. The remaining eight chapters apply these skills and strategies to specific types of on-the-job communication, starting with letters and memorandums, in Chapter 10, and going on through the most common types of informal and formal reports, methods of doing research (including interviewing and the design and use of questionnaires), and various other kinds of specialized communication: internal and external proposals, job descriptions, minutes of meetings, and the design of business forms. Chapter 15 takes up the preparation of tables, charts, and other visual aides. Chapter 16 discusses not only the preparation and delivery of oral presentations but also a vitally important skill that is too often ignored: effective listening. The last text chapter is a step-by-step, highly practical guide to job seeking, with an emphasis on the preparation of effective résumés and of application and follow-up letters. Sample résumés are provided both for students who have had little or no job experience and for those who may have had a great deal of experience.

Finally, in line with its utilitarian approach, *Writing That Works* includes a highly accessible, seventy-five-page Handbook of grammar, composition, and punctuation. The Handbook is based on materials drawn from the same authors' *Handbook of Technical Writing* and *The Business Writer's Handbook* (both published by St. Martin's Press).

We would like to acknowledge the help of the following people during the preparation of the manuscript: Diana C. Reep, Holy Redeemer College; Jerre Collins, Janet Jesmok, and Cynthia V. Sommer, of the University of Wisconsin—Milwaukee; and Bonnie Ewing, Judy Boerger, and Carolyn Brown, all of Good Samaritan Hospital in Dayton, Ohio. We are deeply indebted, as well, to a number of excellent critics whose anonymous comments and suggestions were solicited by St. Martin's Press during the development of the manuscript. In addition, we would like to express our appreciation for the valuable assistance of Nancy Perry and Susan Joseph, of St. Martin's Press. Finally, any acknowledgment would be incomplete without special thanks to Thomas V. Broadbent, director of the College Department of St. Martin's, for his guidance in matters large and small connected with this text.

Walter E. Oliu
Charles T. Brusaw
Gerald J. Alred

Contents

Writing That Works

How to Write Effectively on the Job

1

Before Writing

Christine Thomas was aware of a problem at the Riply Advertising Agency. As an administrative assistant, Christine often typed standardized letters over and over so that every recipient would get a freshly typed copy. At times, the number of copies she typed ran into the hundreds. Christine's supervisor, Harriet Sullivan, often hired temporary secretarial help and rented extra typewriters to meet the deadlines. But the use of temporary help and the pressure of meeting the deadlines brought the normal office routine to a halt until all the letters were typed and mailed. Realizing that the problem would grow worse as the number of direct mailings increased, Christine decided to search for a solution.

Christine had heard about several types of automated typing systems, but she knew little about them. So she sought the advice of an instructor of office systems at the local community college she was attending part-time. The instructor told Christine about the Bently XL-100 System, which used convenient magnetic-coded cards and could type repetitive material four times as fast as a human typist. The instructor even gave her the name and address of the manufacturer of the Bently XL-100. Christine wrote a letter to the manufacturer asking for information and, while she waited for a reply, gathered some facts about the cost of temporary help and rental typewriters.

Finally, with all the information at hand and entirely convinced of the value of her suggestion, Christine wrote the following memo to Harriet Sullivan, the office manager:

1

MEMORANDUM

To: Harriet Sullivan
From: Christine Thomas
Date: December 3, 19--
Subject: Purchase of a Bently XL-100 System

The number of direct mailings that require each recipient to receive an original copy is increasing. Every time we call in temporary help to get out such a mailing, the result is much confusion and many frayed nerves. In addition, the expense is great, and the normal office work does not get done.

A Bently XL-100 System could do the same job, at less cost, without disturbing the normal office routine.

Please consider my suggestion that we purchase a Bently XL-100 System.

Two days later, Christine's memo was returned to her with the note "Not practical for our small volume" written across the bottom.

Christine was not only disappointed but also puzzled. She knew that the solution she had offered was practical because she had checked all the facts before writing the memo. Yet she had failed to convince Harriet.

In writing her memo, Christine committed the most common of all mistakes made by people who write on their jobs: she overlooked the needs of her reader and lost sight of the purpose of her memo. Christine had been so convinced of the rightness of her solution that she forgot that her reader needed to be convinced with the same facts that had convinced her. Had she kept her reader and her purpose clearly in mind, Christine might have succeeded in getting her automated typing system.

Chuck Milton sat at his desk chewing on a pencil. It was 1:00 in the afternoon, and he had been sitting there since 9:00 A.M. After drinking three cups of coffee, cleaning his desk, and passing up two invitations to go out for lunch, he finally gave in to an uncontrollable urge to clean the keys of his typewriter. Nothing he did, however, prompted him to begin writing the circular he had hoped to give his supervisor at the end of the day.

Chuck, a management trainee for a regional chain of hardware stores, had been asked to write a circular for the clerks who worked for the chain. The purpose of the circular was to introduce and explain the metric system to the clerks so that they would be able to answer their customers' questions. Chuck had recently taken a workshop on metrics, and he was anxious to prove himself. But writing was not easy for Chuck. What he needed, he thought, was inspiration.

Unfortunately, Chuck believed the old and persistent myth that writing is the product of inspiration. It is not. Good writing results from knowing how to structure and develop ideas on paper so that they make sense to a reader. And effective structure and development, in turn, require preparation. Chuck had the purpose of his writing and the needs of his readers clearly in mind when he sat down at his desk. If only he had gone ahead and jotted down his main ideas, organized them, and filled in the supporting details, he would not have wasted four valuable hours waiting for inspiration to strike. Preparation, not inspiration, is what Chuck needed.

How do writers prepare? Successful writers do three essential things before they begin to write: they determine their *purpose* for writing, they determine the *needs of their reader,* and they establish their *scope* (the extent to which they will cover the subject to accomplish that purpose with that reader).

DETERMINING YOUR PURPOSE

Everything you write is written for a purpose. You want your reader to know or be able to do something when he or she has finished reading your writing. Determining purpose is the first step in preparing to write, for unless you know what you hope to accomplish by your writing, you cannot possibly know what information your writing should contain.

Purpose, then, gives direction to your writing. And the more precisely you can state your purpose at the outset, the more successful your writing will be. Suppose, for example, that you are going on vacation and a temporary employee will take your place. Your boss tells you to "write about the procedures of your job for your replacement." What would be the purpose of your writing? Although you may be writing only because "my boss told me to write about my job procedures," this is not a precise purpose. Why is it important to write about the procedures? Even to say that your purpose is "to explain my job procedures" is not precise enough. You must go one step further and ask yourself why you must explain the procedures. If you answer that you are writing "to explain the procedures of my job so that my reader (a temporary employee) can function independently in my absence," you now have a precise purpose. With this purpose to guide you, you will include enough detail in your writing to enable the person replacing you to follow the procedures of your job without asking unnecessary questions.

To make sure that your purpose is precise, it is helpful to write a statement of purpose. In most cases, you can use the following pattern to guide you:

My purpose is to _____ so that my reader _____.

This is the pattern that the vacationing employee used:

My purpose is to *explain the procedures of my job* so that my reader (a temporary employee) *can function independently in my absence.*

This pattern is also useful in determining the purposes for other writers described in this chapter.

> *For Christine Thomas:*
> My purpose is to *show the superiority of the Bently XL-100 System to our present typing method* so that my reader (Harriet Sullivan) *will be persuaded to buy it.*

> *For Chuck Milton:*
> My purpose is to *explain the metric system* so that my readers (hardware-store clerks) *will be able to answer their customers' questions about it.*

If Christine Thomas had kept such a purpose clearly in mind as she prepared to write her memo, she would have included the convincing facts (such as the cost of the machine versus the cost of temporary help) for Harriet Sullivan to evaluate. Instead, Christine said only that "a Bently XL-100 System could do the same job, at less cost, without disturbing normal office routine." This statement might have been enough if Christine's purpose had been simply to get Harriet to investigate the Bently XL-100 System, but Christine had already made an investigation. Now she needed to provide the evidence that would convince Harriet to *buy* the new system.

DETERMINING YOUR READER'S NEEDS

If you have stated the purpose of your writing precisely, you are aware that you have a reader. It may sound simpleminded to say that *every* piece of writing has a reader. Yet all too often writers forget their readers and, essentially, write to themselves. Remember that your job as a writer is to express your ideas so clearly that *your reader* cannot fail to understand them. Christine Thomas, for example, did not fully realize that the information she included about the Bently XL-100 System was not sufficient to convince anyone but herself of the system's value.

The point is that when you write, you cannot achieve your purpose unless you provide your reader with sufficient information. The amount and type of information you include depend on the needs of your reader.

To determine the needs of your reader, you must identify *who* your reader is. Keep in mind that different readers have different needs, often depending on their jobs. Operators of equipment, for example, need safety warnings with the instructions that accompany equipment. Buyers of equipment need information about the costs and efficiency of the equipment. And mechanics who repair equipment need explanations of the equipment's working parts. Each of these readers needs a specific kind of information. For your writing to be successful—that is, to achieve your purpose—you must provide your reader with the kind of information he or she needs.

Another consideration in determining the needs of your reader is your reader's knowledge of the subject. A reader who is familiar with your subject will need less detail than a reader who is not. The amount of detail you need to include, therefore, often depends on your reader's training and experience. Specifically, if you are describing a new technique for repairing a vibration dampener to an experienced auto mechanic, you do not need to explain standard terms and procedures of auto repair. But if you are describing the new technique to a car owner who wants to make the repair himself or herself, these terms and procedures require fuller explanation. Your purpose would be the same in both pieces of writing—to describe a new technique for repairing a vibration dampener so that your reader will be able to make the repair. Yet to achieve this purpose, you have to give one reader more information than you give the other.

Always write directly to your reader. If you have more than one reader, as in a report to several people, learn as much as you can about their needs and backgrounds. Then create in your mind a typical person from your group of readers, and imagine that you are writing to only that person. By writing as if to a single reader, you will have less difficulty deciding what information to include in your writing. Chuck Milton, writing to nearly one hundred clerks, could have used this technique to help him get his circular started.

Consider how Chuck could have aimed his writing at his readers. What did he know about his readers? He knew that their experience and training varied. Although some were longtime hardware clerks, many others were college students working part-time. He also knew that his readers were familiar with nonmetric weights and measures because they used them every day. But few of them, his boss had told him, had any knowledge of the metric system. Chuck needed to make the subject understandable for these readers and to emphasize its value to them. By imagining that he was writing to one person who was typical—that is, a person who had limited experience selling hardware, who was familiar with nonmetric weights and measures, and who knew little about the metric system and might be afraid to learn it—Chuck could have written the circular that appears on pages 6–8.

Notice how this circular meets the needs of Chuck's readers and accomplishes his objective. His readers were not generally familiar with the metric system. So Chuck lists some applications of the metric system with which they are familiar (100-millimeter cigarettes, athletic events that use metric measurements, metrics in the space program). For those of Chuck's readers who may have thought that it would not be worth their while to learn the metric system, he explains that it is quite likely that "someday soon" some customers may ask for hardware items in metric units. He further assures his readers that learning metric is not as difficult as they might think, since "only a few words . . . have to be learned for everyday use." Chuck then reinforces his purpose by providing his readers with a chart that they can post in some convenient place for future reference.

FRANKLIN HARDWARE STORES

Circular Number 109

MODERNIZED METRIC

If a customer came into your store and asked whether to buy ¼-inch or ½-inch screws to support 10-pound shelves, you would have little trouble understanding him. Someday soon, however, this same customer may ask whether 5-<u>millimeter</u> or 10-<u>millimeter</u> screws should be used with 4-<u>kilogram</u> shelves.

You may be uncomfortable with these new terms because you learned the traditional language of weights and measures so long ago. You have probably forgotten the day you first understood the meaning of <u>inch</u>, <u>foot</u>, <u>year</u>, and <u>mile</u>; of <u>ounce</u>, <u>pound</u>, <u>ton</u>; of <u>cup</u>, <u>pint</u>, <u>quart</u>, and <u>gallon</u>; of <u>second</u>, <u>minute</u>, and <u>hour</u>; and of <u>degree</u> <u>Fahrenheit</u>. These are familiar units of the "customary" system of measurements that we have traditionally shared with other nations.

The worldwide trend today is toward a comparatively new system of measurement called the <u>modernized metric system</u>. The names of the units sound strange to the American ear at first, but fortunately there are only a few words that have to be learned for everyday use. These are the <u>millimeter</u>, <u>centimeter</u>, <u>meter</u>, and <u>kilometer</u> for describing length and distance; the <u>milliliter</u> and <u>liter</u> for capacity or volume; the <u>gram</u>, <u>kilogram</u>, and <u>tonne</u> for weight; the <u>kilometer/hour</u> for highway speed; and the <u>degree Celsius</u> (formerly called <u>Centigrade</u>) for temperature.

You already encounter the metric system more frequently than you probably realize. You know about 35-millimeter film and cigarettes that are 100 millimeters long——or even a millimeter longer than that. In international athletic competition, such as swimming and field and track events, distances are measured in meters rather than in yards or feet. Our astronauts, from the surface of the moon, excitedly told a worldwide audience how far their rockets had landed from a lunar hill—in meters. If your automobile is imported, and perhaps even if it is domestic, the end wrenches or socket wrenches that you need to work on the car are metric.

To help familiarize yourself with the modernized metric system, keep the following conversion chart handy:

LENGTH

U.S. Unit	Metric Unit
1 inch	25.4 millimeters
1 inch	2.54 centimeters
1 foot	30.48 centimeters
1 foot	0.3048 meter
1 yard	0.9144 meter
1 mile	1609.3 meters
1 mile	1.6093 kilometers
0.03937 inch	1 millimeter
0.3937 inch	1 centimeter
39.37 inches	1 meter
3.2808 feet	1 meter
1.0936 yards	1 meter
3280.8 feet	1 kilometer
1093.6 yards	1 kilometer
0.62137 mile	1 kilometer

WEIGHT

U.S. Unit	Metric Unit
1 grain	0.064799 gram
1 avoirdupois ounce	28.350 grams
1 troy ounce	31.103 grams
1 avoirdupois pound	0.45359 kilogram
1 troy pound	0.37324 kilogram
1 short ton (0.8929 long ton)	907.18 kilograms
	0.90718 tonne
1 long ton (1.1200 short tons)	1016.0 kilograms
	1.0160 tonnes
51.432 grains	1 gram
0.035274 avoirdupois ounce	1 gram
0.032151 troy ounce	1 gram
2.2046 avoirdupois pounds	1 kilogram
0.98421 long ton	1 tonne
1.1023 short tons	1 tonne

LIQUID MEASURE

U.S. Unit	Metric Unit
1 fluid ounce	29.573 milliliters
1 quart	0.94635 liter
1 gallon	3.7854 liters
0.033814 fluid ounce	1 milliliter
33.814 fluid ounces	1 liter
1.0567 quarts	1 liter
0.26417 gallon	1 liter

```
                          DRY MEASURE


        U.S.  Unit                 Metric  Unit
        1 quart                    1.1012  liters
        1 peck                     8.8098 liters
        1 bushel                   35.239 liters
        0.90808 quart              1 liter
        0.11351 peck               1 liter
        0.028378 bushel            1 liter
```

ESTABLISHING YOUR SCOPE

Once you have determined the purpose of your writing and identified the needs of your reader, you are ready to establish your scope. *Scope* is the depth and breadth to which you cover your subject. When you establish scope, you decide how much detail to include to satisfy your reader's needs and achieve the purpose of your writing.

Suppose, for example, that you were writing an explanation of how to pour a concrete foundation for a do-it-yourself homebuilder. This reader probably has had no experience in pouring concrete foundations. Therefore, to achieve your purpose (to enable the homebuilder to pour the foundation), you must include numerous details telling your reader the kinds and amounts of materials to purchase, the proper tools to use, the procedure for preparing the foundation and building the form, the proportions for the concrete mixture, the method for mixing and pouring the concrete, and the technique for finishing and curing the concrete once it has been poured. In other words, the scope of your writing must be broad.

If you state your purpose precisely and consider the needs of your reader carefully, you will have no difficulty establishing the scope of your writing. Had Christine Thomas taken the time to think about her purpose and reader, she would have quickly realized that her memo needed more information (broader scope), including:

the cost advantage of the Bently XL-100
the accuracy of the XL-100
the efficiency of the XL-100
the positive effect on employee morale of the XL-100
the speed of the XL-100 as an aid in meeting deadlines
the corresponding disadvantages of the present typing method

By listing the kinds of information you need to include in your writing, you clearly see the depth and breadth to which you must cover your subject. In other words, you establish your scope.

BRAINSTORMING

With your scope established, the next step is to expand the list of necessary
information into a detailed list of specific items you wish to cover. You can
often create such a list by simply writing down as many items as you can think
of as they occur to you—a process called *brainstorming*. For Christine, the
following list of items could have resulted from brainstorming:

> The Bently XL-100 costs $1,495.
> Temporary typists cost $3,700 last year.
> Temporary typists make errors.
> Deadlines are disturbing our routine.
> Employee morale is down.
> Rental typewriters cost $560 last year.
> XL-100 does not produce errors.
> Magnetic cards cost $9.95 each.
> XL-100 types four times faster than human typists.
> Operator of XL-100 need type in only the address.
> Include a copy of the brochure.

Once you have created a list of items like this one, group the related items.
Then arrange the groups in the most logical order based on what you know
about your reader and your purpose. As you group the items, you may add,
remove, or rearrange points or ideas to fit your reader's needs and your purpose. Christine, for example, might have recognized that cost was more important to her reader than efficiency and decided to present information about
cost first:

> *Cost:*
>
> Bently XL-100 costs $1,495.
> Magnetic cards cost $9.95 each.
> Temporary typists last year cost $3,700.
> Rental typewriters last year cost $560.
> Total savings first year: $2,527.
> Total savings following years: $3,000.
>
> *Efficiency:*
>
> XL-100 types four times faster than human typists.
> XL-100 makes no errors, unlike temporary help.
> Deadlines are disturbing employee morale and office routine.
> XL-100 would free office staff for normal work.

(To organize larger and more complex subjects, it is often helpful to create an
outline. Chapter 13 discusses the outlining technique in detail.)

From these groups of items, Christine could have written a rough draft
and polished it into a final memo that not only might have achieved its purpose but also would have demonstrated Christine's skill and effectiveness to
her boss.

SUCCESSFUL WRITING

Late in the afternoon of the day she received the disappointing response to her memo, Christine got the courage to step into Harriet's office. Christine explained, "I've really investigated the XL-100 thoroughly, and I'm sure it would solve our problem. Perhaps if I gave you more information, you'd reconsider my suggestion." Harriet thought for a moment and then said, "All right. Give me the figures and major benefits tomorrow. If what you say is true, I'll talk to Fred Sadowski, our purchasing agent, as soon as I get the chance." Christine left Harriet's office both relieved and determined that this time she would convince Harriet.

After writing a statement of purpose, determining the needs of her reader, and establishing her scope, Christine listed and organized the items she wanted to cover. She then wrote the following memo:

MEMORANDUM

To: Harriet Sullivan
From: Christine Thomas
Date: December 5,19—
Subject: Advantages of the Bently XL-100 System

The following details show the savings and efficiency of the Bently XL-100 System compared with our present method of handling the typing for our direct mailings. Based on these details, I suggest we consider purchasing this system.

Cost Savings

Purchase of the Bently XL-100 System would result in savings of over $2,500 in the first year, as shown below:

Purchase price of Bently XL-100	$1,495.00	
Cost of one-year supply of XL-100 magnetic cards	$238.00	
	$1,733.00	TOTAL
Cost of temporary typists from Wilson Secretarial Agency last year	$3,700.00	
Temporary typewriter rental from World Office Machines last year	$560.00	
	$4,260.00	TOTAL
Savings for the first year	$2,527.00	

```
    Since purchase of the Bently XL-100 would be a
    one-time investment, the savings would increase
    to over $3,000.00 a year after the first year--
    even considering the cost of magnetic cards and
    repairs.

    Efficiency

        The Bently XL-100 System types without error
    and four times faster than a human typist.
    Because it requires only one operator, the
    XL-100 would eliminate the need for temporary
    typists. It would also eliminate the confusion
    caused by our training these typists while
    attempting to meet our own deadlines. In short,
    we could carry on with our normal office routine.
    A normal routine would not only improve our
    employees' morale but also increase their
    efficiency.
        I am enclosing a brochure that describes the
    Bently XL-100 System in detail.
```

CHAPTER SUMMARY

Successful writing on the job is not the product of inspiration; it is the result of careful preparation and logical organization. Successful writers prepare by precisely defining the *purpose* of their writing, clearly determining the identity and needs of a specific *reader,* and thereby establishing their *scope.* They organize their writing by listing and then logically grouping the facts and ideas the reader will need in order to do what the writer wants done or understand what the writer wants understood. Once organized, the facts and ideas can be converted to a rough draft, then polished into final form. These two steps—writing and revising—are the subjects of the next two chapters.

EXERCISES

1. Write an essay, of assigned length, in which you explain an operation with which you are familiar—how to clean typewriter keys, how to lay out a garment pattern, how to start a car, and so on. Before you begin to write, state your purpose in writing, identify your reader or readers, establish your scope, and brainstorm the list of specific information you will include.

2. Follow the procedure outlined in exercise 1, but this time describe a device or object with which you are familiar—a kitchen utensil or other household object, a stapler or other desk-work item, a piece of athletic equipment, and so on.

3. Write a letter, of assigned length, to a local consumer-affairs office in which you either endorse or complain about a product that you have been using regularly. Before you write, state your purpose, identify your reader, establish your scope, and brainstorm the details you will include. (See Chapter 10 for a sample letter format.)

4. Write a letter, of assigned length, to your school's faculty or administration in which you make suggestions for a change in a current procedure in one of the following areas (or you may select an area of particular interest to you): training programs run in conjunction with local industry; registration, library, or other procedure in school; athletic, cultural, or recreational programs. Or, if you work, you may prefer to write a memorandum suggesting a change in a procedure on the job. In either case, before you begin to write, state your purpose, identify your reader, establish your scope, and brainstorm the information you will include. (See Chapter 10 for sample letter and memorandum formats.)

5. Select a magazine that you read regularly because it is informative, entertaining, or otherwise useful to you. In an essay, of assigned length, convince someone you know who is unfamiliar with this magazine that he or she should read it too.

6. Find an article on a subject of interest to you in two different types of publications—for example, a newspaper and a newsmagazine, a magazine like *Popular Science* and a technical journal, and so on. After you have read the two articles, answer the following questions:

   a. State the purpose of each article and explain how the two articles differ as to purpose.
   b. Compare the approach taken in each article. What do differences in vocabulary and in information presented suggest about the intended audience for each article?
   c. How does the scope of information of each article suit its author's purpose and audience?

2

Writing

As illustrated in Chapter 1, grouping the facts and details you wish to include in your writing is essential to effective organization. But this grouping process serves a further function. Once you have determined which facts and details illustrate and support which main ideas of your writing, you are ready to construct your paragraphs—the major building blocks of any piece of writing.

Suppose you were responsible for writing the report of a committee examining possible locations for a new distribution center. One group of details might concern the way the committee narrowed thirty possible locations to three.

> Committee considered thirty locations.
> Twenty locations eliminated because of labor supply, tax structure, and so forth.
> Committee selected three cities to visit.
> Committee visited Chicago, Minneapolis, and Salt Lake City.
> Committee's observations follow in the report.

From this group of items, you could write the following paragraph:

> The committee initially considered thirty possible locations for the new distribution center. Of these, twenty were eliminated almost immediately for reasons ranging from unfavorable tax structures to inadequate labor supplies. Of the remaining ten locations, the committee selected for intensive study the three cities that seemed to offer the best transportation and support facilities: Chicago, Minneapolis, and Salt Lake City. The committee then visited these three cities, and its observations on each follow in this report.

Because the sentences in the paragraph evolved from the items listed in the group, every sentence is directly related to one central idea—narrowing the selection of possible locations for the distribution center to three cities. Notice that the paragraph does not contain the committee's final recommendation or the specific advantages of each of the three cities. Those details will follow later in the report. To include such details in this paragraph would make the paragraph stray from its one central idea. In fact, the function of any paragraph is to develop a single thought or idea within a larger piece of writing.

PARAGRAPH UNITY

When every sentence in a paragraph contributes to developing one central idea, the paragraph has *unity*. If a paragraph contains sentences that do not develop the central idea, the paragraph lacks unity. The following is a later paragraph from the report evaluating possible locations for the new distribution center. Does this paragraph have unity?

Probably the greatest advantage of Chicago as the location for our new distribution center is its excellent transportation facilities. The city is served by three major railroads. In fact, Chicago was at one time the hub of cross-country rail transportation. Chicago is also a major center of the trucking industry, and most of the nation's large freight carriers have terminals there. We are concerned, however, about the delivery problems that we've had with several truck carriers. We've had far fewer problems with air freight. Both domestic and international air cargo service is available at O'Hare International Airport. Finally, except in the winter months when the Great Lakes are frozen, Chicago is a seaport, accessible through the St. Lawrence Seaway.

Every sentence in this paragraph should have been about *the advantages of Chicago's transportation facilities*. Three sentences, however, do not develop that central idea: the sentence about Chicago as the former hub of rail transportation and the two sentences about delivery problems. These three sentences are italicized below:

Probably the greatest advantage of Chicago as the location for our new distribution center is its excellent transportation facilities. The city is served by three major railroads. *In fact, Chicago was at one time the hub of cross-country rail transportation.* Chicago is also a major center of the trucking industry, and most of the nation's large freight carriers have terminals there. *We are concerned, however, about the delivery problems that we've had with several truck carriers. We've had far fewer problems with air freight.* Both domestic and international air cargo service is available at O'Hare International Airport. Finally, except in the winter months when the Great Lakes are frozen, Chicago is a seaport, accessible through the St. Lawrence Seaway.

Now read the paragraph without the italicized sentences. Each of the remaining sentences is directly related to the central idea, and the paragraph has unity.

> Probably the greatest advantage of Chicago as the location for our new distribution center is its excellent transportation facilities. The city is served by three major railroads. Chicago is also a major center of the trucking industry, and most of the nation's large freight carriers have terminals there. Both domestic and international air cargo service is available at O'Hare International Airport. Finally, except in the winter months when the Great Lakes are frozen, Chicago is a seaport, accessible through the St. Lawrence Seaway.

The Topic Sentence

One way to make sure that your paragraph has unity is to provide a topic sentence. A *topic sentence* is a sentence within a paragraph that clearly states the central idea of that paragraph. If every sentence in the paragraph directly relates to the topic sentence, the paragraph will have unity.

Notice that all the sentences in the following paragraph directly relate to the topic sentence:

> *Probably the greatest advantage of Chicago as the location for our new distribution center is its excellent transportation facilities.* The city is served by three major railroads. Chicago is also a major center of the trucking industry, and most of the nation's large freight carriers have terminals there. Both domestic and international air cargo service is available at O'Hare International Airport. Finally, except in the winter months when the Great Lakes are frozen, Chicago is a seaport, accessible through the St. Lawrence Seaway.

Beginning a paragraph with the topic sentence helps both the writer and the reader. The writer has no difficulty constructing a unified paragraph because every sentence can be measured against the topic sentence and the central idea it expresses. And the reader knows immediately what the paragraph is about because the opening sentence states the central idea. Busy readers, especially, appreciate being told at once what a paragraph is about. For this reason, topic sentences are usually the first sentences of paragraphs in on-the-job writing.

Occasionally, however, a topic sentence may be placed somewhere other than at the beginning of a paragraph. A topic sentence may be the last sentence of a paragraph, for example. Placing the topic sentence at the end of a paragraph emphasizes the central idea because all the sentences build up to that idea. Notice how the sentences in the following paragraph build up to the topic sentence:

A study by the Department of Agriculture revealed that insect damage in our region increased from 15 percent to 23 percent between 1975 and 1977. This past year many farmers reported a 30 percent increase in insect damage over the previous year. Furthermore, another recent study found that certain destructive insects are migrating north into our area. *Clearly, we should prepare for increased insect damage in the coming year.*

Although a topic sentence placed at the end of a paragraph provides a forceful conclusion, it also makes reading the paragraph more difficult. Especially in on-the-job situations, where time is at a premium, the reader may become irritated at having to plow through details to reach the main point of a paragraph. Therefore, it is best to place topic sentences at the ends of paragraphs only occasionally.

PARAGRAPH COHERENCE

An effective paragraph not only has unity but also has *coherence;* that is, it takes the reader logically and smoothly from one sentence to the next. When a paragraph is coherent, the reader clearly recognizes that one sentence or idea logically leads to the next, and that that sentence or idea leads to the following one, and so on. Consider the following paragraph. Does each sentence or idea lead logically and clearly to the one that follows?

Most adjustable office chairs have nylon hub tubes that hold metal spindle rods. To ensure trouble-free operation, lubricate these spindle rods occasionally. Loosen the set screw in the adjustable bell. Lift the chair from the base so that the entire spindle rod is accessible. Lubricant should be applied to the spindle rod and the nylon washer. Use the lubricant sparingly to prevent dripping. Be sure that you tighten the set screw after the chair is replaced.

Because each sentence in the paragraph says something about how to lubricate an adjustable office chair, the paragraph has unity. Yet the paragraph does not move smoothly from one sentence to the next. It lacks coherence.

If a paragraph lacks coherence, you should check first to see if the ideas are presented in a logical order. Does one idea lead logically to the next? In the previous example, the ideas are arranged logically: the instructions for lubricating the spindle rods are arranged in exactly the order in which they must be performed.

Transitional Devices

Next check to see if the paragraph contains adequate transitional devices. *Transitional devices* are words and phrases that help the reader to move smoothly from one sentence to the next and to see the logical relationship between the sentences. Notice how the italicized words and phrases give coherence to the following paragraph:

> Most adjustable office chairs have nylon hub tubes that hold metal spindle rods. To ensure trouble-free operation, lubricate these spindle rods occasionally. *First,* loosen the set screw in the adjustable bell. *Then* lift the chair from the base so that the entire spindle rod is accessible. *Next,* apply the lubricant to the spindle rod and the nylon washer, using the lubricant sparingly to prevent dripping. *When you have finished,* replace the chair and tighten the set screw.

Now, because the transitional devices provide coherence, the reader can follow the writer's step-by-step instructions easily. The word *first* indicates that the statement following is the first step in lubricating the rods. The words *then* and *next* point out the logical, step-by-step relationship of the instructions that follow. The phrase *when you have finished* tells the reader that the lubricating process is finished and that a new instruction will follow.

The following list includes other words and phrases that function as transitional devices:

- To express result: *therefore, as a result, consequently, thus, hence*
- To express example: *for example, for instance, specifically, as an illustration*
- To express comparison: *similarly, likewise*
- To express contrast: *but, yet, still, however, nevertheless, on the other hand*
- To express addition: *moreover, furthermore, also, too, besides, in addition*
- To express time: *now, later, meanwhile, since then, after that, before that time*
- To express sequence: *first, second, third, then, next, finally*

Each of these words and phrases has its own special meaning. Be sure that the transitional device you choose conveys the precise meaning you intend.

Another transitional device is the use of pronouns, such as <u>he, she, they,</u> and *it*. Because pronouns refer to a person or thing mentioned in a previous sentence, they bind sentences and ideas together. Notice the use of pronouns as transitional devices in the following paragraph:

It refers to punch press.

> We have recently discovered a problem with the #41 *punch press. It* consistently fails to retract fully when *it* is shut off at the end of the second shift. *First-shift employees* are concerned that this condition poses a safety hazard. *They* believe that the press could go through a cycle after the power has been turned on. *Bill Taylor,* a second-shift supervisor, reports that the maintenance department does not consider the problem to be a safety hazard. *He* has pointed out to me, however, that when the power is turned on, the safety shield is not in place. *He* believes that this fact warrants a thorough analysis of the problem.

They refers to first-shift employees.

He refers to Bill Taylor.

Although pronouns can be excellent transitional devices, they confuse the reader if the person or thing to which the pronoun refers is not perfectly clear.

CONFUSING   Midcity College is located in the central business district of the city. *It* is very large.

It is confusing because the reader must guess whether *it* refers to the college, the business district, or the city. In such a case, repeating a word is better.

BETTER   Midcity College is located in the central business district of the city. The *college* is very large.

The problem of pronoun reference is discussed in Chapter 7.

Another transitional device that links sentences and ideas is the repetition of key words and phrases. Notice how repetition of the key words and phrases in the paragraph below moves the paragraph forward:

Over the past several months, I have heard complaints about the Merit Award *Program*. Specifically, many employees feel that this *program* should be linked to annual *salary increases*. They believe that *salary increases* would provide much better incentive than the current $150 to $300 *cash awards*. In addition, these *employees believe* that their supervisors consider the *cash awards* adequate compensation when recommending salary increases. Although I don't think this practice is widespread, the fact that the *employees believe* that it is justifies a reevaluation of the Merit Award Program.

TRANSITION BETWEEN PARAGRAPHS

Transitional devices used to link sentences can also be effective for transition between paragraphs. The repetition of a key phrase, for example, connects the first paragraph below with the one that follows.

Consumers spend more money for plumbing repairs than for any other service. The most common repair that plumbers make is the clearing of drains. Since the kitchen *sink drain* is used more often than any other drain in the home, that is the drain that is most often clogged.

Clearing the *sink drain* yourself is easier than you might expect. You probably have all the tools you need. . . .

Another transitional device for linking paragraphs is to begin a paragraph with a sentence that summarizes the preceding paragraph. In the following excerpt from a report, notice how the first sentence in the second paragraph summarizes the ideas presented in the first paragraph:

Each year, forest fires in our region cause untold destruction. For example, wood ashes washed into streams after a fire often kill large numbers of fish. In addition, the destruction of the vegetation along streambanks causes water temperatures to rise, making the stream unfit for several varieties of cold-water fish. Forest fires, moreover, hurt the tourist and recreation business, for vacationers are not likely to visit flame-blackened areas.

These losses, and many other indirect losses caused by forest fires, damage not only the quality of life but also the economy of our region. They also represent a huge drain on the resources and manpower of the Department of Natural Resources. For example, our financial investment last year in fighting forest fires . . .

The opening sentence summarizes the specific examples of the previous paragraph.

If used sparingly, another effective transitional device between paragraphs is to ask a question at the end of one paragraph and answer it at the beginning of the next. This device works well in the following example:

Automation has become an ugly word in the American vocabulary because it has sometimes meant the displacement of employees from their jobs. But the all-important fact that is so often overlooked is that automation invariably creates many more jobs than it eliminates. The vast number of people employed through automation in the American automobile industry compared with the number of people that had been employed in the harness-and-carriage-making business is a classic example. Almost always, the jobs that have been eliminated by automation have been menial, unskilled jobs, and those who have been displaced have been forced to increase their skills, which has resulted in better and higher-paying jobs for them. *In view of these facts, is automation really bad?*

There is no question that automation has made our country the wealthiest and most technologically advanced nation the world has ever known. Furthermore, it has freed many people from boring and repetitive work . . .

Transition using a question and answer.

When you use this transitional device, make sure that the second paragraph does, in fact, answer the question posed in the first. And, again, do not use this device too often. Your reader may find it monotonous and gimmicky.

PARAGRAPH LENGTH

Paragraph length should be tailored to the reader's convenience. Specifically, a paragraph should help the reader by providing a physical break on the page as well as by signaling a new idea. Long paragraphs can intimidate your reader by failing to provide manageable subdivisions of thought. Short paragraphs make it difficult for the reader to see the logical relationship of ideas in your writing. A series of short paragraphs can also sacrifice unity by breaking a single idea into several pieces.

Although there are no rules for the length of paragraphs, paragraphs in on-the-job writing average about one hundred words each, with two or three paragraphs to a double-spaced, typewritten page. Paragraphs in letters tend to be shorter; two- or even one-sentence paragraphs are not unusual in letters. The best advice is that a paragraph should be just long enough to deal adequately with the central idea stated in its topic sentence. A new paragraph should begin whenever the subject changes significantly.

WRITING AN OPENING

What should the opening statement of your writing do? It should (1) identify your subject and (2) catch the interest of your reader.

Most readers of on-the-job writing are preoccupied with other business when they begin to read a memo, letter, or report. Therefore, you must catch their interest and focus their attention on the subject you are writing about. Even if your readers are required to read what you've written, catching their interest at the outset will help ensure that they pay close attention to what follows. And if you are attempting to persuade your readers, you *must* catch their interest if your writing is to succeed.

To catch your reader's interest, you first must know your reader's needs (as discussed in Chapter 1). Those needs will help you determine which details your reader will find important and thus interesting. Consider the following opening from a memo written by a personnel manager to her supervisor. This opening not only states the subject of the report but also promises that the writer will offer solutions to a specific problem. And solutions to problems are always of interest to a reader.

```
                     MEMORANDUM
To: Paul Route, Corporate Relations Director
From: Sondra L. Rivera, Personnel Manager
Date: November 1, 19—-
Subject: Decreasing Applications from Local College
         Graduates

This year only twelve local college graduates have
applied for jobs at Benson Tubular Steel. Last year over
thirty graduates applied, and the year before fifty
applied. After talking with several college counselors, I
am confident that we can solve the problem of decreasing
applications from local colleges.

First, we could resume our advertisements in local student
newspapers . . .
```

For most types of writing done in offices, shops, and laboratories, openings that simply get to the point are more effective than those that provide detailed background information. Furthermore, the subject of a memo or report is often, by itself, enough to catch the reader's interest. The following openings are typical; however, do not feel that you must slavishly follow these patterns. Rather, always first consider the purpose of your writing and the needs of your reader and then tailor your opening accordingly.

Correspondence

```
Mr. George T. Whittier
1720 Old Line Road
Thomasbury, WV 26401

Dear Mr. Whittier:

You will be happy to know that we have corrected the error
in your bank balance. The new balance shows . . .
```

Progress Report Letter

```
William Chang, M.D.
Phelps Building
9003 Shaw Avenue
Parksville, MD 29099

Dear Dr. Chang:

To date, eighteen of the twenty-six specimens you
submitted for analysis have been examined. Our preliminary
analysis indicates . . .
```

Longer Progress Report

```
          PROGRESS REPORT ON REWIRING THE SPORTS ARENA

     The rewiring program at the Sports Arena is
continuing on schedule. Although the costs of certain
equipment are higher than our original bid had indicated,
we expect to complete the project without exceeding our
budget, because the speed with which the project is being
completed will save labor costs.

Work Completed

     As of August 15th, we have . . .
```

Memorandum

```
                    MEMORANDUM

To: Jane T. Meyers, Chief Budget Manager
From: Charles Benson, Assistant to the Personnel Director
Date:  June 12, 19--
Subject: Budget Estimates for Fiscal Year 19--

The personnel budget estimates for fiscal year 19--
are as follows: . . .
```

Notice that all of these openings get directly to the point; they do not introduce irrelevant subjects or include unnecessary details. They give the readers exactly what they need to focus their attention on what is to follow. (For examples of openings for special types of writing such as application letters, complaint letters, and formal reports, refer to the index under appropriate subjects.)

WRITING A CLOSING

A closing not only ties your writing together and ends it emphatically but also may make a significant point. A closing may recommend a course of action, offer a value judgment, speculate on the implications of your ideas, make a prediction, or summarize your main points. Even if your closing only states, "If I can be of further help, please call me" or "I would appreciate your comments," you are showing consideration for your reader and thereby gaining your reader's goodwill.

The way you close depends on the purpose of your writing and the needs of your reader. For example, the committee report on possible locations for a new distribution center could end with a recommendation. A report studying a company's annual sales could end with a judgment about why sales are up or down. A report for a retail department store about consumer buying trends could end by speculating on the implications of these trends, perhaps even suggesting new product lines that the store might carry in the future. A lengthy report could end with a summary of the main points covered to pull the ideas together for the reader.

The following closings are typical.

Correspondence

```
Mr. George T. Whittier
1720 Old Line Road
Thomasbury, WV 26401

Dear Mr. Whittier:

You will be happy to know that we have corrected the error
in your bank balance. The new balance shows . . .
```

Polite, help-
ful closing
```
Please accept our thanks for your continued business, and
let us know if we can be of further help.

                               Sincerely,

                               Michael Fosse

                               Michael Fosse
                               Branch Manager
```

Progress Report Letter

William Chang, M.D.
Phelps Building
9003 Shaw Avenue
Parksville, MD 29099

Dear Dr. Chang:

To date, eighteen of the twenty-six specimens you
submitted for analysis have been examined. Our preliminary
analysis indicates . . .

**Closing that
recommends
a response**

These results indicate that you may need to alter your
testing procedure to eliminate the impurities we found
in specimens A–G and K.

Sincerely,

Marion Lamb

Marion Lamb
Research Assistant

Longer Progress Report

PROGRESS REPORT ON REWIRING THE SPORTS ARENA

The rewiring program at the Sports Arena is
continuing on schedule. Although the costs of certain
equipment are higher than our original bid had indicated,
we expect to complete the project without exceeding our
budget, because the speed with which the project is
being completed will save labor costs.

Work Completed

As of August 15th, we have . . .

**Closing that
makes a
prediction**

Although my original estimate on equipment
($20,000) has been exceeded by $2,300, my original labor
estimate ($60,000) has been reduced by $3,500; therefore,
I will easily stay within the limits of my original bid.
In addition, I see no difficulty in having the arena
finished for the December 23 Christmas program.

Memorandum

MEMORANDUM

To: Jane T. Meyers, Chief Budget Manager
From: Charles Benson, Assistant to the Personnel Director
Date: June 12, 19—
Subject: Budget Estimates for Fiscal Year 19—

The personnel budget estimates for fiscal year 19— are
as follows: . . .

**Closing that
offers a
judgment**

Although our estimate calls for a substantially higher
budget than in the three previous years, we believe that
it is justified by our planned expansion.

MEMORANDUM

To: Paul Route, Corporate Relations Director
From: Sondra L. Rivera, Personnel Manager
Date: November 1, 19——
Subject: Decreasing Applications from Local College
         Graduates

This year only twelve local college graduates have applied
for jobs at Benson Tubular Steel. Last year over thirty
graduates applied, and the year before fifty applied.
After talking with several college counselors, I am
confident that we can solve the problem of decreasing
applications from local colleges.

First, we could resume our advertisements in local student
newspapers . . .

Closing that summarizes main points

As this report has indicated, we could attract more recent
graduates by (1) increasing our advertising in local
student newspapers, (2) resuming our co-op program,
(3) sending a representative to career day programs at
local colleges and high schools, (4) inviting local
college instructors to teach in-house courses here in
the plant, and (5) encouraging our employees to attend
evening classes at various colleges.

As these examples show, a good closing is concise and ends your writing emphatically, making it sound finished. Any of the methods for closing can be effective, depending on the purpose of your writing and the needs of your reader. Be careful, however, not to close with a cliché or a platitude, such as "While profits have increased with the introduction of this new product, *the proof is in the pudding.*" Also be careful not to introduce a new topic in your closing. A closing should always relate to and reinforce the ideas presented in your writing.

CHAPTER SUMMARY

Grouping the facts and details you wish to include in your writing (discussed in Chapter 1) leads naturally to the construction of paragraphs. To be effective, paragraphs must have unity and coherence. <u>Unity</u> is achieved when every sentence in a paragraph relates to the single central idea stated in the topic sentence. <u>Coherence</u> is achieved when the ideas are arranged in a logical order and transitional devices link sentences and paragraphs, enabling the reader to move smoothly from sentence to sentence and from paragraph to paragraph.

Good openings identify the subject of the writing and catch the reader's interest. Good closings not only show consideration for the reader but may recommend a course of action, make a prediction, offer a value judgment, speculate on the implications of the ideas presented in the writing, or summarize the main points.

EXERCISES

1. Read the following paragraph and then complete the exercises pertaining to it.

> Frequently, department managers and supervisors recruit applicants without working through the corporate personnel office. Personnel departments around the country have experienced this problem. Recently, the manager of our tool design department met with a graduate of MTI to discuss an opening for a tool designer. The graduate was sent to Personnel, where she was told that no such position existed. When the tool design manager asked the Personnel Director about the matter, the manager learned that the company president had ordered a hiring freeze for two months. I'm sure that our general employment situation will get better. As a result of the manager's failure to work through proper channels, the applicant was not only disappointed but bitter.

   a. Underline the topic sentence of the paragraph.
   b. Cross out any sentences that do not contribute to paragraph unity.

2. Underline the topic sentences in the following paragraphs.

   a.   Whether you use a hand mower, a power reel mower, or a rotary power mower to cut your lawn, the blades should be sharp enough to trim the grass cleanly without bruising or tearing the leaves. Both the cutting edge of the bedknife or reel-type mower and the reel blades should be sharp, and the reel should be set firmly against the bedknife. Make any necessary adjustments of the bedknife or of the roller (which determines the height of cut) on a flat surface, such as a concrete walk or floor. Rotary mower blades in particular require frequent sharpening. On most rotary mowers height of cut is fixed by adjusting the wheels in holes or slots on the mower frame.

   b.   One property of material considered for manufacturing processes is hardness. Hardness is the internal resistance of the material to the forcing apart or closing together of its molecules. Another property is ductility, the characteristic of material that permits it to be drawn into a wire. The smaller the diameter of the wire into which the material can be drawn, the greater the ductility. Material may also possess malleability, the property which makes it capable of being rolled or hammered into thin sheets of various shapes. Engineers, in selecting materials to employ in manufacturing, must consider their properties before deciding on the most desirable for use in production.

c.   Raisers of houseplants must periodically replace the soil that serves as the growing medium for most indoor plants. When the soil of plants housed in small pots needs to be replaced, the plant is usually "potted up"—that is, transplanted to a pot of the next size. The plant, with its rootball intact, is removed from the small pot, and fresh dirt is piled into the larger container, with space allowed for the rootball. The plant is then carefully inserted into the new soil. For plants already in the largest-sized pots, the indoor gardener may take the plant, along with its root-ball, out of the pot, discard the remaining earth, put in a similar amount of fresh dirt, and then return the plant to its original container.

3. Underline the transitional words and phrases in the following paragraphs.

express result

contrast

a.   Homeowners should know where the gutters on their houses are located and should be sure to keep them in good repair, because gutters are vulnerable to various weather conditions. On many houses, gutters are tucked up under or into the eaves, so that they appear as little more than another line or two of trim. As a result, many homeowners are not even aware that their house has gutters. Unless the gutters are well maintained, however, the thousands of gallons of water that may fall onto the roof of the average house each year can easily damage or weaken the gutters. During the winter months, the weight of snow and ice may pull gutters away from the house or loosen the downspout straps. Clogged and frozen downspouts may also develop seam cracks. When spring comes, these seam cracks sometimes create leaks that may allow heavy rains to flood the yard or the house instead of draining properly into the sewer system. In addition, melting snow flowing freely off the roof may go down the house wall, wetting it sufficiently to cause interior wall damage.

b.   The causes of global climate change remain in dispute. Existing theories of climate, atmospheric models, and statistical data are inadequate to provide planners with information on future weather patterns. In the long run, research may lead to reliable forecasts of climate. For the present, however, planners have no choice but to heed expert judgments about future world climate and its effect on agriculture and other sectors of the economy.

4. The following pairs of sentences lack transition from the first sentence to the second. From the list of transitional devices on page 19, select the most appropriate one for each sentence pair.

consequently or therefore

a. Ms. Silvenski arrived at the post office just before closing time. She was not able to mail her package because it had not been wrapped according to post office specifications.

b. An improperly cut garment will not hang attractively on the wearer. When you sew, you should be sure to lay out and cut your pattern accurately and carefully.

"likewise"
hence

contrast

on the other hand
but
however

   c. Doctors Clinic was able to reach its fund-raising goal on time this
      year.
      Mercer Street Hospital was forced to extend its fund-raising dead-
      line for three months.
   d. The branch manager explained to the new tellers how to deal with
      impatient customers.

for example; for instance,
specifically

      The personal-banking assistant told the new employees that they
      should consult her if they had difficulty handling those customers.
   e. There are several reasons why a car may skid on ice.
      The driver may be going faster than road conditions warrant.

sequence

for example

5. The sentences in the following paragraphs have been purposely placed in
   the wrong order. Rearrange the sentences in each paragraph so that the
   paragraphs move smoothly and logically from one sentence to the next.
   Indicate the correct order of the sentences by placing the sentence numbers in the order in which the sentences should appear.

   a.   ②(1) When wind speed exceeds the maximum that the mill is de-
           signed to handle, the propeller is positioned at an angle to the wind so
           that it no longer turns. (2) Because of their aerodynamic characteristics,
           vertical-axis windmills go into a stall in high winds. (3) To balance cost
           and performance, windmills are designed to obtain power from winds
           within certain speed ranges. (4) If this did not occur, the propeller would
           continue to speed up and the machine would eventually be destroyed.

   b.   ⑨(1) Each atrium is connected to the ventricle below by a valve that
           allows blood to flow in only one direction. (2) The two upper chambers
           are called atria, and the two lower chambers are called ventricles.
           ⑤(3) The ventricles are also connected by one-way valves to the main
           outgoing blood vessels. (4) The organ is divided into four chambers.
           ①(5) The heart is a fist-sized, heavily muscled organ located approximately
           in the center of the chest.

6. Write a paragraph developing one of the following topic sentences. Be
   sure that the paragraphs are unified and coherent; follow the guidelines
   offered in the text.

   a. Job-advancement opportunities for employees are created by
      company growth.
   b. Good relations between management and labor, along with higher
      productivity, are mandatory for the creation of new jobs.
   c. Every successful industrial organization has at least one "bread
      and butter" product that sells well year in and year out.
   d. A ——— technician must perform a variety of duties.

7. Write an opening paragraph for two of the following topics. The audience for each topic is specified in parentheses.

    a. Safety on the job (your immediate supervisor)
    b. Ways to save energy on the job (your immediate supervisor)
    c. The advantages of budgeting an income (a spendthrift friend)
    d. What to look for in a first apartment (a friend who's looking)
    e. The advantages and disadvantages of your school's career-counseling program (the administrator in charge of the program)
    f. Job opportunities in your locality for people in your career field (article for the student newspaper of the high school from which you graduated)

3

Revising

One of the enduring legends of American history is that Abraham Lincoln wrote the Gettysburg Address as he made the train trip from Washington, D.C., to Gettysburg. The address is a remarkable accomplishment, even for a writer as gifted as Lincoln. It is the eloquent testimony of a leader with a powerful intellect and a compassionate heart.

But the facts of how the Gettysburg Address was composed do not support the legend. Lincoln actually worked on the address for weeks and revised the draft many times.[1] What Lincoln was doing on the train to Gettysburg was nothing more than what any of us must do before our writing is finally acceptable: he was revising. What is remarkable about the address is that Lincoln made so many revisions of a speech of well under three hundred words. Obviously he wanted it to fit the occasion for which it was intended, and he knew that something written "off the cuff" would not do the job.

This principle is as true for anyone who writes on the job (which, of course, is what the president was doing) as it was for Lincoln. The more natural a piece of writing sounds to the reader, the more effort the writer has put into revising it.

EFFECTIVE REVISION

Have you ever written a first draft that you knew wasn't the best you could do, but that you did not know how to improve? If your answer is yes, you are not alone. All writers—even professional writers—have the same problem at some time or another.

[1] Tom Burnam, *The Dictionary of Misinformation* (New York: Ballantine Books, 1977), pp. 104–106.

31

The problem has a simple explanation, however. Immediately after you write a rough draft, the ideas are so fresh in your mind that you cannot read the words, sentences, and paragraphs objectively. That is, you cannot sufficiently detach yourself from the ideas to be able to look at the writing critically. And to revise effectively, you *must* be critical. You cannot allow yourself to think, "Because my ideas are good, the way I've expressed them must also be good." The first step toward effective revision, then, is to develop a critical frame of mind—to become objective.

As professional writers have learned, there are a number of ways to put distance between yourself and your writing and become objective. Here are two methods that you should always employ:

1. *Allow for a "cooling" period.* Allow a period of time to go by between writing a rough draft and revising it. The ideas will not be as fresh in your mind then, and you can look at the writing itself more objectively. A "cooling" period of a day or two is best, but if you are pressed for time, even a few hours will help.
2. *Pretend that a stranger has written your draft.* Since it is always easier to see faults in others than in yourself, pretend that you are revising someone else's draft. If you can look at your writing and ask, "How could *he* or *she* have written that?" you are in the right frame of mind to revise.

Of course, you may discover your own methods of becoming objective. One student, for example, can be more critical if she writes her first draft on yellow paper. Another student types his first draft because he cannot be critical when he is looking at his own handwriting. Some students like to revise with felt-tip pen; others prefer using red or green pencils. Experiment and find out what helps you. It is not so important which methods work for you. What is important is that you develop some technique for becoming objective about your writing—and then use it.

Once you have put the necessary distance between yourself and your writing, you are ready to revise. Again, there is no single method that *every* writer uses. The following two techniques, however, invariably prove effective:

1. *Revise in passes.* Make several passes through your draft as you revise. The first time you read the draft, look at only one aspect of your writing, such as accuracy or completeness. Then make additional passes, looking at a different aspect, such as grammar or spelling, each time. Often, you can spot problems more quickly if you look for only one than if you look for several at the same time.
2. *Be alert for your most frequent errors.* Closely related to revising in passes is looking first for the errors that you typically make. One of the most important benefits of taking a writing course is that you can learn what your weak points are. Make a list of the problems your instructor has pointed out in your writing, and use that list to guide you as you revise.

As you revise your draft, there are certain aspects of your writing that you must carefully examine. You cannot be confident that your writing is as good as you can make it unless you have checked for accuracy, for completeness, and for grammatical correctness.

CHECK FOR ACCURACY

Above all else, your information must be accurate. Although accuracy is important in all types of writing, it takes on special significance when you write on the job. One misplaced decimal point, for example, can create a staggering budgetary error. Incorrect or imprecise instructions can cause injury to a worker. At the very least, you will quickly lose the confidence of your reader if your writing is not accurate. Your reader will be annoyed, for example, if a figure or fact in your writing differs from one in a chart or graph. These kinds of inaccuracies are easily overlooked as you write the draft, so it is essential that you correct them during revision.

CHECK FOR COMPLETENESS

You must also make sure that you have given your reader the information he or she needs, based on the purpose of your writing. For example, an omitted step in a set of instructions, like an inaccurate one, can cause damage and even injury. And if an instruction is omitted, chances are that your purpose will not be achieved—your reader will not be able to complete the procedure successfully. Similarly, if you are writing to convince your reader of something you consider important, the omission of a supporting detail may defeat your case.

Revision is the time to insert any missing facts or ideas. Check your draft against the list you made when you were preparing to write. If any of the main ideas or supporting details you listed are missing from your draft, rewrite your sentences and paragraphs as necessary to incorporate the information.

In revising your draft for completeness, you may also think of new information that you failed to include when you were preparing and writing your draft. Always carefully consider such new information in light of your reader and purpose. If the information will help satisfy your reader's need and accomplish the purpose of your writing, by all means add it now. But if the information—no matter how interesting—does not serve these ends, it has no place in your writing.

CHECK FOR GRAMMATICAL CORRECTNESS

Grammatical errors, like inaccurate facts or incomplete information, can confuse or irritate your reader and cause him or her to lose confidence in you.

Even worse, many of the errors discussed in this chapter are so severe that they can actually alter the meaning of a sentence. Therefore, it is essential that in revising your draft, you check for grammatical correctness.

If, as you read the following sections, you do not understand a term used in an explanation of an error, you can refer to the Handbook at the end of this book.

Agreement

Agreement means that the parts of a sentence, like the pieces of a jigsaw puzzle, fit together properly. For example, you would write "she *is* the supervisor" not "she *are* the supervisor." The word *is* fits the sentence pieces together correctly; the word *are* does not. Of course, you would not be likely to make this mistake because the sentence is very simple. But the problem can easily occur when a sentence is more complicated. The following discussion points out the types of sentences in which problems of agreement occur often.

1. **Subject-verb agreement.**   A *verb* must agree with its *subject*. A singular subject requires a singular verb; a plural subject requires a plural verb. Do not let intervening phrases and clauses mislead you.

REVISE
> The *use* of insecticides, fertilizers, and weed killers, although they offer unquestionable benefits, often *result* in unfortunate side effects.

TO
> The *use* of insecticides, fertilizers, and weed killers, although they offer unquestionable benefits, often *results* in unfortunate side effects. (The singular verb *results* must agree with the singular subject of the sentence, *use,* not with the plural subject of the preceding clause, *they.*)

Be careful to avoid making the verb agree with the noun immediately in front of it if that noun is not its subject. This problem is especially likely to occur when a modifying phrase containing a plural noun falls between a singular subject and its verb.

EXAMPLES
> Only *one* of the emergency lights *was* functioning when the accident occurred. (The subject is *one,* not *lights.*)
>
> *Each* of the switches *controls* a separate circuit. (The subject is *each,* not *switches.*)
>
> The *advice* of two engineers, one lawyer, and three executives *was* obtained prior to making a commitment. (The subject is *advice,* not *engineers, lawyer,* and *executives.*)

Words like *type, part, series,* and *portion* take singular verbs even when such words precede a phrase containing a plural noun.

EXAMPLES A *series* of meetings *was* held to decide the best way to market the new product.

A large *portion* of most annual reports *is* devoted to promoting the corporate image.

Subjects expressing measurement, weight, mass, or total often take singular verbs even though the subject word is plural in form. Such subjects are treated as a unit.

EXAMPLES *Four years is* the normal duration of the apprenticeship program.

Twenty dollars is the wholesale price of each unit.

When such subjects refer to the individuals that make up the unit, however, a plural verb is required.

EXAMPLE If you're looking for oil, *three quarts are* on the shelf in the garage.

Similarly, collective subjects take singular verbs when the group is thought of as a unit and plural verbs when the individuals are thought of separately.

EXAMPLES The *committee is* holding its meeting on Thursday. (*Committee* is thought of as a unit.)

The *majority are* opposed to delivering their reports at the meeting. (*Majority* is thought of as separate individuals.)

A relative pronoun (*who, which, that*) may take either singular or plural verbs depending upon whether its antecedent (the noun to which it refers) is singular or plural.

EXAMPLES He is an *employee* who *takes* work home at night.

He is one of those *employees* who *take* work home at night.

A *compound subject* is one that is composed of two or more elements joined by a conjunction such as *and, or, nor, either . . . or,* or *neither . . . nor.* Usually, when the elements are connected by *and,* the subject is plural and requires a plural verb.

EXAMPLE *Chemistry and accounting are* prerequisites for this position.

There is one exception to the *and* rule. If the elements connected by *and* form a unit or refer to the same person, the subject is regarded as singular and takes a singular verb.

EXAMPLES *Bacon and eggs is* a high-cholesterol meal.

His *secretary and biographer was* also his toughest critic. (The same person was his secretary and his biographer.)

A compound subject with two singular elements joined by *or* or *nor* requires a singular verb.

EXAMPLES   Either a *ruler* or a *tape measure is* in the drawer.

Neither the *wiring* nor the *plumbing was* completed on schedule.

A compound subject with a singular and a plural element joined by *or* or *nor* requires that the verb agree with the element nearest to it.

EXAMPLES   Neither the office manager nor the *secretaries were* there.

Neither the secretaries nor the office *manager was* there.

Either they or *I am* going to write the report.

Either I or *they are* going to write the report.

2. **Pronoun-antecedent agreement.** A *pronoun* must agree with its *antecedent,* the noun to which it refers. For example, like subjects and their verbs, a pronoun must agree with its antecedent in number (singular or plural). If the antecedent is singular, the pronoun must be singular. If the antecedent is plural, the pronoun must be plural. Many problems in agreement are caused by expressions that are not clear in number.

REVISE   Although the typical *engine* runs well in moderate temperatures, *they* often stall in extreme cold.

TO   Although the typical *engine* runs well in moderate temperatures, *it* often stalls in extreme cold.

Use a singular pronoun when its antecedent is a word like *everybody, everyone, each, anyone,* unless to do so would be illogical because the meaning is obviously plural.

EXAMPLES   *Everyone* pulled *his* share of the load.

Everyone laughed at my sales slogan, and I really couldn't blame *them*.

Collective nouns may be singular or plural, depending on meaning.

EXAMPLES   The *committee* arrived at the recommended solutions only after *it* had deliberated for days.

The *committee* quit for the day and went to *their* respective homes.

A compound antecedent joined by *or* or *nor* is singular if both elements are singular and plural if both elements are plural.

EXAMPLES   Neither the *technician* nor the *draftsman* could do *his* job until *he* understood the new concept.

Neither the *supervisors* nor the *employees were* pleased at the performance of *their* division.

When one of the antecedents connected by *or* or *nor* is singular and the other is plural, the pronoun agrees with the nearer antecedent.

EXAMPLES   Either the supervisor or the *operators* will have *their* licenses suspended.

Either the operators or the *supervisor* will have *his* license suspended.

A compound antecedent with its elements joined by *and* requires a plural pronoun.

EXAMPLE   *Jim and Ed* took *their* layout drawings with *them*.

A pronoun must also agree with its antecedent in gender (masculine, feminine, or neuter).

EXAMPLE   Mr. Swivet in the Accounting Department acknowledges *his* responsibility for the misunderstanding, but Ms. Barkley in the Research Division should acknowledge *her* responsibility for *it* also.

There is a longstanding tradition of using a masculine, singular pronoun to agree with such indefinite antecedents as *each, one, anyone,* and *person*.

EXAMPLE   *Each* may stay or go as *he* chooses.

Many people are now sensitive to implied sexual bias in such usage. When graceful alternatives are available, use them. One solution is to rewrite the sentence in the plural.

REVISE   Every *employee* will have *his* supervisor sign *his* slip.

TO   All *employees* will have *their* supervisors sign *their* slips.

Be careful not to change the pronoun to the plural but leave its antecedent in the singular. The pronoun and its antecedent must always agree.

REVISE   A *technician* can expect to advance on *their* merit.

TO   *Technicians* can expect to advance on *their* merit.

Other possible solutions are to use *his or her* instead of *his* alone or to omit the pronoun completely if it isn't essential to the meaning of the sentence.

REVISE   *Everyone* must submit *his* expense report by Monday.

TO   *Everyone* must submit *his or her* expense report by Monday.

OR   Everyone must submit *an* expense report by Monday.

However, *he or she* can become monotonous when constantly repeated, and a pronoun cannot always be omitted without changing the meaning of a sentence. The best solution, then, is the first one—to use the plural whenever possible.

Consistency

Much like agreement errors, illogical shifts in *person* or *tense* can confuse the reader. You would be confused, for example, if someone wrote to you: "If *you* show the guard *your* pass, *one* will be allowed to enter the gate" (shift in person) or "When the contract *was* signed, the company *submits* the drawings" (shift in tense). Your confusion would disappear, however, if the sentences were revised as follows:

EXAMPLES   If *you* show the guard your pass, *you* will be allowed to enter the gate. (consistent use of person)

When the contract *was* signed, the company *submitted* the drawings. (consistent use of tense)

Consistency of tense.   *Tense* refers to the forms of a verb that indicate time distinctions. A verb may express past, present, or future time. Be consistent in your use of tense; an unnecessary and illogical change of tense within a sentence confuses the reader.

EXAMPLE   Before he *installed* the circuit board, he *cleans* the contacts.

This sentence, for no apparent reason, changes from the past tense (*installed*) to the present tense (*cleans*). To be both correct and logical, the sentence must be written with both verbs in the same tense.

REVISE   Before he *installed* the circuit board, he *cleans* the contacts.

TO   Before he *installed* the circuit board, he *cleaned* the contacts.

OR   Before he *installs* the circuit board, he *cleans* the contacts.

The only acceptable change of tense within a sentence records a real change of time.

EXAMPLE   After you *have assembled* Part A [past tense, because the action occurred in the past], *assemble* Part B [present tense because the action occurs in the present].

Consistency of person.   *Person* refers to the forms of a personal pronoun that indicate whether the pronoun represents the speaker, the person spoken to, or the person (or thing) spoken about. If the pronoun represents the *speaker,* the pronoun is in the *first person.*

EXAMPLE   *I* could not find the answer in the manual.

If the pronoun represents the person or persons spoken *to,* the pronoun is in the *second person.*

EXAMPLE   *You* are going to be a good supervisor.

If the pronoun represents the person or persons spoken *about*, the pronoun is in the *third person*.

EXAMPLE   *They* received the news quietly.

Identifying pronouns by person helps you avoid illogical shifts from one person to another. A very common error is to shift from the third person to the second person.

REVISE   *People* should spend the morning hours on work requiring mental effort, for *your* mind is freshest in the morning.

TO   *People* should spend the morning hours on work requiring mental effort, for *their* minds are freshest in the morning.

OR   *You* should spend the morning hours on work requiring mental effort, for *your* mind is freshest in the morning.

Dangling Modifiers

A *dangling modifier* occurs when a modifying phrase does not clearly and logically refer to the correct noun or pronoun.

EXAMPLE   While eating lunch in the cafeteria, the computer malfunctioned.

Although the idea of a computer eating lunch in a cafeteria is ridiculous, that is what the sentence actually states. With the dangling modifier corrected, the sentence would read as follows:

EXAMPLE   While *I* was eating lunch in the cafeteria, the computer malfunctioned.

Dangling modifiers often can be humorous, as in the first example. But they can also cause such confusion that your reader misinterprets the meaning of your sentence completely.

One way to correct a dangling modifier is to add a noun or pronoun for the phrase to modify.

REVISE   After finishing the research, the job was easy. (The phrase *after finishing the research* has nothing to modify. Who finished?)

TO   After finishing the research, *we* found the job to be easy. (The pronoun *we* tells the reader who finished.)

REVISE   Having evaluated the feasibility of the project, the centralized plan was unanimously approved. (Who evaluated the feasibility of the project?)

TO   Having evaluated the feasibility of the project, the *committee* unanimously approved the centralized plan.

REVISE	Keeping busy, the afternoon passed swiftly. (Who was keeping busy?)
TO	Keeping busy, *I* felt that the afternoon passed swiftly.

A dangling modifier can also be corrected by making the phrase a clause.

REVISE	After finishing the research, the job was easy.
TO	*After we finished the research* [clause], the job was easy.
REVISE	Having evaluated the feasibility of the project, the centralized plan was unanimously approved.
TO	*Once the committee had evaluated the feasibility of the project* [clause], the centralized plan was overwhelmingly approved.
REVISE	Keeping busy, the afternoon passed swiftly.
TO	*Because I kept busy* [clause], the afternoon passed swiftly.

Occasionally, a subject and verb are omitted from a dependent clause, forming what is known as an *elliptical clause*. If the omitted subject of the elliptical clause is not the same as the subject of the main clause, the construction dangles. Simply adding the subject and verb to the elliptical clause solves the problem. (Or you can rework the whole sentence.)

REVISE	When ten years old, his father started the company. (Could his father have started the company at age ten?)
TO	When *Bill Krebs was* ten years old, his father started the company.
OR	Bill Krebs was ten years old when his father started the company.

Misplaced Modifiers

A modifier is misplaced when it modifies, or appears to modify, the wrong word or phrase. A misplaced modifier differs from a dangling modifier in that a dangling modifier cannot logically modify *any* word in the sentence because a word or group of words is missing. The best general rule for avoiding misplaced modifiers is to place modifiers as close as possible to the words they are intended to modify.

A misplaced modifier can be a word, a phrase, or a clause.

Misplaced words.   Adverbs are especially likely to be misplaced because they can appear in several positions within a sentence.

EXAMPLES	We *almost* lost all the parts.
	We lost *almost* all the parts.

The first sentence means that all the parts were *almost* lost (but they were not), while the second sentence means that a majority of the parts (*almost* all) were in fact lost. Possible confusion in sentences of this type can be avoided by placing the adverb immediately *before* the word it is intended to modify.

Misplaced phrases.   To avoid confusion, place phrases near the words they modify. Note the two meanings possible when the phrase is shifted in the following sentences:

EXAMPLES   The equipment *without the accessories* sold the best. (Different types of equipment were available, some with and some without accessories.)

The equipment sold the best *without the accessories*. (One type of equipment was available, and the accessories were optional.)

Either of these sentences could be correct, of course, depending on the meaning the writer intends.

Misplaced clauses.   To avoid confusion, clauses should be placed as close as possible to the words they modify.

REVISE   We sent the brochure to four local firms *that had three-color illustrations.*

TO   We sent the brochure *that had three-color illustrations* to four local firms.

Sentence Fragments

A sentence that is missing an essential part (*subject* or *predicate*) is called a *sentence fragment.*

EXAMPLES   He quit his job. (Sentence: *He* is the subject; *quit his job* is the predicate.)

And left for Australia. (Fragment: subject is missing.)

But having a subject and a predicate does not automatically make a group of words a sentence. The word group must also make an independent statement. "If I work" is a fragment because the subordinating conjunction *if* turns the statement into a dependent clause.

Sentence fragments are often introduced by relative pronouns (*who, whom, whose, which, that*) or subordinating conjunctions (such as *although, because, if, when,* and *while*). The presence of any one of these words should alert you to the fact that what follows is a dependent clause, not a sentence, and must be combined with a main clause.

REVISE	The new manager instituted several new procedures. *Many of which are impractical.* (*Many of which* must be linked to *procedures.*)
TO	The new manager instituted several new procedures, many of which are impractical.

A sentence must contain a main, or finite, verb. Verbals, which are forms derived from verbs but different in function, will not do the job. The following examples are sentence fragments because they do not contain main verbs. *Providing, to work, waiting* are verbals and cannot perform the function of a main verb.

REVISE	*Providing* all employees with hospitalization insurance.
TO	The company *provides* all employees with hospitalization insurance.
REVISE	*To work* a forty-hour week.
TO	The new contract *requires* all employees to work a forty-hour week.
REVISE	The customer *waiting* to see you.
TO	The customer waiting to see you *is* from the Labatronics Corporation.

Fragments usually reflect incomplete and sometimes confused thinking. The most common type of fragment is the careless addition of an afterthought.

REVISE	The workload increased. By 40 percent.
TO	The workload increased by 40 percent.

The following examples are common types of sentence fragments. As these examples show, a fragment should usually be part of the preceding sentence.

REVISE	Some of our customers prefer to pay at the time of purchase. *While others find installment payments preferable.*
TO	Some of our customers prefer to pay at the time of purchase, while others find installment payments preferable.
REVISE	The union board approved the contract. *After much discussion.*
TO	The union board approved the contract after much discussion.
REVISE	We reorganized the department. *Distributing the work load more evenly.*
TO	We reorganized the department, distributing the work load more evenly.
REVISE	We consider your proposal excellent. *One of the best this year.*
TO	We consider your proposal excellent, one of the best this year.

REVISE   The executive committee met yesterday for only one purpose.
           To consider the proposed merger with the Acme Corporation.

TO   The executive committee met yesterday for only one purpose:
           to consider the proposed merger with the Acme Corporation.

A hopelessly snarled fragment simply has to be rewritten. The most effective way to revise is to pull the main points out of the fragment, list them in the proper sequence, and then rewrite the sentence.

REVISE   Financing the new project and allocating funds to it during the
           coming year by means of a transfer of a portion of the research
           and development budget, but several new products must not be
           developed if we do.

MAIN   1. There is a new project.
POINTS
           2. The new project must be financed.

           3. Research and development money can be used to finance it.

           4. If research and development money is used, the develop-
              ment of several new products must be stopped.

TO   The new project can be financed during the coming year by
           transferring funds from the research and development budget;
           however, doing so would require that the development of sev-
           eral new products be stopped.

Run-on Sentences

A *run-on sentence*, sometimes called a *fused sentence*, is made up of two or more independent clauses (sentence elements that contain a subject and a predicate and could stand alone as complete sentences) without punctuation to separate them.

INCORRECT   The new manager instituted several new procedures some were
              impractical.

Run-on sentences can be corrected in the following ways:

1. Create two separate sentences.

   CORRECT   The new manager instituted several new procedures.
               Some were impractical.

2. Join the two clauses with a semicolon if they are closely related.

   CORRECT   The new manager instituted several new procedures;
               some were impractical.

3. Join the two clauses with a comma and a coordinating conjunction.

> CORRECT   The new manager instituted several new procedures, but some were impractical.

4. Subordinate one clause to the other.

> CORRECT   The new manager instituted several new procedures, some of which were impractical.

5. Join the two clauses with a conjunctive adverb preceded by a semicolon and followed by a comma.

> CORRECT   The new manager instituted several new procedures; however, some were impractical.

Comma Errors

The most common punctuation problem is the misuse of the comma. This is understandable because the comma has such a wide variety of uses: it links, it encloses, it separates, and it indicates omissions. (For a complete discussion of the comma and all other marks of punctuation, see the Handbook at the end of this book.) The following guidelines will help you to use the comma correctly and effectively.

Comma splice.   When two independent clauses are joined with only a comma, the error is known as a *comma splice.* Like a run-on sentence, which also contains improperly connected clauses, a comma splice can be corrected in several ways: (1) joining the two clauses with a comma and a coordinating conjunction, (2) subordinating one clause to the other, (3) joining the two clauses with a semicolon if they are closely related, (4) joining the two clauses with a conjunctive adverb preceded by a semicolon and followed by a comma, or (5) creating two separate sentences.

REVISE   It was five hundred miles to the facility, we made arrangements to fly. (comma splice)

TO   It was five hundred miles to the facility, so we made arrangements to fly. (comma plus coordinating conjunction)

OR   Because it was five hundred miles to the facility, we made arrangements to fly. (one clause subordinated to the other)

OR   It was five hundred miles to the facility; we made arrangements to fly. (semicolon)

OR   It was five hundred miles to the facility; therefore, we made arrangements to fly. (semicolon, conjunctive adverb, comma)

OR   It was five hundred miles to the facility. We made arrangements to fly. (two sentences)

When correcting a comma splice, be sure that the solution you choose correctly conveys the intended meaning of the original sentence.

Superfluous commas. Do not place a comma everywhere you pause. Although it is true that commas usually signal pauses, *it is not true that pauses necessarily call for commas.* A number of common errors involve placing commas where they do not belong.

Do not place a comma between a subject and its verb or between a verb and its object.

REVISE　　　　The cold conditions, made accurate readings difficult. (The comma incorrectly separates the subject, *conditions,* from its verb, *made.*)

TO　　　　　The cold conditions made accurate readings difficult.

REVISE　　　　He has often said, that one company's failure is another's opportunity. (The comma incorrectly separates the verb, *said,* from its object, *that one company's failure is another's opportunity.*)

TO　　　　　He has often said that one company's failure is another's opportunity.

Do not place a comma between the two parts of a compound subject or a compound predicate.

REVISE　　　　The director of the Engineering Department, and the supervisor of the Quality Control Section were both opposed to the new schedules. (The comma incorrectly separates the parts of the compound subject, *director* and *supervisor.*)

TO　　　　　The director of the Engineering Department and the supervisor of the Quality Control Section were both opposed to the new schedules.

REVISE　　　　The director of the Engineering Department listed five major objections, and asked that the new schedules be reconsidered. (The comma incorrectly separates the parts of the compound predicate, *listed five major objections* and *asked that the new schedules be reconsidered.*)

TO　　　　　The director of the Engineering Department listed five major objections and asked that the new schedules be reconsidered.

Do not place a comma after a coordinating conjunction such as *and* or *but.*

REVISE　　　　The chairman formally adjourned the meeting, but, the members of the committee continued to argue. (The word *but* is part of the second clause and should not be separated from it by a comma.)

TO   The chairman formally adjourned the meeting, but the members of the committee continued to argue.

REVISE   I argued against the proposal. And, I gave good reasons for my position. (The word *and* is part of the sentence and should not be separated from it by a comma.)

TO   I argued against the proposal. And I gave good reasons for my position.

Do not place a comma before the first item in a series or after the last item in a series.

REVISE   We are considering a number of new products, such as, calculators, typewriters, and cameras.

TO   We are considering a number of new products, such as calculators, typewriters, and cameras.

REVISE   It was a fast, simple, inexpensive, process.

TO   It was a fast, simple, inexpensive process.

PHYSICAL APPEARANCE

The most thoughtfully prepared, carefully written, and conscientiously revised writing will quickly lose its effect if it has a poor physical appearance. In the classroom or on the job, a sloppy appearance will invariably lead your reader to assume that your work is also sloppy. In the classroom, that carelessness will reflect on you; on the job, it can reflect on your employer as well.

Consider Christine Thomas's memo to Harriet Sullivan in Chapter 1. Christine wanted to persuade Harriet. A memo written in sloppy or illegible handwriting on coffee-stained paper would not have helped Christine accomplish her purpose. Similarly, your writing will not accomplish its purpose if it has a poor physical appearance. Neatness counts!

Unless your instructor provides other specific instructions, use the following guidelines to give your writing a neat and pleasing appearance:

1. Use good quality paper—ruled if you write by hand or white bond if you type.
2. Type if at all possible. Otherwise, make sure that your handwriting is neat and readable.
3. If you type, make sure that the ribbon is fresh and the keys are clean so the letters will not fade or smudge.

4. Use at least one-inch margins on the sides of the paper and one and one-half inch margins on the top and bottom.
5. Handle the paper carefully with clean hands so it does not get crumpled or marked with fingerprints.
6. Make sure that the writing is not crowded and that ample white space separates sections.

Good physical arrangement of specific types of writing, such as letters or formal reports, is discussed elsewhere in the book. Refer to the table of contents or the index for page numbers.

CHAPTER SUMMARY

Like all good writers, you must revise your writing carefully. The first step toward careful revision is to become objective about your writing—allow for a cooling period and then view your draft as if it were written by a stranger. Then revise your draft in passes, examining one aspect of your writing at a time, and look for your worst errors first.

As you revise, it is essential that you check your writing for accuracy and completeness. In addition, you need to examine your writing for grammatical correctness. Check for agreement of subjects and verbs and of pronouns and antecedents, consistency of tense and of person, and clear pronoun reference, and eliminate dangling modifiers, misplaced modifiers, sentence fragments, run-on sentences, and basic comma errors.

Even with the most careful revision, however, you will lose your reader's confidence unless your writing has a neat and pleasing physical appearance.

EXERCISES

1. In each of the following sentences, select the correct word or words from the two items in parentheses. In some sentences, the choice involves the correct pronoun; in other sentences, it involves the correct verb.

    a. The supervisor asked each employee to decide whether (he/they) wanted to work overtime to finish the project.
    b. Her job during the negotiations (was/were) to observe and then report her observations to the manager.
    c. Our line of products (is/are) sold in the West and in the Midwest.
    d. Reports that present only one side of a question (does/do) an injustice to the reader.
    e. Neither John nor Peter remembered to submit (his/their) work on time.

    f. The Association of Corporate Employees failed because (they/it) never received full support from the member companies.

    g. The hidden cameras, which had been objected to by the defense attorney, (were/was) removed from the room.

    h. Inside the warehouse (was/were) many valuable parts.

    i. Any employee who has not completed (his/their) time sheet must do so now.

    j. A number of beneficial products (has/have) resulted from the experiment.

    k. That these figures are contradictory anyone in (their/his) right mind can see.

    l. The benefits and the pay (is/are) difficult to resist.

    m. A staff member is held responsible for any errors (he or she/they) may introduce.

    n. Neither a liquid cleaner nor a hand auger (remove/removes) this type of blockage.

2. Revise the following sentences to correct any errors in agreement. The errors may be in subject–verb agreement or in pronoun–antecedent agreement.

    a. A common sight on Monday mornings are a line of applicants waiting for the employment office to open.

    b. A discussion of the advantages and disadvantages of the new technique are published in the July newsletter.

    c. A survey of residents in the selected communities show a large potential market for our product.

    d. Each employee must submit their vacation schedule by January 15.

    e. After each of the printed characters are translated, the report is given to the word-processing department.

    f. The committee is planning to submit their recommendations before the end of the week.

    g. The course instructs students in the basics of the subject and provides him with hands-on time.

    h. An applicant must always consider the kind of job they will accept.

    i. A project engineer must be able to justify the changes they make in a technician's drawing.

    j. Neither of the two production assistants was able to attend the staff conference yesterday.

3. Each of the following sentences contains either a dangling modifier or a misplaced modifier. Locate the errors and correct them. Add any necessary words.

a. An experienced technician, the company was anxious to hire her.
b. To test it effectively, all types of applications must be considered.
c. Before taking the training course, it is recommended that the operator read the *Operator's Manual.*
d. After evaluating the 38 answers, the test was found by the production manager to reveal a serious deficiency.
e. Hoping to be promoted for her contribution to the project, the vice president's report represents three months of work.
f. We must buy pencil lead for the draftsmen that won't break.
g. We purchased the store's merchandise that was going out of business.
h. We are going to install a desk chair for our assistant with a swivel seat.
i. When writing a business letter, the tone of the correspondence reflects the outlook of the firm.
j. While having my teeth examined, the dentist told me that two wisdom teeth would have to be pulled.

4. Correct any sentence fragments or run-on sentences in this exercise. Add words and punctuation as necessary.

a. You cannot consider submitting the report, If you have not typed it.
b. Hoping to hear from you soon.
c. Supplies are needed to operate and maintain the printout device. Among them ribbon shields, forms, and print bands.
d. I spray the trees twice a year. Once in the late spring and again in early fall.
e. The hydraulic lift raises the elevator to the top floor. And then lowers it again.
f. The stenographic reporter read back the transcript. Because the members of the jury wanted to hear the evidence once more.
g. Almost half of their sales are of nonbook materials. Including science kits, films, tapes, and experimental animals.
h. Two points need further discussion. Volume as a measure of success and the regulation of commissions.
i. Use these accepted signs consistently the typesetter will not understand any others.
j. You are not a physician you should not act like one.

5. Correct the comma faults in the following sentences by adding, changing, or deleting words and punctuation as needed.

a. The electric voltage in the line was too high, he dared not risk touching it.
b. An emergency occurs, another committee is born.

    c. Members may pay their dues immediately, ~~they~~ *or* may choose to have a statement mailed to their homes or offices.

    d. The computer's printer has a red, and tan cabinet.

    e. One should never be ashamed to be somewhat sentimental, for, a certain amount of sentimentality makes a person human.

    f. The new law did not put all accountants behind bars, it did make some accountants fearful, though.

    g. The engine overheated, the operator turned it off. *or semicolon*

    h. The operator needs only to press a button, or turn a knob.

    i. The operator turns the knob, when the machine is to be stopped.

    j. The report must be submitted today, the company will not accept it after 5 p.m.

4

Organizing Your Information

When a motion picture is filmed, the scenes are usually shot out of the sequence in which they will appear in the finished film. Different shooting locations, actors' schedules, weather conditions, and many other circumstances make shooting out of sequence necessary. If it were not for a skilled film editor, the completed film would be a jumble of randomly shot scenes. But the film editor, following the script, carefully splices the film together so that the story moves smoothly and logically from one event to the next, as the screen writer planned. Without a plan, no such order would be possible. For a film, the script is the plan. Without it, the film editor would have no guide for organizing the thousands of feet of film.

Organizing a film and organizing a piece of writing are obviously different tasks, but they have one element in common—both must be planned ahead of time. For a film, planning means creating a script. For a piece of writing, it means organizing the information into a sequence appropriate to the subject, the purpose, and the reader.

Organizing your information before you write has two important advantages. First, it forces you to reexamine the information you plan to include in your writing. You can check to be sure that you have sufficient facts and details to satisfy your reader's needs and achieve the purpose of your writing. Then it forces you to order the information so that your reader understands it as clearly as you do.

The method of organization will come naturally for many types of writing. Instructions for operating a piece of machinery will be arranged step by step. A trip report will usually follow chronological, or time, sequence. When a subject does not lend itself to one particular sequence, you can choose the best sequence, or combination of sequences, by considering your purpose in writing and your reader's needs. Suppose, for example, that you report on a trip to several offset-printing companies to gather information on the most efficient way to arrange equipment in the printing shop where you work. You would probably organize the report of the trip chronologically, but your description of the various shop layouts, emphasizing the physical location of the equipment, would be organized spatially. If you went on to make recommendations about the most workable arrangement for your shop, you would present the most efficient arrangement first, the second most efficient arrangement next, and so on. Thus the recommendations portion of the report would be organized according to decreasing order of importance.

The best way to plan your writing is to organize, or *sequence,* your information into a simple outline. For most on-the-job writing, it is sufficient to list the points you will take up and then arrange them in the order that you think will be clearest. Each example discussed in the chapter is preceded by such an outline. For longer reports that require more elaborate outlines, see the discussion of outlining in Chapter 13.

The most common ways to organize, or sequence, information in on-the-job writing are the following: step by step, chronological, spatial, decreasing order of importance, increasing order of importance, general to specific, and specific to general.

STEP BY STEP

In the step-by-step sequence, you divide your subject into steps and then present the steps in the order which most logically explains the subject. This arrangement is the most effective way to describe a mechanism in operation, such as an internal combustion engine, or to explain a process, such as the administration of cardiopulmonary resuscitation. Step by step is also the logical method for writing instructions. For example, the instructions for using a pay telephone follow a step-by-step sequence.

For Local Calls:

1. Deposit coin.
2. Listen for dial tone.
3. Dial number.

The greatest advantage of presenting your information in a step-by-step sequence is that it is easy for your reader to understand and follow. This is because the sequence of steps in your writing corresponds to the natural sequence of the process. If you were to write instructions for the proper way to clean teeth, for example, you would present the information in a step-by-step sequence:

```
                          OUTLINE

            The Proper Way to Clean Your Teeth

      Step 1.   Obtain proper brush.
      Step 2.   Use correct amount of toothpaste.
      Step 3.   Follow up-and-down brushing technique.
      Step 4.   Floss teeth to remove remaining particles.
      Step 5.   Brush soon after meals.
```

Having divided the information into steps, you could then write the instructions as follows:

The Proper Way to Clean Your Teeth

Step 1
Proper tooth cleaning begins with the proper equipment. Choose a brush stiff enough to remove particles from between your teeth, yet soft enough to massage your gums without making them bleed. A toothbrush labeled "medium" will usually accomplish both objectives.

Step 2
Squeeze out a bead of toothpaste just long enough to cover the bristles of your brush. Too much paste will prevent sufficient contact between the bristles and your teeth and gums.

Step 3
Brush your teeth with an up-and-down motion. The American Dental Association's Council on Dental Therapeutics recommends this technique to remove food particles from between the teeth and to give gums adequate stimulation.

Step 4
Rinse your mouth after brushing. Then use dental floss to remove food particles between your teeth that the toothbrush may have missed. Begin by wrapping the floss securely around your forefinger. Using a gentle back-and-forth motion, insert the floss between your teeth and move it gently up and down. Be sure to floss in the area where the teeth and gums meet.

Step 5
To maintain good oral hygiene, brush your teeth within one hour after each meal. If brushing is not possible after meals, rinse your mouth thoroughly instead.

When you present your information in steps, you must carefully consider the needs of your reader. Do not assume that your reader is as familiar with your subject as you are. Even for a simple process, be sure that you list *all* steps and that you explain each in adequate detail. Sometimes you must also indicate the purpose of a step, as well as explaining how it is performed or how it functions. Step 4 of the instructions for the proper way to clean teeth, for example, told the reader the purpose of flossing.

In some instructions or process descriptions, the steps can be presented in one sequence only. The steps for using a pay telephone, for example, must be carried out in the sequence in which they are listed. In other instructions or process descriptions, the steps can be presented in the sequence that the writer thinks is most effective. Some dentists recommend that teeth be flossed before they are brushed. This preference would require a different sequence of steps from the one given on the tooth-cleaning instructions you just read.

CHRONOLOGICAL

In a chronological sequence, you arrange events in the order in which they occur in time, beginning with the first event, going on to the next event, and so on until you have reached the last event. Trip reports, work schedules, minutes of meetings, and certain accident reports are among the types of writing in which information is organized chronologically.

In the following report, a fire fighter describes the events of a fire at a lumber mill. After providing important background information, the writer presents the events according to their time of occurrence.

```
                    OUTLINE

            Woodworking Plant Fire

1.  Setting
        Pile of combustible by-products stored near two
            buildings.
        Fire building used as electric shop and storage
            area for lumber.
        Fire building contained flammable liquids.
        Fire building contained sprinkler system.
2.  Cause of Fire
        Spontaneous ignition of combustible by-products,
            which spread to second building.
        Fire aided by 40-mph wind.
3.  Events of Fire
        6 A.M.: Fire first noticed.
        7 A.M. (approx.): Plant superintendent arrived and
            wet smoldering area.
        1:20 P.M. Fire resumed in same area.
        1:20 P.M. (approx.): Fire department called.
        Fire spread to second building; pumping equipment
            activated 15 to 30 minutes later.
```

WOODWORKING PLANT FIRE[1]

Exposed Building Destroyed   July 24, 19--

Notification Delayed   Burney, California

Setting   Wood bark, sawdust, and wood chips were stored in three piles about 100 feet south of one building at this lumber mill and 150 feet west of a second building. The second building, called the "panel plant," consisted of one story and a partial attic and was used in part as an electric shop, and in part for the storage of finished lumber. About six pallet loads of Class I flammable liquids in 55-gallon drums were stored in the western section. The building contained a sprinkler system.

[1] "Bimonthly Fire Record, *Fire Journal* 72 (March 1977), 24.

Cause of Fire

Fire, caused by spontaneous ignition of the piled bark, spread to saw-dust and chip piles, then to the chip-loading facilities, and finally to the panel plant. A 40-mph wind was blowing in the direction of the panel plant.

First Fire
Noticed

A watchman first noticed the fire in the bark pile about 6:00 a.m. He notified the plant superintendent, who arrived more than an hour later, hosed down the smoldering bark pile, and set up several irrigation sprinklers to wet the area.

Fire Depart-
ment Called

At about 1:20 p.m., smoke was seen at the further end of the bark pile. The hose was not long enough to reach this area and the local fire depart-ment was called, nearly eight hours after the fire was originally discovered.

Start of Pump-
ing Equipment
Delayed

The fire burned up into the hollow joisted roof of the panel plant. The sprinklers were on a dry system and, from accounts of witnesses, it is esti-mated that the fire pump was not started until after the fire had been burning in the panel plant for 15 to 30 minutes.

The plant was a $350,000 loss. . . .

This report follows a chronological sequence because the time in which the events occurred and the interval between events are crucial to an under-standing of how the fire developed. Consequently, the chronological se-quence is the best method for organizing this report.

SPATIAL

In a spatial sequence, you describe an object or a process according to the physical arrangement of its features. Depending upon the subject, you may describe the features from top to bottom, from side to side, from east to west (or west to east), from inside to outside, and so on. Descriptions of this kind rely mainly on dimension (height, width, length), direction (up, down, north, south), shape (rectangular, square, semicircular), and proportion (one-half, two-thirds). Features are described in relation to one another:

> One end is raised six to eight inches higher than the other end to permit the rain to run off.

Features are also described in relation to their surroundings:

> The lot is located on the east bank of the Kingman River.

The spatial method of organization is commonly used in descriptions of laboratory equipment, proposals for landscape work, construction-site prog-ress reports, and, in combination with a step-by-step sequence, in many types of instructions.

The following instructions, which explain how a two-person security team should conduct a methodical room search, make use of spatial sequencing:

```
                         OUTLINE
           Conducting a Methodical Room Search
```

1.   First, divide the room for the search.
        Divide it as nearly as possible into two equal
           parts.
        Base division on number of objects in room, not on
           room size.
        Divide room with imaginary line extending from one
           object to another.
2.   Select search height for first search.
        Base the height on average height of objects resting
           on floor--table and desk tops, chair backs, etc.
           (usually hip high).
3.   First room sweep
        Go to one end of imaginary dividing line, the
           starting point for first and all subsequent
           searches.
        Work way around room along walls to other end of the
           imaginary line.
          Check all floor and wall objects.
          Check floor under rugs.
        At end point, return to starting point and search
           the middle of the room to the first search
           height.
        Use electronic or medical stethoscope for all
           searches.
4.   Second room sweep
        Establish second search height (usually hip to chin
           or top of head of searchers).
        Return to starting point and repeat search up to
           second search height.
          Include objects hanging on walls, built-in storage
           areas, etc.
5.   Third room sweep
        Establish third search height (usually from top of
           head to ceiling).
        Return to starting point and repeat search up to
           ceiling.
          Include light fixtures, ceiling-mounted air
           conditioning ducts, etc.
6.   Fourth room sweep
        Perform if room has false ceiling or suspended
           ceiling.
          Check flush or ceiling-mounted light fixtures,
           structural frame members, etc.

Conducting a Methodical Room Search

First, look around the room to decide how the room should be divided for the search and to what height the first searching sweep should extend. The first sweep should include all items resting on the floor up to the selected height.

As nearly as possible, divide the room into two equal parts. Base the division on the number and type of objects in the room, not on the size of the room. Divide the room with an imaginary line that extends from one object to another—for example, the window on the north wall to the floor lamp next to the south wall.

Next, select a search height for the first sweep. Base this height on the average height of the majority of objects resting on the floor. In a typical room, this height is established by such objects as table and desk tops, chair backs, and so on. As a rule, the first sweep will be made hip high and below.

After dividing the room and establishing the first search height, go to one end of the agreed upon room division. This point will be the starting point for the first and all subsequent search sweeps. Beginning back to back, work your way around the room along the walls toward the other team member at the other end of the imaginary dividing line. Check all items resting on the floor adjacent to the walls; be sure to check the floor under the rugs. When you meet your partner at the other end of the room, return to the starting point and search all items in the middle of the room up to the first search height. Include all items mounted in or on the walls in the first search sweep, such as air conditioning ducts, baseboards, heaters, built-in storage units, and so on. During this and all subsequent searches, use an electronic or a medical stethoscope.

Then determine the search height for the second search sweep. This height is usually set at the chin or at the top of the head of the searchers. Return to the starting point and repeat the searching technique up to the second search height. This sweep typically covers objects hanging on walls, built-in storage units, tall standing items on the floor, and the like.

Next, establish the third search height. This area usually includes everything in the room from the top of the researcher's head to the ceiling. In this sweep, features like hanging light fixtures and mounted air conditioning units are examined.

Finally, if the room has a false or suspended ceiling, perform a fourth sweep. Check flush or ceiling light fixtures, air conditioning or ventilation ducts, speaker systems, structural frames, and so forth.

DECREASING ORDER OF IMPORTANCE

When you organize your information by a decreasing order of importance, you begin with the most important fact or point, then go on to the next most important, and so on, ending with the least important. Newspaper readers are familiar with this sequence of information. The most significant information always appears first in a news story, with related but secondary information completing the story.

Decreasing order of importance is an especially appropriate method of organization for a report addressed to a busy decision maker, who may be able to reach a decision after considering only the most important points— and who may not even have time to read the entire report. This sequence of

information is useful, too, for a report written for a variety of readers, some of
whom may be interested in only the major points and others in all the points.

OUTLINE

1. Most Qualified Candidate
        Mildred Bryand, Acting Chief, Claims Processing
        Section
            12 years' experience
            knows the department's operations
            strong production record
            supervisory experience
            contributions to automating claims records
            served as acting chief for several sections within
                the department
            continually ranked "outstanding" on job appraisals
2. Second Most-Qualified Candidate
        Michael Bastik, Claims Coordinator
            able administrator
            7 years' experience in department's operations
            currently enrolled in management-training courses
            OBJECTIONS: no on-the-job supervisory experience
            most recent work indirectly related to claims
                processing
            had difficulty adapting to automated claims record
                system
3. Third Most-Qualified Candidate
        Jane Fine, Administrative Assistant
            skilled administrator
            3 years' experience
            OBJECTIONS: lacks supervisory experience
            also lacks broad knowledge of claims procedures

MEMORANDUM

     To: Mary Vincenti, Chief, Personnel Department
   From: Frank W. Russo, Chief, Claims Department
   Date: November 13, 19---
Subject: Selection of Chief of the Claims Processing
          Section

The most qualified candidate for Chief of the Claims
Processing Section is Mildred Bryand, who is at present
Acting Chief of the Claims Processing Section. In her
twelve years in the Claims Department, Mrs. Bryand has
gained wide experience in all facets of the department's
operations. She has maintained a consistently high
production record and has demonstrated the skills and
knowledge that are required for the supervisory duties she
is now handling in an acting capacity. A number of
additional qualifications also make her the best
candidate: her valuable contributions to and cooperation
during the automation of the department's claims records;
her performance on several occasions as acting chief in

other sections of the Claims Department; the continual rating of "outstanding" she has received in all categories of her job—performance appraisals.

Michael Bastik, Claims Coordinator, our second choice, also has strong potential for the position. An able administrator, he has been with the company for seven years. For the past year he has been enrolled in several management—training courses at the university. He is ranked second, however, because he lacks supervisory experience and because his most recent work has been with the department's maintenance and supply components. He would be the best person to fill many of Mildred Bryand's responsibilities if she should be made full—time Chief of the Claims Processing Section.

Jane Fine, our third—ranking candidate, has shown herself a skilled administrator in her three years with the Claims Consideration Section. Despite her obvious potential, my main objection to her is that, compared with the other top candidates, she lacks the breadth of experience in claims processing that would be required of someone responsible for managing the Claims Processing Section. Jane Fine also lacks on—the—job supervisory experience.

INCREASING ORDER OF IMPORTANCE

When you want the most important of several ideas to be freshest in your reader's mind at the end of your writing, organize your information by increasing order of importance. This sequence begins with the least important point or fact, then moves to the next least important, and builds finally to the most important point at the end.

Writing organized by increasing order of importance has the disadvantage of beginning weakly, with the least important information, which can cause your reader to become impatient before reaching your main point. But for writing in which you build a case in which the ideas lead, point by point, to an important conclusion, increasing order of importance is an effective method of organization. Reports on production or personnel goals are often arranged by this method, as are oral presentations.

```
                        OUTLINE
    1.   Staffing problem: too few qualified electronics
         technicians
            new recruiting program necessary
    2.   Heavy reliance on veterans in past
            fewer veterans now available
               no draft
               attractive reenlistment opportunities for
                  technicians on active duty
            want—ad campaign less and less successful
```

3. Apprentice program providing too few new technicians
       school enrollments declining
       fewer high school graduates to enter apprentice
            program
       Career Day recruiting has not attracted enough
            interested high school graduates
4. Local and regional technical schools provide best
       pool of skilled personnel
          graduates are highly motivated
          training and experience are first-rate
          competition for these graduates is great
          recommend that we step up recruiting among this
               group
          meet with vice president to discuss details of new
               recruitment campaign

MEMORANDUM

To: William D. Vane, Vice President for Operations
From: Harry Matthews, Personnel Department
Date: December 3, 19--
Subject: Recruiting Qualified Electronics Technicians

To keep our company staffed with qualified electronics
technicians, we will have to redirect our recruiting
program.

In the past dozen years, we have relied heavily on the
recruitment of skilled veterans. An end to the military
draft, as well as attractive reenlistment bonuses for
skilled technicians now in uniform, has all but eliminated
veterans as a source of trained employees. Our attempts
to reach this group through ads in service newspapers and
daily newspaper ads has not been successful recently. I
think that the want ads should continue, although
each passing month brings fewer and fewer veterans as job
applicants.

Our in-house apprentice program has not provided the
needed personnel either. High school enrollments in the
area are continually dropping. Each year, fewer high
school graduates, our one source of trainees for the
apprentice program, enter the shop. Even vigorous Career
Day recruiting has yielded disappointing results. The
number of students interested in the apprentice program
has declined proportionately as school enrollment goes
down.

The local and regional technical schools produce the
greatest number of qualified electronics technicians.
These graduates tend to be highly motivated, in part
because many have obtained their education at their own
expense. The training and experience they have received
in the tech programs, moreover, are first-rate. Competition for these graduates is keen, but I recommend that
we increase our recruiting efforts and hire a larger share
of this group than we have been doing.

I would like to meet with you soon to discuss the details
of a more dynamic recruiting program in the technical
schools. I am certain that with the right recruitment
campaign we can find the skilled personnel essential to
our expanding role in electronics products and service.

GENERAL TO SPECIFIC

In a general-to-specific sequence, you begin your writing with a general statement and then provide facts or examples to develop and support that statement. For example, if you begin a report with the general statement "Companies that diversify are more successful than those that do not," the remainder of the report would offer examples and statistics that prove to your
reader that companies that diversify are, in fact, more successful than companies that do not.

A memorandum or report organized in a general-to-specific sequence
discusses only one point—the point made in the opening general statement.
All other information in the memo or report supports the general statement, as
in the following example:

OUTLINE

Locating Additional Circuit Suppliers

The company needs to locate additional suppliers of
circuits due to several related events.
1.   The current supplier is reducing output.
2.   Domestic demand for our calculators continues to
     increase.
3.   We are expanding into the foreign market.

Locating Additional Circuit Suppliers

General statement

Based on information presented at the Supply Committee meeting on
April 14, we recommend that the company locate additional suppliers of
integrated circuits. Several related events make such an action necessary.

Our current supplier, ABC Electronics, is reducing its output. Specifically, we can expect a reduction of between 800 and 1,000 units per
month for the remainder of this fiscal year. The number of units should
stabilize at 15,000 units per month thereafter.

Supporting information

Domestic demand for our calculators continues to grow. Demand during the current fiscal year is up 25,000 units over the last fiscal year. Sales
Department projections for the next five years show that demand should
peak next year at 50,000 units and then remain at that figure for at least the
following four years.

Finally, our overseas expansion into England and West Germany will
require additional shipments of 5,000 units per quarter to each country for
the remainder of this fiscal year. Sales Department projections put calculator
sales for each country at double this rate, or 20,000 units in a fiscal year, for
the next five years.

Examples and data that support the general statements are frequently accompanied by charts and graphs. Guidelines for creating and presenting illustrations are given in Chapter 15.

SPECIFIC TO GENERAL

When you organize information in a specific-to-general sequence, you begin with a specific statement and build to a general conclusion. The examples, facts, and statistics that you present in your writing support the general conclusion that comes at the end. This method of organization is somewhat like increasing order of importance in that it carefully builds its case and does not actually make its point until the end.

OUTLINE

The Facts About Seat Belts

1. Study of 4,500 accidents involving nearly 13,000 people showed only 20 percent of those involved wore seat belts.
2. Shoulder belts worn by only 4 percent.
3. Studies show passengers without belts are 4 times as likely to be killed as passengers wearing belts.
4. Estimated 40 percent of front-seat passenger car deaths could be prevented if seat belts were worn.
5. Survival chances in an accident are greater with seat belts.

The Facts About Seat Belts[2]

Statistic   Recently the Highway Safety Foundation studied the use of seat belts in 4,500 accidents involving nearly 13,000 people. Nearly all these accidents occurred on routes which had a speed limit of at least 40 mph. Only 20 percent of all the vehicle occupants were wearing any kind of seat belt.

Statistic   The shoulder-type belts were even more unpopular than the lap belts, and only 4 percent of the occupants who had shoulder belts were wearing them.

Statistic   In this study, as in other studies, it was found that vehicle passengers not using seat belts were more than 4 times as likely to be killed as those using them. The driver in some cases escaped a more serious injury by being thrown against the steering wheel.

General conclusion   A conservative estimate is that 40 percent of the front-seat passenger car deaths could be prevented if everyone used the seat belts, which the law requires the manufacturer to put into each automobile. If you are in an accident, your chances of survival are far greater if you are using your seat belt.

[2] *The Safe Driving Handbook* (New York: Grosset & Dunlap, 1970), pp. 84–85.

CHAPTER SUMMARY

This chapter presents the most commonly used methods of organizing information in job-related writing: step by step, chronological, spatial, decreasing
order of importance, increasing order of importance, general to specific, and
specific to general. Some subjects lend themselves naturally to a particular
method. Other subjects can be organized in more than one way; you must
choose the best method based on your reader's needs and the purpose of
your writing.

A simple outline will help you organize the information into a logical
sequence before you begin to write. Preparing an outline gives you a chance
to reexamine your information and order it in such a way that your reader
will understand it as clearly as you do.

EXERCISES

1. *Step by Step*
   Create an outline for one of the following topics, organizing it by a step-by-
   step sequence. Using the outline, write a paper of assigned length on the
   topic.

   a. changing a washer in a wash basin faucet
   b. starting and banking a fire in a wood-burning stove
   c. tuning a six-string acoustic guitar
   d. opening a checking account
   e. sharpening a chain-saw blade
   f. splicing together two pieces of movie film
   g. bathing a bedridden adult
   h. repairing a broken window
   i. borrowing money on a life-insurance policy
   j. how a monarch butterfly egg becomes an adult

2. *Chronological*
   Create an outline for one of the following topics, organizing it by a chronological sequence. Using the outline, write a paper of assigned length on the
   topic.

   a. the log of a typical day in which you have classes or in which you
      have both classes and work
   b. the report of an accident
   c. the report of a trip you have made either on the job or on your
      own
   d. instructions for breeding, raising, and selling puppies or other pets
   e. the life cycle of a typical fruit, from blossom to ripe fruit, in one
      growing season

3. *Spatial*
   Create an outline for one of the following topics, organizing it in a spatial sequence. Using the outline, write a paper of assigned length on the topic. Without relying on illustrations, describe the topic clearly enough so that a classmate, if asked, could create an accurate drawing or diagram based on your description.

   a. the layout of your apartment or of a floor in your home
   b. the layout of the reference room or other area of the school library
   c. the dimensions and pertinent features of the grounds of a public building
   d. the layout of a vegetable or flower garden
   e. the layout of the shop, office, or laboratory where you work
   f. instructions for disinfecting a hospital room, exterminating insects in a kitchen or other area, or painting or wallpapering a room

4. *Decreasing Order of Importance*
   Create an outline for one of the following topics, organizing it by decreas-ing-order-of-importance sequence. Using the outline, write a paper of assigned length on the topic.

   a. your job qualifications
   b. the advantages to you of living in a particular city or other area
   c. the importance of preventive maintenance of a machine or piece of equipment with which you are familiar
   d. the importance of preventive care in one area of health (diet, exer-cise, dental care, and so on)

5. *Increasing Order of Importance*
   Create an outline for one of the following topics, organizing it by increas-ing-order-of-importance sequence. Using the outline, write a paper of assigned length on the topic.

   a. the college courses you believe will be the most important to your career (discuss no more than five)
   b. why smoking should or should not be permitted in the classroom or on the job
   c. the advantages of learning to pilot a small airplane
   d. the reasons why you need a pay raise
   e. the advantages of a home solar-heating system
   f. a proposal to change a procedure where you work

6. *General to Specific*
   Choose one of the following statements, which you then go on to support with pertinent facts, examples, anecdotes, and so on. Outline the informa-

tion and write a paper of assigned length based on the outline.

    a. practice makes perfect
    b. volunteer jobs provide valuable experience in the working world
    c. for families on limited means, budgeting is essential
    d. the mark of a capable administrator is the willingness to delegate authority.

7. *Specific to General*
Draw your own conclusions, which you state in a plausible general statement, from your observations of trends or patterns as presented in one of the following sets of data. Outline the information that supports your conclusion and write a paper of assigned length based on your outline. Or you may select other information as a basis for this exercise from lists and tables in current yearbooks, almanacs, or newspapers.

    a. Deaths from Motor Vehicle Accidents in the U.S.

1978	51,500
1977	48,849
1976	44,520
1975	45,853
1974	46,402
1973	55,511
1972	56,278

    b. Vocational Training in the U.S., 1979

Type of Training	Men (18–24)	Women (18–24)
Office	300,000	1,100,000
Nursing, Health	63,000	432,000
Trades	1,100,000	384,000
Engineering	277,000	19,000
Agric. and Home Ec.	83,000	46,000
Other	153,000	93,000

5

Writing for a
Specific Purpose

In the previous chapter you learned that writers must sequence, or organize, their material to make it clear and readable: information that is not arranged in a meaningful order will leave the reader more confused than informed. But planning the organization of your material is not the only preparation you must make before you begin to write. You must also establish a *purpose* in writing. Depending on what kind of material you wish to present and on who your reader will be—and on how familiar he or she is with your subject—you can determine what your purpose is and then decide upon the most effective way to present your material.

We'll consider, in this chapter, a variety of on-the-job writing objectives. You may want to tell your reader how to perform a certain task, or you may need to explain how something works. You may want to describe something, or compare it with something else. Sometimes your subject will be easier for your reader to grasp if it is first divided into logical parts, or if the subject's key terms are defined. Or you may want to examine the cause of some event. Finally, your writing goal may be to persuade your reader to accept a particular viewpoint. The techniques discussed in this chapter should help you, first, to establish your purpose, and then to present your information in a way that will be clear and convincing to your reader.

INSTRUCTIONS

When you tell someone how to do something—how to perform a specific task—you are giving instructions. If your instructions are based on clear thinking and careful planning, they should enable your reader to carry the task out successfully.

To write accurate and easily understood instructions, you must thoroughly understand the task you are describing. Otherwise, your instructions could prove embarrassing or even dangerous. For example, the container of a brand-name drain cleaner carried the following warning:

Use Only as Directed

The instructions then directed the user to

Fill sink with one to two inches of cold water, then close off drain opening.

Users would certainly find it difficult to raise the water level in the sink *before* they closed the drain! Because most users simply ignored the instructions and performed the task according to common sense, no real harm resulted. But suppose that such confusing information were to appear on a bottle of intravenous fluid or in the instructions for assembling a piece of high-voltage electrical equipment. The results of inaccurate wording could be both costly and dangerous.

The writer of the drain-cleaning instructions was probably just being careless. Sometimes, though, a writer may not understand an operation well enough to write clear, accurate directions. If you are unfamiliar with a task for which you are writing instructions, watch someone who is familiar with it go through each step. As you watch, ask questions about any step that is not clear to you. Direct observation should help you write instructions that are exact, complete, and easy to follow.

In instruction writing, as in all job-related writing, you should be aware of your reader's level of knowledge and experience. Is the reader skilled in the kind of task for which you are writing instructions? If you know that your reader has a good deal of technical background, you might feel free to use fairly specialized, technical vocabulary. If, on the other hand, your reader has little or no technical knowledge of the subject, it would be more appropriate to use simple, everyday language—to avoid specialized or technical terms as much as possible.

To test the accuracy and clarity of your instructions, it's a good idea to ask someone who is not familiar with the operation to follow the directions you've written. A first-time user can spot missing steps or point out passages that should be worded more clearly. You may find it helpful, as you observe your tester, to make a note of any steps that seem especially puzzling or confusing.

To make your instructions easy to follow, divide them into short, simple steps. Be sure to arrange the steps in the proper sequence. Steps can be organized in one of two ways. (1) You can label each step with a sequential number.

1. Connect each black cable wire to a brass terminal . . .
2. Attach one 4-inch green jumper wire to the back . . .
3. Connect both jumper wires to the bare cable wires . . .

(2) Or you can use words that indicate time or sequence.

First, determine what the problem is that the customer is reporting to you. *Next,* observe and test the system in operation. *At that time,* question the operator until you believe that the problem has been explained completely.

Keeping the steps in the proper order is not always easy. Sometimes two operations must be performed at the same time. You should either state this fact in an introduction to the instructions or include both operations in the appropriate step.

WRONG   4. Hold the CONTROL key down.

                 5. Press the BELL key before releasing the CONTROL key.

RIGHT   4. While holding the CONTROL key down, press the BELL key.

You may find that the clearest, simplest instructions are those whose steps are phrased as "commands." Your instructions will be less wordy, and easier to follow, if you address each sentence directly to your reader.

INDIRECT   The operator should raise the access lid.

DIRECT   Raise the access lid.

Make instructions concise, but do not phrase them as if they were telegrams. You can write shorter sentences by leaving out articles (*a, an, the*) and some pronouns (*you, this, these*) and verbs, but sentences that have been shortened in this way often have to be read more than once to be understood. The following instruction for cleaning a computer punch card assembly, for example, is not easily understood at first reading.

Pass card through punch area for debris.

The meaning of the phrase *for debris* needs to be made clearer. Revised, the instruction is understandable at once.

Pass *a* card through *the* punch area *to clear away* any debris.

Since many people fail to read a set of instructions completely through before beginning a project, you should be aware of this tendency and plan ahead for your reader. If a process in step 9 is affected by instructions in step 2, say so in step 2. Otherwise your reader may reach step 9 before discovering that an important piece of information that should have been given in advance was not.

If any special tools or materials are needed for the project, tell your reader so at the beginning of the instructions. List any essential equipment at the beginning, in a section labeled "Tools Required" or "Materials Required." The reader should not get three-fourths of the way through a project only to discover that a special wrench is necessary for the final steps. The following list of materials appeared at the beginning of a set of instructions for developing film at home.

Materials Required

Exposed film	Clothespins
Developing tank and reel	Towel (paper or cloth)
Photographic thermometer	Scissors
Timer (clock or watch)	Glassine negative sleeves
Funnel (glass or plastic)	D-76 developer solution
Measuring cup (glass or plastic)	Fixing solution (hypo)
Vicose sponge	Water
String	Storage containers for D-76 and
	fixing solution (plastic, glass, or
	stainless steel)

The instructions, which were written for beginners, continued with a discussion of those terms likely to confuse inexperienced film developers: *developing tank and reel, developer solution,* and *fixing solution.*

In any operation, certain steps must be performed with more exactness than others. Anyone who has boiled a three-minute egg for four minutes understands this principle. Alert your reader to steps that require precise timing or measurement.

You also must warn readers of potentially hazardous steps or materials. If the instructions call for materials that are flammable or that give off noxious fumes, let the reader know before he or she reaches the step for which the material is needed. Warned in advance, your reader will be able to take the necessary precautions to avoid harm. You might use a warning technique like the one that appeared in a consumer-service booklet on cleaning fabric stains: it provided an information block labeled PRECAUTIONS. In it, the writer discussed the dangers of using solvents that are poisonous if swallowed, dangerous if inhaled, or flammable.

Finally, clear, well-thought-out illustrations can make instructions for even the most complex operations quickly understandable. Illustrations can simplify instructions by reducing the number of words necessary to explain something. Appropriate pictures and diagrams will enable your reader to identify parts and the relationships between parts more easily than will long explanations. They'll also free you, the writer, to focus on the steps making up the instructions rather than on descriptions of parts. Not all instructions require illustrations, of course. Whether illustrations will be useful depends on your reader's needs and on the nature of the project. Instructions for inexperienced readers should be more heavily illustrated than those for experienced readers. For a full discussion of how to create effective illustrations, see Chapter 15.

The following instructions guide the reader through the steps of "streaking" a saucer-sized disk of material (called *agar*) used to grow bacteria colonies. The object is to thin out the original specimen (the inoculum) so that the bacteria will grow in small, isolated colonies. The streaking process makes certain that part of the saucer is inoculated heavily, while its remaining portions are inoculated progressively more lightly. The streaking is done by hand with a thin wire, looped at one end for holding a small sample of the inoculum.

INSTRUCTIONS

Distribute the inoculum over the surface of the agar in the following manner:

(1) Beginning at one edge of the saucer, thin the inoculum by streaking back and forth over the same area several times, sweeping across the agar surface until approximately one quarter of the surface has been covered.

(2) Sterilize the loop in an open flame.

(3) Streak at right angles to the originally inoculated area, carrying the inoculum out from the streaked areas onto the sterile surface with only the first stroke of the wire. Cover half of the remaining sterile agar surface.

(4) Sterilize the loop.

(5) Repeat as described in step (3), covering the remaining sterile agar surface.

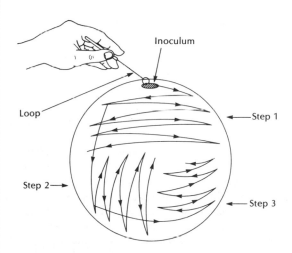

FIGURE 5–1. Progressive steps in making a streaked plate

EXPLAINING A PROCESS

When you prepare instructions, your goal is to enable your reader to complete a specific task by following the step-by-step procedure you have outlined. You know that your reader will use your directions to become a *doer*. If you are asked to write an explanation of a process, on the other hand, you will have a different purpose in mind: you will be telling your reader how something works or how something is done—but probably not something that your reader will actually do himself or herself. The process you explain might be an event that occurs in nature (the tidal pull of the moon), a function that requires human effort (rice harvesting), or an activity in which men and women operate machinery to produce goods or services (automobile assembly-line production).

Just as it is essential for you to be familiar with a task before you can write clear instructions for carrying it out, so you must thoroughly understand a process yourself before you can explain it to your reader. And, as in all work-related writing, you must aim your writing at a level appropriate to your reader's background. Beginners, you will probably find, require more basic information, and less technical vocabulary, than do experienced workers.

The explanation of a process has something else in common with written instructions: both kinds of writing are composed of steps. The steps in a process explanation should be as clear, accurate, and complete as those in a set of instructions.

In your opening paragraph, tell your reader why it is important to become familiar with the process you are explaining. Before you explain the steps necessary to form a corporation, for example, you could cite the tax savings that incorporation would permit. To give your reader a framework for the details that will follow, you might present a brief overview of the process. Finally, you might describe how the process works in relation to a larger whole of which it is a part. In explaining the air brake system of a large dump trunk, you might note that the braking system is one part of the vehicle's air system, which also controls the throttle and transmission-shifting mechanisms.

A process explanation can be long or short, depending on how much detail is necessary. The following description of the way in which a camera controls light to expose a photographic film fits into one paragraph.

> The camera is the basic tool for recording light images. It is simply a box from which all light is excluded except that which passes through a small opening at the front. Cameras are equipped with various devices for controlling the light rays as they enter this opening. At the press of a button, a mechanical blade or curtain, called a shutter, opens and closes automatically. During the fraction of a second that the shutter is open, the light reflected from the subject toward which the camera is aimed passes into the camera through a piece of optical glass called the *lens*. The lens focuses, or projects, the light rays onto the wall at the back of the camera. These light reflections are captured on a sheet of film attached to the back wall.

Many process explanations require more details and will, of course, be longer than a paragraph. The following example discusses several methods of surface mining for coal. The writer begins with an overview of the elements common to all the processes, defines the terms important to the explanation, and then describes each separately. Transitional words and phrases serve to achieve unity within paragraphs, and headings mark the transition from one process to the next.

SURFACE MINING OF COAL

The process of removing the earth, rock, and other strata (called <u>overburden</u>) to uncover an underlying mineral deposit is generally referred to as surface mining. Strip mining is a specific kind of surface mining in which all the overburden is removed in strips, one cut at a time. Three types of strip mining methods are used to mine coal: <u>area</u>, <u>contour</u>, and <u>mountain-top removal</u>. Which method is used depends upon the topography of the area to be mined.

Area Strip Mining

Area strip mining is used in regions of flat to gently rolling terrain, like those found in the Midwest and West. Depending on applicable reclamation laws, the topsoil may be removed from the area to be mined, stored, and later reapplied as surface material during reclamation of the mined land. Following removal of the topsoil, a trench is cut through the overburden to expose the upper surface of the coal to be mined. The length of the cut generally corresponds to the length of the property or of the deposit. The overburden from the first cut is placed on unmined land adjacent to the cut. After the first cut is completed, the coal is removed and a second cut is made parallel to the first. The overburden (now referred to as spoil) from each of the succeeding cuts is deposited in the adjacent pit from which the coal was just removed. The final cut leaves an open trench equal in depth to the thickness of the over- burden plus the coal bed, bounded on one side by the last spoil pile and on the other side by the undisturbed soil. The final cut may be as far as a mile from the first cut. The overburden from all the cuts, unless graded and leveled, resembles the ridges of a giant washboard.

Contour Strip Mining

In areas of rolling or very steep terrain, such as in the eastern United States, contour strip mining is used. In this method, the overburden is removed from the mineral seam in a pattern that follows the contour line around the hillside. The overburden is then deposited on the downslope side of the cut until the depth of the overburden becomes too great for economical recovery of the coal. This method leaves a bench, or shelf, on the side of the hill, bordered

on the inside by a highwall (30 to 100 feet high) and on
the outer side by a high ridge of spoil.

A method of mining that is often used in conjunction
with contour mining is <u>auger mining</u>. This method is employed
when the overburden becomes too thick and renders contour
mining uneconomical and when extraction by underground
mining would be too costly or unsafe. In auger mining an
instrument bores holes horizontally into the coal seam. The
coal can then be removed like the shavings produced by a
drill bit. The exposed coal seam in the highwall is left
with a continuous series of bore holes from which the coal
was removed.

Mountain—Top Removal

In areas of rolling or steep terrain an adaptation of
area mining to conventional contour mining is used; it is
called the mountain—top removal method. With this method
entire mountain tops are removed down to the coal seam by a
series of parallel cuts. This method is economical when the
coal lies near the tops of mountains, ridges, or knobs. If
there is excess overburden that cannot be stored on the
mined land, it may be transported elsewhere.

DESCRIPTION

When you give your reader information about an object's size, shape, color,
method of construction, or other feature of its appearance, you are describing
it. The kind of descriptions you will write on the job depends, of course, on
where you work and on what you do. Office administrators describe office
space and layouts. Equipment maintenance workers write parts and equipment descriptions. And police descriptions of accident scenes are routinely
used in court cases. The key to effective descriptions is the accurate presentation of details. To select appropriate details, determine what use your reader
will make of the description. Will your reader use it to identify something? Will
your reader have to assemble or repair the object you are describing? Which
details you include, then, depends on the task the reader will perform.

Descriptions can be brief and simple, or they can be highly complex. Simple descriptions usually require only a simple listing of key features. A purchase order is a typical example of simple descriptive writing.

PURCHASE ORDER

Part No.	Description	Quantity
GL/020	Trash compactor bags, 31" × 50" tubular, non—transparent, 5—mil thickness, including 100 tie wraps per carton	5 cartons @ 100 per carton

Purchase-order descriptions should be clear and specific. An inaccurate or omitted detail may result in the delivery of the wrong item. Even an order for something as ordinary as trash compactor bags needed, in addition to the part number, five specific descriptive details.

Complex descriptions, of course, require even more details than do simple descriptions. The details you select should accurately and vividly convey what you are describing. If it is useful for your reader to visualize an object, for instance, include details—like color and shape—that appeal to the sense of sight. The example that follows is a description of the leaf abnormalities that occur when trees are planted in soil lacking the necessary minerals. The writer, a forester, offers precise details of the changes in color that he has observed.

> Foliage of the black cherry trees showed striking and unusual discolorations in mid-August. Bright red margins extended one half the distance to the midrib and almost to the tip of the leaf. Nearly all leaves were similarly discolored and showed a well-defined line of demarcation between the pigmentation and the normal coloration. By late September, the pigmentation margins had widened and extended to the tips of the leaves. The red deepened in intensity and, in addition, blue and violet hues were apparent for the first time.

The description of leaf abnormalities concentrates on appearance—it tells the reader what the discolored leaves looked like. Sometimes, however, you may want to describe the physical characteristics of an object and at the same time itemize the parts that go into its makeup. If you intended to write a description of a piece of machinery, for example, you would probably find this approach, called the *whole-to-parts* technique, the most useful for your purpose. You would first present a general description of the device, since an overall description would provide your reader with a frame of reference for the more specific details that follow—the physical description of the various parts and the location and function of each in relation to the whole. The description would conclude with an explanation of the way the parts work together to get their particular job done.

The following paragraph describes the assembly of an electronic typewriter that feeds coded tape or punch cards into the machine. Intended for the typewriter mechanic, this description includes an illustration of the assembly mechanism.

The Die Block Assembly (Figure 5-2) consists of two machined block sections, eight Code Punch Pins, and a Feed Punch Pin. The larger section, called the Die Block, is fashioned of a hard, non-corrosive beryllium-copper alloy. It houses the eight Code Punch Pins and the smaller Feed Punch Pin in nine finely machined guide holes. The guide holes at the upper part of the Die Block are made smaller to conform to the thinner tips of the Punch Pins. Extending over the top of the Die Block and secured to it at one end is a smaller, arm-like block called the Stripper Block. The Stripper Block is made from hardened tool steel, and it also has been drilled through with nine finely machined guide holes. It is carefully fitted to the Die Block at the factory so that its holes will be precisely above those in the Die Block and so that the space left between the blocks will measure .015" (plus or minus .003"). This space should be barely wide enough to allow the passage of a tape or edge-card. It is here, as the Punch Pins are driven up through the media and into the Stripper Block, that the actual cutting, or punching, of the code and feed holes takes place. The residue (chad) from the hole punching operation is pushed out through the top of the Stripper Block and guided out of the assembly by means of a plastic Chad Collector and Chad Collector Extender.

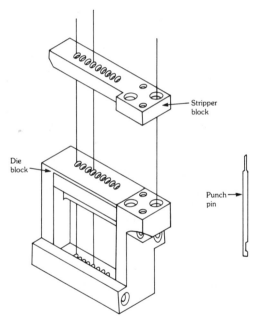

FIGURE 5-2. Die Block Assembly

Illustrations can be powerful aids in descriptive writing, especially when they show details too cumbersome to explain in writing. Do not hesitate to use an illustration with a complex description if the illustration creates a clearer image. Detailed instructions on the use of illustrations appear in Chapter 15.

COMPARISON

To explain something on the job, you may have to tell how it is like or unlike something else. When you do you are making a comparison; you are saying A is like B.

EXAMPLE   A direct-read water meter gives at-a-glance totals of cubic feet used, just as the odometer of a car provides cumulative readings of miles driven.

Comparisons that point out how things differ are also useful.

EXAMPLE   Air-powered filters attract dust, pollen, and pollutants electro-statically; *they differ from electronic filters in using moving air instead of electricity to generate a charge.*

Comparisons come naturally to us. Think of how often you use comparisons yourself. You regularly compare the merits of TV shows, athletic teams, candidates for political office, and the like. In deciding which of two or more items is most suitable for a specific purpose, you automatically weigh the advantages and disadvantages of each one. On the job, you may be called upon to select the best product, the least expensive messenger service, or even the applicant most qualified for a position.

To be sure that your choice will be the best one, you must first determine on what basis you will make the comparison. If you were responsible for the purchase of chain saws for a logging company, you would have a number of factors to take into account in order to establish your bases for comparison. Because loggers use the equipment daily, you would have to select durable saws, with the right-size engine for the type of wood most frequently cut. Large hardwood trees require high-horsepower saws with thick chains and long bars. Saws used on softwood trees, or used primarily for cutting limbs rather than trunks, can be smaller and lighter. Since chain saws produce noise and vibration, you would want to compare the quality and cost of the various silencers on the market. In considering the various features of chain saws, you would *not* include in your comparison such irrelevant factors as color or place of manufacture. Taking all of these elements into account, you would establish a number of bases for choosing from among the available chain saws— engine size, chain thickness, bar length, antivibration mountings, and noise mufflers.

Once you have decided on what basis (or bases) you will make the comparison, you can determine the most effective method of organization to use. Comparisons can be organized several ways, but two methods that present the information in proper balance between likeness and difference appear most frequently. In the *whole-by-whole method,* all the relevant characteristics of one item are discussed before those of the next item are considered. In the *part-by-part method,* the relevant features of each item are compared one by one. The following discussion of typical woodworking glues, organized according to the whole-by-whole method, describes each type of glue and its characteristics before going on to the next type.

COMMON WOODWORKING ADHESIVES

WHITE GLUE is the most useful all-purpose adhesive for light construc-tion, but it should not be used on projects that will be exposed to moisture, high temperature or great stress. Wood that is being joined with white glue must remain in a clamp until the glue dries, which will take about 30 minutes.

ALIPHATIC RESIN GLUE has a stronger and more moisture-resistant bond than white glue. It must be used at temperatures above 50°F. The wood should be clamped for about 30 minutes. . . .

PLASTIC RESIN GLUE is the strongest of the common wood adhesives. It is highly moisture resistant—though not completely waterproof. Sold in powdered form, this glue must be mixed with water and used at temperatures above 70° F. It is slow setting and the joint should be clamped for four to six hours. . . .

CONTACT CEMENT is a very strong adhesive that bonds so quickly it must be used with great care. It is ideal for mounting sheets of plastic laminate on wood. It is also useful for attaching strips of veneer to the edges of plywood. Since this adhesive bonds immediately when two pieces are pressed together, clamping is not necessary, but the parts to be joined must be very carefully aligned before being placed together. Check the label before you work with this adhesive. Most brands are quite flammable and the fumes can be harmful if inhaled. For safety's sake, work in a well-ventilated area, away from flames or heat.[1]

As is often the case when the whole-by-whole method is used, the purpose of this comparison is to weigh advantages and disadvantages of each glue for certain kinds of woodworking. The comparison could be expanded, of course, by the addition of other types of glue. If, on the other hand, your purpose were to consider, one at a time, the various characteristics of all the glues, the information might be arranged according to the part-by-part method:

CHARACTERISTICS OF WOODWORKING ADHESIVES

   Woodworking adhesives are rated primarily according to their bonding strength, moisture resistance, and setting times.
   Bonding strengths are categorized as very strong, moderately strong, or adequate for use with little stress. Contact cement and plastic resin glue bond very strongly, while aliphatic resin glue bonds moderately strongly. White glue provides a bond least resistant to stress.
   Moisture resistance of woodworking glues is rated as high, moderate, and low. Plastic resin glues are highly moisture-resistant. Aliphatic resin glues are moderately moisture-resistant; white glue is least moisture-resistant.
   Setting times for these glues vary from an immediate bond to a four-to-six hour bond. Contact cement bonds immediately and requires no clamping. Because the bond is

[1] *Space and Storage* (Alexandria, Va.: Time-Life Books, 1977), p. 61.

```
immediate, surfaces being joined must be carefully aligned
before being placed together. White glue and aliphatic
resin glue set in thirty minutes; both require clamping to
secure the bond. Plastic resin, the strongest wood glue,
sets in four to six hours and also requires clamping.
```

The part-by-part method could accommodate further comparisons. Comparisons might be made according to temperature ranges, special warnings, common uses, and so on.

DIVISION AND CLASSIFICATION

An effective way to approach a complex subject is to divide it into manageable parts and then go on to explain each part separately. Although this technique is especially well suited to subjects that can be readily broken down into units, it can be used as the method of organization in a good deal of job-related writing. You might use this approach, called *division,* to describe a physical object, like a machine; to examine an idea, like the terms of a new labor – management contract; to explain a process, like the stages of an illness; or to give instructions, like the steps necessary to prepare a rusty metal surface for painting.

To explain the different types of printing processes currently in use, for example, you could divide the field into its major components and, where a fuller explanation was required, subdivide those (see Figure 5-3). The emphasis in division is on the breaking down of a complex whole into a number of like units—because it is easier to consider smaller units and to examine the relationship of each to the other.

The process by which a subject is divided is similar to the process by which a subject is classified. While division involves the separation of a whole

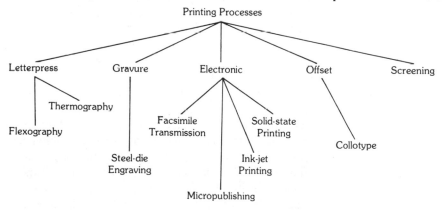

FIGURE 5-3

into its component parts, *classification* is the grouping of a number of units (people, objects, ideas, and so on) into related categories. Consider the following list:

Triangular file	Steel tape ruler
Needle-nose pliers	Vise
Pipe wrench	Keyhole saw
Mallet	Tin snips
C clamps	Rasp
Hacksaw	Plane
Glass cutter	Ball-peen hammer
Steel square	Spring clamp
Claw hammer	Utility knife
Crescent wrench	Folding extension ruler
Slip-joint pliers	Crosscut saw
Tack hammer	Utility scissors

How would you group the items in the list? You would begin by asking what they have in common. The most obvious characteristic they share is that they all belong in a carpenter's tool chest. With that observation as a starting point, you can begin to group the tools into related categories. Pipe wrenches belong with slip-joint pliers because both tools grip objects. The rasp and the plane belong with the triangular file because all three tools smooth rough surfaces. By applying this kind of thinking to all the items in the list, you can group each tool according to function (see Figure 5-4).

In dividing or classifying a subject, you must observe some basic rules of logic. First, divide the subject into its largest number of equal units. The basis for division depends, of course, on your subject and your purpose. If you are describing the *structure* of the Wankel rotating combustion engine, for example, you might begin by dividing the subject into its three major parts—the triangular-shaped rotor, the crank shaft, and the housing that contains them. If a more detailed explanation were needed, each of these parts, in turn, might be subdivided into its components. A discussion of the *function* of the same engine, on the other hand, would require a different logical basis for the division; such a breakdown would focus on the way in which combustion engines function: (1) intake, (2) compression, (3) combustion and expansion, and (4) exhaust.

Once you have established the basis for the division, you must apply it consistently. Put each item in only one category, so that items do not overlap categories. An examination of the structure of the rotary combustion engine that listed the battery as a major part would be illogical. Although it is part of the car's ignition system (which starts the engine), the battery is not a part of the engine itself. And a discussion of the parts of the ignition system which omitted the battery would be just as illogical.

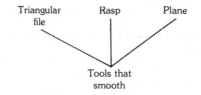

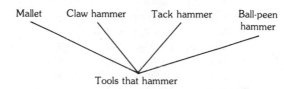

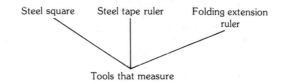

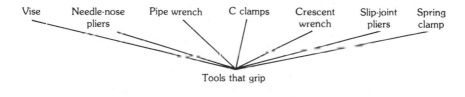

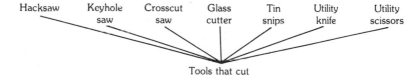

FIGURE 5-4

In the following example, two Canadian park rangers classify typical park users according to four categories; the rangers then go on to discuss how to deal with potential rulebreaking by members of each group. The rangers could have classified the visitors in a variety of other ways, of course: as city and country residents, backpackers and drivers of recreational vehicles, United States and Canadian citizens, and so on. But for law-enforcement agents in public parklands, the size of a group and the relationships among its members were the most significant factors.

DEALING WITH GROUPS

First, recognize the various types of campers. They can be broken down as follows:

, A. Family for weekend stay
   B. Small groups ("a few of the boys")
   C. Large groups or conventions
   D. Hostile gangs

Persons in groups A and B can probably be dealt with on a one-to-one basis. For example, suppose a member of the group is picking wild flowers, which is an offense in most park areas. Two courses of action are open. You could either issue a warning or charge the person with the offense. In this situation, a warning is preferable to a charge. First, advise the person that this action is an offense but, more importantly, explain why. Point out that the flowers are for all to enjoy and that most wild flowers are delicate and die quickly when picked.

For large groups, other approaches may be necessary. Every group has a leader. The leader may be official or, in informal or hostile groups, unofficial. If the group is organized, seek the official leader and hold this person responsible for the group's behavior. For informal groups, seek the person who assumes command and try to deal with this person.[2]

DEFINITION

Accurate definitions are crucial to many kinds of writing, especially for readers unfamiliar with your subject. Depending on your reader's needs, your definition can be formal, informal, or extended.

A *formal definition* is a form of classification. In it, you place a term in a class of related objects or ideas and show how it differs from other members of the same class.

DEFINITIONS

Term	Class	Difference
spoon	eating utensil	that consists of a small shallow bowl on the end of a handle.
auction	public sale	in which property passes to the highest bidder through successively increased offers.
annual	plant	that completes its life cycle, from seed to natural death, in one growing season.

[2] A. W. Moore and J. Mitchell, "Vandalism and Law Enforcement in Wildland Areas," in *Proceedings of the Wildland Recreation Conference,* Feb. 28–March 3, 1977, Banff Centre, Alberta, Canada.

In an *informal definition,* a familiar word or phrase is used as a synonym for an unfamiliar word or phrase.

EXAMPLES   An invoice is a *bill.*

Many states have set aside wildlife habitats (or *living space*).

Plants live in a *symbiotic,* or mutually benefiting, relationship with certain kinds of bacteria.

Dental *amalgam* is the material dentists use most frequently to fill tooth cavities.

The advantage of informal definitions is that they permit you to explain the meaning of a term with a minimum of interruption in the flow of your writing. Informal definitions should not be used, however, if the completeness of a formal definition is needed to make the term easier to understand.

When more than a phrase or a sentence or two is needed to explain an idea, use an *extended definition,* which explores a number of qualities of the item being defined. Some extended definitions may take only a few sentences, while others may run for several paragraphs. How long an extended definition ought to be depends on your reader's needs and on the complexity of the subject. A reader familiar with a topic or an area might be able to handle a long, fairly technical definition, whereas a newcomer to a topic would require simpler language and more basic information.

Compare the language and detail provided in the following two definitions, which explain the chemical concept *pH.* The first definition is intended for people in the graphic arts who need a general understanding of the concept but not a detailed explanation of the principles underlying the concept.

> **pH.** A number used for expressing the acidity or alkalinity of solutions. A value of 7 is neutral in a scale ranging from 0 to 14. Solutions of a lower value are considered acid, while those higher are alkaline.[3]

The second definition of pH, from an article about hydrogen ion activity in human blood, is intended for chemistry students and clinical laboratory technicians. The author assumes that his readers are familiar with chemical symbols (H^+), abbreviations (*mol/liter*), and terms (*ions*).

> About 70 years ago, the pH scale was devised to express hydrogen ion concentration in convenient numbers. The pH value, the exponent of the H^+ concentration in mol/liter with the sign changed from minus to plus, increases as hydrogen ion concentration increases. The normal pH of blood lies between 7.38 and 7.42, and a small change in pH can mean a big change in the H^+ concentration. For example, when pH changes from 7.4 to 7.0, the H^+ concentration increases 2½ fold, from 4×10^{-8} to 10×10^{-8} mol/liter.[4]

[3] International Paper Company, *Pocket Pal—A Graphic Arts Production Handbook,* 11th ed. (N.Y.: International Paper Company, 1974), p. 179.

[4] John A. Lott, "Hydrogen Ions in Blood," *Chemistry* 51 (May 1978), 6.

Perhaps the easiest way to define a term is to give specific examples of it. A landscape architect, for example, performed a land-use analysis of a regional park for officials of the Parks Department. Crucial to the analysis were a number of abstract concepts like *form, line,* and *color,* used in precise ways not necessarily corresponding to their everyday use. Without an understanding of these concepts, the officials would be unable to understand the analysis. Specific examples and easy-to-picture details bridge the gap between writer and reader, as in this definition of *form.*

> Form, which is the shape of landscape features, can best be represented by both small-scale features, such as *trees and shrubs,* and by large-scale elements, such as *mountains and mountain ranges.*

Another way to define a difficult concept, especially when you are writing for nonspecialists, is to link the unfamiliar to the familiar by means of an analogy (resemblance in some aspects between things that are otherwise not alike). Defining radio waves in terms of their length (long) and frequency (low), a writer develops an analogy to show why a low frequency is advantageous.

> The low frequency makes it relatively easy to produce a wave having virtually all its power concentrated at one frequency. Think, for example, of a group of people lost in a forest. If they hear sounds of a search party in the distance, they all will begin to shout for help in different directions. Not a very efficient process, is it? But suppose that all the energy which went into the production of this noise could be concentrated into a single shout or whistle. Clearly the chances that the group will be found would be much greater.

Some terms are best defined by an explanation of their causes. Writing in a professional journal, a nurse describes an apparatus used to monitor blood pressure in severely ill patients. Called an indwelling catheter, the device displays blood-pressure readings on an oscilliscope and on a numbered scale. Users of the device, the writer explains, must understand what a *dampened wave form* is.

> The *dampened wave form,* the smoothing out or flattening of the pressure wave form on the oscilliscope, is *usually caused by an obstruction* that prevents blood pressure from being freely transmitted to the monitor. The obstruction might be *a small clot or bit of fibrin* at the catheter tip. More likely, *the catheter tip has become positioned against the artery wall* and is preventing the blood from flowing freely.

The most significant point about the occurrence of a dampened wave form is that it is usually the result of a potentially dangerous obstruction. The definition, therefore, emphasizes cause and indicates what factors may, in turn, produce the obstruction in blood-pressure transmission.

Expanding a formal definition by breaking a concept into manageable parts makes it easier to understand.

Formal definition

Fire is the visible heat energy released from the rapid oxidation of a fuel. A substance is "on fire" when the release of heat energy from the oxidation process reaches visible light levels.

Division into component elements

The classic fire triangle illustrates the elements necessary to create fire: *oxygen, heat,* and *burnable material* or *fuel.* Air provides sufficient oxygen for combustion; the intensity of the heat needed to start a fire depends on the characteristics of the burnable material or fuel. A burnable substance is one that will sustain combustion after an initial application of heat to start it.

The techniques for dividing the elements of a concept follow the guidelines discussed earlier in this chapter.

Under certain circumstances, the meaning of a term can be clarified and made easier to remember by an exploration of its origin. Scientific and medical terms, because of their sometimes unfamiliar Greek and Latin roots, benefit especially from an explanation of this type. Tracing the derivation of a word can also be useful when you want to explain why a word has favorable or unfavorable associations—particularly if your goal is to influence your reader's attitude toward an idea or an activity.

Efforts to influence legislation generally fall under the head of *lobbying,* a term that once referred to people who prowl the lobbies of houses of government, buttonholing lawmakers and trying to get them to take certain positions. Lobbying today is all of this, and much more, too. It is a respected —and necessary—activity. It tells the legislator which way the winds of public opinion are blowing, and it helps inform him of the implications of certain bills, debates, and resolutions he must contend with.[5]

Sometimes it is useful to point out what something is *not* in order to clarify what it *is.* A what-it-is-not definition is effective only when the reader is familiar with the item with which the defined item is contrasted. If you say *x* is not *y,* your readers must understand the meaning of *y* for the explanation to make sense. In a crane operators' manual, for instance, a "negative definition" is used to show that, for safety reasons, a hydraulic crane cannot be operated in the same manner as a lattice boom crane.

A hydraulic crane is *not* like a lattice boom crane in one very important way. In most cases, the safe lifting capacity of a lattice boom crane is based on the *weight needed to tip the machine.* Therefore, operators of friction machines sometimes depend on signs that the machine might tip to warn them of impending danger.

This is a very dangerous practice with a hydraulic crane. . . .[6]

[5] Bill Vogt, *How to Build a Better Outdoors* (New York: David McKay Company, Inc., 1978), p. 93.

[6] *Operator's Manual* (Model W-180), Harnishfeger Corporation.

When you use a definition as a means of presenting your material, you should keep in mind a few "don'ts"—pitfalls that may result in confusing, inaccurate, or incomplete definitions.

Avoid *circular definitions,* which merely restate the term to be defined and therefore fail to clarify it.

CIRCULAR   *Spontaneous combustion* is fire that begins spontaneously.

REVISED   *Spontaneous combustion* is the self-ignition of a flammable material through a chemical reaction like oxidation and temperature buildup.

Avoid "is when" and "is where" definitions; such definitions overlook one of the three elements of formal definition—they do not *classify* the term being defined.

"IS WHEN"   A *contract* is when two or more people agree to something.
DEFINITION

REVISED   A *contract* is a binding agreement between two or more people. (*Binding agreement* is the class of which *contract* is a member.)

"IS WHERE"   A *day-care center* is where working parents can leave their pre-
DEFINITION   school children during the day.

REVISED   A *day-care center* is a facility at which working parents can leave their preschool children during the day. (*Facility* is the class of which *day-care center* is a member.)

Do not use definitions made up of terms your readers won't understand. Even informally written material will occasionally require the use of a term in a special sense unfamiliar to your readers; such terms should be defined too.

> In these specifications, the term *safety can* refers to an approved container of not more than five-gallon capacity having a spring-closing spout cover designed to relieve internal pressure when exposed to fire.

CAUSE AND EFFECT

When your purpose is to explain why something happened, or why you think something will happen, cause and effect analysis is a useful writing strategy. If you were asked to report on why the accident rate for the company truck fleet rose by 30 percent this year over last year, you would use cause and effect analysis. In this case, you would be working from an effect (higher accident rate) to its cause (bad driving weather, inexperienced drivers, poor truck maintenance, and so on). If, on the other hand, your purpose were to report on the possible effects that the switch to a four-day workweek (ten hours per day) would have on the office staff, you would also use cause and effect analysis—but this time you would start with cause (the new work schedule) and look for possible effects (changes in morale, in productivity, in absenteeism, and the like).

The goal of cause and effect analysis is to make the relationship between a situation and either its cause or its effect as plausible as possible. The conclusions you draw about the relationship will be based on the evidence you have gathered. *Evidence* is any pertinent fact or argument that helps explain the circumstances of an event. Because not all evidence will be of equal value to you as you draw conclusions, it's a good idea to keep some guidelines in mind for evaluating evidence.

Evidence Should Be Pertinent

The facts and arguments you gather should be pertinent, or relevant, to your topic. That is, even if the evidence you collect is accurate, you should be careful not to draw from it a conclusion that it does not lead to or support. You may have researched some statistics, for example, which show that an increasing number of Americans are licensed to fly small airplanes. But you cannot use this information as evidence that there is a slowdown in interstate highway construction in the United States—the evidence does not lead to that conclusion. Other, more relevant evidence is available to explain the decline in interstate construction—greatly increased construction costs, opposition from environmental groups, new legislation that transfers highway construction funds to mass transportation, and so on. Statistics on the increase in small-plane licensing may be relevant to other conclusions, however. You could argue that the upswing has occurred because small planes save travel time, provide easy access to remote areas, and, once they are purchased, are economical to operate.

Evidence Should Be Sufficient

Incomplete evidence can lead to false conclusions.

> Driver training classes in the schools do not help prevent auto accidents. Two people I know who completed driver training classes were involved in accidents.

Although the evidence cited to support the conclusion may be accurate, there is not enough of it, even to make a statement about the driver training program at one school. A thorough investigation of the usefulness of driver training classes in keeping the accident rate down would require many more than two examples. And it would require a comparison of the driving records of those who had completed driver training with drivers who had not.

Evidence Should Be Representative

If you conduct a survey to obtain your evidence, be sure that you do not solicit responses only from individuals or groups whose views are identical to yours —that is, be sure you obtain a representative sampling. A survey of backpackers in a national park on whether the park ought to be open to off-the-road vehicles would more than likely show them overwhelmingly against the idea. Such a survey should include opinions from more than one interested group.

Evidence Should Be Plausible

Two events that occur close to each other in time or place may or may not be causally related. Thunder and black clouds do not always signal rain, but they do so often enough that if we are outdoors and the sky darkens and we hear thunder, we seek shelter unless we're prepared to get wet. If you walk under a ladder and shortly afterward sprain your ankle on a curb, however, you cannot conclude that walking under a ladder brings bad luck—unless you are superstitious. Although the two events occurred close to one another in time, the first did not cause the second. Merely to say that X caused Y (or will cause Y) is inadequate. You must demonstrate the relationship with pertinent facts and arguments. For example, a driver lost control of his car one summer day and crashed into a tavern. He told the police that the accident occurred because his car had been in the sun so long and absorbed so much solar energy that he could no longer control it. The cause the driver gave for the accident cannot be taken as either plausible or objective. A careful examination of the event would probably reveal that the driver had been a patron of the tavern shortly before the crash took place. But even this explanation would have to be demonstrated with convincing facts. The police would have to interview other tavern patrons and test the driver to determine breath and blood alcohol levels. If the patrons identified the driver as a recent customer in the tavern, and if the breath and blood tests showed intoxicating levels of alcohol in his system, the evidence would be sufficient to explain how the car hit the tavern.

Linking Causes to Effects

To show a true relationship between a cause and an effect, you must demonstrate that the existence of the one *requires* the existence of the other. It is often difficult to establish beyond any doubt that one event was *the* cause of another event. More often, a result will have more than one cause. As you research your subject your task is to determine which cause or causes are most plausible.

When several probable causes are equally valid, report your findings accordingly, as in the following article on the use of an energy-saving device called a furnace-vent damper. The damper is a metal plate fitted inside the flue or vent pipe of natural-gas or fuel-oil furnaces. When the furnace is on, the damper opens to allow the gases to escape up the flue. When the furnace shuts off, the damper closes, thus preventing warm air from escaping up the flue stack. The dampers are potentially dangerous, however. If the dampers fail to open at the proper time, they could allow poisonous furnace gases to back into the house and asphyxiate anyone in a matter of minutes. Tests run on several dampers showed a number of probable causes for their malfunctioning.

> One damper was sold without proper installation instructions, and another was wired incorrectly. Two of the units had slow-opening dampers (15 seconds) that prevented the [furnace] burner from firing. And one damper jammed when exposed to a simulated fuel temperature of more than 700 degrees.[7]

The investigator located more than one cause of damper malfunctions and reported on them. Without such a thorough account, recommendations to prevent similar malfunctions would be based on incomplete evidence. Suppose, for instance, that you were conducting a survey of drivers in your town to determine if they drive more slowly because of a recent and well-publicized police department decision to use unmarked police vehicles to catch speeders. If you question twelve drivers and all of them say that they now drive more slowly because of the unmarked police vehicles, you cannot report that "Every driver questioned says that he or she drives more slowly because of the presence of unmarked police vehicles." Such a blatant assertion is obviously misleading; it is also unnecessary. Accurately phrased, the statement would still have a significant impact: "All twelve drivers surveyed say they drive more slowly because of the presence of unmarked police vehicles."

PERSUADING YOUR READER

Suppose you and a friend are arguing over whether the capital of Maine is Portland or Augusta. The issue is a simple question of fact that can be easily checked in an almanac or an atlas. (It's Augusta.) But suppose you are trying

---

[7] Don DeBat, "Save Energy But Save Your Life, Too," *Family Safety* (Fall 1978), 27.

to convince your company that it ought to adopt flexible working hours for its employees. A quick look in a reference book will not settle the issue. Like Christine Thomas in Chapter 1, you will have to *persuade* management that your idea is a good one. And to achieve your goal—to convince your company to accept your suggestions and act on them—you will probably have to put your recommendations in writing.

In all on-the-job writing, it is important to keep your reader's needs, as well as your own, clearly in mind. This is especially true in persuasive writing, where your purpose may often be to ask your reader to change his or her working procedures or habit. You may think, as Christine Thomas did, that most people would automatically accept a recommendation for an improvement in the workplace. But improvement means change, and people tend to resist change. What you see as an improvement others may see as change for the sake of change. ("We've always done it this way. Why change?") The idea you are proposing may be a threat to a staff member's pet project, or it may make the knowledge and experience a veteran employee has accumulated seem out of date—so both will probably resist your suggestion. To overcome their resistance, you'll have to convince them that your suggestion has merit. You can do this most effectively by establishing the need for your recommendation and by supporting it with convincing, objective evidence.

Keep in mind, as you seek to persuade your reader, that the way you present your ideas is as important as the ideas themselves. Be thoughtful of your reader's needs and feelings by applying some basic manners in your writing. Avoid sarcasm or any other hostile tone that will offend your reader. If anger shows through in your writing, you will quickly turn the reader against your point of view. Also avoid being overly enthusiastic. Your reader may interpret such an attitude as insincere or presumptuous. Of course, you should not conceal justified annoyance or genuine enthusiasm; just be careful not to overstate them.

The following memorandum was written by a supervisor to overcome resistance on the part of employees who had done an excellent job but who were now being asked to change their work habits.

```
                      MEMORANDUM
      TO:  Parts Distribution Section Employees
    FROM:  Bernadine Kovak, Supervisor
    DATE:  April 8, 19—
 SUBJECT:  Plans for Automated Inventory Control

     As you all know, our work load has jumped by 30
percent in the past month. It has increased because we
have begun to centralize parts distribution here at
Edgewood Division. We no longer have to get parts from the
home plant in Lexington.
     For us, centralized parts distribution has meant more
work. In the next few months the work load will increase
```

```
another 30 percent. Even a staff as experienced as you are
cannot handle such a work load without help——nor will
you be asked to.
        In the next few weeks we will be installing
electronic equipment for the automation of inventory
control. Instead of the present manual system of keeping
track of parts storage, a small computer will do the
memorizing and searching for us.
        The new system, unfortunately, will cause some
disruption at first. We will have to move most of our
parts stock to the new warehouse. We will also have to
reorganize the area once the stock is moved. And all of us
will have to learn to operate some new equipment.
        I would like to put your knowledge and experience to
work by having you help the new system get into operation.
Let's meet in my office to discuss these improvements
on Friday, April 12, at 1 P.M. I'll have details of the
plan to discuss with you. I'm also eager to get your
comments, suggestions, and——most of all——your cooperation.
```

Notice that not everything in this memorandum is painted a rosy hue. Change brings disruption and the writer points out that fact.

Do not overlook opposing points of view. Most issues have more than one side, and you should acknowledge them. If you were listing reasons why flexible working hours are a good idea, for example, it would be a mistake to overlook the added paperwork that might be required to keep track of separate schedules for all employees. It would be most effective to admit that the paperwork will increase—and then go on to show that the added burden would be more than made up for by improved employee morale and perhaps by even greater productivity. By including differing points of view, you gain several advantages. First, you show your reader that you are honest enough to recognize opposite views when they exist. Second, you can demonstrate the advantage of your viewpoint over others. And by bringing up opposing views *before* your co-workers do, you may be able to blunt some of their objections.

CHAPTER SUMMARY

Writing on the job is writing with a purpose. The purpose will always be specific and practical.

When you give someone instructions on how to perform a task, be sure that you understand the task thoroughly. Then present the information at a level appropriate to your reader's background in the subject. Write concisely, addressing yourself directly to the reader. Divide the task into steps and present each step in its correct sequence. Mention any necessary preparations at the beginning and provide appropriate warnings where necessary. Use illustrations when they will add clarity.

Most of the guidelines for writing instructions apply to the writing of process explanations as well. Introduce the process by giving the reader pertinent information about its purpose or significance. Then divide the process into steps and present each step in its proper sequence.

Descriptive writing requires the careful selection of pertinent details. Simple descriptions should be specific and detailed. Complex descriptions require greater selectivity of details. The whole-to-parts method may be the most effective one for providing your reader with a framework for the explanation of large or complex subjects. Illustrations can be used to clarify descriptive material.

Comparisons show how two or more things are like or unlike one another. For the comparison to be effective, its basis must be valid and consistently applied. Comparisons can be organized on a whole-by-whole or on a part-by-part basis, depending on your reader's needs. The type of organization chosen should be used consistently to avoid confusing the reader.

A complex subject can be made more understandable if it is divided into its largest number of equal parts. Continue the breakdown until it is sufficiently detailed to explain the subject clearly. Classification can be used to group people, ideas, or objects on the basis of their common characteristics. For subjects that can be divided or classified in more than one way, select the basis for the division or grouping that best represents your writing objective. Dealing with all pertinent parts, apply the basis for the division or classification consistently.

Define terms that may be unfamiliar to your readers. Terms can be defined formally, informally, or by extended definition, depending, again, on your reader's needs. To define a term formally, state which grouping, or class, the term belongs to and show how it differs from all other members of the class. To define a term informally, substitute familiar words and phrases for the unfamiliar term. Difficult or important terms can be explained by a variety of methods that extend the original definition. Terms used in a sense different from their accustomed meaning should also be defined. Avoid circular definitions and "is when" and "is where" definitions.

In cause and effect explanations, your goal is to establish a plausible relationship between an event and its cause, or between an event and its likely effect. Such explanations require a careful evaluation of the evidence. Is it pertinent? Is it representative? Is it sufficient? Is it merely coincidental? When your evidence is accurate and applicable, state your conclusions carefully. Overstated conclusions will misrepresent your evidence regardless of how pertinent it is.

In persuasive writing, the way in which the ideas are presented is as important as the ideas themselves. Take your reader's feelings into account. Avoid a hostile tone and appeal instead to the reader's good sense. In controversial issues, acknowledge other points of view. The reader will appreciate your honesty and you can then demonstrate the advantage of your views over the other views.

EXERCISES

1. Choose one of the following topics to write about and, first, decide whether you will develop the topic as a *set of instructions* or as *an explanation of a process.* Then, based on the approach you have selected, write a paper, of assigned length, on the topic. Assume that your reader has no knowledge of the topic. Use illustrations where they would be helpful to the reader.

    a. operation of a photocopy machine
    b. blood pressure measurement
    c. how automobile-battery terminals are cleaned
    d. how a bicycle-tire inner tube is repaired
    e. preparation of sour-dough starter
    f. directions from the nearest commercial airport to your home

2. Write a *description* of one of the following items or of an item of your choice. Specify who your reader will be and write the description in sufficient detail to permit your reader either to visualize or to locate the item without further assistance. Do not illustrate this assignment.

    a. the prominent features (of face, body, clothing, and so on) of a close friend or relative for a "missing persons" bulletin
    b. a small mechanical device with no more than five moving parts (pencil sharpener, can opener, etc.)
    c. a nonmechanical household or recreational device (rolling pin, tennis racquet, etc.)
    d. a piece of land. First give an overview, then establish its location relative to city street or natural boundaries; complete the description with significant details of the land.

3. Write a paper, of assigned length, on one of the following topics by *comparing* the two items in the topic. Before you begin to write, specify who your reader will be. Make the comparison detailed enough to suit the needs of the reader.

    a. two career choices
    b. two job offers
    c. two products or services with which you are familiar
    d. two persons who are being considered for promotion to the same position
    e. a comparison of your choice, organized either by the whole-by-whole method or the part-by-part method (for example, a comparison of two products or appliances designed to do the same job)

4. Choose one of the following topics to write about and, first, decide whether you will develop the topic through *division* (separation of a complex whole

into several smaller units) or *classification* (grouping of a number of small units into larger, related categories). Then, based on the approach you have selected, write a paper, of assigned length, on the topic. Before you begin to write, be sure that you have determined who your reader will be and what your scope will be.

    a. road signs in your area
    b. home-heating methods
    c. hand-held calculators
    d. a community service organization in your locality
    e. 35-mm cameras
    f. recreational or athletic programs in your community
    g. a college library
    h. safety regulations where you work
    i. fire extinguishers
    j. the set-up of an office, hospital, or other organization with which you are familiar

5. Write an *extended definition* of a key concept or term related to an occupation or a school subject. Use some or all of the techniques discussed in the chapter for creating extended definitions. Assume that your reader is unfamiliar with the term.

6. Choose one of the following topics to write about and, first, decide whether you will develop the topic through *cause and effect* or *persuasion*. Then, based on the approach you have selected, write a paper, of assigned length, on the topic. Before you begin to write, be sure that you have determined who your reader will be and what your scope will be.

    a. A dangerous practice or condition in your office or school is likely to cause an accident.
    b. You ought to be promoted to a job with greater responsibility.
    c. Businesses should be encouraged to locate in your community.
    d. The setting up of job-training programs in connection with a college will lead to higher employment in your community.
    e. Some aspects of your present job (such as working conditions, equipment, availability of help, organization of your work area) should be changed.
    f. Some aspect of your school (such as the grading system, the library facilities, work programs) should be changed.
    g. Smoking should (or should not) be permitted in public places.

6

Writing Emphatic Sentences

Effective writing is *emphatic* writing—it highlights the facts and ideas the writer considers to be most important and downplays those the writer considers less significant. By focusing the reader's attention on the key elements in a sentence, emphatic writing enables the reader to determine how one fact or idea in a sentence is related to another. Emphatic writing, then, is a technique by which writers can make their material more accessible to their readers.

There are a number of methods writers employ to achieve emphasis in their sentences; a few of the devices are discussed in this chapter: the active voice; subordination; unusual word order; introductory words and phrases; capital letters, underlining, and other mechanical features; and parallel structure.

ACTIVE AND PASSIVE VOICE

If you were going to relate the information contained in the following two sentences to someone in conversation, which version would you use?

EXAMPLE 1 The complicated equipment is operated skillfully by the x-ray technician.

EXAMPLE 2 The x-ray technician operates the complicated equipment skillfully.

You would probably choose example 2 because it conveys its message more directly than example 1. By making the x-ray technician the *actor* (or *doer*) in the sentence, example 2 readily communicates the fact that it is the technician's initiative that turns the equipment into a working tool. Example 1, on the contrary, downplays the role of the operator; the focus of the sentence is on the x-ray equipment as the *receiver* of the action. The technician, though still the performer of the action, appears in a *by* phrase at the end of the sentence, rather than as the subject of the sentence.

What accounts for the difference in "feel" between the two sentences is that example 2 is in the active voice, while example 1 is in the passive. A sentence is in the *active voice* if the subject of the sentence acts; it is in the *passive voice* if the subject is acted upon.

In general, the active voice is the more emphatic of the two. The reader can move quickly and easily from *actor* to *action performed* (the verb) to *receiver of the action* (direct object); in passive-voice sentences the reader often has to reach the end of the sentence to find out who (or what) performed the action that the subject received.

ACTIVE VOICE   Sheila Cohen made the layout design for the new pump. (The subject, *Sheila Cohen,* acts on *the layout design*—the direct object.)

PASSIVE VOICE   The layout design for the new pump was made by Sheila Cohen. (The subject, *the layout design,* receives the action.)

Passive-voice sentences tend to be longer than active-voice sentences, for two reasons: first, because a verb in the passive voice is always made up of at least two forms (like *was made*), whereas a verb in the active voice may consist of just one word (*made*); second, because passive-voice sentences frequently require a *by someone* or *by something* phrase to complete their meaning. The active-voice version of the *Sheila Cohen* sentence contains ten words; the passive-voice version has twelve.

The chief advantage of the active voice is that, by clearly stating who is doing what, it gives the reader information quickly and emphatically. A straightforward style is especially important in writing instructions. Compare the following two versions of a paragraph that provides nurses with directions for treating a serious burn. The first version is written entirely in the passive voice; the second uses the active.

PASSIVE VOICE   The following action must be taken when a serious burn is treated. Any loose clothing on or near the burn is removed. The injury is covered with a clean dressing, and the area around the burn is washed. Then the dressing is secured with tape. Burned fingers or toes are separated with gauze or cloth so that they are prevented from sticking together. Medication is not applied unless it is prescribed by a doctor.

ACTIVE
VOICE
Take the following action when treating a serious burn. Remove any loose clothing on or near the burn. Cover the injury with a clean dressing and wash the area around the burn. Then secure the dressing with tape. Separate fingers or toes with gauze or cloth to prevent them from sticking together. Do not apply medication unless a doctor prescribes it.

If you were the nurse who must follow these instructions, which version would you find easier to read and understand?

Occasionally, of course, the passive voice can be useful. There are times, for example, when the doer of the action is less important than the receiver of the action, and the writer can emphasize the receiver of the action by making it the subject of the sentence.

EXAMPLE
The new medical secretary was recommended by several doctors.

The important person in this sentence is the medical secretary, not the doctors who made the recommendation. To give the secretary—the receiver of the action—the needed emphasis, the sentence should be written in the passive voice.

The passive voice is also useful when the performer of the action either is not known or is not important.

EXAMPLE
The valves were soaked in kerosene for twenty-four hours. (*Who* soaked them is not important.)

The wheel was invented thousands of years ago. (*Who* invented it is not known.)

Another common use of the passive voice is to avoid identifying the performer of an action.

EXAMPLE
The guilty employee was placed on disciplinary probation. (The writer does not want to say *who* placed the guilty employee on probation.)

As you write—and as you revise—select the voice, active or passive, that is appropriate to your purpose. In most cases you can express your ideas more simply and more emphatically in the active voice, especially if you are writing instructions or making a report in which you intend to emphasize *who did what* (for example, which employee performed which task of a large project). And if you are describing a complicated piece of equipment, the active voice will probably make it clearer how one part interacts with another part. If, on the other hand, you are explaining a process in which the *doer* is not known or is not important, the passive voice is likely to be more effective. In whatever kind of writing you do, though, be careful to maintain a consistency of voice.

Avoid making an awkward switch, either in one sentence or between sentences, from active to passive (or vice versa).

REVISE   After the test for admission to the training program had been taken by ten applicants, each one wrote a brief essay on his or her career plans.

TO   After the ten applicants had taken the test for admission to the training program, each one wrote a brief essay on his or her career plans.

SUBORDINATION

Read the following passage.

The computer is a calculating device. It was once known as a mechanical brain. It has revolutionized industry.

Reading the passage—a group of three short, staccato sentences—is something like listening to a series of drum beats of identical tone. The writing, like the music, is monotonous, because every sentence has the same subject – verb structure, and, like the music, it is unemphatic, because every idea is given equal weight. But the passage can be revised to eliminate the monotonous sentence structure and to place stress on the most important idea, that the computer has revolutionized industry.

The computer, *a calculating device once known as a mechanical brain,* has revolutionized industry.

The key to transforming a series of repetitive, unemphatic sentences is *subordination,* a technique in which a fact or an idea is subordinated to—that is, made less important than—another fact or idea in the same sentence. There are three basic ways to subordinate an element in a sentence: to make it a clause, to make it a phrase, or to make it a single modifier. In all three methods, the less-important element can be combined with the more-important element to form one unified sentence.

Types of subordination

Clauses.   A *subordinate clause* (also called a *dependent clause*) has a subject and a predicate, but by itself is not a sentence. Rather, it must be joined to a sentence by a connecting word (the sentence to which a subordinate clause is joined is called an *independent clause*). Thus, when two sentences are joined by subordination, one sentence becomes the independent clause, and the other sentence, introduced by a connecting word, becomes the dependent clause. The words most commonly used to introduce subordinate clauses are *who, that, which, whom, whose* (relative pronouns) and *after, although, because, before, if, unless, until, when, where, while* (subordinating conjunctions). A few word groups are also used to introduce subordinate clauses—*as soon as, even though, in order that, so that.*

In the following examples, two sentences are turned into one sentence that contains a subordinate clause.

REVISE   Virginia Kelly has become a printing press operator at the Granger Printing Company. She graduated from the Midcity Graphic Arts School last month.

TO   Virginia Kelly, *who graduated from the Midcity Graphic Arts School last month,* has become a printing press operator at the Granger Printing Company.

REVISE   Their credit union has a lower interest rate on loans. Our credit union provides a fuller range of services.

TO   *Although their credit union has a lower interest rate on loans,* our credit union provides a fuller range of services.

Phrases.   The second type of subordination is the phrase. A *phrase* is a group of related words that does not have either a subject or a predicate and that acts as a modifier. In the following groups of two-sentence passages, one sentence is turned into a subordinate phrase that modifies an element in the other sentence.

REVISE   The Beta Corporation now employs 500 people. It was founded ten years ago.

TO   The Beta Corporation, *founded ten years ago,* now employs 500 people.

REVISE   Roger Smith is a forest ranger for the State of Michigan. He spoke at the local Kiwanis Club last week.

TO   Roger Smith, *a forest ranger for the State of Michigan,* spoke at the local Kiwanis Club last week.

Single modifiers.   The third type of subordination is the single modifier. A *single modifier* may be either one word or a group of words.

REVISE   The file is obsolete. It is using valuable storage space.

TO   The *obsolete* file is using valuable storage space.

REVISE   The police radio was out of date. It was auctioned to the highest bidder.

TO   The *out-of-date* police radio was auctioned to the highest bidder.

Subordination to Achieve Emphasis

Depending on the context of your writing—your subject, your purpose, and your reader—you may find that, in a sentence, one type of subordination is more effective than another. In general, a subordinate single modifier achieves some emphasis, a subordinate phrase achieves more emphasis, and a subordinate clause achieves the most emphasis of all. In the following example, one idea has been subordinated three ways.

REVISE	The display designer's report was carefully illustrated. It covered five pages.
TO	The display designer's *five-page* report was carefully illustrated. (single modifier subordinated)
OR	The display designer's report, *covering five pages,* was carefully illustrated. (phrase subordinated)
OR	The display designer's report, *which covered five pages,* was carefully illustrated. (clause subordinated)

Just as you can determine the kind of subordinate element you think is most appropriate in a given sentence, so you can decide, according to the context in which you are writing, which ideas you should emphasize and which ones you should subordinate. In the following sets of examples, two sentences have been combined into one, in two different ways. Notice how the emphasis varies in each set.

REVISE	Blast furnaces are used mainly in the smelting of iron. They are in use all over the world.
TO	Blast furnaces, *which are in use all over the world,* are used mainly in the smelting of iron. (Subordinates the extent of the use and emphasizes the purpose for which they are used.)
OR	Blast furnaces, *which are used mainly in the smelting of iron,* are in use all over the world. (Subordinates the purpose and emphasizes the extent.)
REVISE	The document explains how to install the gear. It is written for the mechanic.
TO	The document, *which is written for the mechanic,* explains how to install the gear. (Subordinates the intended reader and emphasizes the purpose.)

OR   The document, *which explains how to install the gear,* is written for the mechanic. (Subordinates the purpose and emphasizes the intended reader.)

REVISE   Henry Ford was a pioneering industrialist. He understood the importance of self-esteem.

TO   Henry Ford, *who understood the importance of self-esteem,* was a pioneering industrialist. (Subordinates the subject's understanding and emphasizes his pioneering work.)

OR   Henry Ford, *who was a pioneering industrialist,* understood the importance of self-esteem. (Subordinates the subject's pioneering work and emphasizes his understanding.)

Avoiding Overloaded Sentences

Subordination is a helpful technique that can enable you to write clear, readable sentences. But, like many useful devices, it can be overdone. Be especially careful, in your writing, not to pile one subordinating clause on top of another. A sentence that is overloaded with subordination will force your reader to work harder than necessary to understand what you are saying. The following sentence is difficult to read because the bottleneck of subordinate clauses prevents the reader from moving easily from one idea to the next.

REVISE   When the two mechanics, who had been trained at the company's repair center in Des Moines, explained to Margarita that the new word-processing machine, which Margarita had told them was not working properly, needed a new part, Margarita decided that until the part arrived the department would have its sales letters reproduced by an independent printing supplier.

TO   Margarita told the two mechanics that the new word-processing machine was not working properly. The mechanics, who had been trained at the company's repair center in Des Moines, examined the machine and explained to Margarita that it needed a new part. Until the part arrived, Margarita decided, the department would have its sales letters reproduced by an independent printing supplier.

Subordinating everything is as bad as subordinating nothing. For example, study the next three examples of the same letter from a garage owner to a parts supplier. The first one has too little subordination, the second one has too much subordination, and the third one illustrates effective subordination.

Haley's Garage
1449 Banes Pike
Walleye, Wisconsin 49321
April 14, 19--

Elm Auto Parts
129 Westport Street
Milwaukee, Wisconsin 45341

Attention: Parts Department

I am returning the parts you sent me, and I am enclosing the invoice that came with them. You must have confused my order with someone else's. I ordered spark plugs, condensers, and points, and I received bearings, piston rings, head gaskets, and valve-grinding compound. I don't need these parts, but I need the parts I ordered. Please send them as soon as possible.

Sincerely,

Walter G. Haley

Walter G. Haley

Haley's Garage
1449 Banes Pike
Walleye, Wisconsin 49321
April 14, 19--

Elm Auto Parts
129 Westport Street
Milwaukee, Wisconsin 45341

Attention: Parts Department

You must have confused my order with someone else's, because although I ordered spark plugs, condensers, and points, I received bearings, piston rings, head gaskets, and grinding compound; therefore, I am returning the parts you sent me, along with the invoice that came with them, in the hope that you will send me the parts that I need as quickly as possible because this delay has already put me behind schedule.

Sincerely,

Walter G. Haley

Walter G. Haley

Haley's Garage
1449 Banes Pike
Walleye, Wisconsin 49321
April 14, 19--

Elm Auto Parts
129 Westport Street
Milwaukee, WI 45341

Attention: Parts Department

I am returning the parts you sent me, along with the invoice that came
with them, because you must have confused my order with someone else's.
Although I ordered spark plugs, condensers, and points, I received
bearings, piston rings, head gaskets, and grinding compound. Since I
need the parts I ordered and this mix-up is causing an unexpected delay,
please send me the parts that I ordered as quickly as possible.

Sincerely,

Walter G. Haley

Walter G. Haley

UNUSUAL WORD ORDER

You can sometimes call attention to an idea simply by stating it in a sentence that varies from the most common word order in our language. Most sentences, of course, follow a subject-verb-object pattern.

EXAMPLE   I (subject) never saw (verb) a smoother-running machine (object).

Because so many sentences follow this pattern, readers learn to expect it, and their familiarity with the pattern helps them understand what they are reading. In the example sentence, the reader recognizes the subject and the object by their positions in relation to the verb. But a reader who comes across a sentence like this

EXAMPLE   A smoother-running machine (object) I (subject) never saw (verb).

may sit up and take notice. The rearrangement of the three sentence elements prompts the reader to pay more attention to the sentence—to think about it more carefully—than he or she ordinarily would.

In your work, you may find that unusual word order can be effective as a means of stressing an idea—if you keep in mind two cautionary notes: (1) unusual word order has the greatest impact in relatively short sentences, and (2) like any technique that depends upon deviation from a normal pattern, it should not be overused.

INTRODUCTORY WORDS AND PHRASES

Another way to vary sentence structure to achieve emphasis is to begin a sentence with an introductory element—a modifying word or phrase that contains the idea you wish to stress. Such a modifier would normally occur later in the sentence.

EXAMPLES   Sales have been good recently.
            Recently, sales have been good.
            You must work hard to advance.
            To advance, you must work hard.
            She found several errors while reading the report.
            Reading the report, she found several errors.

When you use introductory words and phrases, though, there are two dangers that you must watch for. (1) Beginning a sentence with a modifying word or phrase may lead you to write a dangling modifier (for a fuller discussion of dangling modifiers, see pages 39–40). The first sentence below, for instance, contains a dangling modifier, because the phrase *to advance* cannot logically modify *hard work*. The second sentence corrects the error by making it clear that *to advance* modifies the pronoun *you*.

REVISE   To advance, hard work is required.

TO   *To advance,* you must work hard.

(2) Beginning a sentence with a modifying word or phrase may cause you to change the meaning of your sentence accidentally. The first of the following sentences instructs the reader to measure the oil that drains over a time period that lasts fifteen seconds. The second sentence instructs the reader to wait fifteen seconds before measuring the amount of oil that drains into the container —a completely different thought.

EXAMPLES   Measure the amount of oil that drains into the container in fifteen seconds.

In fifteen seconds, measure the amount of oil that drains into the container.

Once again, make sure that your sentences say exactly what you intend them to say.

OTHER WAYS TO ACHIEVE EMPHASIS

You can create a feeling of anticipation in your reader by arranging a series of facts or ideas in *climactic order*. Begin such a series with the least important idea and end it with the most important one.

REVISE   The hurricane destroyed thousands of homes, ruined some crops, and interrupted traffic.

TO   The hurricane interrupted traffic, ruined some crops, and destroyed thousands of homes.

Emphasis is added at each step as the reader is led from the minor inconvenience of traffic tie-ups, to the more serious problem of partial crop failure, and finally to the hurricane's most devastating impact: the destruction of thousands of homes.

An abrupt change in sentence length can also achieve effective emphasis.

EXAMPLE   We have already reviewed the problems the bookkeeping department has experienced during the past year. We could continue to examine the causes of our problems and point an accusing finger at all the culprits beyond our control, but in the end it all leads to one simple conclusion. *We must cut costs.*

Sometimes, simply labeling ideas as important creates emphasis.

EXAMPLE   There are a number of things we can do that will help us achieve
               our goal. We can conduct sales contests in the field; in the past,
               such contests have been quite successful. We can increase our
               advertising budget and hope for a proportionate increase in
               sales. We can be prepared to step up production when the in-
               crease in sales makes it necessary. But *most important,* we can
               do everything in our power to make sure that we are producing
               the best dictating equipment on the market.

If you don't overuse them, direct statements like *most important* should make
your reader take particular notice of what follows.

    Another kind of direct statement is the warning to your reader that some-
thing dangerous is about to follow. Warnings most often appear in instructions, where they may be brought to the reader's attention by a special format
—the material may be boxed off, for instance—or by attention-attracting
devices like all-capital letters or a distinctive typeface. Many offices are
equipped with typewriters, like the IBM Selectric, that have changeable type,
usually a "golf ball" that contains the letters of the alphabet in **boldface** and
italic, as well as standard, typefaces.

```
                        WARNING


          DO NOT proceed to the next
          instruction until you have
          checked to be sure that the
          equipment has been unplugged.
          The electrical power generated
          by this unit CAN KILL!
```

    Other mechanical devices can achieve a certain amount of emphasis. A
dash within a sentence, for example, can alert the reader to what follows it (on
the typewriter, the dash is made by striking the hyphen twice, with no space
between the two).

EXAMPLES   The job will be done--after we are under contract.
               The manager pointed out that our conduct could have
               only one result--dismissal.

Italics (indicated on the typewriter by underlining) can be used occasionally to
emphasize a word or phrase.

EXAMPLE   Sales have <u>not</u> improved since we started the new
               procedure.

The problem with devices like italics and the dash is that they are so easy to use that we tend to rely on them too readily.

EXAMPLE   Sales have <u>not improved</u> since we started the new procedure and are <u>not likely</u> to improve unless we initiate a more <u>aggressive</u> advertising campaign.

Overuse of mechanical devices may cancel their effectiveness; the reader quickly learns not to count on the writer to use the signals to point out only really important material.

PARALLEL STRUCTURE

Parallel structure requires that sentence elements—words, phrases, and clauses—that are alike in function be alike in structure as well. In the following example, the three locations in which a cable is laid are all expressed as prepositional phrases.

EXAMPLE   The cable was laid *behind the embankment, under the street,* and *into the building.*

Parallel structure can produce an economy of language, clarify meaning, indicate the equality of related ideas, and, frequently, achieve emphasis. Parallel structure allows your reader to anticipate the sense of a series of units within a sentence.[1] The reader realizes, for instance, that the relationship between the second unit (*under the street,* in the *cable* sentence) and the subject (*cable*) is the same as that between the first unit (*behind the embankment*) and the subject. A reader who has sensed the pattern of a sentence can go from one idea to another more quickly and confidently.

Parallel structure can be achieved with words, with phrases, and with clauses. Whether you use words, phrases, or clauses in parallel structure depends, as it does with subordination, upon the degree of emphasis you wish to create. In general, words in parallel structure produce some emphasis, phrases produce more emphasis, and clauses produce the most emphasis of all.

EXAMPLES   If you want to earn a satisfactory grade in the training program, you must be *punctual, courteous,* and *conscientious.* (parallel words)

If you want to earn a satisfactory grade in the training program, you must recognize the importance *of punctuality, of courtesy,* and *of conscientiousness.* (parallel phrases)

If you want to earn a satisfactory grade in the training program, *you must arrive punctually, you must behave courteously,* and *you must study conscientiously.* (parallel clauses)

[1] Occasionally a paragraph may contain a series of sentences that are parallel in structure.

To make the relationship among parallel units clear, repeat the word (or words) that introduces the first unit.

REVISE   The advantage is not in the pay but the greater opportunity.

TO   The advantage is not *in* the pay but *in* the greater opportunity.

REVISE   The study of electronics is a necessity and challenge to the technician.

TO   The study of electronics is *a* necessity and *a* challenge to the technician.

REVISE   Supervisors have it in their power to do great good or much mischief.

TO   Supervisors have it in their power *to do* great good or *to do* much mischief.

Parallel structure can contribute greatly to the clarity of your writing. But it is more than just a helpful device—sentences that contain faulty parallel structure are often awkward and difficult to read.

REVISE   Adina Wilson was happy about her assignment and getting a pay raise.

TO   Adina Wilson was happy *about her assignment* and *about her pay raise.*

REVISE   Jason advises his employees to work hard and against relying on luck.

TO   Jason advises his employees *to work hard* and not *to rely* on luck.

REVISE   The manufacturer promises to sell us the parts and that the cost will not be excessive.

TO   The manufacturer promises *that it will sell us the parts* and *that the cost will not be excessive.*

CHAPTER SUMMARY

Effective writing is *emphatic* writing—it places stress on those facts and ideas the writer wishes to highlight. There are a number of techniques a writer can use to make his or her sentences emphatic.

Ordinarily, the *active voice,* in which the subject of a sentence *performs* the action, provides greater emphasis than the *passive voice,* in which the subject *receives* the action. Unless you have a particular reason to use the passive voice, use the active.

Subordination is a device in which one element in a sentence is given greater stress than another. The less-important element may be expressed as a clause, introduced by words like *who, which, that,* and *although, when, where;* as a phrase; or as a single modifier. Subordination can turn a series of short, subject-verb sentences into one emphatic sentence that pinpoints the relationship of the sentence elements.

Other ways in which writers emphasize the key ideas in a sentence include unusual word order (as in the sentence *Never would I have expected such a result*); introductory words and phrases (*By keeping a record of the traffic flow through the office,* staff members can better determine the department's space needs); climactic order; direct statement; and several mechanical devices—the dash, all-capital letters, and underlining (italics).

Parallel structure, finally, can achieve economy of language, clarify meaning, indicate the equality of related ideas, and, often, create emphasis. Like subordination, parallel structure may be expressed in words, phrases, and clauses. It's important to note, too, that parallel structure is not just a stylistic device; it's often a necessity in a sentence, to avoid awkward or unclear writing.

EXERCISES

1. Rewrite the following sentences so that the verb is in the *active voice.* Supply a subject in those sentences that will need one when the sentence is rewritten.

    a. The report should be submitted to Sid Miner on Friday.
    b. The motion was passed by the delegates unanimously.
    c. A bonus of one thousand dollars for every year of service was voted by the board.
    d. Relocation pay must be approved by company officials.
    e. The sink in the bathroom has just been scrubbed.
    f. The new board of directors was approved by the stockholders at the annual meeting on May 22.
    g. It is greatly feared by employees that those who lose their jobs will not receive adequate compensation.
    h. It was felt by the committee that Jim Talbott should represent the company in New York.
    i. At the end of the presentation, the speaker was greeted with a loud burst of applause.
    j. It was announced by the advertising agency that the new package is an effective sales tool.
    k. The process of oxidation is speeded up by the presence of certain metals.
    l. You have been given an additional week by the vice-president to finish the interim report.
    m. After the operator inserts a check, the check-endorsement message is printed by the terminal.
    n. All current data should be analyzed before the decision is made.

Create 2 sets of 2 sentences - reverse it

, emphasize a sub. sentence

2. In each of the following, combine the series of short sentences into one unified sentence. Use *subordination* (1) to indicate how the ideas expressed in the sentence relate to each other and (2) to emphasize the most important idea or ideas.

  a. I recorded my speech on a cassette tape. The cassette tape can be recorded over. It does not need to be erased.
  b. It rained this morning. The construction crew stayed indoors. Members played a game of hearts. Valdez won.
  c. It had snowed for a week. I like to ski. I was delighted.
  d. He studied drafting at a technical school. He joined his brother's firm as a draftsman in 1969.
  e. Thomas Edison was one of America's greatest inventors. Teddy Roosevelt was the twenty-sixth president of the United States. Edison and Roosevelt were friends.
  f. Sales of sewing machines were declining. The management of Presto-Seam became worried. The management decided to initiate a TV ad campaign.
  g. The word-processing group had a backlog of work. No one could type my report. My report is due in two days.
  h. The cost of cotton has increased. All the suppliers have increased their prices. The suppliers are wholesalers.

3. Rewrite the following sentences to eliminate excessive subordination.

  a. It was the security guard who warned the police who arrived in time to catch the man who was robbing the safe.
  b. Never before have I known a student who was so ready to help a friend who had gotten into trouble that involved money.
  c. Will your report, in which you outline new developments in the field, be one of the papers which will be put on the agenda that is planned for the conference?

4. Rewrite the following sentences to make elements within them parallel in construction.

2
of your own

  a. The system is large and convenient, and it does not cost very much.
  b. The processor sends either a ready function code or standby function code.
  c. The log is a record of the problems which have occurred and of the service performed.
  d. The committee feels that the present system has three disadvantages: it causes delay in the distribution of incoming mail, dup-

licates work, and unnecessary delays are created in the work of several other departments.

e. In our first list we inadvertently omitted the seven lathes in room B-101, milling machines in room B-117, and from the next room, B-118, we also forgot to include sixteen shapers.

f. This product offers ease of operation, economy, and it is easily available.

g. The manual gives instructions for operating the machine and to adjust it.

h. Three of the applicants were given promotions, and transfers were arranged for the other four applicants.

i. To analyze the data, carry out the following steps: examine all the details carefully, eliminate all the unnecessary details, and a chart showing the flow of work should then be prepared.

j. We have found that the new system has four disadvantages: too costly to operate, it causes delays, fails to use any of the existing equipment, and it permits only one in-process examination.

k. The design is simple, inexpensive, and can be used effectively.

l. Management was slow to recognize the problem and even slower understanding it.

7

Revising for Precision
and Conciseness

In Chapter 3 you learned the importance of revising—of examining your work to see whether you've made any of the errors in mechanics that writers most frequently make. When you revise, you should also make sure that your meaning is unmistakable and your writing clear, direct, and uncluttered with unnecessary words and phrases. As you go over your work, ask yourself three questions: Can any of the passages be interpreted as expressing a meaning other than the one I had intended to express? Do any of the passages contain more words than are needed to convey my message? Do any of the passages contain pretentious or inappropriately technical language? If you answer Yes to the first question, your writing is vague—it lacks *precision,* or exactness. If you answer Yes to the second and third questions, your writing is wordy—it lacks *conciseness.* It hasn't been trimmed of unnecessary or overly fancy words and phrases. In this chapter, then, we'll examine some of the ways you can achieve precision and conciseness as you revise your work.

ACHIEVING PRECISION

Writing that is precise is so clear that your reader should have no difficulty understanding exactly what you want to say. In checking for precision, look for three likely trouble spots, enemies of precision that may give rise to misinterpretation on your reader's part: ambiguity, unclear pronoun reference, and imprecise word choice.

113

Ambiguity

The following sign once hung on the wall of a restaurant.

CUSTOMERS WHO THINK OUR WAITERS ARE RUDE
SHOULD SEE THE MANAGER

Several days later the sign was removed after customers continued to chuckle at the sign's unintended suggestion: that the manager was even ruder than the waiters.

In the case of the sign, of course, the customers understood the point that the restaurant owner had wanted to make. But in many types of job-related communication—a report or a letter, for instance—the reader may have difficulty deciding which of several possible meanings the writer had intended to convey. When a sentence (or a passage) can be interpreted in two or more ways and the writer has given the reader no clear basis for choosing from among the alternatives, the writing is *ambiguous*. Ambiguity is a common source of vagueness in on-the-job writing. Two of the most frequent causes of ambiguity in writing are faulty comparisons and inaccurately placed modifiers.

Faulty comparison.   When you make a comparison, be sure that your reader understands which elements are included in the comparison.

REVISE   Ms. Jones values rigid quality-control standards more than Mr. Johnson. (Does Ms. Jones value the standards more than she values Mr. Johnson, or does she value the standards more than Mr. Johnson values them?)

TO   Ms. Jones values rigid quality-control standards more than Mr. Johnson *does.*

When you compare two persons, things, or ideas, be sure that they are elements that can logically be compared with each other.

REVISE   The *accounting textbook* is more difficult to read than *office management.* (A textbook is not the same as a field of study.)

TO   The *accounting textbook* is more difficult to read than the *office management textbook.*

Inaccurately placed modifiers.   Another source of ambiguity occurs in the placement of certain modifiers. The modifiers (words that describe, explain, or qualify an element in a sentence) that are most likely to create ambiguity are *only, almost, just, hardly, even,* and *barely.* When you use one of these terms in a sentence, be sure that it modifies the word or element that you had intended it to. In most cases, place the modifier directly in front of the word it is supposed to qualify.

EXAMPLES   Katrina was the *only* engineer at Flagstead Industries. (The sentence says that Flagstead had one engineer, and she was Katrina.)

Katrina was *only* the engineer at Flagstead Industries. (The sentence says that Katrina had a position at Flagstead no higher than that of engineer.)

Anna Jimenez *almost* wrote a million dollars in insurance policies last month. (The sentence says that although Anna Jimenez came close to writing a million dollars in insurance policies, she actually didn't write *any*.)

Anna Jimenez wrote *almost* a million dollars in insurance policies last month. (The sentence says that Anna Jimenez wrote *nearly* a million dollars in insurance policies last month—a very different matter.)

A different kind of ambiguous modifier is the "squinting modifier"—a modifier that could be interpreted as qualifying either the sentence element before it or the sentence element following it.

EXAMPLE   We agreed *on the next day* to make the adjustments.

The reader doesn't know which of the following possible interpretations the writer had intended.

MEANING 1   *On the next day* we agreed to make the adjustments.
MEANING 2   We agreed to make the adjustments *on the next day.*

Unclear Pronoun Reference

A *pronoun* is a word that is used as a substitute for a noun. The noun for which the pronoun substitutes is called its *antecedent.* Using a pronoun to replace a noun eliminates the monotonous repetition of the noun. When you use a pronoun, though, be sure that your reader knows which noun the pronoun refers to. If you do not make it clear what word, or group of words, a pronoun is standing for, your reader may be uncertain of your meaning. When you revise your sentences for unclear pronoun reference, look especially for three types of errors: ambiguous reference, general (or broad) reference, and hidden reference.

Ambiguous reference.   In *ambiguous reference,* it is not clear to the reader which of two or more nouns a pronoun is referring to.

REVISE   Studs and thick treads make snow tires effective. *They* are installed with an air gun. (*What* are installed with an air gun—studs, treads, or snow tires? The reader can only guess.)

TO   Studs, which are installed with an air gun, and thick treads make snow tires effective. (Now it is clear that only studs are installed with an air gun.)

REVISE   We made the sale and delivered the product. It was a big one. (Does *It* refer to the sale or to the product?)

TO   We made the sale, which was a big one, and delivered the product. (Now it is clear that the sale, not the product, was a big one.)

REVISE   Jim worked with Tom on the report, but *he* wrote most of it. (*Who* wrote most of the report, Tom or Jim?)

TO   Jim worked with Tom on the report, but Tom wrote most of it.

General (or broad) reference. In a *general (or broad) reference* the pronoun, frequently one like *this, that, which,* or *it,* does not replace an easily identifiable antecedent; instead, it refers in a general way to the preceding sentence or clause.

REVISE   He deals with social problems in his work. *This* helps him in his personal life. (The pronoun *this* refers to the entire preceding sentence.)

TO   Dealing with social problems in his work helps him in his personal life.

REVISE   Mr. Bacon recently retired, *which* left an opening in the accounting department. (The pronoun *which* refers to the entire preceding clause.)

TO   Mr. Bacon's recent retirement left an opening in the accounting department. (Revising the sentence to eliminate the pronoun makes the meaning clear.)

Hidden reference. The third cause of unclear pronoun reference is the *hidden reference.* In sentences that contain a hidden reference, the antecedent of the pronoun is implied but never actually stated.

REVISE   In spite of the fact that our tractor division had researched the market thoroughly, we didn't sell *many.* (Many what? The pronoun *many* has no stated antecedent in the sentence. The writer assumes that the reader understands that *many* refers to tractors.)

TO   In spite of the fact that we had thoroughly researched the market for tractors, we didn't sell *many.* (Now the pronoun *many* has an antecedent, *tractors.*)

OR   In spite of the fact that our tractor division had researched the market thoroughly, we didn't sell many *tractors.* (Revising the sentence so that *many* becomes an adjective modifying *tractors* makes the meaning clear too.)

eylan

Imprecise Word Choice

The United States Congress no longer takes recesses. It's not that the two houses of Congress have stopped going on vacation. Rather, senators and representatives simply call the eight periods a year when they are not in session by another name. The House now has "district work periods," while the Senate goes into "nonlegislative periods." Why all the fuss over a simple word like *recess*? Certainly "vacation" is one of the meanings of *recess*. But another meaning of the word is "a brief period during the school day, for rest, play, or lunch." For many people the second meaning brings to mind the image of a schoolyard full of noisy children. It was probably to avoid this association that Congress decided to drop *recess* in favor of more serious-sounding terms. The change of label, though small, goes to show that the association which a word carries may be as important as its dictionary definition.

When you write, be alert to the effect a word may have on your reader— and try to avoid words that might, by the suggestions they carry, confuse or distract your reader. In describing a piece of machinery your company recently bought, for example, you might refer to the item as *cheap*—meaning inexpensive. But because *cheap* often suggests "of poor quality," or "shabbily made," your reader may picture the new piece of equipment as already needing repairs.

In selecting the appropriate word, you will want to keep in mind the context—the "setting" in which the word appears. Suppose you call the new machine "inexpensive" or "moderately priced." Your reader may have confidence that the equipment will work, but may ask, "What does the writer *mean* by inexpensive?" An electric typewriter at $300 might be inexpensive; a small printing press at $30,000 would also be a good buy. The exact meaning of *inexpensive* would depend upon the context. For readers who are unfamiliar with the costs of heavy machinery to learn that a $30,000 press was reasonably priced might come as a surprise. It would be up to you, the writer, to provide your readers with a context—to let them know, in this case, what the relative costs of printing equipment are.

The context will also determine whether a word you choose is *specific* enough. When you use the word *machine,* for instance, you might be thinking of an automobile, a lathe, a cash register, a sewing machine—the variety of mechanical equipment we use is almost endless. *Machine,* in other words, is an imprecise term that must be qualified, or explained, unless you want to refer, in a general way, to every item included in the category *machine.* If you have in mind a particular kind of machine, then you must use more precise language.

REVISE	The maintenance contract covers all the *machines* in Building D.
TO	The maintenance contract covers all the *electric typewriters* in Building D.

Depending upon the context, you might need to choose a term even more specific than *electric typewriters*. Just how specific a particular context might require you to be is illustrated by Figure 7-1, which goes from most general, on the left, to most specific, on the right.

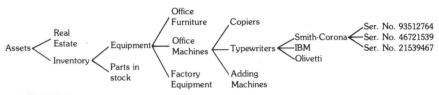

FIGURE 7-1

The figure represents seven levels of reference; which one would be appropriate depends on your purpose in writing and on the context in which you are using the word. For example, a company's annual report might logically use the most general term, *assets,* to refer to all the property and goods the firm owns: shareholders would probably not expect a further breakdown. Inter-office memos between the company's accounting and legal departments would appropriately call the firm's holdings *real estate* and *inventory.* To the company's inventory control department, however, the word *inventory* is much too broad to be useful, and a report on inventory might contain the more specific categories *equipment* and *parts in stock.* But to the assistant inventory control manager in charge of *equipment,* that term is still too general; he or she would speak of several particular kinds of equipment: *office furniture, factory equipment,* and *office machines.* The breakdown of the types of *office machines* the inventory control assistant is responsible for might include *copiers, adding machines,* and *typewriters.* Even this classification wouldn't be specific enough to enable the company's purchasing department to obtain service contracts for the normal maintenance of its typewriters, though. Because the department must deal with different typewriter manufacturers, *typewriters* would have to be listed by brand name: *Olivetti, IBM,* and *Smith-Corona.* And the Smith-Corona technician who performs the maintenance must go one step further and identify each Smith-Corona typewriter by serial number. As Figure 7-1 shows, then, a term may be sufficiently specific at one of the seven levels—but at the next level it becomes too broad. Your purpose in writing and your intended reader will determine how specific you should be.

Purpose and audience may sometimes require a general rather than a specific term. It would be inappropriate, of course, to include typewriter serial numbers in a company's annual report, to include a detailed parts list in a sales brochure, or to include highly technical language in a letter to the accounting department. In all the writing you do, you must decide what your purpose is and who your reader will be, and then select the term that is neither too general nor too specific for the occasion.

Remember that it may sometimes be necessary to define terms for your reader. If, for example, you are making a proposal to your boss, who must pass your proposal along to his or her boss for final approval, you may be using terms that your boss's superior will not recognize, because you work at a level of detail that someone two levels above may rarely come in contact with. If you want your proposal to be approved, you'd better do everything you can to be sure that your ideas are readily understandable. You would be wise, therefore, to define any terms that might be unclear.

How you go about defining the terms that need explanation depends upon the context. It may often be sufficient to give a brief explanation, in everyday language, of a technical or specialized term.

EXAMPLE   The program then spools the first file (*stores the file on magnetic tape until the program is ready to print it*) and opens the second file.

Or you may find it easiest to provide a dictionary-type definition.

EXAMPLE   The property includes approximately 1700 feet of waterside (land bordering any body of water).

Sometimes it may be necessary to provide a formal definition of a word. To write a formal definition, place the term in a category and show how the term differs from other members of that category.

EXAMPLE   A lease [*term*] is a contract [*category*] that conveys real estate for a specified period of time at a specified rent [*how "lease" differs from other contracts.*]

A definition will be clear and complete only if you include all three items (term, category, difference).

REVISE   A *kiln* is where you dry things. (Because this sentence does not assign the term *kiln* to a category and show how the word differs from other members of the category, it is not a definition.)

TO   A kiln [*term*] is a heated chamber [*category*] in which wood, clay, and other products are dried [*difference*].

Avoid circular definitions, those that merely restate the term and therefore fail to define it.

REVISE   A rectifier tube rectifies. (incomplete)

TO   A rectifier tube [*term*] is an electrical device [*category*] for converting alternating current to direct current [*difference*].

ACHIEVING CONCISENESS

Vagueness and ambiguity interfere with communication by requiring the reader to decide which of two (or more) possible ideas the writer had intended. *Wordiness,* too, can act as a barrier between reader and writer: writing that is wordy—that contains more words than are necessary to convey an idea, or that employs stilted or pretentious language—can slow the reader down and make relatively straightforward ideas difficult to understand. You can achieve conciseness (the opposite of wordiness) by eliminating from your work any words, phrases, or clauses that do not contribute to your meaning and any expressions that are excessively fancy or obscure. While a concise sentence is not guaranteed to be an effective one, a wordy sentence, because of the extra load it carries, always loses some of its readability and clarity. As you revise your work, be on the alert in particular for four types of wordiness: *redundancy,* or the use of a word or words that do no more than repeat the meaning of something already stated (*round circle* is an example of redundancy—*circle* contains the idea of roundness); *padded phrases,* which express in several words an idea that could easily be said in one (*due to the fact that* for *because* is an example of a padded phrase); *jargon,* the specialized, often highly technical vocabulary of a particular field—business, education, science, and the like (*provides the capability of performing the printing function* for *can print* is an example of jargon); and *excessive formality* (*The writer believes* instead of *I believe*).

Redundancy

When a modifying word, phrase, or clause adds no new information to what a sentence already says, the modifier is redundant.

REVISE	To complete the circuit, join the wires *together* with solder. (The word *together* repeats the thought contained in the word *join.*)
TO	To complete the circuit, join the wires with solder.
REVISE	*Modern* students of *today* consider work experience to be as valuable as classroom attendance. (The phrase *of today* repeats the thought expressed by the word *modern.*)
TO	*Modern* students consider work experience to be as valuable as classroom attendance.
OR	Students *of today* consider work experience to be as valuable as classroom attendance.
REVISE	Our imported products, *which come from abroad,* all have limited warranties. (Since *imported products* can be assumed to be manufactured *abroad,* the clause is not needed.)
TO	Our imported products all have limited warranties.
REVISE	We moved the storage cases into the empty warehouse, *which had nothing in it.* (*An empty warehouse* is understood to have nothing in it.)
TO	We moved the storage cases into the empty warehouse.

When they are selected carefully, modifiers—whether adjectives, adverbs, prepositional phrases, or subordinate clauses—can make the words they describe vivid and specific. Modifiers to avoid are those that simply repeat the idea contained in the word they modify. Studying the following list of *redundant expressions* may sharpen your ability to spot this kind of wordiness.

blue *in color*	to resume *again*
square *in shape*	brief *in duration*
to plan *ahead*	*tall* high rise
basic essentials	small *in size*
descended *down*	to attach *together*
visible *to the eye*	to cooperate *together*

Padded Phrases

When an idea that could be stated in one word is buried in an expression that takes several words—and is no clearer than the single word—a padded phrase results.

REVISE	The committee will meet *at an early date.*
TO	The committee will meet *soon.*
REVISE	The contractor will issue regular progress reports *during the time that* the contract is in effect.
TO	The contractor will issue regular progress reports *while* the contract is in effect.
REVISE	I recently met with the city attorney *with reference to* your case.
TO	I recently met with the city attorney *about* your case.
REVISE	We missed our deadline *due to the fact that* a strike occurred.
TO	We missed our deadline *because* a strike occurred.
REVISE	We cannot accept new clients *at the present time.*
TO	We cannot accept new clients *now.*
REVISE	We have received four complaints *in connection with* the project.
TO	We have received four complaints *about* the project.
REVISE	*In order to* meet the deadline, we must work overtime.
TO	*To* meet the deadline, we must work overtime.
REVISE	She was thinking *in terms of* subcontracting much of the work.
TO	She was thinking *of* subcontracting much of the work.

There are times, however, when the longer wording is desirable.

EXAMPLES	The committee must know the estimated costs *in order to* evaluate the feasibility of the project.
	In terms of gross sales, the year has been successful; *in terms of* net income, however, it has been discouraging.

Expressions like these must be evaluated individually. If the expression does not contribute to the meaning of the sentence, use its simpler substitute.

A half-dozen terms are the particular villains of wordiness. When they occur, you should examine your work critically for padded phrases. The words are *case, fact, field, factor, manner,* and *nature.*

REVISE	*In many cases,* students profit from writing a term paper.
TO	Students *often* profit from writing a term paper. (Sometimes it is necessary, when revising a sentence, to shift the location of the modifier.)
REVISE	I was not certain *of the fact that* your cousin is a steelworker.
TO	I was not certain *that* your cousin is a steelworker.
REVISE	I have been interested *in the fields of* drafting and electronics for several years.
TO	I have been interested *in* drafting and electronics for several years.
REVISE	Speed is also *an important factor.*
TO	Speed is also *important.*
REVISE	The skids were stacked *in an unsafe manner.*
TO	The skids were stacked *unsafely.*
REVISE	The committee seldom considered grievances *of a controversial nature.*
TO	The committee seldom considered *controversial* grievances.

Jargon

Jargon, the specialized, technical vocabulary of an occupational group, can be both an aid and a stumbling block to communication. If you are writing for members of an occupational group, you can reasonably expect your readers to know certain specialized terms and therefore can concentrate on presenting your ideas without having to stop and define the terms.[1] What you should be on the lookout for, in your writing, is *inappropriate jargon*—language that is more technical than the occasion requires. Jargon-laden writing is characterized by high-sounding but essentially meaningless expressions that may distract from your message and sometimes actually obscure it.

The use of jargon is *the* most serious problem in on-the-job writing, because many people apparently feel that inflated language lends a degree of formality, and thereby authority, to their writing. Nothing could be further from the truth. Pretentious—or "highfalutin"—language simply creates a smokescreen that the reader must penetrate to get to the writer's meaning.

[1] As you learned in the section on definition (pages 82–86), there are times when you may have to use technical terms that you cannot expect your reader to be familiar with. In such cases, of course, the best approach is to define the words clearly and concisely.

REVISE   It is the policy of the company to provide the proper telephone
              apparatus to enable each employee to conduct the interoffice
              and intra-business communication necessary to discharge his or
              her responsibilities; however, it is contrary to company practice
              to permit telephones to be utilized for employee personal com-
              munications.

TO   Your telephone is provided for company business; do not use it
              for personal calls.

Most people would have to read the first version of the sentence several times
before deciphering its message. The meaning of the revised version, which
uses direct, simple, and precise language, is evident at a glance.

In your own writing, avoid jargon as much as possible. Even if your
reader is a co-worker or a member of your occupational group, do not use
jargon as a substitute for simple, well-thought-out language. Take a critical
look at what you've written to see whether any of the wording should be de-
flated—replaced with clearer, shorter, down-to-earth words and phrases.

REVISE   I hereby authorize the above repair work to be done along with
              the necessary materials, and hereby grant you and/or your em-
              ployees permission to operate the car or truck herein described
              on streets, highways, or elsewhere for the purpose of testing
              and/or inspection.

TO   You have my permission to make repairs listed on this work
              order and to use the necessary materials. You or your em-
              ployees may drive my car or truck to test its performance.

Notice the absence in the revised version of the "high-sounding" phrases *I
hereby authorize, hereby grant, herein described, the above repair work,
and/or.* And notice that when it is translated into straightforward English the
statement gains in clarity what it loses in pomposity. Consider another jargon-
laden sentence.

REVISE   The Model 3211 is a device which provides the capability of
              performing the printing function to produce reports.

TO   The Model 3211 prints reports.

The first sentence reads like an important pronouncement. Stripped of its pretentious phrases, however, it is actually a simple statement.

Excessive Formality

Some writers feel that, especially in job-related writing, it is immodest or inappropriate to use the first-person point of view—that is, to speak of themselves as *I, me.* They believe that their material will sound more "objective" or
"businesslike" if they refer to themselves in the third person, employing such
terms as *the writer, the technician, the reporter,* or if they use the passive

voice. Writing of this sort tends to sound stuffy and unnatural, however. In most cases your message will be clearer and easier to follow if you speak of yourself as *I*.

REVISE   *The technician* will complete the wiring and test the system at the end of June.

TO   *I* will complete the wiring and test the system at the end of June.

REVISE   The tests described in the attached report *were all performed by the writer.*

TO   *I* performed all the tests described in the attached report.

It is also generally better, in on-the-job writing, to avoid the use of *one* as a pronoun, because it is inexact, it is indirect, and it sounds pretentious. The use of *one* does not make your writing more objective; it merely makes a statement sound impersonal, almost as if some nameless, formless being, rather than you yourself, were expressing an idea or making a suggestion.

REVISE   *One* can only conclude that the new valves are not effective on the old fire trucks.

TO   *I* can only conclude that the new valves are not effective on the old fire trucks.

The use of an impersonal *it is* expression to avoid the pronoun *I* has the same kind of stuffy effect as *the writer* and *one*.

REVISE   *It is regrettable that* the material shipped on the 12th is unacceptable.

TO   *I regret that* we cannot accept your shipment of the 12th.

The second version is more direct, and suggests that the writer is not trying to avoid taking responsibility for what he or she has stated.

Some writers, looking for ways to make their work sound more authoritative or more serious, introduce expressions like *It should be noted that* or *I am inclined to think that* in their writing. Expressions like these only add wordiness.

REVISE   *It should be noted that* the gaskets tend to turn brittle after six months in the warehouse.

TO   The gaskets tend to turn brittle after six months in the warehouse.

REVISE   *I am inclined to think that* each manager should attend the meeting to hear the committee's recommendations.

TO   I think that each manager should attend the meeting to hear the committee's recommendations.

There is never any valid reason to make your writing sound formal. On the contrary, the more natural your writing sounds, the more effectively it will communicate.

CHAPTER SUMMARY

In revising, make sure that you have expressed the exact meaning that you had intended to express and that you have trimmed your writing of unnecessary words and stilted phrases. Make sure, in other words, that your writing is *precise* and *concise.*

To achieve *precision,* eliminate the ambiguity that faulty comparisons and inaccurately placed modifiers may produce; supply an immediately recognizable antecedent for a pronoun whenever it is not clear which word or words the pronoun is referring to; and, according to the context, select words that have no inappropriate associations and are neither too general nor too specific for the context. And, if you use specialized or technical terms that your reader may be unfamiliar with, provide definitions or explanations of the terms.

To achieve *conciseness,* strike from your work any redundant modifiers —modifiers that contribute no additional meaning to the words they qualify— and any padded phrases—expressions that take several words to convey an idea that one or two words would express just as effectively. Do not use inappropriate jargon (high-sounding but often empty phrases) as a substitute for direct, well-thought-out language. Finally, avoid excessive formality; in most cases it is preferable to speak of yourself as *I* than as *the writer* or *one* (*I believe* is more straightforward than *the writer believes* or *one believes*).

EXERCISES

1. Each of the following sentences contains a faulty comparison. Rewrite each sentence to eliminate the error.
    a. The shipping department's absentee rate was higher than the storeroom.
    b. The Bodkins' van is cleaner than Jim.
    c. The word-processing machine in the Direct Mail Department operates more efficiently than the Customer Relations Department.
    d. The production manager expressed greater appreciation for the temporary help than the sales manager.
    e. Julia Valenti, the personnel manager, felt that the applicant was better qualified than Charles Crane, the director of Office Services.

2. Each of the following sentences contains a "squinting modifier"—that is, a modifier that may qualify either of two elements within the sentence. Locate the squinting modifier and rewrite the sentence in two ways.

    a. The transformer that was sparking violently shocked the line operator.
    b. The man who was making calculations hastily rose from the desk and left the room.
    c. After the committee decided that the work must be completed by Monday, in spite of other commitments, it adjourned immediately.
    d. He planned after the convention to take a short vacation.

3. Each of the following sentences or pair of sentences contains an unclear pronoun reference. Rewrite the sentence or sentences to eliminate the error.

   a. Many members complained that their representatives made decisions secretly without considering them.
   b. Technology has so simplified computer operation that it is now being used in homes.
   c. The crane operator did not file a safety grievance and does not plan it.
   d. Our company decided to relocate in Grandview Hills, after rejecting Westville and Dale City, which was a difficult decision to make.
   e. Anita has held stenographic positions in two insurance companies and in an auto-rental firm, and it should help her in finding a new job.
   f. Mrs. Jardina wanted to dictate a letter to her assistant, Mrs. Sanfredini, but she was unable to begin work until after lunch.
   g. If you feel that you would like to become a dental hygienist, by all means take a course in it.

4. In the sentences that follow, substitute for the word in italics one that has a *more* favorable association.

   a. A good project engineer *controls* the new drafting mechanic in every step of the assignment.
   b. Because the display unit occupies such a small space, the device is ideal for *secret* viewing.
   c. The group leader was *stubborn* in his determination to finish the job on time.
   d. The plant superintendent complained that the quality-assurance program was *killing* production.

5. In the following sentences, substitute for the word in italics one that has a *less* favorable association.

   a. The *dignitary* announced to the group that the economy was suffering.
   b. The customer would not admit that he had *misrepresented* the facts.
   c. The workers complained that the new manager was *carefully watching* everything they did.
   d. They *adjusted* their prices to keep them in line with increased costs.

6. For each of the following terms, supply four words that provide a specific example of the category the term covers. The first item has been done for you.

a. a building	d. a vehicle	i. unit of
police headquarters, YMCA,	e. a liquid	measure
City Hall, a private house	f. a tool	j. a job
b. an appliance	g. food	
c. a fabric	h. furniture	

7. Each of the following sentences contains a redundant word, phrase, or clause. Rewrite the sentences to eliminate the redundant element.

    a. Our experienced salespeople, who have many years of work behind them, will plan an aggressive advertising campaign to sell the new product.

    b. Any two raceway assemblies can be connected together with the plate as shown.

    c. The radio announcer kept repeatedly saying, "Buy PDQ brand pretzels!"

    d. Dissatisfied employees should give their complaints to the manager who is in charge as supervisor.

    e. If you are interested in economics, do not neglect to read the above-mentioned book, which was discussed previously.

8. Each of the following sentences contains a padded phrase. Rewrite the sentences to eliminate the padded phrase.

    a. We began the project in the month of April.

    b. He opened the conversation with a reference to the subject of inflation.

    c. The field of engineering is a profession that offers great opportunities.

    d. The fact that the chemicals were impure caused the delay.

    e. The personnel manager spoke to the printing-plant supervisor with regard to the scheduling of employee vacations.

    f. Due to the fact that Monday was a holiday, we will not be able to complete the job until Wednesday.

    g. The committee postponed the decision until the fall season.

9. Each of the following passages contains some jargon. Rewrite the passages to eliminate the jargon.

    a. With reference and regard to the matter that management has declared to be in the best interests of the furtherance of company – employee relations, the president has been authorized and empowered to grant each and every employee, upon the attainment of thirty years of continued and uninterrupted service to the company and its aforementioned management, an additional period of vacation that shall be of one week's duration.

b. I hereby designate Mr. Samson, who has been holding the position and serving in the capacity of assistant technical supervisor, to be named and appointed to the position and function of deputy director of Customer Relations. In his newly elevated position Mr. Samson will report, in the first instance, directly to the department director—that is, to myself.

c. Purchasers of the enclosed substance should carefully and thoroughly follow the instructions provided herein for the use of the substance, and should in no case whatsoever consume, or otherwise partake of, said substance without proceeding in the prescribed manner as set forth on the accompanying and attached circular of instructions.

8

Spelling

Personnel managers often reject candidates who make spelling errors on employment applications, résumés, and covering letters. Consider, for example, the true story of a college graduate who applied for the position of Assistant Director of Personnel and was rejected for misspelling the word *personnel*.

The reason potential employers react so strongly to spelling errors is simple. Poor spelling reflects negatively on an employee—and, by association, on the employer as well. Everyone makes an occasional error, of course, but a personnel manager may conclude that someone who has overlooked a spelling mistake on something as important as a job application may be careless in his or her work too. Keep in mind that when you apply for a job, an employer must make a judgment based primarily on your résumé, your letter of application, and your interview.

But an even more important reason to learn to be a careful speller is that accuracy in spelling can help you keep the bargain you, as a writer, make with your readers: to assist them in understanding what you are saying. Your job as a writer is to remove roadblocks from the path of communication between you and your readers—and spelling errors, because they can confuse and slow your readers down, create roadblocks.

As you write a first draft, you needn't be concerned about spelling words correctly. Your attention then should focus on what you are saying; to worry about spelling at that point would be a distraction. You can check for and correct spelling errors when you revise; in fact, you should proofread once *just for spelling*. Guard against the natural tendency to concentrate on complex words; pay as much attention to words in common use as you do to "hard" words. It is often the words you use most frequently that trip you up.

To proofread for spelling errors, go over your writing slowly, using a pencil to focus on each word. The trick in this kind of proofreading is the pace at which you read. Read slowly. Concentrate on the words rather than on the ideas they express.

Like building a vocabulary, learning to spell requires a systematic effort on your part. The following system will help you learn to spell correctly; the effort you must provide.

1. Keep a dictionary handy, and use it regularly. If you are unsure about the spelling of a word, don't rely on memory or guesswork—consult the dictionary. When you look up a word, focus on both its spelling and its meaning.
2. After you have looked in the dictionary for the spelling of the word, write the word from memory several times. Then check the accuracy of your spelling. If you have misspelled the word, repeat this step. If you do not follow through by writing the word from memory, you lose the chance of retaining it for future use. Practice is essential.
3. Keep a list of the words you commonly misspell, and work regularly at whittling it down. Do not load the list with exotic words; many of us would stumble over *asphyxiation* or *pterodactyl.* Concentrate instead on words like *calendar, maintenance,* and *unnecessary.* These and other frequently used words should remain on your list until you have learned to spell them.
4. Study the following common sets of words that sound alike but differ in spelling and meaning.*

affect (verb: to influence)
effect (noun: a result)
all ready (We are *all ready* to go.)
already (Have you finished the work *already*?)
brake (noun: device for stopping)
break (verb: to crack; noun: period of relaxation)
cite (verb: use as proof of something)
sight (noun: view; something to look at)
site (noun: location)
cent (noun: coin)
scent (noun: smell)
sent (verb: past tense of *send*)
coarse (adjective: rough)
course (noun: direction; adverb in *of course*)
complement (noun: something that completes something else)
compliment (noun: praise; verb: to give praise)
fair (noun: exhibition; adjective: light-hued, beautiful)

* The meanings given here are for identification only—they are not intended to represent every meaning a word may have.

fare (noun: cost of a trip; food served)
forward (adjective and adverb: near or toward the front)
foreword (noun: introduction to a book)
hear (verb: to listen to)
here (adverb: in this place)
its (possessive pronoun: Does the dog have *its* bone?)
it's (contraction* of *it is*: *It's* good to see you.)
lead (noun: a metal—rhymes with *bread*)
lead (verb: to be first—rhymes with *breed*)
led (verb: past tense of verb *to lead*)
may be (verb: It *may be* true, but it's hard to believe.)
maybe (adverb: perhaps—*Maybe* he will visit us.)
pair (noun: set of two)
pare (verb: to trim)
pear (noun: fruit)
peace (noun: absence of war)
piece (noun: small amount)
plain (adjective: ordinary-looking, simple; noun: large field)
plane (noun: aircraft)
plane (verb: to make smooth)
principal (adjective: primary, main; noun: school official)
principle (noun: a controlling idea or belief)
right (adjective: correct)
rite (noun: ritual)
write (verb: to create with words)
road (noun: street)
rode (past tense of verb *to ride*)
rowed (past tense of verb *to row*—to propel a small boat)
stationary (adjective: not moving)
stationery (noun: writing paper and envelopes)
their (possessive pronoun—Do you know *their* telephone number?)
there (adverb: at that place)
they're (contraction of *they are*—They're going to meet us at the movies.)
to (preposition: toward)
too (conjunction: also; adverb: excessively)
two (number)
weak (adjective: not strong)
your (possessive pronoun—Is this *your* book?)
you're (contraction of *you are*—You're a fine friend!)

---

* In a *contraction,* two words are combined and one or more letters are omitted. An apostrophe (') indicates where the letter or letters have been dropped. Contractions are appropriate in some informal writing, but it is best to avoid them in formal contexts.

> **week** (noun: seven days)
> **weather** (noun: atmospheric conditions)
> **whether** (conjunction: if)
> **who's** (contraction of *who is*—Do you know *who's* coming?)
> **whose** (possessive pronoun—*Whose* coat is this?)

The following pages contain a number of rules and some advice to help you improve your spelling. It would be pointless to try to memorize all the rules and reminders. If you have specific problem areas in spelling, however, you would be wise to learn the rules that apply to your particular needs.

The Silent *e* Rule

Words of one syllable that have a long vowel sound usually end in silent *e*. (A *long vowel* is one that is pronounced like the letter's name.) Adding silent *e* to a one-syllable word that has a *short vowel sound* ordinarily gives the vowel a long sound. (Dictionaries vary in the symbols they use to indicate how a word is pronounced. Examine the pronunciation key in the dictionary you use.)
    Compare the words in the two lists below.

Short-vowel sounds	Long-vowel sounds
fat	fate
pet	Pete
bit	bite
dot	dote
cut	cute

The silent *e* rule also applies to the accented syllable in some longer words.*

| com · plete′ | con · trive′ | en · ve · lope′ |
| re · fuse′ | su · per · sede′ | |

The silent *e* rule does not apply in longer words in which the final syllable is *not* accented.

| com · pos′ · ite | gran′ · ite | hes′ · i · tate | op′ · pos · ite |
| prac′ · tice | ser′ · vice | ul′ · ti · mate | |

If endings are added to the basic word, the silent *e* rule still holds, even if the silent *e* is dropped when the ending is added.

late   later
complete   completed
hope   hoping

---

* An *accented syllable* receives the emphasis when the word is spoken. The symbol ′ is used here to indicate the accented syllable. Check your dictionary for the symbol it uses.

Hard and Soft Sounds

The letter c can sound like a k ("hard" c) or like an s ("soft" c). The letter g can sound like "guh" ("hard" g) or like a j ("soft" g).

Hard Sound	Soft Sound
attic	ace
cog	cogent
rag	rage
sac	suffice

Hard c and soft c. Hard c and soft c cause problems mostly at the ends of words. The following guidelines will help you to distinguish between hard c and soft c.

1. The sound of c is always hard when it is the last letter of a word.

   automatic   economic   electric   spastic   specific

2. A long vowel followed by a k sound is always spelled with a k and a silent e.

   take   eke   like   woke   fluke

3. A short vowel followed by a k sound is always spelled ck when another syllable follows.

   beckon   bracket   picket   pocket   trucker

4. An e after a c almost always indicates a soft c.

   ace   ice   piece   puce   place

Hard g and soft g. Hard g and soft g cause problems mostly at the beginnings of words. The following guidelines should help you to distinguish between hard g and soft g.

1. Any g followed by a consonant is a hard g.

   ghetto   gladly   grain   green

2. The g in the combinations gu and go is always hard.

   cargo   goblet   guess   guide

3. The g in the combination ga is always hard except in the word margarine.

   gale   gape   garage   gate

4. The g in the combination gi can be either hard or soft.

   fragile   gibber   gift   give

5. The g in the combination ge is usually soft.

   cage   garage   general   germinate   gesture

6. The g in the combination gy is soft.

   gymnasium   gypsum   gyrate   gyroscope

Adding to Basic Words

Words may change spelling according to the way they are used in a sentence. The following rules can serve as a guide in choosing the correct spelling of a plural noun, a verb form, an adverb formed from an adjective, and the comparative and superlative forms of some adjectives (*nicer, nicest*).

Plurals of nouns.   You may have no difficulty spelling a word like *tax, brush,* or *ox.* You may encounter some trouble, though, in spelling the plural form of these and other words. The general rules for forming the plural of nouns are as follows.

1. To form the plural of *most* nouns, add *s.*
    - circumstance/circumstances   hat/hats   mule/mules
      pen/pens   tie/ties   tool/tools

2. To form the plural of nouns that end in *ch, s, sh, ss, x, z,* or *zz,* add *es.*
    bus/buses   branch/branches   brush/brushes
    buzz/buzzes   glass/glasses   tax/taxes

3. To form the plural of nouns that end in *y* preceded by a vowel, add *s.*
    boy/boys   monkey/monkeys

    But if the *y* is preceded by a consonant, change the *y* to *i* and then add *es.*
    filly/fillies   fly/flies

4. To form the plural of most nouns that end in *f* and all nouns that end in *ff,* add *s.*
    reef/reefs   roof/roofs   cuff/cuffs

    For a few nouns that end in *f,* change the *f* to *v* and add *es.*
    leaf/leaves   loaf/loaves   sheaf/sheaves
    shelf/shelves   wolf/wolves

    If a noun ends in *fe,* change the *f* to *v* and add *es.*
    knife/knives   life/lives   wife/wives

    Note: If there is a *v* in the plural form of a noun, you can usually hear it in the spoken word.

5. Some commonly used nouns have a special plural form.
    child/children   foot/feet   ox/oxen
    tooth/teeth   woman/women

Consult your dictionary for other plural forms that may be troublesome: nouns ending in *o,* foreign words used in English, a number of scientific and medical terms, and so on.

Adding verb, adjective, and adverb endings. The general rules for adding endings to verbs, for forming adverbs from adjectives, and for adding the comparative (*er*) and superlative (*est*) endings to adjectives are as follows.

1. If the word ends in a consonant, simply add the ending.

   long + er = longer   small + est = smallest
   want + ed = wanted   burn + ing = burning
   catch + es = catches

2. If the word ends in silent *e* and the ending begins with a vowel (including *e*), drop the silent *e* of the basic word.

   note + ed = noted   fine + est = finest
   landscape + er = landscaper base + ic = basic
   advise + ory = advisory   desire + able = desirable
   enclose + ure = enclosure   guide + ance = guidance
   continue + al = continual   serve + ice = service
   write + ing = writing   distribute + ing = distributing

3. If the basic word ends in silent *e* and the ending begins with a consonant, simply add the ending.

   like/likely   use/useless   care/carefully

   There are a few exceptions to this rule.

   true/truly   argue/argument   nine/ninth

4. If the basic word ends in a consonant and the ending begins with the same consonant, keep both consonants.

   cool/coolly   tail/tailless   jewel/jewellike

5. If the basic word ends in *y* preceded by a vowel, simply add the ending.

   betray/betrays/betrayed/betraying
   obey/obeys/obeyed/obeying

   Note: There are three important exceptions to this rule:

   lay/lays/laying *but* laid   pay/pays/paying *but* paid
              say/says/saying *but* said

6. If the basic word ends in *y* preceded by a consonant, change the *y* to *i* before adding the ending, *unless the ending begins with i.*

   copy/copies/copied/copying
   try/tries/tried/trying

7. If a verb ends in *ie*, add *s* or *d* directly to the word.

   die/dies/died   tie/ties/tied
   But change *ie* to *y* before adding *ing*.
   die/dying   tie/tying

8. When you add *ly* to most adjectives to form an adverb, simply add the ending. The word *truly* is an exception to this rule.

careful/carefully   complete/completely   dim/dimly
nice/nicely   sure/surely   useless/uselessly

When you add the ending *ly* to most adjectives ending in *cal,* be sure to retain the *a* and both *l*'s.

magical/magically
medical/medically
practical/practically

9. When you add *er, est,* or *ly* to an adjective that ends in *y,* change the *y* to *i* before adding the ending.

happy/happier/happiest/happily
noisy/noisier/noisiest/noisily

10. When you add *ly* to adjectives ending in *ble,* drop the *e* and add only the *y.*

able/ably   favorable/favorably   incredible/incredibly

Doubling Final Consonants

Knowing when and when not to double a final consonant before adding an ending is important. Three things affect the decision: (1) whether the vowel in the basic word is long or short, (2) which syllable in longer words receives the accent, and (3) whether the basic word ends in more than one consonant.

The effect of the vowel in the basic word.   For most words of one syllable, double the final consonant only if the preceding vowel is *short.*

plan/planning	mate/mated
let/letting	cede/ceding
rip/ripped	ripe/ripen
flop/flopped	tone/toner
sun/sunning	tune/tuning

Never double the final consonant of a word if the consonant is immediately preceded by two vowels.

appear/appeared/appearing/appearance
treat/treated/treating/treatment

The effect of the word's accent.   In longer words, whether the final consonant is doubled depends on which syllable is accented. When the accent falls on the last syllable of a word, double the final consonant before adding the ending.

com · pel'/compelled/compelling
ad · mit'/admitted/admitting
oc · cur'/occurred/occurring
pre · fer'/preferred/preferring

When the accent does not fall on the last syllable, do not double the final consonant before adding the ending.

pro'fit/profited/profiting   ex · hib'it/exhibited/exhibiting
dif'fer/differed/differing   fo'cus/focused/focusing

The effect of final consonants.   When a word ends in more than one consonant, *do not double* the final consonant when adding an ending.

confirm/confirmed/confirming
depend/depended/depending/dependence
plump/plumper/plumpest

When a word ends in a double consonant, keep both consonants when adding the ending.

embarrass/embarrassed/embarrassing/embarrassment
enroll/enrolled/enrolling/enrollment

Prefixes and Suffixes

A *prefix* is a form like *dis, un, anti* placed in front of a word to change its meaning. A *suffix* is a form like *able, ible,* placed at the end of a word (or word part) to change its meaning. To avoid making spelling errors when you use words that contain prefixes and suffixes, study the following rules.

1. When you attach a prefix like *dis, im, mis, un* to a word that begins with the same letter as the *last* letter of the prefix, be sure to retain the double letters.

   dis + similar = dissimilar   im + movable = immovable
   mis + spell = misspell   un + natural = unnatural

2. When you attach a suffix that begins with a vowel to a word that ends in silent *e,* the *e* is usually dropped.

   sane/sanity   advise/advisory
   enclose/enclosure   continue/continual
   base/basic   value/valuable
   desire/desirable   guide/guidance

3. When you attach the suffix *able* or *ible* to a word that ends in a soft *c* or a soft *g* sound, retain the *e* of the original word.

   change/changeable   notice/noticeable
   manage/manageable   service/serviceable

4. When you attach suffixes like *ness* and *less,* be sure you spell the original word correctly.

drunken + ness = drunkenness (retain both *n's*)
care + less = careless (retain the *e*—otherwise you are spelling *carless,* "without a car")
Note: In a word like *lioness,* the suffix is *ess* (to indicate female), not *ness.*

Words with *ie* or *ei*

Among the trickiest words in the English language to spell are *ie* and *ei* words. The following rules of thumb should help you recognize the correct spelling of these words.

1. In most cases, the correct combination following the letter *c* is *ei.*

| ceiling | conceive | perceive | receive |

2. Many words that are pronounced *ee* are spelled *ie.*

| achieve | brief | cashier | field |
| piece | relieve | tier | yield |

3. Many words that are pronounced as a long *a* are spelled *ei.*

eight	freight	weight
rein	veil	vein
neighbor	reign	sleigh

4. Words that are pronounced as a long *i* are always spelled *ei.*

| height | seismograph | sleight |

Contractions

A *contraction* is a form that combines two words, omitting one or more letters, and uses an apostrophe (') to indicate where the letter or letters have been dropped.

cannot/can't	is not/isn't
it is/it's	they are/they're
were not/weren't	who is/who's
would not/wouldn't	

Remember to place the apostrophe exactly where the letter is deleted.
Be careful not to confuse contractions with words that have the same pronunciation as the contractions.

whose/who's   theirs/there's   its/it's   their/they're

And do not confuse the presence of the apostrophe to form a contraction with the use of the apostrophe to show possession.

	Contraction	*Possession*
	can't (can + not)	the woman's voice
	don't (do + not)	a student's book

In a contraction, the apostrophe indicates that a letter has been left out. In a possession form, the apostrophe indicates ownership.

Abbreviated Spellings

In very informal writing, certain words are sometimes spelled in an abbreviated form: *thru (through), til (until), tho (although),* and *nite (night).* Such abbreviated spellings should be avoided in all job-related writing.

Word Groups of Frequently Misspelled Words

Words Ending in ery

creamery	bravery	effrontery (note double *f*)
hatchery	imagery	nursery

Words Ending in ary

arbitrary	complementary	complimentary	documentary
elementary	fragmentary	imaginary	library
monetary	necessary	primary	tributary

Words Ending in able

acceptable	agreeable	avoidable	changeable
dependable	manageable	profitable	valuable

Note: Remember to keep the *e* in *changeable* and *manageable.*

Words Ending in iable

appreciable	enviable	justifiable
liable	reliable	variable

Words Ending in ible

audible	compatible	combustible	credible
divisible	eligible	feasible	forcible	illegible
indelible	invincible	negligible	reducible
visible

Words Ending in ise

advertise	advise	comprise	compromise
excise	exercise	franchise	revise	supervise

Note: Note the spelling of the nouns *supervisor* and *adviser* or *advisor.*

Words Ending in ize

authorize	energize	familiarize	magnetize
notarize	organize	specialize	standardize
stabilize	subsidize	summarize	synchronize

Words Ending in yze

analyze   paralyze

Note: The noun forms are *analysis* and *paralysis*.

Words Ending in eous

courteous	erroneous	gaseous	heterogeneous
homogeneous	instantaneous	outrageous	
spontaneous			

Words Ending in ious

cautious	contagious	curious	laborious
mysterious	nutritious	previous	repetitious

Words Ending in ous

anonymous	callous	dangerous	disastrous
grievous	hazardous	intravenous	mischievous
monotonous			

Words Ending in sion

compulsion	conclusion	conversion	diversion
erosion	expansion	expulsion	extension
occasion	persuasion	propulsion	provision
reversion			

Words Ending in ssion:

accession	admission	concession	discussion
omission (note one *m*)		recession	remission
succession	transmission		

Note: Be sure to distinguish between *intersession* (the period between two *sessions* of the school year) and *intercession* (intervention on behalf of someone).

Words ending in cede and ceed are sometimes troublesome. Study the following lists.

Words Ending in cede

accede   concede   intercede   precede (to go ahead
of someone or something)   recede   secede

The *ing* forms of these words follow the silent *e* rule: *acceding, conceding, interceding, preceding, receding, seceding.*

Words Ending in ceed

exceed   proceed (to go forward)   succeed

The *ing* forms are *exceeding, proceeding, succeeding.*

Note: The word *supersede,* "to take the place of something that went before," is often misspelled. It is the only word in common use that has a *sede* ending.

Words Ending in ence

magnificence   maleficence   permanence
    persistence   pertinence

Words Ending in ance

dissonance   malfeasance   perseverance

Words Ending in scence

effervescence   luminescence   phosphorescence

CHAPTER SUMMARY

Incorrect spelling in on-the-job writing reflects poorly on both you and your employer. But an even more important reason to learn to spell correctly is that spelling errors often confuse and distract your readers and slow their progress. As you revise your written work, you should check carefully for spelling errors.

Keep a dictionary handy, and use it; don't rely on guesswork or memory. When you look up a word, learn its spelling, its pronunciation, and its meaning. Write the word from memory several times, and then check the accuracy of your spelling. Keep a list of the words you commonly misspell, and work regularly at reducing it. Memorize the dozen or so sets of words, like *course* and *coarse,* that sound alike but differ in spelling and meaning.

If you know that you are weak in spelling, carefully study the rules included in the chapter.

EXERCISES

1. Give the plural form of the following nouns.

   blush   crisis   disk   donkey   guess
   hoof   spy   task   tomato   utterance

2. Add the ending *-ful* to the following nouns to form adjectives.

   bliss   care   hope   respect   spite   tact

3. Add the ending *-ly* to the following adjectives to form adverbs.

   accidental   grateful   intentional   invisible
   remote   shrill   sincere   probable
   unlike

4. Add the comparative ending (*-er*) and superlative ending (*-est*) to the following adjectives.
   silly   roomy   fancy   friendly

5. Add prefixes to the following words as indicated.

   dis + able   dis + satisfy   dis + service   dis + taste
   im + mobile   interchange + able   mis + match
   mis + statement   profit + able   un + intended
   un + necessary

6. Add the endings as indicated to the following words.
   argue + ment   continue + al   dismiss + al   erase + ure
   intense + ity   five + teen   pleasure + able   refer + al
   replace + ment   sane + ity

7. Give the *-ed* form of the following verbs.

   cancel   cope   defer   depend   fine   flatten
   frighten   mop   mope   occupy   plan   plunk
   promote

8. Give the *-s* form of the following verbs.

   die   dye   elate   fry   relay   wait

9. Give the *-ing* form of the following verbs.

   beat   compel   feed   fly   focus   fume
   infer   press   remain   rip   stem

9

Acquiring a Useful Vocabulary

Trying to get along with a limited vocabulary is like trying to prepare a five-course meal with only one utensil and a pan. The limited equipment prevents you from dealing successfully with the range of situations you'll find yourself in. A limited vocabulary is a handicap, but it is one you can overcome. The emphasis here is on you because there is no magic formula for vocabulary building. It must be done because you want it done. It must also be done systematically and over a period of time. This chapter provides a system; you must provide the time and desire.

If you stop to think about it, you'll realize that you use at least three different vocabularies, perhaps four. Your largest vocabulary is your *recognition vocabulary*, which includes all the words you recognize and understand in your reading. Your next largest vocabulary is your *writing vocabulary,* which takes in all the words you use in your writing. The third largest is your *speaking vocabulary;* it is smaller than your writing vocabulary because you may consider some words from your writing vocabulary too formal for conversation. And, finally, you may have a limited vocabulary, of from 50 to 1,000 words, that are unique to the particular trade or profession in which you are (or will be) engaged.

You will probably have no trouble in learning your trade, or professional, vocabulary, but you may need to work on improving the other three—especially your writing and recognition vocabularies. One excellent way to do so is by increasing the amount of reading you do and keeping a good dictionary nearby for looking up unfamiliar words. The movement of a word from your recognition vocabulary to your writing vocabulary should be relatively easy. Another effective way to increase your vocabulary is to take a word-part approach, learning the meanings of prefixes and roots of words and, on the basis of those meanings, figuring out the meaning of a new word that contains them. The following pages explore these two methods of improving your vocabulary.

CHOOSING THE RIGHT WORD

Your guideline in choosing the right word should be appropriateness. Is the word or expression you are considering appropriate to both your reader and your subject? When in doubt about the correct use, exact meaning, or pronunciation of a word, consult a recent edition of a good college or desk dictionary. A compact paperback dictionary may be convenient for checking the spelling of a word, but for a wide range of detailed information about a term, a hardback desk dictionary is essential. The following are considered good desk dictionaries.

The American Heritage Dictionary of the English Language. New York: American Heritage Publishing Company, 1969.

Funk and Wagnall's Standard College Dictionary. Rev. ed. New York: Funk and Wagnall's, 1974.

The Random House College Dictionary. New York: Random House, 1975.

Webster's New Collegiate Dictionary. Rev. ed. Springfield, Mass.: G. & C. Merriam Company, 1977.

Webster's New World Dictionary of the American Language. Second college ed. Cleveland: World Publishing Company, 1976.

Get into the habit of using a dictionary. Like any reference tool, the more you know about it, the more useful it will be to you. The following is a list of the kinds of information a dictionary entry may provide. Both the order in which the information is given and the form in which it is presented vary; most dictionaries supply a note near the beginning of the volume that explains how the information is arranged and presented in the work. Many dictionaries also include a key to the signs, symbols, and abbreviations used in the dictionary. In addition, most dictionaries include, before and after the entry section, a variety of information, such as a pronouncing gazetteer (names of places), a list of common English given names, the names of colleges and universities, and a history of the English language.

1. *Spelling.* Each entry is printed in **bold type.** Occasionally, when there is more than one acceptable spelling, both are given: *catalog, catalogue.*
2. *Syllables.* The word is divided into syllables (if it contains more than one): ox · y · gen. This division provides the correct *hyphenation* of the word—it indicates how the word is divided at the end of the line.

3. *Pronunciation.* The word's pronunciation (how it sounds when spoken) is given, usually in parentheses, by a combination of standard alphabet letters and symbols (the combination is called a *respelling*). Each letter and symbol represents one specific sound; a key to the symbols ordinarily appears at the bottom of every page or every second page of the dictionary. The pronunciation of the word *reserve,* for example, is indicated by the form rĭ·zûrv'.

4. *Accent.* An accent mark (' or ') indicates which syllable is emphasized when the word is spoken: pri·mar'·i·ly. The accent mark ordinarily appears as part of the *respelling* of the word.

5. *Part of Speech.* An abbreviation identifies the part or parts of speech the word belongs to: *v.* for *verb; n.* for *noun; pron.* for *pronoun; adj.* for *adjective; adv.* for *adverb; prep.* for *preposition; conj.* for *conjunction; interj.* for *interjection.* If a word functions as more than one part of speech, the different parts of speech are included in the entry.

6. *Definition.* When a word has more than one meaning, each definition is listed, in numbered sequence. The order in which a word's meanings are listed varies. Some dictionaries present the meanings in historical order, with the oldest meaning first and the most recent meaning last; other dictionaries list the most recent meaning first and the oldest meaning last. (The dictionary's explanatory notes will tell you in what order the meanings are arranged.) If a word has two or more fundamental, and unrelated, meanings, each word is listed as a separate entry; any additional related meanings of each word are numbered consecutively within the entry. The word *fan,* for instance, has two separate entries in *The Random House Dictionary:* the first entry includes both the noun that signifies "a device for moving air" and the verb meaning "to move the air"; the second entry applies to the noun *fan* that refers to an "enthusiastic follower."

When a word has one or more specific meanings in one or more special fields (biology, music, literature, architecture, religion, telecommunications, to name just a few), the definitions are introduced by a label that identifies the field. The entry for the word *rest* in *The American Heritage Dictionary,* for example, first defines the word according to its most general use—the act of ceasing from work; sleep; death, and so on—and then goes on to define the word according to the way it is used in the specific fields of music, prosody, billiards, and the military.

7. *Example.* To help you understand exactly how a word may be used, some dictionaries provide examples of the word, usually in a phrase or a sentence. The word *serried,* for instance, is defined in *The American Heritage Dictionary of the English Language* as "pressed together in rows; in close order." The example sentence that follows is "Troops in *serried* ranks assembled."

8. *Picture.* Occasionally, the definition of a word is accompanied by a

drawing or a photograph of the object. *The American Heritage Dictionary* in particular has numerous pictures.

9. *Usage.* Usage labels provide information about the standing a word has in relation to current standards of speech. Such a label might indicate that a word is obsolete (no longer in use), primarily British, slang, and so on. Since usage standards change over time, the date of the dictionary is an important factor in determining the accuracy of a given label.

10. *Special Uses.* Special uses of a word, or its use in certain expressions, may follow the main body of the definition. The entry for the word *court* in *The American Heritage Dictionary,* for instance, indicates that the word appears in the expressions *out of court* and *pay court to;* each expression is defined.

11. *Synonyms.* For some words, *synonyms* (words that are similar in meaning) are listed and discussed; the discussion, by providing an explanation of the differences in meaning among the synonyms, can help you select the precise word you need.

12. *Antonyms.* For some words, *antonyms* (words that are opposite in meaning) are supplied. The listing may sometimes aid you in selecting the exact word for your context.

13. *Origin.* The origin and history of a word (its *etymology*) appears in some dictionaries following the last definition and in other dictionaries following the part-of-speech indicator.

The following is a typical dictionary entry. It is taken from The Random House Dictionary (revised edition, 1975).

> **op·er·a·tion** (op/ə rā/shən), *n.* **1.** the act or an instance, process, or manner of functioning or operating. **2.** the state of something that operates or is in effect (usually prec. by *in* or *into*): *a rule no longer in operation.* **3.** the exertion of force or influence: *the operation of alcohol on the mind.* **4.** a process of a practical or mechanical nature. **5.** *Surg.* a process or act of operating on the body of a patient. **6.** *Math.* a mathematical process, as addition, multiplication, etc., or an instance of its application. **7.** *Mil.* **a.** a campaign, mission, maneuver, or action. **b.** Usually, **operations.** the conduct of a campaign, mission, etc. **c. operations,** a place from which a military campaign or the like is planned and controlled. **8.** a business transaction in securities or commodities, esp. one of a speculative nature or on a large scale. [ME *operacioun* < L *operātiōn-* (s. of *operātiō*)]

Once you've become familiar with the dictionary, make using it a habit. A dictionary can provide great help to you as speaker, reader, and writer. Remember, too, that one of the most effective ways to build a good vocabulary is to read. You will, of course, sometimes run into terms that even a good desk dictionary does not define—especially those terms related to a particular occupation. Many occupations have created special vocabularies to serve their particular requirements, and a number of these vocabularies are large enough and widely enough used to necessitate the publication of specialized dictionaries. If such a dictionary exists in your field, locate one and use it regularly.

WORD-PART APPROACH

One effective way to increase your vocabulary is to call on the *word-part* approach when you come across a word you don't know. The technique enables you to work out the meaning of many words when you first see them. A large number of words contain a root, or part, that expresses its primary meaning. In the word *dictate,* for example, *dict-,* the root, means "say," "tell," "speak."

The meaning of a word frequently changes when a prefix and a suffix is added to the root. A *prefix* is a word part that is placed in front of a root to modify the word's meaning. *Sure* is made *unsure* by the addition of the prefix *un-.* A *suffix* is a word part that is placed after a root. It often tells you what part of speech the word is. Nouns are formed by suffixes like *-ness (tightness),* *-ment (impediment),* and *-ion, (coordination).* Many verbs end in *-ate (dictate),* *-ize (minimize),* and *-ify (qualify).* Adverbs are usually recognized by their *-ly* suffixes *(slowly, privately),* while for adjectives the endings *-ous, -ful,* and *-less* are common *(famous, colorful, colorless).*

Sometimes a root can have more than one prefix or suffix. The root *new* and the prefix *re-* form *renew.* The addition of the prefix *non-* and the suffix *-able* makes the word *nonrenewable.* Less common words follow the same pattern. The root *aqua* means "water." This root forms the basis for many words: An *aqualung* is a device used for breathing under water. An *aquacade* is a water sports spectacle in which an *aquaplane* (a board being towed swiftly across water) may be used. An *aquarium* is an enclosure for fish and other *subaqueous* creatures; chemicals dissolved in water form an *aqueous* solution. Once you learn to identify a group of roots and their prefixes and suffixes, you can often work out the meaning of a complex word you have never seen before.

The remainder of this chapter presents sections on roots, prefixes, and suffixes. The word-part under study is listed, defined, and followed by examples of its use in typical sentences. Exercises are provided periodically to help you measure your grasp of the material.

ROOTS

1. **act**

   The root *act* means "do," "move," "put in motion." Typical words are *actuary* (one who calculates insurance premiums) and *activate* (to make active or more active; to put someone on active duty).

   EXAMPLES

   My insurance agent said that an *actuary* would have to determine the new rates.

   To *activate* the mechanism, press the button.

2. cap, cip

The roots *cap* and *cip* means "take." Typical words are *capacity* (the ability to take something; the amount that can be contained), *incapacitated* (unable to take on usual work or responsibility), and *recipient* (one who takes or receives).

EXAMPLES

Most babies do not have a *capacity* for large amounts of food.

The injury kept Randall *incapacitated* for weeks.

The *recipients* of the questionnaire were asked to complete it and return it within ten days.

3. cede, ceed

The roots *cede* and *ceed* mean "go" or "move." Typical words are *precede* (to go before), *intercede* (to act on someone's behalf; to attempt to settle a dispute between two people or groups), *proceed* (to go forward), and *exceed* (to move or go beyond).

EXAMPLES

The union stated that negotiations must *precede* any decision.

The attorney attempted to *intercede* on behalf of the juvenile defendant.

After visiting the museum, we will *proceed* to a quaint little café for lunch.

The motorist had *exceeded* the speed limit.

4. chron

The root *chron* means "time." Typical words are *synchronize* (to arrange two or more things to make them come together in time), *chronic* (continuing over a period of time) and *chronology* (time sequence).

EXAMPLES

The two governments *synchronized* their announcements of the new treaty.

Johnson's *chronic* lateness to work prevented him from receiving a promotion.

The *chronology* of the events was clear from a reading of the pilot's log.

5. claim, clam

The roots *claim* and *clam* mean "shout." Typical words are *reclaim* (to make available for use; to rescue), *disclaim* (to deny responsibility for or association with something), and *proclamation* (an official public announcement).

EXAMPLES

The urban renewal project will *reclaim* many decaying areas of the city.

Norman *disclaimed* any knowledge of the mistake.

The governor's *proclamation* declared next Monday a state holiday.

6. **clude**

The root *clude* means "shut" or "close." Typical words are *include* (to close or contain within), *exclude* (to shut out or refuse admission), and *preclude* (to shut out, or make impossible, beforehand).

EXAMPLES

The warranty *included* both parts and labor.

The new warranty will *exclude* labor.

A busy schedule coming up in October will *preclude* our attending the national convention.

I. Exercises*

activate; actuary; capacity; chronic; chronology; disclaim; exceed; exclude; incapacitated; include; intercede; precede; preclude; proceed; proclamation; recipient; reclaim; synchronize

Fill in the appropriate words from the list above.

a. The newspaper printed a _____ of the events leading up to the outbreak of war.

b. The accident left the athlete _____ for nearly three months.

c. It is not always wise to _____ in a quarrel between a husband and wife.

d. The president's heavy public-relations schedule _____ her participation in the daily operation of the company.

e. A _____ issued by the White House announced the appointment of the new ambassador.

f. Certain brands must be _____ from the sale.

g. The _____ of the award was asked to make a brief acceptance speech.

h. The manufacturer _____ any responsibility for the accident.

i. The heavy smoker suffered from _____ bronchitis.

j. A manager's responsibilities _____ personnel evaluation.

k. This bill for repairs _____ your original estimate.

---

* The correct answers may be slight variations of the words discussed—for example, a verb may be in the past or the future tense rather than in the present, or may end in -s, -ed, or -ing; a noun may be in the plural; an adjective or adverb ending (-ical, -ically, and so on) may be added to the word.

l. Attempts to _____ wilderness lands are difficult in industrialized societies.

m. The governor _____ the Ninth National Guard Division to deal with the problem.

n. Certain ceremonies will _____ the formal signing of the contract.

o. Since we planned to meet at the airport exactly at 3 P.M., we _____ our watches before we separated.

p. The tank's _____ was 26 gallons.

q. Being an _____ requires an aptitude for working with figures.

r. The police officer _____ to write the ticket in spite of the motorist's protests.

7. **cred**
   The root *cred* means "believe." Typical words are *credible* (believable), *credence* (believability), *incredible* (not believable), and *credulous* (tending to believe too readily).

EXAMPLES

Vera's version of the event was the most *credible.*

The press gave little *credence* to the official's explanation.

The statistics, *incredible* as they seemed, were nonetheless accurate.

If you are too *credulous*—if you believe everything you hear—you may become the victim of many practical jokes.

8. **cur**
   The root *cur* means "run." Typical words are *current* (that which runs or flows; at the present time), *cursory* (hasty, not thorough), *recurrent* (occurring or happening again), and *concurrent* (occurring together or at the same time).

EXAMPLES

The rate at which electric *current* flows through the conducting wire is measured in amperes.

The mechanic was not able to determine, from a *cursory* examination, just what had caused the machine to break down.

A *recurrent* dream haunted him all his life.

The *concurrent* scheduling of the meetings meant that we could attend only one of them.

9. **dict**

The root *dict* means "speak." Typical words are *dictate* (to speak for recording and transcription; to issue an order or command), *edict* (a proclamation or order), and *jurisdiction* (the area in which one is qualified or has the right to exercise power).

EXAMPLES

Once a week the dietitian calls and *dictates* an order for groceries.

The presidential *edict* commanded citizens not to go out after 10 P.M.

The personnel manager's *jurisdiction* is not restricted to the hiring of employees; he or she administers the medical-insurance programs as well.

10. **frag, fract**

The roots *frag* and *fract* mean "break." Typical words are *fragile* (easily breakable) and *infraction* (the breaking of a rule).

EXAMPLES

The instrument is extremely *fragile* and must be handled with great care.

Although the *infraction* of the rule was not serious, the teacher felt that it should not be allowed to go unnoticed.

11. **gress**

The root *gress* means "step" or "go." Typical words are *progressive* (favoring change or improvement, especially in political or social affairs; increasing step by step), *digress* (to depart from the subject), and *egress* (the exit or the way out).

EXAMPLES

The *progressive* actions taken by the new administration were praised by the press.

The audience became restless when the speaker *digressed* from the announced topic.

The fire department considered the matter of an emergency *egress* from the building to be a primary concern.

12. **ject**

The root *ject* means "to throw." Typical words are *inject* (to force a fluid into a passage; to introduce something new or different into a conversation or other matter), *eject* (to throw out), and *reject* (to refuse to accept).

EXAMPLES

The virus can be controlled by *injecting* medication directly into the bloodstream.

The pilot survived because he was *ejected* from the cockpit moments before the crash.

Jerry worked hard on the proposal, but his boss *rejected* it.

II. Exercises

concurrent; credence; credible; credulous; current; cursory; dictate; digress; edict; egress; eject; fragile; incredible; infraction; inject; jurisdiction; progressive; recurrent; reject

Fill in the appropriate words from the list above.

a. The publisher needed only a _____ glance at the manuscript to see that it had been well written.

b. The employees who failed to sign the attendance sheet were informed that they had committed a(n) _____ of the company's rules.

c. The _____ of the audience from the auditorium began at ten o'clock and lasted two hours.

d. The _____ was so swift that they lost control of the canoe.

e. By _____ sex into the issue, the press turned the story of the governor's rapid political rise into a scandal.

f. The convicted felon served _____ sentences for assault and grand larceny.

g. In the consumer-affairs course, students were warned about being too _____ of any sales pitch or advertisement.

h. The company has a _____ hiring policy: it offers on-the-job training to those who have had no work experience.

i. The crystal was wrapped carefully and placed in a carton marked "_____."

j. The cartridge is designed to be _____ automatically at the end of the tape.

k. The story sounds _____ enough to me; what is your reason for *not* believing it?

l. Finding well-qualified staff members was a _____ problem for the firm; every few months new transcribers and word processors were needed.

m. The union _____ the contract offer and made a counter-proposal.

n. Custom _____ that weekend visitors send thank-you notes to their hosts.

o. The judge said that such a matter was outside the _____ of the court.

p. The detective gave little _____ to the theory that the burglar had entered through the front door.

q. Bill's account of the adventure was so _____ that none of us could take him seriously.

r. The _____ issued by the governor allowed the citizens free access to the state parklands.

s. If you continue to _____ from the topic, you'll never finish the story.

13. **mit**

The root *mit* means "send." Typical words are *emit* (to send out or send forth), *remit* (to send back, especially money), and *transmit* (to send from one point to another).

EXAMPLES

The electronic cash register *emits* a signal to a central processor.

Please *remit* a total payment of $14.95.

The information is *transmitted* over commercial telephone lines.

14. **sed**

The root *sed* means "sit." Typical words are *sedentary* (involving much sitting) and *sediment* (substance that settles to the bottom of a liquid).

EXAMPLES

Data, Incorporated, is conducting a survey to determine how many people have *sedentary* occupations and how many people have jobs requiring physical work.

Sediment accumulated at the bottom of the pool.

15. **solv**

The root *solv* means "free from" or "loosen." Typical words are *absolve* (to free from, especially of guilt), *dissolve* (to loosen or break up), and *solvent* (an agent used to loosen or to dissolve).

EXAMPLES

After the car accident in which his passenger was killed, he was never to feel completely *absolved* of guilt.

A liquid *solvent* was used to *dissolve* the paint.

16. **spec**

The root *spec* means "look at." Typical words are *aspect* (the particular view from which something is considered), *inspect* (to look at closely and critically), *perspective* (an accurate way of looking at things; a point of view that considers the relative proportion of the various elements of a scene), and *specification* (a detailed definition of the requirements of a project or a description of the parts of a whole).

EXAMPLES

The monetary *aspect* of the job was the least of his concerns.

The highway patrol arrived to *inspect* the scene of the accident.

From the *perspective* of the purchaser, the warranty was not a good one.

The *specifications* for the job were published for the benefit of all potential bidders.

17. **tempor**

The root *tempor* means "time." Typical words are *contemporary* (existing at the same time, of the same age; modern), *temporary* (for a short time), and *temporize* (to stall for time).

EXAMPLES

Although the two authors were *contemporaries,* their attitudes were centuries apart in political understanding.

Ms. Kenka has taken a *temporary* job, from June to September, when she plans to return to school.

The negotiator had instructions to *temporize* until more information could be obtained.

18. **vis**

The root *vis* means "to see." Typical words are *vision* (the ability to see), *advice* (to give a suggestion or a recommendation to someone), *improvise* (to do a thing on the spur of the moment), and *supervise* (to oversee the activities of others).

EXAMPLES

The patient was relieved that he still had full *vision* after the eye operation.

Attorneys are appointed by the court to *advise* those who cannot afford to hire their own legal counsel.

Because we had run out of storage space, we *improvised* a cabinet from the paper boxes.

College students were hired to *supervise* the playgrounds.

III. Exercises

absolve; advise; aspect; contemporary; dissolve; emit; improvise; inspect; perspective; remit; sedentary; sediment; solvent; specification; supervise; temporary; temporize; transmit; vision

Fill in the appropriate words from the list above.

a. The flood left a four-inch layer of _____ on the basement floor.

b. Jazz musicians are proud of their ability to _____ during a performance.

c. Late for work, the commuter did not wait for the sugar to _____ in his coffee.

d. Although the governor continued to _____, the legislature proceeded as though the bill had already been signed.

e. _____ the equipment carefully before signing a receipt for it.

f. The lawyer was hired to _____ company management on legal matters.

g. An exceptionally strong _____ was used to remove the stain.

h. Eyeglasses improved her _____ considerably.

i. The author and the inventor were _____; both lived from about 1900 to 1965.

j. The lawyer glossed over several _____ of the case, emphasizing only those that would benefit his client.

k. The buzzer _____ an unpleasant tone.

l. The foreman may not _____ more than twenty workers.

m. The original suspects were _____ of blame when the real culprits were found.

n. The electrical _____ were printed on a metal plate near the base of the unit.

o. The health lecturer warned that leading an overly _____ life could seriously damage the heart.

p. Please _____ the agreed-upon amount immediately.

q. The potential buyer crossed the street to view the house from another

_____.

r. The CB radio _____ signals from one moving vehicle to another.

s. The revision is only _____, until a permanent improvement can be made.

PREFIXES

1. **a-, an-**
   The prefixes *a-* and *an-* mean "without." Typical words are *anemia* (without sufficient red blood cells or volume of blood), *apathy* (complete lack of interest or feeling), *anesthetic* (a drug that dulls the senses, especially the sense of pain).

   EXAMPLES
   A blood test revealed that the patient suffers from *anemia.*
   When only 10 percent of the voting public go to the polls, civic *apathy* is evident.
   Before pulling the tooth, the dentist administered an *anesthetic.*

2. **ab-, abs-**
   The prefixes *ab-* and *abs-* mean "from." Typical words are *abnormal* (removed from the normal), *abstract* (relating to ideas rather than to facts or objects), and *abstain* (to keep oneself away from).

   EXAMPLES
   The man's *abnormal* behavior was caused by excessive drinking.
   The report moved quickly from *abstract* concepts to concrete examples.
   Drivers are advised to *abstain* from alcohol.

3. **ad-** (sometimes spelled **ag-, al-, at-** when combined with roots that begin with *g, l,* or *t*)
   This prefix means "to" or "toward." Typical words are *adjoining* (joined to something else), *aggressive* (marked by forceful or angry action), *allocate* (to assign to; to distribute something according to a plan), and *attract* (to draw to or toward).

   EXAMPLES
   The two families knew each other well because they lived in *adjoining* apartments.
   Every city must *allocate* a large sum of money for its transportation system.
   Insects are *attracted* to food.

The attack by the riot police was prompted by the *aggressive* behavior of the crowd.

4. **ante-**
   The prefix *ante-* means "before." Typical words are *anterior* (in or near the front), *anteroom* (a room that comes before another room, as a waiting room), and *antecedent* (an event that occurs before another; the word or phrase to which a pronoun refers).

EXAMPLES
The tumor was located in the *anterior* lobe of the brain.
My *antecedents* were farmers who lived in Wales.
Because many patients had come to see the doctor, the *anteroom* of the office was crowded.

5. **anti-, ant-** (before a vowel)
   The prefix *anti-* (*ant-*) means "against" or "opposite." Typical words are *antibiotic* (a medicine that acts against a virus), *antipathy* (a feeling of strong dislike), *antacid* (medicine that acts against acid in the body), *antonym* (a word that means the opposite of another word).

EXAMPLES
Her fever was lower a few hours after she took the *antibiotic*.
Because I have an *antipathy* to crowds, I avoid the beach on July 4.
He felt better after taking the *antacid* to soothe his upset stomach.
Part of the assignment was to find *antonyms* for a given list of words.

6. **bi-**
   The prefix *bi-* means "two." Typical words are *biped* (animals with two feet), *bigamy* (marriage to two people at the same time), *biannual* (two times each year), and *biennial* (every two years).

EXAMPLES
Humans, monkeys, and apes are *bipeds*.
The man was charged with *bigamy* because he had one wife in Akron and another in Indianapolis.
The *biannual* event was held twice a year.
The *biennial* event was held every other year.

7. **cata-**
   The prefix *cata-* means "down." Typical words are *catalog* (a written list; to write down an orderly listing), *catalyst* (a substance that brings about a chemical change), and *catastrophe* (a sudden and severe downturn in fortune; a disaster).

EXAMPLES

The *catalog* listed all the products manufactured by the company.

The sodium chloride was a *catalyst* that allowed the other two substances to interact freely.

The sudden drop in the stock was a *catastrophe* for many small investors.

IV. Exercises

abnormal; abstain; abstract; adjoining; aggressive; allocate; anemia; anesthetic; antacid; antecedent; anterior; anteroom; antibiotic; antipathy; antonym; apathy; attract; biannual; biennial; bigamy; biped; catalog; catalyst; catastrophe

Fill in the appropriate words from the list above.

a. If you have eaten too many rich foods, you probably need a(n) _____.

b. The purpose of the _____ was to break down the other chemicals.

c. The animal world includes a number of _____, such as gorillas.

d. By being _____, the sales staff doubled the volume of sales last year.

e. General _____ is a loss of interest in nearly everything.

f. The programmer _____ a portion of the computer's memory to data that must be processed.

g. Beauty is a(n) _____ concept that cannot be defined in concrete terms.

h. The _____ of a pronoun should usually precede it in the sentence.

i. The stock market crash of October 1929 was the beginning of an economic _____.

j. Those who become partners in two marriages at the same time are legally guilty of _____, in our society, although some societies permit it.

k. If you have a(n) _____ to loud music, perhaps you should not attend the concert.

l. The magnet _____ the iron filings.

m. The ——————— portion of the device contained a small opening.

n. The ——————— meetings are held during odd-numbered years.

o. Some dictionary entries include ———————.

p. ——————— is a condition in which the patient does not have an adequate supply of red blood cells.

q. The store manager in charge of inventory prepared a ———————
   of all the items for sale in all the company's branches.

r. ——————— hotel rooms sometimes share a bathroom.

s. The ——————— meetings are held in February and in August.

t. Novocain is a commonly used local ———————.

u. The ——————— was used against the virus, but the symptoms did
   not go away.

v. The reformed alcoholic ——————— from drink.

w. The small ——————— served as a lobby for the auditorium.

x. The behavior of an emotionally disturbed person may sometimes seem

   ———————.

8. **circum-**
   The prefix *circum-* means "around." Typical words are *circumference*
   (the distance around a circular object), *circumlocution* (a word or expression that says something in a roundabout rather than a straightforward
   way), *circumspect* (proceeding carefully; taking the consequences of a
   deed into account before acting), and *circumvent* (to go around a problem or an obstacle and thus avoid it).

EXAMPLES
After measuring the round library table, Jessica announced that its *circum-
ference* was 12 feet.
A person who uses *circumlocution* is probably trying to avoid an issue.
Recognizing the importance of the question, the shop steward tried to be as
circumspect as possible in answering it.
By apologizing to Ed, Martin hoped to *circumvent* further unpleasantness.

9. **co- col-, com-, con-**
   These prefixes are all variations of *cum,* meaning "with" or "together."
   Typical words are *cooperate* (to work together), *coordinate* (to regulate

together), *collaborate* (to work jointly with someone else), *collate* (to put together in order), and *compound* (something formed by the joining of elements or parts).

EXAMPLES

The problem could be solved if the two sides would *cooperate*.

The nationwide United Fund is a *coordinated* attempt to raise funds for charitable organizations.

The two designers agreed to *collaborate* on the layout drawing.

The office bought a machine that can *collate* a sixteen-page document.

The glossy finish was achieved by the application of a rubbing *compound*.

10. **contra-, contro-, counter-**

These prefixes mean "against" or "opposite." Typical words are *contrary* (consistently against), *controversy* (a dispute between those of opposing views), and *countermand* (to cancel or reverse an order).

EXAMPLES

The views expressed in the book were *contrary* to everything Michael believed.

The superintendent *countermanded* the foreman's orders.

The school bond issue created a *controversy* in the town; there were strong feelings on both sides of the matter.

11. **de-**

The prefix *de-* means "down" or "reverse of." Typical words are *decelerate* (to slow down), *demote* (to move down to a lower rank), and *descend* (to go down).

EXAMPLES

He ran the car off the road because there was no time to *decelerate*.

Unfavorable sales figures forced the company to *demote* several of its junior officers.

The lineman *descended* from the pole after completing the repairs.

12. **dia-**

The prefix *dia-* means "across," "thoroughly," or "through." Typical words are *diagonal* (across from corner to corner, slanted), *diagnose* (to identify the nature of an illness; to investigate the cause of something), and *diathermy* (a treatment that sends heat through the body).

EXAMPLES

The editor drew a *diagonal* line across the page that was to be omitted from the manuscript.

Lennie was examined by four specialists before one of them was able to *diagnose* his ailment.

A heating pad is one simple device for administering *diathermy*.

13. **dis-** (also spelled **di-, dif-**)

This prefix means "apart" or "not." Typical words are *dilate* (to make larger), *differentiate* (to tell apart), *disjointed* (disconnected, lacking unity), *dissent* (lack of agreement; to disagree), and *disrupt* (to interrupt, especially in a noisy way; to throw into confusion).

EXAMPLES

The medicine the eye doctor administered caused the pupils of her eyes to *dilate*.

The students were taught to *differentiate* between the two chemicals.

His account of the incident was so *disjointed* that the police were hardly able to follow it.

Martha Sells was the only member of the committee to *dissent* from the majority report.

Sam seemed determined to *disrupt* the meeting because he did not want the resolution to be passed.

14. **e-, ex-**

The prefixes *e-* and *ex-* mean "out" or "outside." Typical words are *efficacy* (ability to produce a desired result), *exhale* (to breathe out), and *exorbitant* (exceeding the customary amount).

EXAMPLES

The chemist was testing a new cancer drug to determine its *efficacy*.

The doctor instructed the patient to take a deep breath and then *exhale*.

The price of the typewriter was *exorbitant;* we had never paid so much for such a machine.

V. Exercises

circumference; circumlocution; circumspect; circumvent; collaborate; collate; compound; contrary; controversy; cooperate; coordinate; countermand; decelerate; demote; descend; diagnose; diameter; diathermy; differentiate; dilate; disjointed; disrupt; dissent; efficacy; exhale; exorbitant

Fill in the appropriate words from the list above.

a. _____ can sometimes provide relief from neck and back pains.

b. A faulty switching mechanism ——————— service on the subway train this morning.

c. The experts worked for weeks to ——————— the cause of the airplane crash.

d. You'll have to organize your notes more carefully; otherwise, your speech will be completely ———————.

e. Charles Darwin's theories of evolution are ——————— to the Bible's account of creation.

f. Does the drug company guarantee the ——————— of its antisneeze medication?

g. The customer tried to ——————— the complaint desk by going directly to the manager's office.

h. The decade of the 1960s was a time of political ———————.

i. Even their mother found it difficult to ——————— between the twins.

j. It is essential to the efficient running of the office that employees ——————— with one another.

k. Rodgers and Hammerstein ——————— on a number of successful musical comedies.

l. ——————— from the mountain was almost as difficult as climbing it.

m. Do you know the two elements that form the ——————— we call salt?

n. We measured the distance around the lake and found the ——————— to be about four miles.

o. The general manager ——————— the activities of the design and production departments.

p. Being ——————— can be an unpleasant experience; certainly, anyone would prefer to advance on the job.

q. News reporters accused the senator of using ——————— to avoid answering embarrassing questions.

r. You can determine the ——————— of a round piece of fruit, like an orange, by cutting it in half and measuring across its center.

s. The assistants ——————— the manuals, putting the pages together in proper sequence.

t. A human being inhales oxygen and ——————— carbon dioxide.

u. The customer was quite _____ in choosing a new car, first looking at all the different makes and dealers.

v. The company's growth was _____ by a lack of capital.

w. During surgery, the opening to the organ was _____.

x. Because of inflation, costs have risen _____.

y. The order that _____ the company's previous stand was signed by the general manager.

z. Open-admissions policies caused a _____ in the academic community.

15. **in-** (also spelled **il-, im-,** and **ir-**)

    The prefix *in-*, as well as the alternate forms *il-, im-,* and *ir-,* means "not."* Typical words are *insolvent* (not able to pay one's debts; bankrupt), *illegible* (difficult or impossible to read, usually because of unclear or messy copy), *immune* (protected against a disease; not affected by an outcome), and *irrevocable* (irreversible; unable to be reversed or changed).

EXAMPLES

Jim had to move to a less expensive apartment because he had become *insolvent.*

Since the first draft of the paper was *illegible,* I decided to retype my work before I revised it.

Children who have taken flu shots should be *immune* to the disease.

Think carefully before you decide upon a course, since your decision will be *irrevocable.*

16. **inter-**

    The prefix *inter-* means "between." Typical words are *intervene* (to come between; to interfere), *intermittent* (occurring from time to time; alternately starting and stopping), and *interlinear* (inserted between the lines).

EXAMPLES

Since the two lawyers could not settle the dispute, they asked the judge to *intervene* in the matter.

The patient complained of *intermittent* headaches that would come and go during periods of stress.

I've typed this draft triple-spaced so you can easily make *interlinear* corrections or changes.

---

* *In-* as a prefix meaning "in, into, within, or toward," is a separate form.

17. **intra-, intro-**

These prefixes mean "within." Typical words are *intrastate* (within a state), *intravenous* (within the veins), and *introspection* (examination of one's own thoughts and feelings).

EXAMPLES

The trucking firm was awarded a license to operate on an *intrastate* basis only.

The antibiotic can be taken only by *intravenous* injection.

The *introspection* forced on him by a long period of illness made a striking change in his personality.

18. **micro- (micr-** before a root beginning with a vowel)

The prefix *micro-* means "small." Typical words are *microfilm* (a small film) and *micrometer* (an instrument for measuring small things).

EXAMPLES

Microfilm requires the use of special equipment to enable the viewer to see the material, the size of which has been reduced considerably.

The tiny specimen could be measured only with a *micrometer*.

19. **para-**

The prefix *para-* means "alongside." Typical words are *paraprofessional* (someone who works alongside a professional), *paraphrase* (to rephrase or restate something in one's own words), *parasite* (something that lives off another without giving anything useful in return), and *parallel* (alongside of but at an equal distance at every point, never meeting).

EXAMPLES

The use of *paraprofessionals* is becoming common in schools and hospitals.

When taking notes for a term paper, it is better to *paraphrase* the thinking of others than to quote them directly.

The tree was being slowly destroyed by two different *parasites*.

Railroad tracks are *parallel* to each other.

20. **poly-**

Poly- means "many." Typical words are *polygraph* (an instrument that measures changes in heartbeat, blood pressure, and so on at one time and is used as a lie-detector device), *polytechnic* (pertaining to instruction in many arts and sciences), *polyphonic* (combining many different sounds), and *polychromatic* (having many colors).

EXAMPLES

The lie detector test is one of the most common uses of the *polygraph*.

The institute was dedicated to *polytechnic* studies.

The recording technique included a *polyphonic* procedure.
The art department ordered a *polychromatic* scale.

VI. Exercises

illegible; immune; insolvent; irrevocable; interlinear; intermittent; intervene; intrastate; intravenous; introspection; microfilm; micrometer; parallel; paraphrase; paraprofessional; parasite; polychromatic; polygraph; polyphonic; polytechnic

Fill in the appropriate words from the list above.

a. The children had hoped to go to the game, but their mother _____ and told them they had to finish their homework first.

b. Frank has been hired as a _____ and will assist Dr. Converse in the chemistry laboratory.

c. Congress does not ordinarily pass laws affecting _____ commerce; such legislation is within the jurisdiction of the states.

d. The tick is a _____ that lives on the blood of animals.

e. The Russian-language training manual has a(n) _____ English translation.

f. A _____ is an instrument used to measure very small things.

g. I could not recall the quotation exactly, so I had to _____ it.

h. The board of directors decided that the school would be a _____ institute.

i. After a long period of _____, the veteran decided to go to college.

j. If you expect me to understand this _____ letter, you'll have to tell me what it says.

k. The results of a _____ test are not admitted as evidence in court.

l. Nature presents us with a _____ symphony of bird songs, running water, rustling trees, and animal calls.

m. It's a good idea to budget your expenses, to avoid becoming _____ just before payday.

n. The weather forecast called for _____ showers.

o. The governor was _____ opposed to the idea—he said that he would not change his mind under any circumstances.

p. The space needed for files is greatly reduced when records are kept on

_____ .

q. Because the child's parents were teachers at the school, she thought she

was _____ from punishment.

r. _____ lines never meet.

s. The doctor ordered _____ feeding in the final stage of the illness.

t. The field contained a _____ abundance of wild flowers.

21. **post-**
The prefix *post-* means "after." Typical words are *posterity* (that which comes after; future generations), *postmortem* (after death), *postnatal* (after birth), and *postgraduate* (after graduation).

EXAMPLES
We owe it to *posterity* to preserve as much of our natural environment as possible.
The judge ordered a *postmortem* examination to determine the cause of the victim's death.
Postnatal complications can be serious for both the mother and the baby.
The university had acquired a fine reputation for the quality of its *postgraduate* program.

22. **pre-**
The prefix *pre-* means "before." Typical words are *preliminary* (going before and leading up to the main part), *preview* (to look at something before it is officially presented), and *preface* (a brief introduction before the text of a book).

EXAMPLES
The court must set a date for a *preliminary* hearing before the trial can be scheduled.
Employees were given a *preview* of the president's presentation to the stockholders.
The *preface* to the speech captured the audience's full attention.

23. **pro-**
The prefix *pro-* means "forward," or "forth." Typical words are *propose*

(to put forward a suggestion), *proliferate* (to reproduce or increase rapidly), and *profusion* (that which is brought forth in large numbers; an abundance).

EXAMPLES

Frank wanted to *propose* a new method of handling the data, but he could not get the floor.

In the last decade, the use of calculators has *proliferated*; in many offices almost every executive has one.

Grasshoppers appeared that summer in *profusion*.

24. **proto- (prot-** before a root beginning with a vowel)
   Proto- means "first" or "fundamental." Typical words are *prototype* (the first form of something, serving as a model for later forms), and *protozoa* (fundamental forms of animal life).

EXAMPLES

The committee voted funds to begin the project but withheld additional financing until the *prototype* proved whether the plan was practical.

Protozoa can be studied only through a microscope.

25. **super-**
   The prefix *super-* means "over" or "beyond." Typical words are *superior* (far above average; higher in rank or authority), *supersede* (to take the place of something that occurred earlier), and *superfluous* (more than what is needed).

EXAMPLES

The judges declared XYZ brand carwash to be *superior* to LMO brand.

The directive of June 12 *supersedes* the one dated May 5.

The shipwrecked sailors threw away everything that was *superfluous*.

26. **sym-, syn-**
   The prefixes *sym-* and *syn-* mean "together" or "with." Typical words are *sympathy* (shared feeling; concern for another's distress), *symmetrical* (equal in size, shape, or position of parts on opposite sides of a dividing line), and *synthesis* (the combining of varied elements to form a meaningful whole).

EXAMPLES

The students appeared to be in *sympathy* with the protesters.

Organisms whose right and left sides are mirror images of each other are *symmetrical*.

Dr. Markon's theory of personality is a *synthesis* of psychological ideas taken from Freud, Jung, Horney, and Sullivan.

27. **trans-**

The prefix *trans-* means "across," "through," or "beyond." Typical words are *transport* (to carry from one place to another), *transfer* (to send from one person or place to another), *transcend* (to go beyond; to surpass), and *transient* (referring to something that passes away; a visitor, especially to a hotel, who stays only briefly).

EXAMPLES

It is the company's responsibility to *transport* the goods to the customers.

The fee was payment for the *transfer* of the title from the seller to the buyer.

Each new generation of computers *transcends* the achievements of the last generation.

Although the thought was a *transient* one, it had made an impression.

VII. Exercises

posterity; postgraduate; postmortem; postnatal; preface; preliminary; preview; profusion; proliferate; propose; prototype; protozoa; superfluous; supersede; sympathy; symmetrical; synthesis; transcend; transfer; transient; transport

Fill in the appropriate words from the list above.

a. Trucks rather than trains now _____ produce from California to New York.

b. The critics were given a _____ of the movie.

c. The _____ of their friends helped the family through the crisis.

d. _____ are a highly primitive life form.

e. The _____ of the various ideas seemed to present an entirely new theory.

f. In acquiring an education on her own and later becoming a famous writer, she showed that it was possible to _____ the limitations of poverty.

g. If you move an item from one side of the figure to the other, the form will no longer be _____.

h. From the _____ of ideas put forth, the committee was able to select two that were workable.

i. After the _____ tests in the laboratory, the product was subjected to further checking by physicians.

j. The book's _____ stated its purpose.

k. Hotels accommodate mostly _____, although they may also have some permanent residents.

l. The machinist _____ that additional lighting be installed near the new lathe.

m. A _____ examination revealed that the patient had died of a heart attack.

n. Suburbs _____ throughout the United States after World War II.

o. He felt that his _____ studies had been of great value to him in his profession.

p. The manager informed the staff that the new fire-safety regulations posted on the company bulletin board would _____ the old laws relating to emergency exits from the building.

q. The modern airplane had its _____ in the paper gliders made and thrown by schoolchildren.

r. Darlene had many problems during her pregnancy, but fortunately there were no _____ complications.

s. As machines take over more and more work, people of the future may find themselves _____ at the age of thirty-five.

t. The president felt that _____ would judge him kindly, even though he was not popular while he governed.

u. If you would rather work in the accounting department, why don't you ask for a _____ from sales?

SUFFIXES

Although individual suffixes do convey meaning, their chief function is to indicate part of speech. For example, the suffixes -ance, -ion, -ism, -ity, and -ment indicate nouns; the suffixes -ify and -ize indicate verbs; and the suffixes -able, -al, -ical, -ive, and -ous indicate adjectives.

Noun Markers

1. **-ance, -ence**
   Typical words are brilliance (quality of light; great brightness) and emergence (act of coming out).

EXAMPLES

The *brilliance* of the stage lights made the keynote speaker appear unreal.

The river widened at the point of its *emergence* into the sea.

2. **-ion, -ation, -tion**

Typical words are *resolution* (the act of solving a problem), *litigation* (the process of taking court action), and *option* (act or power of choosing; a choice).

EXAMPLES

The *resolution* of the problem was to be decided at a meeting of top management officials.

Ten persons who were seriously injured when the building collapsed began *litigation* to sue for medical expenses and lost wages.

The student has several career *options* after graduation: she can become a production trainee, enlist in the service, or take a degree in accounting.

3. **-ism**

Typical words are *anachronism* (something that is out of its place in time), *socialism* (a political theory that favors society's ownership of factories), and *individualism* (the assertion of one's specialness as an individual being).

EXAMPLES

The image of the Pilgrims traveling to the New World by jet is an *anachronism.*

Under *socialism,* all large industry is controlled by the government.

The company encouraged *individualism* in its employees.

4. **-ity**

Typical words are *facility* (the ability to do something easily), *authenticity* (the condition of being genuine), and *authority* (the power to command).

EXAMPLES

The *facility* with which Susan handled higher mathematics was remarkable.

Do you have proof of the *authenticity* of this painting—or might it be a fake?

The supervisor did not have the *authority* to dismiss an employee.

5. **-ment**

Typical words are *impediment* (an obstacle; something that stands in the way of something else) and *sentiment* (an opinion on a particular matter; a feeling based more on emotion than on thinking).

EXAMPLES
Not knowing how to operate some office machines can be an *impediment* to receiving a promotion.

The *sentiment* among the hospital staff was in favor of working from 8:30 to 4:30 rather than from 9 to 5.

Verb Markers

1. **-ify**

    Typical words are *testify* (to make a statement under oath), *justify* (to show that something is reasonable or correct), and *typify* (to be an example of).

EXAMPLES
Mavine was asked to *testify* during the trial, since she had been a witness to the accident.

You should not try to *justify* your action by claiming that the instructions were so poorly written that you misunderstood them.

I don't believe that the questionable acts of the manager *typify* the company's hiring policies.

2. **-ize**

    Typical words are *legalize* (to make something lawful), *modernize* (to make something current in appearance), and *anesthetize* (to make someone unable to feel pain).

EXAMPLES
The retail industry believed that stores would benefit from *legalized* shopping on Sundays.

The company decided to *modernize* its building, which was old and in poor condition.

Before the operation the patient was *anesthetized* and felt no pain at all during surgery.

Adjective Markers

1. **-able, -ible**

    Typical words are *comparable* (able to be compared; similar or equivalent), *indelible* (not able to be removed), *compatible* (able to live together in peace and harmony), and *inevitable* (incapable of being prevented; bound to happen).

EXAMPLES

Do you know in what ways soccer is *comparable* to football?

The tragic experience left an *indelible* mark on her memory.

The two technicians were *compatible* because they had had many similar experiences.

It seemed *inevitable* that the two companies would merge.

   2. **-al- -ial**

   Typical words are *superficial* (shallow, lacking in depth) and *beneficial* (leading to a favorable outcome; helpful).

EXAMPLES

Because the report did not explore the deep-seated reasons for the decline in sales, it was too *superficial* to be of any real value.

The new product should prove to be *beneficial* to the company and its customers alike.

VIII. Exercises

anachronism; anesthetic; authenticity; authority; beneficial; brilliance; compatible; emergence; facility; impediment; indelible; inevitable; individualism; justify; legalize; litigation; modernize; option; resolution; sentiment; socialism; superficial; testify; typify

Fill in the appropriate words from the list above.

   a. Perhaps we can settle this matter out of court rather than have to take it to

   _____.

   b. _____ has elements both of capitalism and of communism.

   c. The governor supports a bill that would _____ the sale of certain state-owned properties to private business.

   d. The _____ of the noonday sun was blinding.

   e. The laundry marks all items with _____ ink.

   f. A study showed that to _____ the procedure would require the purchase of a new line of equipment.

   g. When negotiations failed, a strike became _____.

   h. An electric clock as part of the stage set of *Julius Caesar* would be a(n)

   _____.

   i. The recently hired manager has a _____ for leadership.

j. Some newborn creatures are less helpless than others upon their

_____ .

k. Although a number of thoughtful people offered advice, the difficult situa-

tion remained without _____ .

l. The witness agreed to _____ in court on behalf of the accused.

m. Did you find it a(n) _____ when you traveled abroad that you
did not know any foreign languages?

n. My _____ are limited in selecting an apartment because I do
not have much money.

o. There is little place in war for peacetime _____ .

p. Those who stress the idea of _____ may not fit well into a
society that encourages everyone to act and dress alike.

q. The _____ of the report was in doubt because the document
was too old to be subjected to certain tests.

r. The _____ the veterinarian gave the colt was half the dosage
needed for a horse.

s. The _____ analysis failed to consider most of the underlying
problems.

t. If the behavior of this animal could be shown to _____ that of
the breed, veterinarians could learn much about the way the animals live.

u. To _____ the expenditure, it was necessary to make an accurate sales forecast.

v. The accident did have one _____ effect; it caused a traffic light
to be installed in the intersection.

w. A new administrator may be uncertain about his or her _____ .

x. Jealousy is not _____ with the formation of lasting friendships.

CHAPTER SUMMARY

You may use as many as four different vocabularies: a vocabulary of words
that you recognize when you read, a vocabulary of words that you use when
you write, a vocabulary of words that you use when you speak, and a small
vocabulary of words that are unique to your occupation.

By using a word–part approach to building your vocabulary, you can
piece together the meaning of a new word because you recognize the meanings of its parts: its prefix, its root, and its suffix.

EXERCISES

Define the italicized word in each of the following sentences. Feel free to use a dictionary.

1. The nurse was instructed to give the patient a *sedative* one hour before surgery.
2. The defendant's *malevolent* stare made the jury uneasy.
3. The scientist attempted to *correlate* the findings of the two research teams.
4. The investigation sought to determine what had *precipitated* the crisis.
5. It was *evident* to the jury that the defendant was guilty.
6. She was well liked on the job because she was both *amiable* and efficient.
7. The department sent a *delegation* to the national convention.
8. He *deluded* himself into thinking he was right even though he had lost the case.
9. Everyone felt that the company would do well because it had made an *auspicious* start.
10. The new personnel manager was *addicted* to working long hours.
11. The *predicament* the technicians found themselves in was the result of inadequate planning.
12. Lack of sleep and poor nutrition can be *detrimental* to one's health.
13. The company's treasurer was *indicted* for attempted bribery.
14. The *configuration* of the equipment resembled the letter *u.*
15. The client insisted on retaining *access* to the files.
16. The nurses learned that *application* of the medicine caused irritation to the skin.
17. The clause in the contract was considered *punitive* by the union.
18. *Density* of population is often measured in square miles.
19. The decision was made in order to *expedite* the processing of the forms.
20. Do you feel that you were given adequate *compensation* for the work you did?
21. The firm received a *dispensation* from the state allowing it to burn a low-grade fuel.
22. The foreign visitor's English was as *impeccable* as a native speaker's.
23. Because Aline had a *propensity* for catching colds, she took regular doses of vitamin C.
24. The citizens' group *endorsed* the new antipollution law.
25. Water that was poured on the material caused it to *disintegrate.*

10

Business Correspondence

Spencerville Tool Company

Bottombrook Road   Spencerville, RI 02813
(401) 867-2038

August 7, 19 – –

Mr. Stewart R. Cassidy
Smith and Jones, Attorneys at Law
1212 Broadway
Hartford, CT 06119

Dear Mr. Cassidy:

In regard to claim on Account #5-861 see enclosed copy of letter received and copy of delivery receipt regarding same. There had been a claim which was disallowed and debtor withheld payment on the bill, and the one we referred to your office for collection, as no pro was mentioned but the one the claim was on was referred to the bill is still open and they still owe Universal, please review and advise.

Sincerely,

Ralph Madison

Ralph Madison

RM/bc
Encl.

This letter, as it appears, was sent to a law firm (the names have been changed). Can you make any sense out of it? The staff at Smith and Jones could not, even though a number of attorneys, paralegals, and secretaries were familiar with the case. Staff members wrote to the sender, the tool company, without success, and finally had to call to find out what the letter was about.

A letter like this wasted the time of a highly paid staff—and may well have caused a delay in service to the tool company. But carelessly written letters, because they project such a poor image of the writer, can result in loss of another kind. A reader's negative reaction to an unclear or messy letter can cost a firm an important contract or an employee his or her job.

If so much hinges on the preparation of an acceptable letter, why do business people write letters at all? Why don't they rely on the telephone, usually a quicker and easier means of communication? (A letter may even be more expensive than a call: a single business letter can cost well over $5 in labor, stationery, and postage.) A good deal of the time, of course, a telephone call is more appropriate than a letter—when, for instance, an immediate response is needed, or when a person-to-person exchange might smooth over a touchy situation. But there are times when a telephone call cannot replace a letter. Letters provide a permanent, written record of a business transaction. Furthermore, a letter represents a commitment on the part of the writer, as the expression "Put it in writing" indicates. A written promise, above the signature of an employee who has the authority to act, carries weight that the recollection of a telephone conversation does not. And there is another, practical reason to write rather than call: traveling salespeople, busy executives, and others may be out of the office, or not at their desks, when the phone rings; but usually they can set aside a convenient time to answer their mail. Finally, just as an unattractive, poorly thought-out letter can result in loss of business and of good will, so an attractive, carefully planned letter can create good will—and sometimes stimulate business.

WRITING LETTERS

Drafting the Letter

The same steps that go into the writing of most business-related materials make up the process of composing a letter or a memorandum. First, prepare an outline; for a letter, an outline may involve little more than jotting down, on a note pad, the points you wish to make in the order you wish to make them. Second, write a rough draft, based on the outline. Third, set aside a "cooling" period (see Chapter 3). The cooling period is especially important in the case of a letter written in response to a problem. Business letters are not the place to vent emotions. A cooling period, even if it is only a lunch hour, gives the writer a chance to remove any hasty and inappropriate statements made in the heat of the situation. One chief executive of a large company always allows the rough draft of a crucial letter to "cool" overnight before revising and mailing it—regardless of the pressure to send it out right away. The executive believes that a slightly delayed—but appropriate—response is preferable to an immediate reply that may cause misunderstanding later. A good idea!

For the fourth step, revising the rough draft, go over your work carefully, checking both for sense and for mechanics (grammar, spelling, punctuation). Since *form* (the arrangement on the page of the parts of a letter) is a basic element in letter writing, it's a good idea, if you can, to type out a preliminary copy of the letter on a sheet of paper the size of the stationery you will be using. Set the typewriter at the margins you will use and, as you type, insert the correct spacing between parts of the letter (see pages 189 – 190). If a secretary or an assistant does your typing, be sure to check his or her work; you will sign the letter, and therefore you are responsible for its appearance and accuracy.

The Tone of a Letter

Business correspondence (letters as well as memorandums) differs in one important way from other kinds of job-related writing: it usually represents a direct communication between one person and another. As a letter writer addressing yourself directly to your reader, you have an opportunity that the writer of, say, a report doesn't have; you are in a very good position to take your reader's needs into account. If you ask yourself, "How might I feel if I were the recipient of such a letter?" you can gain some insight into the likely needs and feelings of your reader—and then tailor your message to fit those needs and feelings. Suppose, for example, you were a department-store manager who received a request for a refund from a customer who forgot to enclose the receipt with the request. In a letter to the customer, you might say, "The sales receipt must be enclosed with the merchandise before the refund can be processed." If you put yourself in your reader's place, however, you might word the request this way: "Please enclose the sales receipt with the merchandise, so that we can send your refund promptly." Notice that the second version uses the active voice: "Please enclose the sales receipt," while the first version contains the passive voice: "The sales receipt must be enclosed." In general, the active voice creates a friendlier, more courteous tone; the passive, on the other hand, tends to sound impersonal and unfriendly. (For a discussion of the active and passive voice, see Chapter 6.)

Consider the following letter, written to an applicant for a job as a dental receptionist. Does the letter sound as if the writer had given much thought to the reader's needs?

Southtown Dental Center

3221 Ryan Road   San Diego, CA 92217
(714) 321-1579

November 11, 19 - -

Mrs. Barbara L. Mauer
157 Beach Drive
San Diego, CA 92113

Dear Mrs. Mauer:

Your application for the position of dental receptionist at Southtown Dental Center has been rejected. We have found someone more qualified than you.

Sincerely,

Mary Hernandez

Mary Hernandez
Office Manager

MH/bt

The letter has a distinctly curt, nasty tone. Even though the letter addresses the reader directly (the writer uses the pronouns *you* and *yours*), the writer has apparently not considered how the recipient (Mrs. Mauer) will feel as she reads the letter. There is no expression of regret that Mrs. Mauer is being rejected for the position, nor any appreciation of her efforts in applying for the job. The letter is, in short, unpleasant and suggests bad manners.

How might the letter have appeared if the writer had been courteous, friendly, and considerate of the reader's needs?

Southtown Dental Center

3221 Ryan Road   San Diego, CA 92217
(714) 321-1579

November 11, 19--

Mrs. Barbara L. Mauer
157 Beach Drive
San Diego, CA 92113

Dear Mrs. Mauer:

Thank you for your time and effort in applying for the
position of dental receptionist at Southtown Dental Center.

Since we needed someone who can assume the duties here
with a minimum of training, we have selected an applicant
with over ten years of experience.

I am sure that with your excellent college record you will
find a position in another office.

Sincerely yours,

Mary Hernandez

Mary Hernandez
Office Manager

MH/bt

This letter carries the same disappointing news as the first, but the writer
is careful to thank the reader for her time and effort, to explain why she was
not accepted for the job, and to offer her encouragement in finding a position
in another office.

The following tips will help you achieve a tone that shows your consideration for your reader.

1. *Be respectful, not demanding.*
   Demanding: Submit your answer in one week.
   Respectful: I would appreciate your answer within one week.

2. *Be modest, not arrogant.*
   Arrogant: My report is thorough, and I'm sure that you won't be able to continue efficiently without it.
   Modest: I have tried to be as thorough as possible in my report, and I hope you find it useful.

3. *Be polite, not sarcastic.*
   Sarcastic: I just received the shipment we ordered *six months ago.* I'm sending it back—we can't use it now. Thanks!
   Polite: I am returning the shipment we ordered on March 12, 1978. Unfortunately, it arrived too late for us to be able to use it.

4. *Be positive and tactful, not negative and condescending.*
   Negative: Your complaint about our prices is way off target. Our prices are definitely not any higher than those of our competitors.
   Positive: Thank you for your suggestion concerning our prices. We believe, however, that our prices are competitive with, and in some cases below, those of our competitors.

Writing Style in Business Letters

Letter-writing style may legitimately vary from informal, in a letter to a close business associate, to formal, or restrained, in a letter to someone you do not know. (Even if you are writing a business letter to a close associate, of course, you must always follow the rules of standard grammar, spelling, and punctuation.)

INFORMAL   It worked! The new process is better than we had dreamed.

RESTRAINED   I am pleased to report that the new process is more effective than we had expected.

You will probably find yourself relying on the restrained style more frequently than on the informal, since an obvious attempt to sound casual may strike the reader as insincere. Do not adopt such a formal style, however, that your letters read like legal contracts. Using legalistic-sounding words in an effort to impress your reader will make your writing seem stuffy and pompous—and may well irritate your reader. Consider the following letter.

Amex Laboratories

327 Wilson Avenue   Birmingham, AL 35211
(205) 743-6218

September 7, 19 – –

Mr. Roland E. Forbes
772 South Wilton Street
Birmingham, AL 35207

Dear Mr. Forbes:

In response to your query, I wish to state that we no longer have an original copy of the brochure requested. Be advised that a photographic reproduction is enclosed herewith.

Address further correspondence to this office for assistance as required.

Sincerely yours,

E.T Hillman.

E. T. Hillman

ETH:knt
Enclosure

The writing style is full of largely out-of-date business jargon; expressions like *query* (for *request* or *question*), *I wish to state, be advised that,* and *herewith* are both old-fashioned and pretentious. Good business letters today have a more personal, down-to-earth style, as the revision of the letter illustrates (page 182).

```
                        Amex Laboratories
            327 Wilson Avenue        Birmingham, AL 35211
                          (205) 743-6218

        September 7, 19--


        Mr. Roland E. Forbes
        772 South Wilton Street
        Birmingham, AL 35207

        Dear Mr. Forbes:

        Because we are currently out of original copies of our
        brochure, I am sending you a photocopy of it.

        If I can be of further help, please let me know.

        Sincerely,

        E.T.Hillman.

        E. T. Hillman

        ETH:knt
        Enclosure
```

The revised version is not only less stuffy; it is also more concise. Being concise in writing is important, but don't be so concise that you become blunt. If you respond to a written request that you cannot understand with "Your request was unclear" or "I don't understand your question," you will probably offend your reader. Instead of attacking the writer's ability to phrase a request, consider that what you are really doing is asking for more information. Say so. "I will need more information before I can answer your request. Specifically, can you give me the title and the date of the report you are looking for?" The second version is a little longer than the first, but it is both more polite and more helpful.

Accuracy in Business Letters

Since a letter is a written record, it must be accurate. Facts, figures, dates, and explanations that are incorrect or misleading may cost time, money, and good will. Remember that when you sign a letter, you are responsible for what it says. Always allow yourself time to review a letter before mailing it. Whenever possible, ask someone who is familiar with the situation to review an important letter. Listen with an open mind to the criticism of others about what you have said. Make the changes you believe are necessary. Again—if you sign the letter, you are responsible for its contents.

A second kind of accuracy to check for is the mechanics of writing—punctuation, grammar, and spelling. In business as elsewhere, accuracy and attention to detail are equated with carefulness and reliability. The kindest conclusion a reader can come to about a letter containing mechanical errors is that the writer was careless. Do not give your reader cause to form such a conclusion.

Appearance in Business Letters

Just as the clothes you wear to job interviews play a part in the first impression potential employers have of you, so the appearance of a business letter may be crucial in influencing a recipient who has never seen you. The rules for preparing a neat, attractive letter are not difficult to master. First, be sure that the typewriter keys are clean and that the ribbon is fresh. Type as neatly as possible and handle the paper with clean hands to avoid smudges. Type on unruled white bond paper of standard size and use envelopes of the same quality. Center the letter on the page so that the space between the top of the page and the first line of typing is about equal to the space between the last line of typing and the lower edge. When you use company letterhead, consider the bottom of the letterhead as the top edge of the paper.

Neat appearance alone will not improve a poorly written letter, but a sloppy appearance will detract from a well-written one.

Parts of the Letter

Almost all business letters have at least five major parts. According to variations in the alignment of the parts on the page, letters may be of one format or another. If your employer recommends or requires a particular format and typing style, use it. Otherwise, follow the guidelines provided here.

Heading. The heading is the writer's full address (street, city and state, zip code) and the date. The writer's name is not included in the heading because it appears at the end of the letter. In giving your address, do not use abbreviations for words like *Street, Avenue, First, West* (as part of a street or city name). You may either spell out the name of the state in full or use the Postal Service abbreviations (see page 184). The date usually goes directly beneath the last line of the address. Do not abbreviate the name of the month.

EXAMPLE
```
1638 Parkhill Drive East
Great Falls, MT 59407
April 8, 19--
```

On the page, align the heading just to the right of center. If you are writing on company letterhead, type in only the date, a double-space below the last line of printed copy.

U.S. POSTAL SERVICE ABBREVIATIONS
OF STATE NAMES

Alabama	AL	Montana	MT
Alaska	AK	Nebraska	NE
Arizona	AZ	Nevada	NV
Arkansas	AR	New Hampshire	NH
American Samoa	AS	New Jersey	NJ
California	CA	New Mexico	NM
Canal Zone	CZ	New York	NY
Colorado	CO	North Carolina	NC
Connecticut	CT	North Dakota	ND
Delaware	DE	Ohio	OH
District of Columbia	DC	Oklahoma	OK
Florida	FL	Oregon	OR
Georgia	GA	Pennsylvania	PA
Guam	GU	Puerto Rico	PR
Hawaii	HI	Rhode Island	RI
Idaho	ID	South Carolina	SC
Illinois	IL	South Dakota	SD
Indiana	IN	Tennessee	TN
Iowa	IA	Trust Territories	TT
Kansas	KS	Texas	TX
Kentucky	KY	Utah	UT
Louisiana	LA	Vermont	VT
Maine	ME	Virginia	VA
Maryland	MD	Virgin Islands	VI
Massachusetts	MA	Washington	WA
Michigan	MI	West Virginia	WV
Minnesota	MN	Wisconsin	WI
Mississippi	MS	Wyoming	WY
Missouri	MO		

SOURCE: U.S. Postal Service

Inside address.   The *inside address* is the recipient's full name and address. You can begin the inside address two lines (or spaces) below the date if the letter is long, or four spaces below the date if the letter is quite short. The inside address should be flush with (or aligned with) the left margin—and the left margin should be at least one-inch wide. Include the reader's full name and title (if you know them) and his or her full address, including zip code.

EXAMPLE
```
Ms. Gail Silver
Production Manager
Quicksilver Printing Company
14 President Street
Sarasota, FL 33546
```

Salutation. Place the *salutation* (or "greeting") two spaces below the inside address, also flush with the left margin. In most business letters, the salutation contains the recipient's title (*Mr., Ms., Dr.,* etc.) and last name, followed by a colon (if you are on a first-name basis with the recipient, you would include his or her title and full name in the inside address but use only the first name in the salutation).

EXAMPLES
```
Dear Ms. Silver:
Dear Mr. Smith:
Dear Dr. Smith:
Dear Captain Smith:
```
(Note that titles like *Captain* and *Professor* are not abbreviated.)
```
Dear Professor Smith:
Dear George:
```
(if you are on a first-name basis)

For women who do not have a professional title, use *Ms.* (for either a married or an unmarried woman). If the woman has expressed a preference for *Miss* or *Mrs.,* honor her preference. In cases where you do not know whether the recipient is a man or a woman, you may use a title appropriate to the context of the letter. The following are examples of the kinds of titles you may find suitable:

EXAMPLES
```
Dear Customer:
```
(letter from a department store)
```
Dear Homeowner:
```
(letter from an insurance agent soliciting business)
```
Dear Parts Manager:
```
(letter to an auto-parts dealer)

In the past, writers to large companies or organizations customarily addressed their letter to "Gentlemen." Today, however, writers who do not know the name or the title of the recipient often address the letter to an appropriate department. Notice, in the following examples, that the name of the department may appear either in an "attention" line or in a "subject" line.

EXAMPLES
```
National Business Systems
501 West National Avenue
Minneapolis, MN 55107

Attention: Customer Relations Department

I am returning three calculators we purchased that
failed to operate when . . .
```

```
National Business Systems
501 West National Avenue
Minneapolis, MN 55107

Subject: Defective Parts for XL-100

I am returning three calculators we purchased that
failed to operate when . . .
```

The body.   The body of the letter is, of course, what the letter is about. Begin the body two spaces below the salutation (or below the heading if no salutation appears). Single-space within paragraphs and double-space between paragraphs. If a letter is very short and you want to suggest a fuller appearance, you may double-space throughout and indicate paragraphs by indenting the first line of each paragraph five spaces from the left. The right margin should be approximately as wide as the left margin. (In very short letters you may increase both margins to about an inch and a half.)

Complimentary close.   Start the complimentary close (or conventional "goodbye") two spaces below the body. Use a standard expression like *Yours truly, Sincerely,* or *Sincerely yours.* (If the recipient is a friend as well as a business associate, you can use a less formal close: *Best wishes, Best regards.*) Only the first word of the complimentary close is capitalized, and the expression is followed by a comma. Four spaces below the complimentary close, and aligned at the left with the close, type your full name. On the next line you may type in your business title, if it is appropriate to do so. Then sign your name in the space between the complimentary close and your typed name. If you are writing to someone with whom you are on a first-name basis, it is acceptable to sign only your given name; otherwise, sign your full name.

EXAMPLE   Yours truly,

Gail Silver

```
Gail Silver
Production Manager
```

Second page.   If a letter requires a second page, carry at least two lines of the body over to Page 2. Do not use a continuation page to type only the complimentary close of the letter. The second page should have a heading too, containing the recipient's name, the page number, and the date (never use letterhead for a second page). The heading may go in the upper-left-hand corner or across the page (see illustrations on the opposite page).

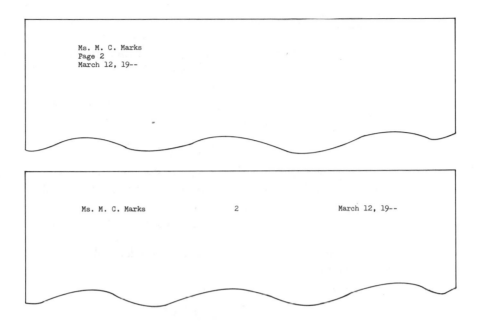

Ms. M. C. Marks
Page 2
March 12, 19--

Ms. M. C. Marks   2   March 12, 19--

Additional information.   Business letters sometimes require additional information—the typist's initials, an enclosure notation, or a notation that a copy of the letter is being sent to one or more named people. Place any such information—the typist's initials, an enclosure notation, or a notation that a copy of the letter is being sent to one or more named people. Place any such information flush left with the margin, two spaces below the last line of the complimentary close in a long letter, four spaces below in a short letter.

Typist's initials follow two basic patterns; no matter which style you choose, however, the letter writer's initials should appear in capital letters and the typist's initials should appear in lower-case letters. (When the writer is also the typist, no initials are needed.)

EXAMPLES   JTR/pst
(Typist's initials are separated from the writer's initials by a slash.)
JTR:pst
(Typist's initials are separated from the writer's initials by a colon.)

Enclosure notations, which indicate that the letter writer is sending material along with the letter (an invoice, an article, and so on), may take several forms. Choose the form that seems most helpful to your readers. Remember, though, that no matter which form you select, the enclosure notation should not replace a reference in the body of the letter to the fact that material is enclosed.

EXAMPLE   Enclosures: Preliminary report invoice
                          Draft contract

(Enclosures are specified in a long, formal letter or if the nature of the enclosed items is not obvious.)

Enclosures (2)

(Enclosures are not specified if letter is short and the nature of the enclosures is obvious to the reader.)

Encs. (or Enc. for a single item)

A *copy notation* tells the reader that a copy (either carbon or photocopy) of the letter is being sent to one or more named individuals.

EXAMPLE   cc: Ms. Marlene Brier
                     Mr. David Williams

A business letter may, of course, contain all three items of additional information.

EXAMPLE   Sincerely yours,

Jane T. Rogers

Jane T. Rogers

JTR/pst
Enclosures: Preliminary report invoice
                   Draft contract
cc: Ms. Marlene Brier

Sample Letter Styles

An important factor in the appearance of a letter is its overall format—the arrangement on the page of the five major parts of the letter. The two most common styles of business letters are the full block and the modified block. The *full block style,* which is easier to type because *every* line begins at the left margin, is suitable only with letterhead stationery. In the *modified block style* the return address, date, and complimentary close are placed just to the right of the center of the page. The remaining elements are aligned at the left margin. All other letter styles are variations of these two basic styles. Again, if your employer recommends or requires a particular style, follow it carefully. Otherwise, choose the style you are most comfortable with and follow it consistently.

only for letterhead stationery

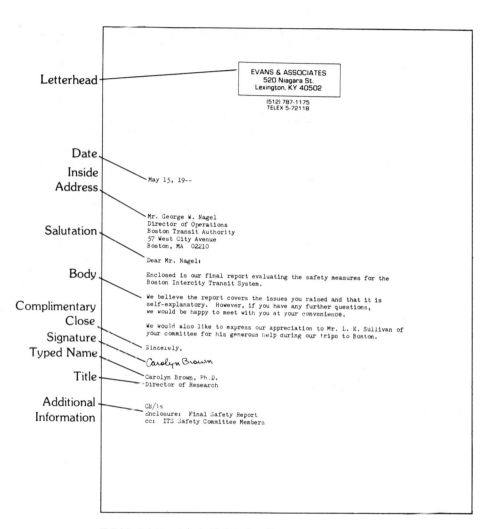

Letterhead —

> EVANS & ASSOCIATES
> 520 Niagara St.
> Lexington, KY 40502
>
> (512) 787-1175
> TELEX 5-72118

Date

Inside
Address

May 15, 19--

Salutation

Mr. George W. Nagel
Director of Operations
Boston Transit Authority
57 West City Avenue
Boston, MA 02210

Dear Mr. Nagel:

Body

Enclosed is our final report evaluating the safety measures for the
Boston Intercity Transit System.

We believe the report covers the issues you raised and that it is
self-explanatory. However, if you have any further questions,
we would be happy to meet with you at your convenience.

Complimentary
Close

We would also like to express our appreciation to Mr. L. K. Sullivan of
your committee for his generous help during our trips to Boston.

Signature

Sincerely,

Typed Name

Carolyn Brown

Title

Carolyn Brown, Ph.D.
Director of Research

Additional
Information

CB/ls
Enclosure: Final Safety Report
cc: ITS Safety Committee Members

Full block letter style (with letterhead)

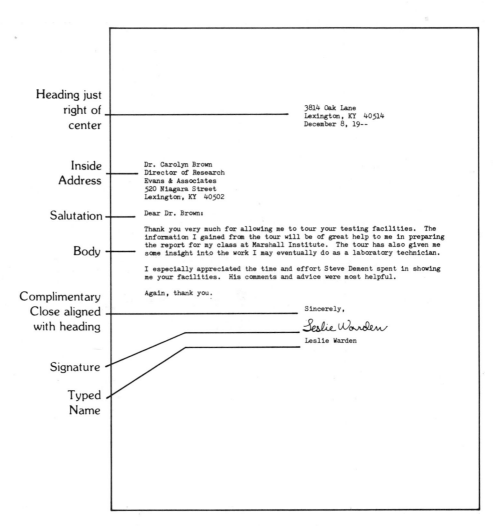

Heading just right of center

3814 Oak Lane
Lexington, KY 40514
December 8, 19--

Inside Address

Dr. Carolyn Brown
Director of Research
Evans & Associates
520 Niagara Street
Lexington, KY 40502

Salutation

Dear Dr. Brown:

Body

Thank you very much for allowing me to tour your testing facilities. The information I gained from the tour will be of great help to me in preparing the report for my class at Marshall Institute. The tour has also given me some insight into the work I may eventually do as a laboratory technician.

I especially appreciated the time and effort Steve Dement spent in showing me your facilities. His comments and advice were most helpful.

Again, thank you.

Complimentary Close aligned with heading

Sincerely,

Leslie Warden

Signature

Leslie Warden

Typed Name

Modified block letter style (without letterhead)

Preparing the Envelope

The most widely used form for typing envelopes is the *block* form. The two illustrations below show the block form used on two different size envelopes.

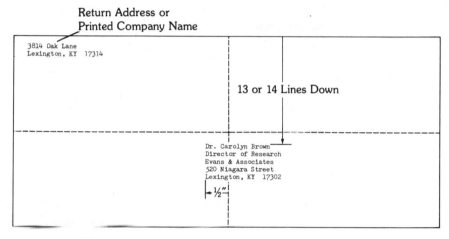

A #10 envelope, addressed

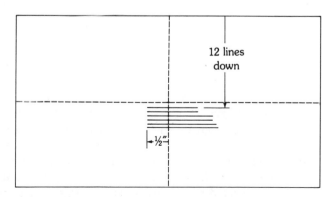

A 6¾" envelope

When you insert the letter into an envelope, be careful not to smudge or crumple the paper. The following illustration shows the proper technique for folding 8½″ × 11″ stationery into a standard (#10 size) business envelope.

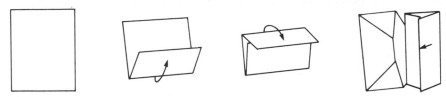

When folding 8½″ × 11″ stationery into a smaller (No. 6¾) envelope, use the following technique.

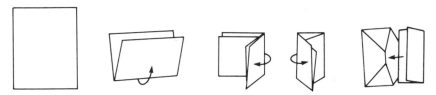

TYPES OF LETTERS

Because the most important business letter most people write is the letter of application, it is discussed separately in Chapter 17, along with other strategies for finding a job. But almost as many types of letters exist as there are reasons for writing. To select the appropriate kind, you must carefully assess both the situation and your reader's needs. Since a number of situations and reasons for writing letters are typical, the remainder of this chapter is devoted to the following common types of letters: the order letter, the order follow-up letter, the inquiry letter, the response to an inquiry, answering a forwarded inquiry letter, the transmittal (or "cover") letter, the acknowledgment letter, the complaint letter, the adjustment letter, and the sales letter.

The Order Letter

One of the commonest reasons for writing a letter, especially if you work for a small organization or are self-employed, is to order supplies or equipment. The equipment may be anything from company letterhead to x-ray film. Obviously, an order letter must be specific and complete if you are to receive the exact item you want. But be careful not to clutter the letter with unnecessary details, such as why you need the items or who will use them. Above all, be accurate. Since a misspelled word or misplaced decimal point could cause a staggering error, proofread carefully and double-check all price calculations.

Make sure that the order letter contains the following information, as it applies to the item or items you are purchasing.

1. The exact name and part number (if appropriate) of the item.
2. Any useful description of the item: size, style, color, and so on.
3. The quantity needed of each item.
4. The price of the item, both unit price and total price, if appropriate.
5. The shipping method: mail, air, express, or, perhaps, the "best route."
6. The date of the order and the date by which you need the item (indicate "rush" or other instructions).
7. The place to which the material is to be shipped (make sure you provide the exact and full shipping address).
8. The method of payment: for example, indicate that you have enclosed a check or money order, that you will pay c.o.d. (usually more expensive), or that you have enclosed a purchase order number and the seller is to bill your company.

If you order several items, list them. A list will make your order easier to read.

The example on page 194 is a typical order letter.

If you receive no response to an order letter within about ten days after the date the item was due, you may need to send a follow-up letter. If you do send a follow-up letter, be courteous and avoid showing irritation. In your follow-up, identify the order by referring to the date of the original letter. It is also wise to include a copy of the letter. The example on page 195 is a typical follow-up letter.

The Inquiry Letter

Another frequently sent business letter is the *inquiry letter,* in which the writer requests information from the recipient. Such a letter may be as simple as a note asking the Far 'N' Wide Travel Bureau for a copy of the free brochure "Inexpensive Fly and Drive Vacations" that was offered in a recent issue of your local newspaper; it may be as complex as a letter asking a financial consultant to define the specific requirements for floating a multimillion-dollar bond issue.

There are two broad categories of inquiry letters. The first kind is of obvious benefit to the recipient—you may be asking, for instance, for information about a product a company has recently advertised. The second kind, on the other hand, primarily benefits the writer; an example would be a request to a nonprofit religious organization to send information on the number of worshippers in a geographical area. If the letter of inquiry you are writing is of the second type, it is particularly important that you be considerate of your reader's needs. Your objective in writing the letter will probably be to obtain,

HOLT TOOL COMPANY
1012 Clarke Street
Phoenix, AZ 85019

(602) 297-3100

September 5, 19--

Downtown Parts Company
109 South State Street
Chicago, IL 60650

Attention: Sales Department

Please send the following items listed in your current parts catalog:

  2 Tempered steel cylinders, 2" diameter and 5" long,
     part number C5789S, @ $12.75 each $25.50

  4 Aluminum castings with corrosion-resistant
     coating, part number S312A, @ $4.89 each $19.56

12 Special tempered sheet metal screws, $1\frac{1}{4}$"
     long with hexagonal heads, @ $.57 each $ 6.84

                                  TOTAL $51.90

The enclosed check for $56.31 covers the price, sales tax, and parcel
post charges.

Please send this material to me by October 1.

Sincerely,

James Siemer

James Siemer
Parts Manager

JS:tb
Enclosure: Check

Order letter

HOLT TOOL COMPANY
1012 Clarke Street
Phoenix, AZ 85019

(602) 297-3100

October 12, 19--

Downtown Parts Company
109 South State Street
Chicago, IL 60650

Attention: Sales Department

On September 5, I sent you a letter in which I placed an
order for a number of parts listed in your current catalog. I
also sent a check for $56.31.

I have enclosed a copy of that letter, and I request that you
please rush this material to me. If for some reason you
cannot send the material, please cancel my order and return
the check.

Thank you.

Sincerely,

James Siemer

James Siemer
Parts Manager

JS:tb
Enclosure: Copy of order letter

Order follow-up letter

P.O. Box 113
University of Dayton
Dayton, OH 45409
March 11, 19--

Ms. Jane Metcalf
Engineering Services
Miami Valley Power Company
P.O. Box 1444
Miamitown, OH 45733

Dear Ms. Metcalf:

Our Systems Design class at the University of Dayton is designing an all-electric, energy-efficient, middle-priced home. The house, which contains 2,000 square feet of living space (17,600 cubic feet), meets all the requirements stipulated in your company's brochure "Insulating for Efficiency." However, we need some additional information on heating systems. Specifically, we need the following information:

1. The proper size heat pump to use in this climate for such a home;

2. The wattage of the supplemental electrical furnace that would be required for this climate; and

3. The estimated power consumption, and current rates, of these units for a calendar year.

We will be happy to send you a copy of our preliminary design report.

Thank you very much.

Sincerely yours,

Kathryn J. Parsons

Inquiry letter

within a reasonable period of time, answers to specific questions. You will be more likely to receive a prompt, helpful reply if you follow two guidelines: keep the number of questions to a minimum, so that you do not intrude unduly on the reader's time; and phrase your questions in such a way that the reader will know immediately what type of information you are seeking, why you are seeking it, and what use you will make of it. Be sure, as you write your questions, that you are asking the ones that you had intended to ask; it will be a waste of the reader's time, and a source of frustration to you later on, if you word your questions in such a way that your reader misinterprets them. And your reader will probably find it easiest to answer your questions one by one if you present them in a numbered list. Your reader may also appreciate it if you offer to send a copy of material (a report or a proposal for a project, for example) that you plan to prepare based, in part, on the information you are requesting. As a courtesy, too, you should promise to keep confidential any personal information you may receive. And at the end of your letter, express your thanks to the reader for taking the time and trouble to respond. Do not forget, also, to include the address to which the material is to be sent (this is most important, of course, if the information will be sent to an address other than the one in your heading). It is sometimes a good idea, in fact, to enclose a stamped, self-addressed return envelope, especially if you are writing to someone who is self-employed. A typical inquiry letter appears on page 196.

Response to an Inquiry Letter

Sometimes, of course, you may be on the receiving end of a letter of inquiry. When you do receive such a letter, read it first quickly to determine whether you are the right person in your organization to answer it—whether, that is, you are the one who possesses both the information and the authority to respond. If you are in a position to answer, do so as promptly as you can, and be sure to answer every question the writer has included. How long your responses should be, and how much technical language you should use, depends, of course, on the nature of the question and on what information the writer has provided about himself or herself. Even if the writer has asked a question that sounds obvious or unimportant to you, be polite. You may point out that the reader has omitted or misunderstood a particular piece of information or has in some other way introduced an error, but be tactful in your correction, so that the reader won't feel foolish or ignorant. If, on the other hand, you see an opportunity to give your reader praise or encouragement, do so. And at the end of the letter, offer to answer any further questions the writer may have (see page 198).

Forwarding an Inquiry Letter

Sometimes a letter of inquiry sent to a large company arrives at the desk of a staff member who realizes that he or she is not the employee best able to answer the letter. If you have received a letter that you feel you can't answer (because you lack the information or the authority or both), you should do two things. First, find out (if you don't know off-hand) who in the company is best equipped to answer the letter. Second, forward the letter to the co-worker. The co-worker's letter answering the inquiry should state in the first paragraph that although the letter was addressed to you, it is being answered

MIAMI VALLEY POWER COMPANY
P.O. BOX 1444
MIAMITOWN, OH 45733

(513) 264-4800

March 15, 19--

Ms. Kathryn J. Parsons
P.O. Box 113
University of Dayton
Dayton, OH 45409

Dear Ms. Parsons:

The project you mentioned in your letter sounds interesting.
Unfortunately, I cannot give you an answer that would apply specifically
to the house you are designing unless I have additional information about
particular design features of the house (one or two stories, number of
windows, number of entrances, for example).

I can, however, estimate the insulation requirement of a typical home of
17,600 cubic feet.

1. We would generally recommend, for such a home, a heat pump capable
    of delivering 40,000 BTUs. Our model AL-42 (17 kilowatts) meets
    this requirement.

2. With the efficiency of the AL-42, you would not need a supplemental
    electrical furnace.

3. Depending on usage, the Al-42 unit averages between 1,000 and 1,500
    kilowatt hours from December through March. To determine the current
    rate for such usage, you will need to check with the Dayton Power and
    Light Company. The Miamitown area is not serviced by DP&L, and
    therefore I do not know what its rates are.

I am sorry that I cannot give you more specific answers. If you could
send me more detailed information, however, I would be happy to provide
you with more precise figures.

Sincerely,

Jane Metcalf

Jane E. Metcalf
Director of Public Information

JEM/mk

Response to an inquiry letter

by someone else in the firm, because he or she is better qualified to respond
to the inquiry. The letter on page 199 is an example of a response to a forwarded inquiry letter.

The Transmittal Letter

When you send (or transmit) a formal report, brochure, or other type of material, you should include with it a short letter called a *transmittal,* or *cover, letter,*

```
                  MIAMI VALLEY POWER COMPANY
                           P.O. BOX 1444
                        MIAMITOWN, OH 45733

                         (513) 264-4800




         March 15, 19--


         Ms. Kathryn J. Parsons
         P.O. Box 113
         University of Dayton
         Dayton, OH  45409

         Dear Ms. Parsons:

         Thank you for inquiring about the heating system we would recommend for
         use in homes designed according to the specifications outlined in our
         brochure "Insulating for Efficiency."

         Since I cannot answer your specific questions, I have forwarded your
         letter to Mr. Michael Stott, Engineering Assistant in our development
         group. He should be able to answer the questions you have raised.

         Sincerely,

         Jane Metcalf

         Jane E. Metcalf
         Director of Public Information


         JEM/mk
         cc:  Michael Stott
```

Response to a forwarded inquiry letter

which identifies what you are sending and why you are sending it. Transmittal letters accompanying reports and proposals may contain the title of the report, a brief description of the report, an acknowledgment of any help received in the preparation of the report, and the authorization or reason for the report. The transmittal letter provides the writer with a record of when and to whom the material was sent.

Written in the form of a standard business letter, the transmittal letter most often opens with a brief paragraph (one or two sentences) explaining

WATERFORD PAPER PRODUCTS
P.O. BOX 413
WATERFORD, WI 53474

(414) 738-2191

January 16, 19--

Mr. Roger Hammersmith
Ecology Systems, Inc.
1015 Clarke Street
Chicago, IL 60615

Dear Mr. Hammersmith:

Enclosed is the report estimating our power consumption for the year as
requested by John Brenan, Vice President, on September 4.

The report is a result of several meetings with the Manager of Plant
Operations and her staff and an extensive survey of all our employees.
The survey was delayed by the temporary layoff of key personnel in
Building "A" from October 1 to December 5. We believe, however, that
the report will provide the information you need to furnish us with a
cost estimate for the installation of your Mark II Energy Saving System.

We would like to thank Diana Biel of ESI for her assistance in preparing
the survey. If you need any more information, please let me know.

Sincerely,

James G. Evans
New Projects Office

JGE/fst
Enclosure

Transmittal letter—long

cover letter

what is being sent and why. The next paragraph contains a brief summary of
the material or stresses some feature that is important to the reader. A letter
accompanying a proposal, for example, might briefly present convincing evidence that your firm is the best one to do the job. The letter may go on to
point out specific sections in the proposal of particular interest to the reader.
You might also want to mention any special conditions under which the material was prepared (limitations in time or money, for instance). The closing paragraph should acknowledge any help received in the preparation of the mate-

```
┌─────────────────────────────────────────────────────────┐
│  ┌──────────────────────────────────────────────────┐   │
│  │        WATERFORD PAPER PRODUCTS                    │   │
│  │              P.O. BOX 413                          │   │
│  │           WATERFORD, WI 53474                      │   │
│  └──────────────────────────────────────────────────┘   │
│                    (414) 738-2191                         │
│                                                           │
│                                                           │
│   November 12, 19--                                       │
│                                                           │
│                                                           │
│   Ms. Nancy Melcher                                       │
│   2021 State Street                                       │
│   Racine, WI  53307                                       │
│                                                           │
│   Dear Ms. Melcher:                                       │
│                                                           │
│   Thank you for your interest in Waterford Paper Products.│
│   The enclosed brochure describes our product line and    │
│   our current prices.                                     │
│                                                           │
│   If I can be of further help, please let me know.        │
│                                                           │
│   Sincerely,                                              │
│                                                           │
│   Lawrence Smith                                          │
│                                                           │
│   Lawrence Smith                                          │
│   Customer Relations                                      │
│                                                           │
│   LS:ik                                                   │
│   Enclosure                                               │
│                                                           │
└─────────────────────────────────────────────────────────┘
```

Transmittal letter—short

rial, offer additional assistance, or express the hope that the material will fulfill its purpose.

These elements are basic to any letter of transmittal. Keep additional remarks brief. The report, pamphlet, or whatever should speak for itself. A transmittal letter should not run beyond a few short paragraphs; it should never exceed one page. The example on page 200 is a typical letter of transmittal. Some letters of transmittal are not as detailed as this one is. They say essentially "here it is." The letter above is typical.

The Acknowledgment Letter

One of the ways to build goodwill in any business is to let customers or clients know that something they sent has arrived. A letter that serves such a function is called an acknowledgment letter. It is usually a short, polite note. The examples on this page and the following page are typical.

Ecology Systems, Inc.
1015 Clarke Street
Chicago, IL 60615

(312) 719-6620

January 21, 19--

Mr. James G. Evans
New Projects Office
Waterford Paper Products
P.O. Box 413
Waterford, WI 53474

Dear Mr. Evans:

I received your report today; it appears to be complete and well done.

When I finish studying it thoroughly, I will send you our cost estimate for the installation of the Mark II Energy Saving System.

Again, thanks for your effort.

Sincerely,

Roger Hammersmith

Roger Hammersmith
Sales Manager

RLH/rlt

Acknowledgment letter I

ECADS, INCORPORATED

501 BEACH STREET
MIAMI, FL 33167

(305) 834-7200

January 18, 19--

Mr. Joel Baker
3078 Terrace Boulevard
Miami, FL 33117

Dear Mr. Baker:

I received in today's mail the defective part that we talked
about last week on the phone.

As soon as one of our engineers can examine it, I will phone
you.

Sincerely,

Marylin Sanches

Marylin Sanches

MS/bk

Acknowledgment letter II

The Complaint Letter

The best complaint letters do not sound complaining. That statement may
sound contradictory, but it's not.

By the time it becomes necessary for you to write a complaint letter
(sometimes called a *claim letter*), you may be irritated and angry. If you write a
letter that reflects *only* your annoyance and anger, however, you may not be

taken seriously—you may simply appear petty and irrational. Remember, too, that the person who receives your letter may not be the one who was directly responsible for the situation about which you are complaining. Venting your anger at someone who was not at fault is neither fair nor useful.

An effective complaint letter—a letter that accomplishes its purpose—should be both firm and well thought out. It should assume, first, that the recipient will be conscientious in correcting the problem. Second, it should present the writer as capable of handling the situation calmly. Finally, the letter should reflect the fact that you expect the situation to be corrected.

Although the circumstances and the severity of the problem may vary, effective complaint letters should generally follow the same pattern. They should

1. Identify the faulty item, including invoice numbers, part names, dates, and so forth. (Often it is a good idea to include a photocopy of the bill, or contract.)
2. Explain logically, clearly, and specifically what went wrong. (Avoid expressing an opinion of why you *think* some problem occurred if you have no way of knowing.)
3. State what you expect the reader to do to solve the problem to your satisfaction.

Large organizations often have special departments, with such names as "Customer Relations," "Consumer Affairs," or "Adjustment," to handle complaints. If you address your letter to one of these departments, it should reach someone in the company who can be of help to you. In smaller organizations, you might write to a vice president in charge of sales or of service. For very small businesses, write directly to the owner. You can assume that persons at high levels of responsibility will take your letter seriously. As a last resort, you may find that a complaint letter photocopied and sent to more than one person in a company will get fast results. Each employee receiving the letter knows (because of the carbon-copy notation) that others, possibly higher in the organization, have received the letter and will notice if the problem is solved.

The letter on page 205 is an example of a complaint letter.

The Adjustment Letter

If you, as the manager of the Customer Relations Department of the television company, receive the letter of complaint from Paul Denlinger, you should take it—and any letter like it—seriously. What is at stake is more than nine tuners. Regardless of how trivial the incident may seem to you, your employer's reputation is on the line. And if the writer, Mr. Denlinger, is satisfied with the way

BAKER MEMORIAL HOSPITAL
Television Services
501 Main Street
Springfield, OH 45321

(513) 683-8100

September 23, 19--

Manager, Customer Relations
General Television, Inc.
5521 West 23rd Street
New York, NY 10062

On July 9th I ordered nine TV tuners for your model MX-15 color
receiver. The tuner part number is TR-5771-3.

On August 2nd I received from your Newark, New Jersey, parts warehouse
seven tuners, labeled TR-413-7. I immediately returned these tuners with
a note indicating the mistake that had been made. However, not only have
I failed to receive the tuners I ordered, but I have also been billed
repeatedly.

Would you please either send me the tuners I ordered or cancel my order.
I have enclosed a copy of my original order letter and the most recent
bill.

Sincerely,

Paul Denlinger
Paul Denlinger
Manager

PD:oj
Enclosures

Complaint letter

you handle his complaint, he may decide that when the hospital next orders
TV sets, he'll place the order with your company. What is at stake, then, are
both the good name of your company and potential orders of several dozen
television sets worth thousands of dollars.

An appropriate response to Mr. Denlinger's letter would be an *adjustment
letter*—a letter that explains to the reader how a complaint he or she has made
will be settled. To prepare an adjustment letter, you must first investigate what

General Television, Inc.
5521 West 23rd Street
New York, NY 10062

Customer Relations
(212) 574-3894

September 28, 19--

Mr. Paul Denlinger, Manager
Baker Memorial Hospital
Television Services
501 Main Street
Springfield, OH 45321

Dear Mr. Denlinger:

Thank you for your letter regarding your order for nine TR-5771-3
tuners. Please accept our apologies for not sending the proper tuners
and for incorrectly billing you.

Evidently when your package arrived at our loading docks, a dock worker
failed to see your letter in the container. He set the box aside with
several boxes of parts destined for our Rebuilt Parts Department.
Regrettably, therefore, your note did not come to the attention of our
parts manager.

We have shipped the correct tuners by United Parcel; you should receive
them shortly after you receive this letter. I have also cancelled your
original order so that you will not be sent overdue notices and so that
we can charge you at our preferred-customer rate -- normally requiring
orders of more than $2,000.

To prevent any further inconveniences, we ask that you send any
packages directly to Mr. Gene Smith, Parts Manager at our Newark facility.

If I can be of any further help, please let me know.

Sincerely,

Susan Siegel

Susan Siegel
Assistant Director

SS/mr

Adjustment letter I

happened and what you can do to satisfy the customer. After you have obtained the facts, you should organize your letter into three basic parts.

1. Refer to the letter of complaint and identify the faulty item or service.
   If your company is responsible for the error, *offer an apology at the
   very beginning.* Doing so will immediately help to regain the customer's good will.
2. Explain clearly why the error occurred or outline the company policy

General Television, Inc.
5521 West 23rd Street
New York, NY 10062

Customer Relations
(212) 574-3894

September 28, 19--

Mr. Fred J. Swesky
7811 Ranchero Drive
Tucson, AZ 85761

Dear Mr. Swesky:

Thank you for your letter regarding the replacement of your KL-71
television set.

You stated in your letter that you used the set on an uncovered patio.
As our local service representative pointed out, this model is not
designed to operate in extreme heat conditions. As the accompanying
instruction manual states and our engineers confirm, such exposure can
produce irreparable damage to this model. Since your set was used in
such extreme heat conditions, therefore, we cannot honor the two-year
replacement warranty.

However, with the enclosed certificate, your local GTI dealer will give
you a trade-in allowance equal to his markup for the set. This means
you can purchase a new set at wholesale, provided you return your
original set.

Sincerely yours,

Susan Siegel

Susan Siegel
Assistant Director

SS/mr
Enclosure

Adjustment letter II

related to the problem, or do both. This is especially important if you
are not able to do everything the customer asks.
3. State specifically what you intend to do or have done to solve the
   problem. If you are not able to do exactly what the customer asks,
   give a partial adjustment at least.

The examples show two circumstances: the first in which the company was at
fault, the second in which the customer was at fault.

The Sales Letter

A sales letter, or letter that promotes a product, service, store, and so on, is probably the most difficult of all types of business letters to write because it requires both a thorough knowledge of the product or service and a keen awareness of the potential customer's needs. For this reason, many businesses (such as department stores) employ specialists to compose their sales letters. If you are employed in a small business or are self-employed, however, you will probably have to write your sales letters yourself.

Whether you write sales letters for a small company or a large one, your first task is to determine who they should be sent to. One good source of names is a list of past and recent customers; those who have, at some time, purchased a product or service from you may become users again. Another source are lists, compiled by companies who specialize in marketing techniques, of people who may be interested in certain products or services. Such lists are drawn from the membership rolls of clubs, fraternal and religious organizations, professional societies, and the like. Because these lists tend to be expensive, however, they should be selected with care.

After you decide who your mailing list will include, you must prepare your letter carefully. As you do, keep the following points in mind.

1. The opening must attract the reader's attention and arouse his or her interest. Start out, for example, by describing a feature of the product or service that you believe would appeal strongly to your reader's needs. A representative of a company that installs home insulation might use the following opening, addressed to "Dear Homeowner":

   ```
   If you've thought that home insulation is a good
   idea but too expensive, think again. We can fully
   insulate your home at no cost to you. Impossible?
   With the new Federal Energy Tax Credit and the
   money that we guarantee you'll save . . .
   ```

   Be careful, of course, that any claim you make in a sales letter is valid. Mail fraud carries heavy legal penalties.
2. Continue to emphasize the benefits of the product to the reader. Don't exaggerate; you will lose the reader's confidence if your claims sound unreasonable. And don't downgrade a competitor; it smacks of unfair tactics.
3. Make it easy and worthwhile for the customer to respond. You might include a local street map to your store, a discount coupon, or instructions for convenient phone-in order and free delivery.
4. Suggest ways the reader can make immediate use of the product or service. A sales letter from a fabric store might give instructions for making pillows, bags, and other home-sewn items.

The sales letters on this and the next page are typical. Notice that they are written in a light, friendly tone—sales letters from small, local businesses frequently are, since their purpose is to make the reader feel comfortable about coming to the shop or office. Notice, too, that sometimes such sales letters are "signed" not by an individual but by the shop itself.

```
                              Janice's Cycle Shop
                               775 First Avenue
                              Ottumwa, Iowa  52501
                                 (515) 273-5111




          April 3, 19--


          Mr. Raymond Sommers
          350 College Place
          Sharpsville, Iowa  52156

          Dear Mr. Sommers:

          Are you ready to go bike riding this Spring -- but your bike isn't?

          Janice's Cycle Shop is ready to get your bike in shape for the
          beautiful days ahead.  We will lubricate all moving parts; check the
          tires, brakes, chain, lights, horn, and all other accessories; and make
          any minor repairs -- all for only ten dollars and the coupon enclosed
          in this letter.

          Just stop in any day, Monday through Saturday, between 8:00 a.m. and
          9 p.m.  We are conveniently located at the corner of First and Walker.
          You can pay with cash, check, or bank credit card.

          If you bring your bike in before 10:00 a.m., you can be enjoying a spring
          bike ride that evening.

          Happy riding.


          Janice's Cycle Shop
```

Sales letter I

Downtown Stationery Supply
101 South Ludlow Street
East Hartford, CT 06207

(203) 321-5000

February 24, 19--

Ms. Marilyn Prentice
Office Manager
Midway Insurance Company
571 State Street
East Hartford, CT   06101

Dear Ms. Prentice:

We have discovered that many office managers frequently spend part of their
lunch hour shopping for office supplies. Although we appreciate the
business, we believe lunch hours are for lunch -- not for business.

Therefore, we are offering a unique service. So you won't have to spend
your lunch hour with us, we'll come to you during regular office hours.

If you'll simply mail the enclosed postcard, indicating the day and time
you will be available, our representative will stop by to take your order.
Your supplies will normally be delivered the same day.

To make your shopping easier we have also enclosed our full-color catalog.
Should you want something not in our catalog, our representative will be
happy to order it.

Enjoy your lunch hour.

Sincerely,

James Larrick

James Larrick
Sales Manager

Sales letter II

THE MEMORANDUM

The most frequently written type of communication between members of the
same organization is the memorandum, called the "memo" for short. Memos
are routinely used for internal communications of all kinds—from short notes

INTEROFFICE CORRESPONDENCE
INDUSTRIAL PUBLISHING CORPORATION

To: Hazel Smith, Publications Manager

From: Herbert Kaufman, Vice President

Date: April 14, 19--

Subject: Time Estimate for Acme Electronics Brochure

Acme Electronics has asked us to prepare a comprehensive brochure for
their Milwaukee office by August 1 of this year. We have worked with
electronic firms in the past, so this job should be relatively easy to
prepare. My guess is that the job will take nearly two months. Ted Harris
has requested time and cost estimates for the project. Fred Moore in
accounting will prepare cost estimates, and I would like you to prepare a
schedule for the estimated time.

Schedule
In preparing the schedule, check production schedules for all staff
writers, compile a list of available free-lance writers we can depend on,
and contact local graphic designers for art work, since our art department
is heavily scheduled through July. Also, don't forget to take staff
vacation time into account. Let me emphasize that we must finish by our
estimated date (most important), that the overall design must have a
uniform format, and that the art work must blend properly with the copy.

Time Estimates
Please give me time estimates by April 19. A successful job done on
time will give us a good chance for the contract to do Acme's publications
for their annual stockholder's meeting this fall.

I know your staff can do the job.

cc: Ted Harris

Memorandum—long

to small reports. In addition to transmitting information, the memo furnishes a
permanent record of decisions made and of actions taken.

In writing a memo, follow the rules for good writing that you would use
for letters and longer works. An outline, even though it may be no more than
a number of items jotted down and arranged in a logical sequence, is essential;
it should enable you to stick to your topic.

```
                              M E M O R A N D U M


           To:  Ben Johnson, Systems Design
           From:  Linda Coleman, Sales and Service
           Date:  February 12, 19--

           Subject:  Meeting with Ackley Brothers & Co.

           I thought you'd like to know that the meeting with Ackley went very
           well.  In fact, I think they'll accept our proposal.

           Keep your fingers crossed.
```

Memorandum—short

A memo should deal only with the subject specified in the subject line. To focus the reader's attention on particular topics, in a long memo, you can insert headings where they are appropriate. Headings divide the material into manageable segments, call attention to the main topics, and signal changes of topic—and they should aid you in organizing your material. If your memo presents a series of items for consideration, you may list them in a numbered sequence.

The tone of a memo can range from formal to informal, depending on your reader. A memo to your general manager would be more formal than a memo to an employee of equal rank in another department who is also a friend. As with other writing, if your reader is not familiar with your subject, or with the background of the problem being dealt with, provide a brief introductory paragraph. In addition, an introduction or background paragraph will provide necessary information months (or even years) later if the memo must be reviewed and you are not there. Generally, longer memos dealing with complex subjects benefit most from this introductory information.

Short memos are organized in simple paragraph form. The above example was written by the manager of the Sales and Service Department and is addressed to the manager of the Systems Design Department. Job titles or department names ("Systems Design" and "Sales and Service") are occasionally omitted if the sender and receiver know each other well. Since memos are often used as records of information, however, it is usually best to include the appropriate titles.

CHAPTER SUMMARY

To write effective business letters, follow the steps of the writing process discussed in Chapters 1–3: make an outline (which may simply be a list of the points you wish to include in the letter); prepare a first draft and then set it aside for a "cooling" period; revise your work, paying attention to both content and mechanics; type your final copy according to standard business-letter form.

In all business-letter writing, it is important to show your reader courtesy and consideration. Ask yourself, "How might I feel if I were the recipient of the letter I am going to write?" Doing so will help you put yourself in your reader's place and enable you to write a letter that is thoughtful of your reader's needs and feelings.

Writing style in business letters can be informal—in a letter to a close business associate—or formal—in a letter to someone the writer has never met.

The level of formality depends on the situation. In general, though, it is better to avoid a style that seems overly "chatty."

Because a business letter is a formal written record, it must be accurate. Make sure that your facts, figures, and dates are correct. Every business letter should follow one of the standard letter formats. The two most common ones are the *full-block style,* in which all parts of the letter begin at the left margin, and the *modified-block style,* in which the return address, the date, and the complimentary close appear just to the right of the center of the page.

There are a number of different types of business letters. Some of the most frequently written kinds include the following.

An *order letter* places a purchase for supplies or equipment. It should be specific, accurate, and complete, but not cluttered with unrelated details.

An *inquiry letter* is a request for information. It should state clearly and concisely what information is wanted, who wants it, and what use will be made of the information.

A *letter of transmittal* accompanies a report, brochure, or other material that is being sent to the recipient. The purpose of the letter is to identify what is being sent and why it is being sent; the letter may also include a brief description of the material, an acknowledgment of assistance received in the preparation of the material, or the authorization for the material.

A *complaint letter* should be businesslike and logical; it should not sound "complaining." It should reflect the fact that the writer is registering the complaint calmly—but that he or she expects the situation will be corrected.

A *letter of adjustment,* often a response to a complaint letter, should explain what caused the problem, specify what is being done to correct it, and, if the company for which the writer works was at fault, apologize for the incident.

A *sales letter* must catch the reader's attention, arouse the reader's interest, emphasize the benefits of the product or service, and invite the reader to respond.

A *memorandum,* or *memo* for short, is the chief means of written communication between members of the same organization. A memo may take the form of a brief note; a longer, letter-like correspondence; or an informal report.

EXERCISES

1. Bring to class one business letter you believe is well written and one that is poorly written. Be prepared to explain your reasons for thinking that one is better than the other. You may be able to find letters in your office (if you are working full or part time), or you might obtain examples from friends or relatives. Watch your own mail too.

2. Rewrite the following statement to make it more positive and less blunt.

   I will not pay you because you have not sent the double-jointed widget. If you do not send the right one right away, I will not pay you at all.

3. Rewrite the following passage to make it less unfriendly.

   I wrote for the record you advertised on television, and it not only took six weeks to get here but it was also the wrong record. Can't you get anything right? I'm canceling payment on my check and sending this record back!

4. Revise the following passage to make it clearer and less pretentious.

   With reference to and in connection with your recent automobile accident, I have been unable to contact you due to the fact that I have been in Chicago on work-related business. I should be back in the office in the neighborhood of the 15th or so. In the unforeseen and unlikely event that I should be delayed, you can utilize Mr. Strawman, of my office, who will also endeavor in your behalf.

5. Prepare a letter of transmittal for either a report or a term paper you are preparing for a course. Address the letter to the appropriate instructor.

6. The following exercises present a situation which you are asked to respond to with different types of correspondence. Based on the events as they are described in exercises a – e, write the letters or memo assigned by your instructor. In all exercises, follow the proper format for business letters. Your instructor may ask you to type your letters and envelopes.

   a. Assume you are writing a letter requesting a free booklet that explains how to clean window-unit air conditioners to achieve better energy efficiency. You must write to an organization called the Energy Conservation Society, located in New York City at 1012 Third Avenue (zip code 10021). You are writing to Nancy Reibold, who is the Executive Director. You learned about this booklet in an article in *Time* magazine (May 25, 1979). You don't remember the precise title of the booklet.

b. Assume that you are Nancy Reibold in exercise a. You have received the inquiry letter asking for the booklet. You are out of copies at the moment, however, because you have received more requests for the booklet than you had anticipated. You expect to receive more copies of the booklet within two weeks. Write a response to the inquiry letter explaining the circumstances and telling the reader that you will send the booklet, entitled "Reducing the Cost of Operating Your Window Air Conditioner," as soon as you can.

c. You are Nancy Reibold's assistant at the Energy Conservation Society (see exercises a and b). You have just received 1,000 copies of the booklet from the Jones Printing Company, 105 East Summit Street, New Brunswick, New Jersey (zip code 08910). Both you and Nancy Reibold are very angry. When you opened the box containing the booklets you discovered that several pages of each booklet had been left unprinted. This is the second printing mistake made by Jones Printing, and the shipment is late as well. Robert Mason, the sales representative for Jones Printing, promised that you would have no problems this time. Nancy Reibold asks you to write a complaint letter to Robert Mason to "get this problem corrected immediately." Write the letter for Ms. Reibold to sign.

d. Assume that you are Robert Mason (see exercise c). You have received the complaint letter about the printing mistake. After checking, you discover that the booklets sent to the Energy Conservation Society had been subcontracted to another printing firm (ILM Printing Company), because of the backlog of printing jobs at Jones. You know that Jones Printing will not be billed for the booklets if you return them to ILM Printing within five working days. You decide that you must write an adjustment letter to Ms. Reibold quickly. You will need to ask her to return the incorrectly printed booklets.

e. Assume that you are Robert Mason (see exercise d). Send a memo to J. R. Jones, your boss and president of Jones Printing, recommending that ILM Printing Company not be used for future subcontracting work. Use the details from the previous exercises to make the memo convincing.

7. As a class, and with the help of your instructor, create a made-up situation similar to the one in exercises 6a –e. From the events and the details you have developed, assign various types of letters to be completed as your instructor requires.

8. Find a catalog for parts or equipment with which you are familiar—stereo components, office supplies, automobile accessories, for example. Photocopy the pages that give you enough information to order items you need (or would like to have). Write an order letter with an envelope and submit the letter, envelope, and photocopies of the pertinent pages to your instructor.

9. Assume that eight weeks have passed since you sent the order letter in exercise 8. Write an order follow-up letter.

10. You have been designated to write a memorandum to Mark Heller, the head of your engineering department, asking for an extension of the deadline originally set for the completion of your engineering group's current project. Your reasons for asking for the extension are that a vendor delivered needed material seven days late and one of the key draftsmen in your group missed two weeks of work because of illness.

11

Informal Reports

Reports make up a large part of on-the-job communication. The successful operation of many firms depends on reports that either circulate within the company or are submitted to customers, clients, and others with whom a company does business. It would be difficult, in fact, to find a job in business or industry that did not require, at least on occasion, the writing of reports.

What is a report? Although the term is used to refer to hundreds of different types of written communication, the word can be defined as an organized presentation of information, serving an immediate and practical purpose by furnishing requested or needed data.

All reports fall into two broad categories: *formal reports* and *informal reports.* Formal reports, which are explained in detail in Chapter 13, are generally the outgrowth of projects that require many months of work and large sums of money, or of projects done on behalf of governmental agencies. Formal reports, which may take several hundred pages, are usually accompanied by a letter of transmittal to the recipient; frequently, such reports have a table of contents and other aids to the reader. Informal reports, on the other hand, normally run from a few paragraphs to a few pages and include only the essential elements of a report (introduction, body, conclusions, recommendations). And informal reports, because of their brevity, are customarily written as a letter (if the report is to be sent outside the company) or as a memorandum (if it is to be distributed within the firm).

WRITING THE REPORT

If you will be writing a report on an activity in which you are participating (a special project, for example), it's a good idea to collect information and keep notes as the activity progresses. You may have trouble obtaining all the information later on, when you prepare to write the report.

In determining what notes to take, include all the information that will meet the objective of your report (for example, whatever information will persuade your boss to adopt the plan of action you are proposing) and the needs of your reader (exactly the information that will enable your boss to understand your proposal and to see the logic and the benefits of it).

The purpose of taking notes is to record, in an abbreviated form, the information that will go into your report. The advantage of taking notes is that you don't have to rely on your memory to recall every detail at exactly the moment when you need to include it in your report. Be careful, however, not to make a note so brief that you forget what you intended when you wrote it. The critical test of a note is whether, a week later, you will still be able to recall all the information and significance that you had in mind when you made the note. (Notetaking is discussed in more detail in Chapter 12.)

Once you have prepared all your notes, organize your outline as explained in Chapter 4. Then work your notes into the appropriate places in your outline.

An informal report is almost always intended for one specific reader or for a small group of readers. Because you will know, in most cases, who your reader will be and how much technical background he or she has, you should be able to determine just how much specialized or technical language it would be appropriate to use. You should also have a good idea of how much background information it will be necessary to supply your reader.

THE PARTS OF THE REPORT

Most reports that you will be called on to write have at least three, and sometimes four, main parts: the introduction, the body, and recommendations and conclusions. The *introduction* should state the subject and the purpose of the report (for a brief informal report, a subject line may be adequate introduction). You may sometimes find it helpful to your reader if you mention in the introduction any conclusions you have drawn. The introduction may, if necessary, also provide any background information your reader might need in following the report. The *body* of the report should present a clearly organized account of the report's subject—the results of a test carried out, the status of a construction project, and so on. The amount of detail to include in the body depends upon the complexity of the subject and on your reader's familiarity with the subject. In the *conclusion* of the report, you should summarize your findings and tell the reader what you think their significance may be. Finally, your *recommendations* would be suggestions that you might make, based upon the data you have presented—suggestions, say, for instituting new work procedures, for setting up new departmental responsibilities, or for hiring new employees.

TYPES OF REPORTS

Because there are so many different types of informal reports, and because the categories sometimes overlap (a trip report, for example, might also be a progress report), it would be unrealistic to attempt to study every type. But it is possible to become familiar with report writing in general and to examine some of the most frequently written kinds of reports. In this chapter we will take up five: the trouble (or accident) report, the special-purpose report, the progress report, the trip report, and the test report. If you master the techniques of writing these five kinds, you should be able to prepare other informal reports as well.

Trouble Report

In almost any kind of work you may do, accidents, equipment failures, and work stoppages will occur. Every such incident must be reported, so that its cause can be determined and any necessary steps taken to prevent a recurrence. The record of an accident or a breakdown—a *trouble report,* or *accident report* as it is also called—may even be used by the police or by a court of law in establishing guilt or liability. Because it can be vital in preventing further injury or disruption in service, and because it may become legal evidence, a trouble report should be prepared as accurately, objectively, and promptly as possible.

The trouble report should normally be in the form of a memorandum written by the person in charge of the site where the incident occurred and addressed to his or her superior.* On the subject line of the memorandum, briefly state the nature of the incident you are reporting.

```
Subject: Personal-Injury Accident in Section A-40,
         October 10, 19--
```

Then, in the memorandum itself, get immediately to the point. State exactly when and where the accident or breakdown took place. Describe any physical injury or any property damage—no matter how slight—that occurred. Itemize any expenses that resulted from the incident (for example, an injured employee may have missed a number of work days, or an equipment failure may have caused a disruption in service to the company's customers). Since insurance claims, worker's compensation awards, and, in some instances, law suits may hinge on the information in a trouble report, be sure to include precise data on times, dates, locations, treatment of injuries, the names of any

---

* Some companies have printed forms for specific types of trouble reports, but even form reports include a section in which the writer must explain in detail what happened.

witnesses, and any other crucial information. Include in the report a detailed analysis of what you believe caused the trouble. Avoid any tone of condemnation or blame. Be thorough, exact, and objective, and support any opinion you offer with facts. Mention what has been or will be done to correct the conditions that may have led to the incident. Finally, present your recommendations for the prevention of a recurrence of the trouble (such as increased safety precautions, improved equipment, or the establishment of training programs). If you are speculating on the cause of the accident, make sure that this is clear to the reader; your guess is no doubt an educated one, but it still should be labeled as a guess.

The following trouble report was written by the foreman of a group of punch press operators and was addressed to the plant's safety officer, at the request of the safety officer. Since there were no witnesses, the foreman obtained the information for the report by talking to the plant nurse, to hospital personnel, and to the victim—and by inspecting the equipment being used by the victim at the time of the accident.

```
                           MEMORANDUM


To: James K. Arburg, Safety Officer
From: Lawrence T. Baker, Foreman of Section A-40
Date: November 30, 19--

Subject: Personal-Injury Accident in Section A-40,
         October 10, 19--


    On October 10, 19--, at 10:15 P.M., Jim Hollander,
operating punch press #16, accidentally brushed the knee
switch of his punch press with his right knee as he swung a
metal sheet over the punching surface. The switch activated
the punching unit, which severed Hollander's left thumb
between the first and second joints as his hand passed
through the punch station. While an ambulance was being
summoned, Margaret Wilson, R.N., administered first aid at
the plant dispensary. There were no witnesses to the
accident.
    The ambulance arrived from Mercy Hospital at 10:45
P.M., and Hollander was admitted to the emergency room at
the hospital at 11:00 P.M. He was treated and kept overnight
for observation, then released the next morning.
    Hollander returned to work one week later, on
October 17. He has been given temporary duties in the tool
room until his injury heals.
```

```
Conclusions About the Cause of the Accident

The Maxwell punch press on which Hollander was working has
two switches, a hand switch and a knee switch, and both
must be pressed to activate the punch mechanism. The hand
switch must be pressed first, and then the knee switch, to
trip the punch mechanism. The purpose of the knee switch
is to leave the operator's hands free to hold the panel
being punched. The hand switch, in contrast, is a safety
feature. Because the knee switch cannot activate the press
until the hand switch has been pressed, the operator cannot
trip the punching mechanism by touching the knee switch
accidentally.
     Inspection of the punch press that Hollander was
operating at the time of the accident made it clear that
Hollander had taped the hand switch of his machine in the
ON position, effectively eliminating its safety function.
He could then pick up a panel, swing it onto the machine's
punching surface, press the knee switch, stack the newly
punched panel, and grab the next unpunched panel, all in
one continuous motion--eliminating the need to let go of
the panel, after placing it on the punching surface, in
order to press the hand switch.
     To prevent a recurrence of this accident, I have
conducted a brief safety session with all punch press
operators, at which I described Hollander's experience and
cautioned them against tampering with the safety features
of their machines.
```

Trouble report

Special-Purpose Report

Although a *special-purpose report* may be written for a variety of reasons, it is most often produced in response to a request for information. You might be asked, for instance, to check the range of prices that companies charge for a particular item, to conduct an opinion survey among customers, to study a number of different procedures for performing a specific operation, to review a recently published work, and so on. You would then present your findings in a special-purpose report.

A special-purpose report is usually prepared as a memorandum. Open with a statement of the information you were seeking. Then define the extent of your investigation.

In the following example, an industrial training manager has asked the senior instructor to investigate and report on a method of preparing repair manuals that eliminates the need to translate the manuals into foreign languages. The report explains how the new method works and offers alternative ways in which it might be adopted by the report writer's company.

MEMORANDUM

To: Noreen Rinaldo, Training Manager
From: Charles Lapinski, Senior Instructor
Date: February 14,19--

Subject: The Addison Corporation's Basic English Program

     As you requested, I have investigated the subject
program to determine whether we might also adopt such a
program. The purpose of the Addison Basic English course is
to teach foreign mechanics who do not speak or read English
to understand repair manuals written in a special 800-word
vocabulary called "Basic English," and thus eliminate the
need for Addison to translate its manuals into a number of
different languages. The Basic English Program does not
attempt to teach the mechanics to be fluent in English but,
rather, to recognize the 800 basic words that appear in the
repair manuals.
     The course does not train mechanics. Students must
know, in their own language, what a word like _torque_ means;
the course simply teaches them the English term for it.
As prerequisites for the course, students must have a basic
knowledge of their trade, must be able to identify a part in
an illustrated parts book, must have served as a mechanic
on Addison products for at least one year, and must be able
to read and write in their own language.
     Students are given the specially prepared instruction
manual, an illustrated book of parts and their English
names, and a pocket reference containing all 800 words of
the Basic English vocabulary plus the English names of parts
(students can write the corresponding word in their language
beside the English words and then use the pocket reference
as a bilingual dictionary). The course consists of thirty
two-hour lessons, each lesson introducing approximately 27
words. No effort is made to teach pronunciation; the course
teaches only recognition of the 800 words, which include
450 nouns, 70 verbs, 180 adjectives and adverbs, and 100
articles, prepositions, conjunctions, and pronouns.
     The 800-word vocabulary enables the writers of the
manuals to provide mechanics with any information that
might be required, because the area of communication is
strictly limited to maintenance, inspection, trouble-
shooting, safety, and the operation of Addison equipment.
All nonessential words (such as _apple_, _father_, _mountain_, and
so on) have been eliminated, as have most synonyms (for
example, _under_ appears, but _beneath_ does not).

Conclusions

I see three possible ways in which we might be able to use
some or all of the elements of the Basic English Program:
(1) in the preparation of all our student manuals, (2) in

the preparation of student manuals for the international students in our service school, or (3) as Addison uses the program.

I think it would be unnecessary to use the Basic English methods in the preparation of student manuals for <u>all</u> our students. Most of our students are English-speaking people to whom an unrestricted vocabulary presents no problem.

In conjunction with the preparation of student manuals for international students, the program might have more appeal. Students would take the Basic English course either before coming to this country to attend school or after arriving but before beginning their technical training.

As for our initiating a Basic English Program similar to Addison's, we could create our own version of the Basic English vocabulary and write our service manuals in it. Since our product lines are much broader than Addison's, however, we would need to create illustrated parts books for each of the different product lines.

Special-purpose report

Progress Report

The purpose of a *progress report* is to keep an individual or a group—usually management—informed of the status of a project. In answering the questions Is the project on schedule? Is it staying within its budget? Is the staff running into any unexpected snags?, the report lets the reader know precisely what work has been completed and what work remains to be done. Often the report will include recommendations for changes in procedure or will propose new courses of action.

Projects that are most likely to generate progress reports are those that last for a considerable period of time and are fairly complex. The construction of a building, the development of a new product, or the opening of a branch office in another part of town are examples of such projects. Sometimes, too, a progress report is a specified requirement in the contract for a project.

The chief value of a progress report is that it allows management not only to check on the status of a project but to make any necessary adjustments in assignments, schedules, and budget allocations while the project is under way. Project reports can make it easier for management to schedule the arrival of equipment and supplies so that they will be available when they are needed. And such reports can, on occasion, avert crises. If a hospital had planned to open a new wing in February, for instance, but a shortage of wallboard caused a two-month lag in construction, a progress report would alert hospital managers to the delay—in time for them to prepare alternate plans.

HOBARD CONSTRUCTION COMPANY
9032 Salem Avenue
Lubbock, Texas 79409

(806) 769-0823

August 17, 19--

John H. Mambert,
City Manager
109 Main Street
Lubbock, Texas 79416

Subject: Rewiring the Sports Arena

Dear Mr. Mambert:

The rewiring program at the Sports Arena is progressing on schedule and within budget. Although the cost of certain equipment is higher than our original bid had indicated, we expect to complete the project without exceeding the estimated costs, because the speed with which the project is being completed will reduce overall labor expenses.

Equipment used up to now has cost $10,800, and labor costs have been $31,500 (including some subcontracted plumbing). Our estimate for the remainder of the equipment, based on discussions with your lighting consultant, is $11,500; remaining labor costs should not be in excess of $25,500.

As of August 15, we have finished the installation of the circuit breaker panels and meters, of level-one service outlets, and of all subfloor wiring. The upgrading of stage-lighting equipment, the installation of level-two service outlets, and the replacement of lighting fixtures are in the preliminary stages (the wiring has been completed, but installation of the fixtures has not yet begun).

We have scheduled the upgrading of stage-lighting equipment to take place from August 16 to October 5, the installation of level-two service outlets from October 6 to November 12, and the replacement of lighting fixtures from November 15 to December 17. We see no difficulty in having the arena finished for the December 23 Christmas program, as specified in our contract.

Sincerely yours,

William L. Hobard

William L. Hobard

WLH/jsi

Progress report

Many projects, of course, will require more than one progress report. In general, the more complicated the project, the more frequently management will want to review it. The reports should be released at regular intervals (once every three weeks, once every two months, and the like), and all reports issued during the life of a project should be of the same format. Project reports to be sent outside the company are normally prepared as letters; otherwise, they can be written as memorandums. The first in a series of reports should identify the project in detail and specify what materials will be used and what procedures will be followed throughout the project. Later reports will contain only a transitional introduction that briefly reviews the work discussed in the previous reports. The body of the reports should describe in detail the current status of the project. And every report should end with any conclusions or recommendations—alterations in schedule, materials, or procedures, for instance.

In the example on page 224, a contractor reports to the city manager on his progress in rewiring a city-owned arena. Notice that the emphasis is on meeting specified costs and schedules.

Trip Report

Many companies require or encourage reports of the business trips their employees take. A *trip report* not only provides a permanent record of a business trip and its accomplishments but also enables many employees to benefit from the information one employee has gained.

A trip report should be in memorandum format, addressed to your immediate superior. On the subject line give the destination and dates of the trip. The body of the report will explain why you made the trip, who you visited, and what you accomplished. The report should devote a brief section to each major event and may include a head for each section (you needn't give equal space to each event but, instead, elaborate on the more important events). Follow the body of the report with any appropriate conclusions and recommendations.

A sample trip report appears on page 226.

Test Reports

The *test report,* also called the *laboratory report* or the *investigative report,* records the results of tests and experiments. Normally, those who write test reports do so as a routine part of their work. Tests that form the bases of reports are not limited to any particular occupation; they commonly occur in many fields, from chemistry to fire science, from physics to home economics, from metallurgy to medical technology, and include studies on cars, blood, mercury thermometers, pudding mixes, smoke detectors—the list is endless.

MEMORANDUM

To: Manuel Cruz, Manager, Customer Relations

From: Isoroku Somoto, Field Service Engineer

Date: May 31, 19—

Subject: Trip to Inspect New Power Unit Installations,
         May 26–30

    The purpose of this trip was to inspect the installa-
tion of Taylor Auxilliary Power Units in five hospitals and
to train the maintenance staffs at those hospitals to
operate the units during a commercial power failure. I
visited the New Orleans General Hospital on the 26th, Our
Lady of Mercy Hospital in San Antonio on the 27th, Dallas
Presbyterian Hospital on the 28th, St. Elizabeth Hospital in
Oklahoma City on the 29th, and the Jefferson Davis Memorial
Hospital in Atlanta on the 30th.
    At each site, I found that the installation of the
equipment had been done properly. I made arrangements, in
each hospital, with the administrative office and then
placed the hospital on auxilliary power for one hour as a
trial run. In every location, the transfer from commercial
power to auxilliary power was made without problems.
    After inspecting the equipment and its installation, I
held a brief training session with the maintenance staff.
The training consisted of instruction in starting the
unit's engine, in operating the generator's controls to
produce 220 volts of electricity at 60 Hertz, and in activat-
ing the operating unit in the event of a commercial power
failure.
    In all five hospitals, both the administrative and
maintenance staffs appeared to have a favorable opinion of
the Taylor Power Equipment Company, its product, and its
field personnel. Our sales staff and installers seem to be
doing a good job.

Trip report

Biospherics, Inc.
4928 Wyaconda Road
Rockville, MD 20852

March 14, 19--

Mr. John Sebastiani, General Manager
Midtown Development Corporation
114 West Jefferson Street
Milwaukee, WI 53201

Subject: Results of Analysis of Soil Samples for Arsenic

Dear Mr. Sebastiani:

Following are the results of the analysis of 22 soil samples for arsenic. The arsenic values listed are based on a wet-weight determination. The moisture content of the soil is also given to allow conversion of the results to a dry-weight basis if desired.

Hole Number	Depth	Percent of Moisture	Arsenic Total As ppm
1	12"	19.0	312.0
2	Surface	11.2	737.0
3	12"	12.7	9.5
4	12"	10.8	865.0
5	12"	17.1	4.1
6	12"	14.2	6.1
7	12"	24.2	2540.0
8	Surface	13.6	460.0

I noticed that some of the samples contained large amounts of metallic iron coated with rust. Arsenic tends to be absorbed into soils high in iron, aluminum, and calcium oxides. The large amount of iron present in some of these soil samples is probably responsible for retaining high levels of arsenic. The soils highest in iron, aluminum, and calcium oxides should also show the highest levels of arsenic, provided the soils have had approximately equal levels of arsenic exposure.

If I can be of further assistance, please do not hesitate to contact me.

Yours truly,

Gunther Gottfried
Chemist

GG/jrm

Test report I

Biospherics, Inc.
4928 Wyaconda Road
Rockville, MD 20852

September 9, 19--

Mr. Leon Hite, Administrator
The Angle Company, Inc.
1869 Slauson Boulevard
Waynesville, VA 23927

Dear Mr. Hite:

On Tuesday, 30 August, Biospherics, Inc., performed asbestos-in-air monitoring at your Route 66 construction site, near Front Royal, Virginia. Six persons and three construction areas were monitored.

All monitoring and analyses were performed in accordance with "Occupational Exposure to Asbestos," U.S. Department of Health, Education, and Welfare, Public Health Service, National Institute for Occupational Safety and Health, 1972. Each worker or area was fitted with a battery-powered personal sampler pump operating at a flow rate of approximately one liter per minute. The airborne asbestos was collected on a 37-mm Millipore type AA filter mounted in an open-face filter holder. Samples were collected over an 8-hour period.

A wedge-shaped piece of each filter was mounted on a microscope slide with a drop of 1:1 solution of dimethyl phthalate and diethyl oxalate and then covered with a cover clip. Samples were counted within 24 hours after mounting, using a microscope with phase contrast option.

In all cases, the workers and areas monitored were exposed to levels of asbestos fibers well below the NIOSH standard. The highest exposure found was that of a driller who was exposed to 0.21 fibers per cubic centimeter. The driller's sample was analyzed by scanning electron microscopy followed by energy dispersive X-ray techniques which identify the chemical nature of each fiber, thereby verifying the fibers as asbestos or identifying them as other fiber types. Results from these analyses show that the fibers present are tremolite asbestos. No nonasbestos fibers were found.

Yours truly,

Gary Willis

Gary Willis
Chemist

GW/jrm
Enclosures

Test report II

Information collected in testing may be used to upgrade products or to stream-line procedures.

Because the accuracy of a test report is essential, be sure to take careful notes while you are performing the test. When you prepare the report, state your findings in clear, straightforward language. Since a test report should be as objective as possible, it is one of the few writing formats in which the passive voice is usually more suitable than the active voice (see Chapter 6). A test report may be either a letter or a memorandum.

On the subject line, identify the test you are reporting on. If the purpose of the test is not obvious to your reader, explain it in the body of the report. Then, if it is helpful to your reader, outline the testing procedures. You needn't give a detailed explanation of how the test was performed; rather, provide just enough information for your reader to have a general idea of the testing methods. Next, present the data—the results of the test. If an interpretation of the results would be useful to your reader, furnish such an analysis in your conclusion. Close the report with any recommendations you are making as a result of the test.

The letter on page 227 is one example of a test report. This report does not explain how the test was conducted, because such an explanation is unnecessary. Compare this report with the one on page 228, which does explain how the tests were performed.

CHAPTER SUMMARY

Much on-the-job writing consists of various kinds of reports. Informal reports, normally no longer than a few pages, may take the form of a memorandum that circulates within an organization or be prepared as a letter to be sent to someone outside the organization.

The *introduction* of an informal report should state the report's subject and its purpose. In addition, the introduction may state the writer's conclusions and recommendations. The *body* of an informal report should present a detailed account of the work or activity being reported on. Any *conclusions* and *recommendations* the writer wishes to offer should close the report.

A *trouble report,* the record of an accident, breakdown, or work stoppage, is usually written as a memorandum. The writer should identify the precise time and place of the trouble, any injury or property damage involved, and any expenses that resulted from the incident. The report should continue with a detailed analysis of the likely cause of the accident or breakdown and conclude with a statement of what is being done or what will be done to prevent a recurrence of the incident.

A *special-purpose report* is, in most cases, the presentation of data that the writer has gathered. The report, ordinarily in memorandum format, opens with a statement of the information the writer has sought and goes on to define the extent of the investigation. The report then presents the writer's findings and an interpretation of them if such an analysis is appropriate. The report ends with conclusions and/or recommendations.

A *progress report* informs the reader of the status of an ongoing project, frequently one that lasts a fairly long period of time and thus may generate a series of progress reports issued at regular intervals. A progress report, by stating precisely what work has been done and what work remains to be completed, can alert the reader to any necessary adjustments in scheduling, budgeting, and work assignments.

A *trip report,* generally a memorandum submitted to the writer's immediate superior following a business trip, includes the destination and the dates of the trip in the subject line. The body of the report explains why the trip was made, who was visited, and what was accomplished. Any conclusions and/or recommendations the writer wishes to present would come at the end of the report.

A *test report* gives the results of a test or experiment. The test reported on is identified in the subject line. The body of the report states the purpose of the test and, if it is appropriate, explains the procedures used to conduct the test. The results of the test, and any interpretations the writer considers helpful to the reader, appear in the body. The report closes with any recommendations the writer may be making as a result of the test.

EXERCISES

1. Write a *trouble,* or *accident, report* in the form of a memo to your instructor on a recent incident or accident with which you are familiar. Be specific and detailed. If appropriate, make recommendations about how similar incidents can be prevented. Your instructor will specify report length.

2. Write one of the following *accident reports* in the form of a memo.

    a. You are the traffic manager of a trucking company that has had four highway accidents within a one-week period. Using the following facts, write a *trouble report* to your company president, Millard Spangler.
    - Your company operates intrastate (your state).
    - The four accidents occurred in different parts of the state and on different dates (specify the date and location of each).
    - Each accident has resulted in damage not only to the truck (specify the dollar amount of the damage) but to the cargo as well (specify the type of cargo and the dollar amount of the damage).
    - Only one of the accidents involved another vehicle (truck swerved into a parked car when a tire blew out). Give the make and year of the damaged car and its owner's name.

- Only one of the accidents involved injury to a company driver (give the name).
- Your maintenance division traced the accidents to faulty tires, all the same brand (identify the brand), and all purchased at the same time and place (identify the place and date).
- The tires have now been replaced and your insurance company, Acme Underwriters, has brought suit against the tire manufacturer to recover damages, including lost business while the four trucks are being repaired (specify the dollar amount of the lost business).

b. You are the dietitian at a hospital. A fire has occurred in the cafeteria, which is under your supervision. Using the following information, write a trouble report to the hospital's administrator, Mildred Garnett.

- The chief cook, Pincus Berkowitz, came to work at 5:30 a.m. (specify the date).
- He turned on the gas jets under the grill. The pilot light had gone out, and the jets did not light.
- The cook went to find a match, neglecting to turn off the gas jets.
- He found matches, returned, and lit a match, thus igniting the accumulated gas under the grill.
- The resulting explosion destroyed the grill (estimate the damage) and injured the cook.
- The fire was put out by the security force, but the fire department was called as a precaution.
- The cook was treated by the emergency room physician, then admitted to the hospital's burn unit as a patient, with second-degree burns on his hands, face, and neck.
- He was hospitalized three days and will be off work four weeks.

3. You have been asked to provide information on *one* of the following topics. Gather the information pertinent to the topic and present the information in a *special-purpose report*. Your instructor will specify the length of the assignment.

   a. your energy-consumption habits at home
   b. your recommendation on the best hotel or motel in your area for out-of-town guests
   c. which of two local garages that have serviced your car you would recommend to a friend
   d. which of two local charities you think more worthy of support (specify from among charities in your area)
   e. which of two or more products or services you use at home or on the job you would recommend to someone and why

4. As the medical staff secretary at a hospital, you must write a *progress report* to the director of the hospital outlining the current status of the annual reappointment of committees. Using the following facts, write the report.

- A total of 19 committees must be staffed.
- The Chief of Staff has telephoned each person selected to chair a committee, and you have sent each of them a follow-up letter of thanks from the Chief of Staff.
- You have written letters to all physicians who are currently on committees but are not being reappointed, informing them of this fact.
- You have written letters to all physicians being asked to serve on committees.
- You expect to receive replies only from those physicians declining the appointment by the 15th of the following month.
- Once committee assignments have been completed, you will type up the membership of all committees and distribute them to the complete medical staff.

5. Write a *trip report* for a trip you have recently taken. The trip may have been a class trip, a job-related trip, or a personal trip.

6. Submit a laboratory *test report,* written in memo form, from a laboratory class that you are taking or have taken.

12

Researching Your Subject

pick out something ∝ quote
paraphrase it
summarize

When Tom Cabines, the production manager, received a memo from Alice Enkend, chief of the Purchasing Department, asking him how many copies of its holiday calendar a customer had commissioned the firm to print, Tom probably had the answer at his fingertips or would be able to find it after a quick look in his production-scheduling book. The *research*—or tracking down of information on the topic—that Tom might have to do would be minimal. Suppose, though, that Tom was asked to review current literature on new developments in printing or marketing techniques and to write a report on the subject. How would he go about obtaining the necessary information? For these tasks he *would* have to do some research. He'd probably go first to the library—either the company library, if the firm had one, or the public library.

This chapter will discuss the research facilities most libraries provide, and then go on to consider several other sources of information for a research report: the personal interview, the questionnaire, first-hand observation, and free or inexpensive materials from private and governmental bodies. The chapter will also discuss techniques for systematically recording your research findings (notetaking), for furnishing proper credit to your sources (footnoting), and for preparing a bibliography (organized list of the books, magazine and newspaper articles, personal interviews, and so on that constituted your research).

IN THE LIBRARY

The key tools of library research are the *card catalog,* which represents a listing of every book the library owns; *periodical indexes,* which furnish the names of articles in journals, magazines, and newspapers; and published *bibliographies,* which contain the names of books and other materials available on a given subject. In addition to the card catalog, indexes, and bibliographies, most libraries have a number of *reference works:* almanacs, atlases, dictionaries devoted to special subjects (of musical terms, medical terms, and so on), encyclopedias, and manuals. You may find reference books especially helpful in providing a brief, easy-to-locate overview of your subject. Many libraries have a reference librarian, who can give you the specific details of the reference works in the library.

Card Catalog

The *card catalog* is a listing of all the books a library owns. A card catalog can furnish the answers to some questions that are vital to you as a researcher: Does the library own a particular book or one or more books by a particular author? What books, if any, on a specific subject does the library own? Where in the library is a given book located?

For most books, there are three cards on file in the catalog: an *author card* (Figure 12-1), a *title card* (Figure 12-2), and a *subject card* (Figure 12-3). Every card is arranged in the catalog alphabetically. Thus, an author card appears under the author's last name; a title card is alphabetized by the first important word in the title (*A, An,* and *The* at the beginning of a title are ignored in alphabetizing); and a subject card is filed alphabetically by the first word of the subject heading. All three types of card contain the book's "vital statistics": author's name; title; date and place of publication; publisher's name; number of pages; the term *illus., bibliography,* or *index* if the book has illustrations, bibliography, or index; the size of the book in centimeters; the major subjects the book covers; and, sometimes, additional information.

If you want to locate a book whose title and/or author you know, you can look in the card catalog for the book under either its title or its author's name. If, on the other hand, you are trying to find a book on a particular subject and do not have a title or an author in mind, you can look through the card catalog

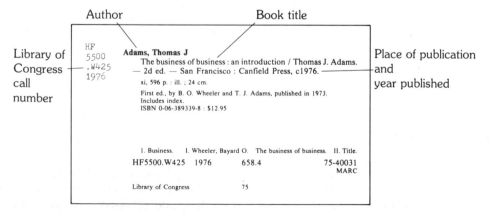

FIGURE 12-1. Author card

Title

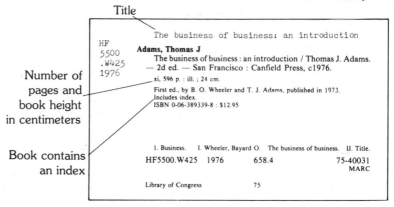

Number of pages and book height in centimeters

Book contains an index

FIGURE 12-2. Title card

Subject category of this book

Subjects that the book covers and other subjects in the card catalog where related information can be found

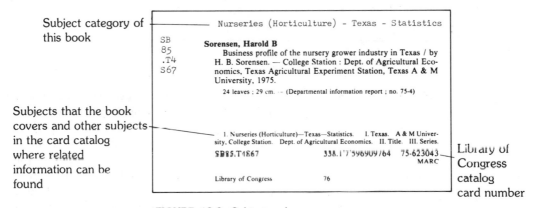

Library of Congress catalog card number

FIGURE 12-3. Subject card

for the subject card or cards that correspond to the subject you are researching. For example, if you were trying to locate information on the plant nursery business, you would look at the cards in back of the letter *N* in the card catalog and go alphabetically through the *N*'s until you reach the subject cards under the heading *Nurseries*. Included under that broad heading would be a number of specific topics. The books under one subject heading are arranged alphabetically by authors' last names.

The sample card in Figure 12-3 refers to a report on the nursery business in Texas.

Some subject cards do not list a particular book but, instead, provide "see also" subject headings that the researcher may want to consult in tracking down additional books (Figure 12-4).

A *call number,* which indicates where on the shelves (or stacks) a book can be found, is located in the upper-left-hand corner of all three cards. The same call number normally appears on the lower portion of the spine of the book itself. Libraries use one or both of two systems of *classification*—that is, the system under which every book is assigned an identifying call number: the

```
        Florida.   State Board of Conservation.
          Marine Laboratory, St. Petersburg.

        see also

        Florida Board of Conservation Marine Research
          Laboratory.
```

FIGURE 12-4. "See also" subject card.

older system is the Dewey Decimal System; the newer system is the Library of Congress System. Check with the librarian about which system or systems your library uses.

You can frequently tell from a book's title what the book is about. Another factor to take into account as you decide whether to include a particular book in your research is the author's reputation: Is the writer considered an authority in the field? Has the author written other, well-thought-of books in the field or in a related field? You might check in the card catalog under the author's name to see what other books, if any, the author has written. And you might ask a librarian, an instructor, or someone you know who is familiar with the subject area whether the author has an established reputation in the field. Still another guide in determining whether the book will be useful to you in your research is the book itself (if necessary, you can examine the book in the library before deciding whether to use it). Does the book have an index? Indexes are indispensable in tracking down specific topics within a book. Does the book have informative diagrams, charts, tables, and so on? Does the book have a comprehensive bibliography that you can use in locating additional material for your research? Is the book reasonably up-to-date? Timeliness is especially important in a fast-changing field like computer technology.

For any book that you decide to include in your research, prepare a 3″ × 5″ note card, with the following information on it: the call number (having the call number handy will enable you to locate the book on the shelves); the author (if the "author" is an organization, indicate that fact); the city of publication; the publisher's name; and the year of publication. When you are ready to prepare a bibliography for your research report, you can do so easily from the information you have recorded on these cards (known as *bibliography*

```
QA
76.5
.K382

          Kemeny, John G.

          Man and the Computer
          N.Y. : Scribner, 1972
```

FIGURE 12-5. Bibliography card—book

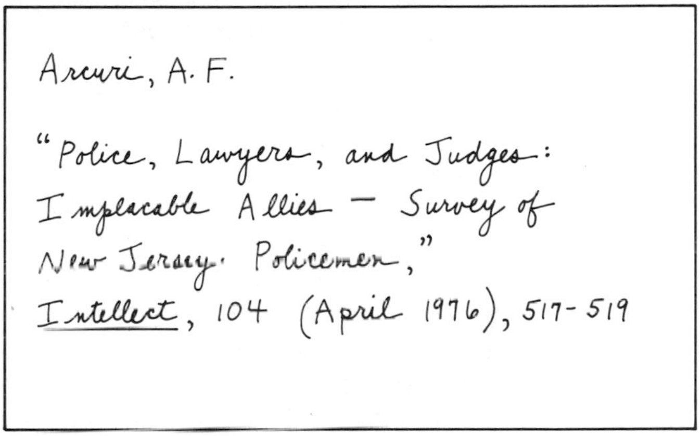

```
Arcuri, A. F.

"Police, Lawyers, and Judges:
I mplacable Allies — Survey of
New Jersey. Policemen,"
Intellect, 104 (April 1976), 517-519
```

FIGURE 12-6. Bibliography card—periodical

cards). See Figure 12-5 for a bibliography card for a book and Figure 12-6 for a bibliography card for an article in a periodical. Having the author's last name near the upper-left-hand corner of the card will assist you in preparing the bibliography, in which the titles of the books and articles you used are arranged alphabetically according to the authors' last names.

Periodical Indexes and Bibliographies

Periodical indexes and bibliographies are lists of journal articles and books. *Periodical indexes* are devoted specifically to journal, magazine, and newspaper articles (the term *periodical* is applied to publications that are issued at regular intervals—daily, weekly, monthly, and so on). *Bibliographies* list books, periodicals, and other research materials published in a particular subject area, such as business, engineering, medicine, the humanities, and the social sciences.

After you have selected the periodical indexes and bibliographies that deal with your subject, consult the instructions in the front of the volume or in the first volume of a series. There you will find a key to the abbreviations and symbols used in the volume and an explanation of the way in which information is arranged in the books, as well as a listing of the specific subjects covered and, for periodical indexes, a listing of the newspapers, magazines, and journals that have been included in the work.

Some of the bibliographies and indexes that you are likely to find useful are the following.

Applied Science and Technology Index (formerly *Industrial Arts Index*), 1913—. (Alphabetical subject listing of over 50,000 periodicals; issued monthly)

Bibliographic Index: A Cumulative Bibliography of Bibliographies, 1937—. (Subject list of bibliographies that appear separately or in books; issued three times a year)

Bibliography and Index to Geology, 1969—. (Bibliography of world literature dealing with the earth sciences; entries are arranged within 29 subject areas; issued monthly)

Bibliography of Agriculture, 1942—. (Listing of literature covering agriculture and allied subjects; issued monthly)

Biological and Agricultural Index, 1964—. (Alphabetical subject listing of biological and agricultural periodicals; issued monthly)

Business Periodicals Index, 1958—. (Alphabetically arranged by subject and title; issued monthly)

Cumulative Index of the National Industrial Conference Board Publications, 1962—. (Subject index of publications of interest to commerce and industrial managers; issued annually)

Cumulative Index to Nursing Literature, 1965—. (Subject and author index to nursing journals)

Engineering Index, 1906. (Alphabetically arranged by subject; issued monthly)

Essay and General Literature Index, 1900—. (Semiannual index to information on all subjects in collections of articles. Organized by subject, but sometimes by title)

Government Reports Index (formerly *U.S. Government Research and Development Reports*), 1965—. (A semimonthly index of reports arranged by subject, author, and report number)

Index of Labor Union Periodicals, 1960—. (Monthly index of articles from labor union periodicals)

Index of Supermarket Articles, 1963—. (Subject index of articles on supermarkets and the food industry)

Monthly Catalog of U.S. Government Publications, 1895—. (Lists unclassified publications of all federal agencies by subject, author, and report number)

New York Times Index, 1851—. (Alphabetically arranged listing of subjects covered in *New York Times* articles; issued bimonthly)

Readers' Guide to Periodical Literature, 1900—. (Monthly index of general U.S. periodicals, arranged alphabetically by subject)

Social Sciences Index, 1974—. (Alphabetical subject and author listing of social science periodicals; issued quarterly)

Wall Street Journal Index, 1958—. (Monthly index of business and financial news covered in the *Journal*)

Perhaps the most frequently used index is *Readers' Guide to Periodical Literature.* As a general-purpose reference, *Readers' Guide* contains entries from a wide range of popular, professional, and scientific periodicals. Articles are indexed alphabetically both by author's name and by subject area. The sample entry below (Figure 12-7), from *Readers' Guide,* deals with articles about the police. The main entry, "Police," is followed by the listing of an article on the general subject of "Police" and then by a number of "see also" subject areas under which additional articles on police-related topics are listed. Then come several subheads, "Attitudes," "Equipment and Supplies," and others, in alphabetical order. Under the subhead "Attitudes," the article "Police, Lawyers, and Judges: Implacable Allies," by A. F. Arcuri, is listed. The article can be found in *Intellect* magazine, volume 104, April 1976, on pages 517–519. The entry includes a brief summary of the article's contents.

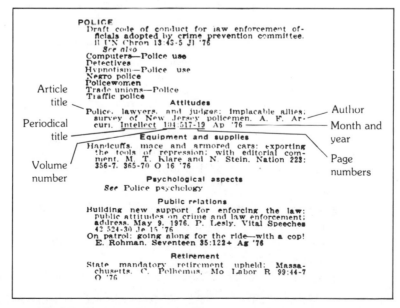

FIGURE 12-7. Entry from *Readers' Guide*

If the Arcuri article seemed useful to your research, you would prepare a 3″ × 5″ note card for the entry, including on the card the information that *Readers' Guide* has provided about the article.

After completing your search for periodical articles, locate the necessary periodical volumes in the stacks. Many libraries shelve periodicals alphabetically by title in a separate section of the library. If the periodicals you need are not in your library, you can submit an interlibrary loan request. This service permits you to borrow books and photocopied periodical articles from other libraries that have the materials you need in their collections. Consult your librarian for specific details of the system.

Reference Works

Additional sources of information that may prove helpful include encyclopedias, specialized dictionaries, handbooks and manuals, various statistical sources, and atlases.

Encyclopedias are comprehensive, multivolume collections of articles, usually arranged alphabetically and often illustrated. Some encyclopedias cover a wide range of general subjects, while others specialize in a particular subject. *General encyclopedias* provide the researcher with an overview of a particular subject that can be helpful to someone new to a subject. As a source of background information, the articles in general encyclopedias usually include the terminology essential to an understanding of the subject. Some articles contain bibliographies that can lead the researcher to additional information. The two best-known general encyclopedias are

Encyclopedia Americana. New York: Grolier. 30 volumes.

Encyclopaedia Britannica. Chicago: Encyclopaedia Britannica, Inc. 24 volumes.

Subject encyclopedias provide detailed information on all aspects of a particular field of knowledge. Their treatment of a subject is sufficiently thorough to make it desirable that the researcher have some background information on the subject in order to use the information to full advantage. There are many more specialized encyclopedias than there are general encyclopedias. The following list indicates the range available.

Encyclopedia of Chemical Technology, 2nd. ed. Completely rev. New York: Interscience Publishers, 1970.

Heyel, Carl, ed. *The Encyclopedia of Management,* 2nd. ed. New York: Van Nostrand Reinhold, 1973.

Hopke, William, ed. *The Encyclopedia of Careers and Vocational Guidance.* Rev. ed. Chicago: Ferguson, 1972. 2 vols.

International Encyclopedia of the Social Sciences. New York: Crowell Collier and Macmillan, 1968. 2 vols.

McGraw-Hill Encyclopedia of Science and Technology. New York: McGraw-Hill, 1971. 15 vols.

Dictionaries contain definitions, arranged in alphabetical order, of a selection of the words in a language or subject. They also contain information on how words are spelled and pronounced, how they are divided into syllables, and where they originated. *General English-language dictionaries* will provide the meanings of terms from numerous fields of knowledge. For the meanings of words too specialized for a general dictionary, a subject dictionary is useful. *Subject dictionaries* define the basic and specialized terms used in a particular field, such as business, geography, architecture, and consumer affairs. Definitions in subject dictionaries are generally more current and complete than those found in general dictionaries.

Chapter 9 lists a selection of desk-size English-language dictionaries. Unabridged dictionaries, which are larger and more comprehensive in their coverage, often contain basic terms from many specialized subjects. The three major up-to-date, unabridged English-language dictionaries are

Funk & Wagnalls New Standard Dictionary. New York: Funk & Wagnalls, 1964.

The Random House Dictionary of the English Language. New York: Random House, 1966.

Webster's New International Dictionary of the English Language. 3rd. ed. Springfield, Mass.: Merriam, 1971.

Following is a selection of subject dictionaries.

A Dictionary of Paper. 3rd. ed. New York: American Pulp and Paper Association, 1965.

Dictionary of the Environmental Sciences. Palo Alto, Calif.: National Press Books, 1973.

Dorland's Illustrated Medical Dictionary. 25th ed. Philadelphia: Saunders, 1974.

Harris, C. M., ed. *Dictionary of Architecture and Construction.* New York: McGraw-Hill, 1975.

McGraw-Hill Dictionary of Scientific and Technical Terms. New York: McGraw-Hill, 1976.

Monkhouse, F. J., ed. *A Dictionary of Geography.* 2nd. ed. Chicago: Aldine, 1970.

University Dictionary of Business and Finance. New York: Thomas Y. Crowell, 1967.

Handbooks and manuals are usually one-volume compilations of frequently used information in a particular field of knowledge. The information can include brief definitions of terms or concepts, explanations of how certain organizations function, graphs and tables that display basic numerical data, maps, and the like. They are a ready source of fundamental information about a subject, although they are usually intended for the researcher with a basic knowledge of the subject, particularly in scientific or technical fields. Every field has its own handbook or manual; the following listing shows some typical examples.

Becker, Ester, and Evelyn Anders. *The Successful Secretary's Handbook.* New York: Harper & Row, 1971.

CRC Handbook of Chemistry and Physics. Cleveland, Ohio: Chemical Rubber Company. Annual.

Environment Regulation Handbook. New York: Special Studies Division of Environment Information Center, 1973.

Merritt, F. S., ed. *Building Construction Handbook,* 3rd. ed. New York: McGraw-Hill, 1975.

Russell, M. M. *The Blue Book of Occupational Education.* New York: CCM Information Corp., 1971.

U.S. Government Manual. Washington, D.C.: Government Printing Office. Annual.

Statistical sources are collections of numerical data. They are the best source for such information as the height of the Washington Monument; the population of Boise, Idaho; the cost-of-living in Aspen, Colorado; and the annual number of motorcycle fatalities in the United States. The answers to many statistical reference questions can be found in almanacs and encyclopedias. The answers to difficult or comprehensive questions, however, can be found in works devoted exclusively to statistical data, a selection of which follows:

American Statistics Index. Washington, D.C.: Congressional Information Service, 1978 to date. Monthly, quarterly, and annual supplements.

The *Statistics Index* lists all statistical publications issued by agencies of the United States government. The publications cited include periodicals, reports, special surveys, and pamphlets.

Bureau of the Census. *County and City Data Book.* Washington, D.C.: Government Printing Office, 1952 to date. Irregular.

The *Data Book* includes a variety of data from cities, counties, congressional districts, metropolitan areas, and the like. The information, arranged by geographic and political areas, covers such topics as climate, dwellings, population characteristics, school districts, employment, and city finances.

Bureau of the Census. *Statistical Abstract of the United States.* Washington,
   D.C.: Government Printing Office, 1879 to date. Annual.

The *Statistical Abstract* includes statistics on the social, political and economic
condition of the United States. Compiled by the Bureau of the Census, the
data covers broad topics like population, education, public land, and vital
statistics. Some state and regional data are included.
   An *atlas* is a collection of maps. Atlases are classified into two broad categories based on the type of information they present—general maps that
represent physical and political boundaries, and thematic maps that represent a special subject, such as climate, population, natural resources, or agricultural products. Listed below are several well-known general atlases.

Hammond Medallion World Atlas. New Census ed. Maplewood, N.J.: C. S.
   Hammond, 1971.
National Geographic Atlas of the World. 3rd. ed. Washington, D.C.: National
   Geographic Society, 1970.
Rand McNally New Cosmopolitan World Atlas. Planet Earth ed. Chicago:
   Rand McNally, 1971.
The Times Atlas of the World. Comprehensive ed. Boston: Houghton Mifflin,
   1971.

The following are thematic atlases.

Department of Agriculture. *Atlas of United States Trees* Washington, D.C.:
   Government Printing Office, 1971.
Environmental Science Services Administration. *Climatic Atlas of the United
   States.* Washington, D.C.: Government Printing Office, 1968.

TAKING NOTES

The purpose of taking notes is to condense and record information from the
books and articles you have chosen for your research. The notes you take will
furnish much of the material for your outline and final written work.
   For your notes, you may use either 3″ × 5″ or 4″ × 6″ cards—but which-
ever you choose, stick to that size, because, when you arrange the cards by
topic later on, you may have trouble handling cards of two different sizes. You
may well find that the larger-size card is handier: it provides more room for the
information, and is readily distinguishable from the 3″ × 5″ bibliography cards.
Make one note per card, on one side of the card only; use ink, since pencil
tends to smudge. Near the bottom of each card, identify the source of the
information: put in the author's last name (include first name or initials if you
have two authors with the same last name) and the page number or numbers
on which the material appears in the original source. If you have consulted

more than one book or article by an author, include the title as well; for long titles, you may use a shortened form to save space on the card. And be sure to put information from only one source on each card.

As you are taking notes, it's a good idea to make a list of the topics that you will be covering in your research. Then, on the upper-left-hand corner of each note card, enter the appropriate identifying topic (these are sometimes called "slugs"). When you arrange the cards by topic in preparation for working up an outline, you can use the "slugs" as a guide in organizing your material.

Notes can be gathered in one of three ways. The information can be quoted word for word from the original source, as a *direct quotation;* it can be *paraphrased,* or restated in the researcher's own words; or it can be *summarized,* or stated by the researcher in a highly condensed (or shortened) form.

Quoting Directly

A *direct quotation* is an exact, word-for-word copy of an original source. Such quotations, which can be of a word, of a phrase, of a sentence, or, occasionally, of a paragraph, should be used sparingly and chosen carefully. A direct quotation is appropriate when the wording of the original source will confirm, or support, a point you are making, or when you feel that your reader will gain some insight from a particularly well expressed passage. In both instances, the quoted material should be fairly brief. In addition, such material as policy state-

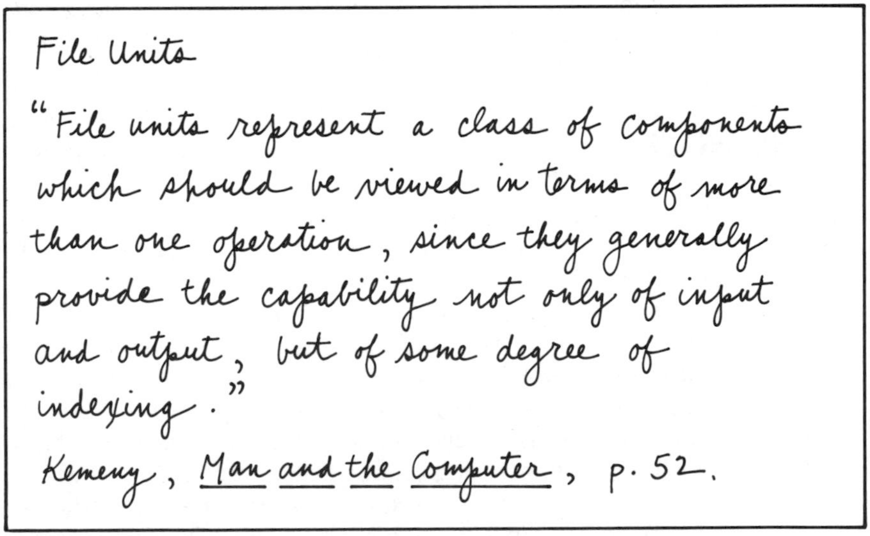

File Units

" File units represent a class of components which should be viewed in terms of more than one operation, since they generally provide the capability not only of input and output, but of some degree of indexing."
Kemeny, Man and the Computer, p. 52.

FIGURE 12-8. Note card—direct quotation

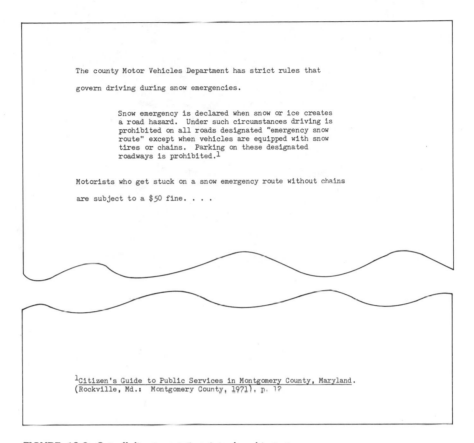

The county Motor Vehicles Department has strict rules that

govern driving during snow emergencies.

> Snow emergency is declared when snow or ice creates
> a road hazard. Under such circumstances driving is
> prohibited on all roads designated "emergency snow
> route" except when vehicles are equipped with snow
> tires or chains. Parking on these designated
> roadways is prohibited.[1]

Motorists who get stuck on a snow emergency route without chains

are subject to a $50 fine. . . .

[1]Citizen's Guide to Public Services in Montgomery County, Maryland.
(Rockville, Md.: Montgomery County, 1971), p. 1?

FIGURE 12-9. Set-off direct quotation, introduced in text.

ments, laws, and mathematical and scientific formulas should ordinarily be quoted exactly. Figure 12-8 shows a note card with a direct quotation on it.

There are two ways of presenting direct quotations. If the quotation you have chosen occupies more than four lines of typed copy, it should be *set off* from your text. Set-off quotations are usually separated from the text by a double-space; *every* line of the quotation is indented ten spaces from the left margin; the quotation is single-spaced, and quotation marks are not needed. It is a good idea to introduce the quotation smoothly—that is, to tell the reader, in your own words, what significance the quotation has for your report (see Figure 12-9).

The second kind of direct quotation, which takes up four lines of typed copy or less, is *run-in* with the text—it is not set off. It is enclosed in quotation marks (see Figure 12-10).

When you are planning your remodeling project, don't forget that
residential construction requires a building permit. To obtain a
building permit in our area, contact the Department of Inspections and
Licenses. "An applicant must submit an application in duplicate, two
sets of blueprints, three plot plans drawn to scale, and an application
for a driveway apron."[2] Once the application has been obtained, it
must be posted at the project site. . . .

[2]Citizen's Guide to Public Services, p. 15.

FIGURE 12-10. Direct quotation, run in.

There may be times when you want to quote directly from only part of a passage. Suppose, for example, you saw a sentence like the following in a company house organ.

    SpeedMail, Incorporated, just hired two junior-level
    copywriters, who will report to the advertising manager,
    and a direct-mail assistant, who will be working closely
    with the director of promotion.

If you wanted to quote only the portion of the sentence that pertains to the direct-mail assistant, you would omit the text relating to the copywriters. When you omit material that falls *within a quoted passage,* you insert *three spaced dots* (called *ellipses*) to indicate where the omission occurs.

    SpeedMail, Incorporated, just hired . . . a direct-mail
    assistant, who will be working closely with the director
    of promotion.

If, on the other hand, you intended to quote the portion of the sentence that deals with the copywriters, you would delete the reference to the direct-mail aide. To mark the omission of material that comes *at the end of a quoted passage,* you place *a period followed by three spaced dots* after the last quoted word.

```
SpeedMail, Incorporated, just hired two junior-level
copywriters, who will report to the advertising
manager. . . .
```

Paraphrasing

A *paraphrase* of a written passage is a restatement of the essential ideas of the passage in the researcher's own words. Because a paraphrase does not quote the source word for word, quotation marks are not necessary. When you use paraphrased material in your own work, however, you must credit the source in a footnote.

As you are getting ready to write a paraphrase, you may find it helpful, after you've read the passage, to put it aside for a moment while you decide how to word the paraphrase; this brief period of reflection will give you a chance both to make sure that you understand the writer's message and to prepare your own version of it. When you start to write, pick up the original and refer to it. Check to be certain that you include every important point in the original that is relevant to your topic.

The passage should be paraphrased, of course, according to your topic and the scope of your written work; if the source contains more information than is pertinent to your subject, paraphrase only the material that relates to your purpose in writing. As an example, consider the following passage and the two paraphrases of it.

> Another industrial application of computers lies in the numerical control of machine tools. A great many parts of machines are produced by either milling or routing, processes in which a cutting tool moves so as to cut some contoured shape out of sheet metal or heavier stock. In conventional methods this demands the constant attention of a skilled machine operator, particularly if the contour to be formed is irregularly curved. Under the control of a computer the cutter can be made to move in any desired path, and it is in principle no more difficult to produce "sculptured" shapes bounded by complex curved surfaces than it is to produce objects with flat faces. The numerical control of machine tools has enjoyed an extraordinary success because it guarantees the reliability and reproducibility of even the most elaborate shapes. The spoilage due to human error is reduced to the vanishing point, and many parts are now practicable that would be prohibitively expensive to produce if a human operator had to monitor the settings of the machine.[1]

[1] Steven Anson Coons, "The Uses of Computers in Technology," in *Information, A Scientific American Book* (San Francisco: W. H. Freeman, 1966), p. 134.

If your purpose in writing were to compare human efficiency on the job with that of a machine, you might paraphrase the passage as in Figure 12-11.

Computer adjusts machines

A skilled machinist must continually monitor machine tools, especially when contoured or sculptured parts are made. Computer-controlled machines produce the same parts without waste. For complex-shaped parts, the computer adjusts machines more cheaply than a machinist can.

Coons, p. 134.

FIGURE 12-11. Note card—paraphrase I

If your purpose in writing were to examine the industrial application of computers, your paraphrase might read as in Figure 12-12.

Machined parts

Computers direct machine tools to cut complex shapes from metals and other materials. Contoured objects are as easily produced as flat objects, and with greater efficiency and less expense than those produced by a skilled machinist. Computer-controlled machines now produce complex parts that were too expensive to produce before.

Coons, p. 134.

FIGURE 12-12. Note card—paraphrase II

Summarizing

A *summary* is a highly condensed (or shortened) version, in the researcher's own words, of an original passage. Summary notes present only the essential ideas or conclusions of the original. As such, they are considerably shorter than paraphrases of the same passage. Like directly quoted and paraphrased material, the source of summarized information must be credited in a footnote.

Examine the summary note of the following passage (see Figure 12-13).

> Now that we have learned something about the nature of elements and molecules, what are fuels? Fuels are those substances that will burn when heat is applied to them. Some elements, in themselves, are fuels. Carbon, hydrogen, sulfur, magnesium, titanium and some other metals are examples of elements that can burn. Coal, charcoal, and coke, for example, are almost pure carbon; hydrogen, another element, is a highly flammable gas. But the most familiar combustible materials are not pure elements; they are compounds and mixtures.
>
> Wood, paper and grass are principally composed of molecules of cellulose, a flammable substance. If we examine the chemical makeup of this compound, we will discover what elements form the basic fuels in most solid materials. The cellulose molecule contains twenty-one atoms: six carbons, ten hydrogens and five oxygen atoms: $C_6H_{10}O_5$. Since oxygen is not flammable (see Oxygen, below), it follows that the carbon and hydrogen found in most common combustible solids are the elements that burn. This conclusion becomes even stronger when we look at common flammable liquids. Gasoline, kerosene, fuel oils and other petroleum compounds are composed of only carbon and hydrogen atoms, in varying amounts. These compounds, called Hydrocarbons (hydrogen + carbon), will all burn.
>
> Other flammable compounds are composed of carbon, hydrogen, and oxygen atoms in a fixed ratio, making it appear as if there is a water molecule

Why fuels burn

The chemical makeup of a substance determines whether it's flammable. Carbon and hydrogen are highly flammable elements, so material made up largely of these elements, called hydrocarbons, are good fuels. Substances made up of carbon, hydrogen, and oxygen, with hydrogen and oxygen in the same proportion as they are in water, are also flammable; they're called carbohydrates. Heat is required before any fuel will burn.

Meidl, pp. 8-9.

FIGURE 12-13. Note card—summary

attached to each carbon atom. A good example is glucose, a common sugar, which has the formula $C_6H_{12}O_6$. Chemists call this type of molecule a "hydrated (watered) carbon," or carbohydrate. Carbohydrates also burn, but are not to be confused with hydrocarbons.

Carbon and hydrogen are only two of the elements which will burn. But, since most common flammable materials contain a combination of carbon and hydrogen fuels, we will limit our discussion of combustion to them at this point.

Fuel, as we have seen, is only one side of the fire triangle. Before it will burn, any fuel requires the addition of heat, another side of the triangle.[2]

Take summary notes to remind you of the substance of a research source. Summarized information can also be useful to your reader, because it condenses passages that give more details than the reader needs.

PLAGIARISM

To use someone else's exact words or original ideas in your writing without giving credit in a footnote reference is known as *plagiarism*. Plagiarism is illegal; in class or on the job it may be grounds for dismissal. Whether the words and ideas come from a published source, or from a fellow student's work, plagiarism is a form of theft for which you can be held accountable.

You may present the words and ideas of another person as long as you give appropriate credit by footnoting the passage. Ideas and facts considered "common knowledge" need not be cited in a footnote. The dates and names of historical events, and many kinds of scientific and statistical information, are common knowledge. Specific examples of common knowledge include the temperature at which water boils, the year the Constitution was ratified, the number of passengers a 747 jetliner can hold, and the area in square miles that Dallas, Texas, occupies.

INTERVIEWING

If you need information that is not readily available in print, you may be able to do some of your research by interviewing someone who is an expert on the subject. If, for instance, your subject is nursing-home care in your community, the logical experts to interview would be the managers or the directors of several local nursing homes. Sources that can help you decide whom to interview —and how to get in touch with them—include membership lists of professional societies (the membership rolls of large professional organizations are available in many libraries); the yellow pages of the local telephone book; and

[2] James H. Meidl, *Flammable Hazardous Materials* (Beverly Hills, Calif.: Glencoe Press, 1970), pp. 8–9.

a firm or organization in the area whose staff includes experts in your subject.

Once you have selected the person or persons you would like to interview, use the following guidelines to help you to obtain the information you need with a minimum of time and trouble for your interviewee and for yourself.

Before the Interview

Always request an interview in advance and make an appointment. You can do so either by telephone or by letter, although a letter may sometimes take too long to permit you to meet a deadline. When you request the interview, explain who you are, what kind of information you are seeking, and why you have chosen to interview this particular expert. Also state that you will schedule the interview at the convenience of the interviewee. Gather some background information about the person and his or her occupation before the interview. You need not exhaust all information sources, of course; let common sense be your guide. How much time will you have before the interview? Is the information difficult to obtain? Be aware, however, that the more preparation you put into an interview, the more you will get out of it.

Your first contact with the interviewee is important because it gives you the opportunity to tell the expert exactly what kind of information you are seeking and allows the interviewee time to prepare for the interview. Some people are made nervous by a tape recorder, so if you would like to use one during the interview, request permission at this point. If the interviewee refuses permission, plan to bring a note pad instead. If you plan to bring a tape recorder, check to see if it's in good working order. Even a tape recorder that works well can malfunction unexpectedly. Prepare for the worst; bring a writing pad and several pens or pencils to the interview as a backup.

After you have made the appointment, prepare a list of specific questions, based on your writing purpose, that you will ask. Avoid the tendency of the beginning interviewer to ask general rather than specific questions. Analyze your questions to be certain that they are direct and to the point. "Tell me about the kinds of people admitted to Hillcrest Nursing Home," is too broad a request. You will probably get a rambling, general answer in reply. Productive questions would be "What is the average age of persons who come to Hillcrest?" "Are the majority from this vicinity?" "What's the ratio of men to women?" And they are much easier to answer than general questions.

Conducting the Interview

Because an interview represents an imposition on someone's time—usually someone who is busy—arrive promptly at the appointed time.

After you arrive and introduce yourself, a few moments of informal conversation will help both you and the interviewee relax. But don't drag this period out; an interview is largely straightforward question and response.

During the interview, use the following guidelines.

1. Be pleasant but purposeful. The interviewee knows you are there to get information, so don't be timid about asking your questions. And don't confuse an elementary question on a subject with an ignorant question. If you are too timid, you will go away empty-handed.

2. Refer to the list of questions you prepared in advance, and follow them—don't let yourself become sidetracked. Avoid being rigid, how-ever; if you realize that a prepared question is no longer suitable, go on to the next question.

3. Let the interviewee do most of the talking. Don't try to impress the interviewee with your knowledge of the subject on which he or she is the expert. And don't rebut every point the interviewee makes; after all, you are there to get information, not to debate.

4. Some answers prompt follow-up questions; ask them. "Mr. Bolchalk, has the automated mail-handling system been as efficient as originally planned?" If the answer is no, you can follow up with "Why?" or "In what specific areas has the system failed?" If the answer is yes, ask details about the difference between the old and the new systems.

5. If the interviewee gets off the subject, be ready with a specific ques-tion to direct the conversation back on the track. Your prepared list of questions will help.

6. Take only the notes you really need. Obviously, you cannot write down every word of the interview, so concentrate on the important ideas and the key facts and figures. You will be the best judge of how pertinent an idea or a statistic is. If the interviewee is talking too fast, ask him or her to speak more slowly. Anyone who wants to be quoted accurately will be glad to. And if you need a clarification of the facts, politely ask the speaker to explain a point.

7. As the interview is reaching a close, take a few minutes to skim your notes. If you feel there is time, ask for a clarification of anything that is still unclear. But be careful not to overstay your welcome.

8. If you use a tape recorder, do not be lulled into a feeling that all your work is being done for you and thereby neglect to ask crucial questions.

After the Interview

As soon as possible after the interview, go over your notes again and fill in any material that is obviously missing. This is the time to summarize the speaker's remarks. Then type or write out the notes in complete sentences. After writing out your notes, select the important information you need and transfer it to your note cards. Observe the same guidelines for creating interview note cards that you used for creating library-research cards. Provide a topic "slug" for each card.

USING A QUESTIONNAIRE

A *questionnaire*—a series of questions on a particular topic, sent out to a number of people—is a sort of interview on paper. It has several advantages over the personal interview, and several disadvantages. A questionnaire allows you to test the thinking of many more people than personal interviews would. It enables you to obtain responses from people in different parts of the country. Even people who live near you may be easier to reach by mail than in person. Those responding to a questionnaire do not face the constant pressure posed by someone jotting down their every word—a fact that could result in more thoughtful answers from questionnaire respondents. And the questionnaire reduces the possibility that the interviewer might influence an answer by tone of voice or facial expression. Finally, the cost of a questionnaire is lower than the cost of numerous personal interviews.

Questionnaires have drawbacks too. People who have strong opinions on a subject are more likely to respond to a questionnaire than those who do not. This factor could slant the results. An interviewer can follow up on an answer with a pertinent question; at best, a questionnaire can be designed to let one question lead logically to another. Furthermore, mailing a batch of questionnaires and waiting for replies take considerably longer than a personal interview does.

The advantages of a questionnaire will work in your favor only if the questionnaire is properly designed. Your goal should be to obtain as much information as possible from your recipients with as little effort on their part as possible. The first rule to follow is to keep the questionnaire brief. The longer the questionnaire is, the less likely the recipient will be to complete and return it. Next, the questions should be easy to understand. A confusing question will yield confusing results, whereas a carefully worded question will be easy to answer. Ideally, questions should be answerable with a "yes" or "no."

```
Would you be willing to work a four-day work week, ten
hours a day, with every Friday off?

        Yes _____

        No _____

        No opinion _____
```

When it is not possible to phrase questions in such a straightforward style, provide an appropriate range of answers.

```
How many hours of overtime would you be willing to work
each week?

    4 hours _____        10 hours _____

    6 hours _____        More than 10 hours _____

    8 hours _____        No overtime _____
```

And questions should be neutral; they shouldn't be worded in such a way as to lead the respondent to give a particular response.

When preparing your questions, remember that you must eventually tabulate the answers; therefore, try to formulate questions whose answers can be readily computed. The easiest questions to tabulate are those for which the recipient does not have to compose an answer. And questions that require a comment for an answer take time to think about and write. As a result, they lessen your chances of obtaining a response. They are also difficult to interpret. Questionnaires should include a section for additional comments, though, where recipients may clarify their overall attitude toward the subject. If the information will be of value in interpreting the answers, include questions about the recipient's age, education, occupation, and so on. Include your name, your address, the purpose of the questionnaire, and the date by which an answer is needed.

A questionnaire sent by mail must be accompanied by a letter explaining who you are, the purpose of the questionnaire, how the questionnaire will be used, and the date by which you would like to receive a reply. If the information provided will be kept confidential, say so in the letter. If the recipient's identity will not be disclosed, state this in the letter too.

Selecting the proper recipients for your questionnaire may be easy or difficult, depending on your needs. If you want to survey the opinions of all the employees in a small shop or a laboratory, you simply send each worker a questionnaire. To survey the members of a club or a professional society, you would mail questionnaires to those who are on a membership list. But to survey the opinions of large groups—for example, all medical technologists working in private laboratories, or all independent garage owners—in the general population is not so easy. Since you cannot include everybody in your survey, you would have to choose a representative cross-section. How would you go about selecting such a cross-section, and how large should such a sample be? Methods of large-scale sampling are beyond the scope of this text. The best sources of information on sampling techniques are research and statistics texts.

The sample questionnaire in Figure 12-14 was sent to employees in a large organization who had participated in a six-month program of flexible working hours. Under the program, employees worked a forty-hour, five-day week, with flexible starting and quitting times. Employees could start the work day between 7 and 9 A.M. and leave between 3:30 and 6:30 P.M., provided that they worked a total of eight hours each day and took a one-half-hour lunch period midway through the day.

October 18, 19--

To: All Company Employees

From: Nelson Barrett, Director
        Personnel Department

Subject: Review of Flexible Working Hours Program

Please complete and return the attached questionnaire regarding Luxwear Corporation's trial program of flexible working hours. Your answers will help my staff and me to decide whether the program is worthwhile enough to continue permanently.

Return the completed questionnaire to Ken Rose, Mail Code 12B, by October 28. Your signature on the questionnaire is not necessary. Feel free to raise additional issues pertaining to the program. All responses will be given consideration.

If you want to discuss any item in the questionnaire, call Pam Peters in the Personnel Department at extension 8812.

1. What kind of position do you occupy?

Supervisory _____

Nonsupervisory _____

2. Indicate to the nearest quarter of an hour your starting time under flexitime.

7 a.m. _____   8:15 a.m. _____

7:15 a.m. _____   8:30 a.m. _____

7:30 a.m. _____   8:45 a.m. _____

7:45 a.m. _____   9 a.m. _____

8 a.m. _____   Other, specify _____

3. Where do you live?

Talbot County _____   Greene County _____

Montgomery County _____   Other, specify _____

4. How do you usually travel to work?

    Drive alone _____   Walk _____

    Taxi _____   Bus _____

    Train _____   Motorcycle _____

    Car pool _____   Other, specify _____

    Bicycle _____

5. Has flexitime affected your commuting time?

    Increase: Approx. number of minutes _____.

    Decrease: Approx. number of minutes _____.

    No change _____

6. If you drive alone or in a car pool, has flexitime increased or decreased the amount of time it takes you to find a parking space?

        Increased _____   Decreased _____

                No change _____

7. Has flexitime had an effect on your productivity?

    a. Quality of work

        Increase _____   Decrease _____

                No change _____

    b. Accuracy of work

        Increase _____   Decrease _____

                No change _____

    c. Quiet time for uninterrupted work

        Increase _____   Decrease _____

                No change _____

8. Have you had difficulty getting in touch with employees who are on different work schedules from yours?

        Yes _____   No _____

9. Have you had trouble scheduling meetings within flexible starting and quitting times?

Yes _____   No _____

10. Has flexitime affected the way you feel about your job?

Feel better about job   Feel worse about job

slightly _____   slightly _____

considerably _____   considerably _____

No change _____

11. How important is it for you to have flexibility in your working hours?

Very _____   Not very _____

Somewhat _____   Not at all _____

12. Has flexitime allowed you more time to be with your family?

Yes _____   No _____   Some _____

13. If you are responsible for the care of a young child or children, has flexitime made it easier or more difficult for you to obtain babysitting or day-care services?

Easier _____   More difficult _____

No change _____

14. Do you recommend that the flexitime program be made permanent?

Yes _____   No _____

15. Do you have suggestions for major changes in the program?

Yes (please specify)   No _____

THANK YOU FOR YOUR ASSISTANCE

FIGURE 12-14. Sample questionnaire.

OTHER SOURCES OF INFORMATION

There are two additional sources of information that may prove fruitful in providing you with materials for your research: first-hand observation and experience, and free or inexpensive materials from private and governmental agencies and organizations.

First-hand Observation and Experience

Why not interview yourself? If your topic deals with something you know well (a hobby or an area of interest, for example), or relates to an occupation you are in or hope to be in, you may already have enough information to get started. Check your home or office for any materials you have acquired on the subject. From your knowledge of the topic, make a rough outline—it will tell you how much you know about the topic and which areas you are strong in and which areas you are weak in. When your flow of ideas turns to a trickle and then stops, you can expand your knowledge from the other sources discussed in this chapter. For topics that involve a great deal of factual data, you should, in addition, check the accuracy of any facts and figures you aren't certain about.

Free or Inexpensive Materials from Private and Governmental Agencies and Organizations

In your search for materials on your topic, do not overlook the field of private and governmental agencies and organizations. These include corporations, business and professional associations, nonprofit organizations, and the numerous bureaus and offices of the federal, state, and local governments. Most of these sources distribute free or inexpensive material on virtually any subject. A reference librarian can show you how to go about obtaining material from the agencies and organizations.

When you request information from governmental or private organizations, you must be specific in describing the material or materials you are seeking. If you know the title of a pamphlet or a booklet you want, refer to the title, and to any other information that will serve to identify the pamphlet, in your letter requesting the item. If you are aware that there is a charge for the material, send a check or money order with the request. Doing so will save time for both you and the recipient, because it won't be necessary for the organization to write to you asking for payment before it can send you the materials. One final note: Requests for information from private and governmental agencies are usually handled by mail, and postal deliveries can be slow. Therefore, do not rely too heavily on such materials for your research, because the deadline for your written work may arrive before the requested material does.

DOCUMENTATION

The final version of a research paper should give complete, accurate credit to your sources of information, in notes either at the bottom of the page or at the end of the report, and should provide an alphabetical listing of all the sources you used in doing your research—that is, a bibliography. Together, footnotes (or endnotes) and bibliography are referred to as *documentation.*

The data to include in footnote references and in the bibliography will come from your bibliography note cards. The sections on pages 260–267 provide examples of standard forms for documentation. It is essential to follow a standard form so that your reader will be able to identify and locate the source materials you have used. The footnote and bibliography details given here are based on the *MLA Handbook for Writers of Research Papers, Theses, and Dissertations* (New York: The Modern Language Association of America, 1977).

Footnotes

In nonscientific writing, credits for sources of information ordinarily go in one of two places: credits that are placed at the bottom, or foot, of the page on which quoted, paraphrased, or summarized material appears are called *footnotes;* when all the credits for a chapter, report, or entire book appear at the end of the chapter, report, or book, they are called *endnotes* or, simply, *notes.* * The term *footnotes,* as it pertains to references, will be used here to indicate both bottom-of-page and end-of-work credits.

In your own work, you may find it easier to use endnotes than footnotes, because the latter require you to fit the credits on the bottom of the page as you type. If your instructor or employer prefers footnotes or endnotes, follow that preference. Otherwise follow the style you are more comfortable with, but be consistent throughout a work.

There is another type of footnote you should be aware of. When you want to add a fact, opinion, or definition to clarify a point in the text, you can do so in an *explanatory footnote.* Usually indicated by an asterisk (*), such footnotes ordinarily appear at the bottom of the page on which the material they refer to appears. An example of an explanatory footnote appears at the bottom of this page.

Footnotes are numbered consecutively, in the order in which the quoted, paraphrased, or summarized material occurs in the text of your report. Footnote numbers in the text are normally raised slightly above the typewritten line of copy. You can position a footnote number correctly by moving the platen (roller) of the typewriter toward you, by hand, about one-quarter of an inch. In scientific writing, footnote numbers are not usually raised above the line and are enclosed in parentheses. Footnote numbers for direct quotations

* In some books, footnote references are given at the end of each chapter; other books list all credits, usually arranged by chapter, at the end of the book.

should follow the closing quotation mark for material that is run in with the text, or the end punctuation mark for material that is set off from the text (see pages 245–246). For paraphrased or summarized material, the footnote number should normally be placed at the end of the paraphrase or the summary, following the end punctuation mark.

The footnote number in the text identifies the numbered note (either at the foot of the page or in the "Notes" section) in which the information source appears. Normally, the first line of a footnote is indented, like a paragraph, five spaces from the left margin; any additional lines of the footnote are typed flush with the left margin. Footnotes that take more than one line of copy are single-spaced; there should be a double space between footnotes.

First-reference footnotes. In your report, you may have occasion to credit a research source—book, article, interview, and so on—just once or more than once. The first footnote (it may be the only one) to a source must give the author's full name (or the names of the authors if the work has more than one); the full title of a book, underscored, or of an article, in quotation marks; the name and location of the publisher of a book or the name of the periodical in which an article appeared; the date of publication (the year for a book; the day, month, and year for a daily or weekly periodical; the month and year for articles from monthly magazines; the volume number and year for journal articles); and the page number on which the footnoted material occurred in the original source.

The following list shows the *MLA* preferred style for first-reference footnotes. For information on handling second-and-later footnotes, see pages 262–263.

Book, One Author

[1]Wayne Hanley, <u>Natural History in America</u> (New York: Quadrangle Press/New York Times Books, 1977), p. 183.

Book, Two Authors

[2]Herbert M. Jelley and Robert O. Herrmann, <u>The American Consumer: Issues and Decisions</u> (New York: McGraw–Hill, 1973), p. 65.

Book, Three or More Authors

[3]Hugo Young, Bryan Silcock, and Peter Dunn, <u>Journey to Tranquility</u> (Garden City, N.Y.: Doubleday, 1970), pp. 8–9.

Book Edition, If Not the First

[4]Wesley E. Woodson and Donald W. Conover, <u>Human Engineering: Guide for Equipment Designers</u>, 2nd ed. (Berkeley: Univ. of California Press, 1964), pp. 2–7.

Multivolume Work

⁵John Bartholemew, ed., <u>Times Atlas of the World</u> (London: Times Publishing, 1955), I, 27.

[The information given in the footnote indicates that the researcher used only one volume, the first, of a multivolume work. The page number, 27, follows the volume number. For other forms of footnotes for multivolume works, consult the *MLA* handbook or another footnote-style guide.]

Corporate Author

⁶Commission on Vocational Education, <u>Job Selection in the 1980's</u> (Washington, D.C.: American Vocational Institute, 1973), p. 12.

Journal Article

⁷Keith D. Gardels, "A Controlled Experiment to Assess Centralized Word Processing," <u>Technical Communication</u> 24 (1977), 5.

[The number *before* the year is the volume number; if a journal uses Roman numerals as its volume number, the figure is often converted to Arabic numerals in footnotes and bibliographies. The number *after* the year is the page number. Note that the abbreviation for *page* is ordinarily not used in journal article footnotes.]

Magazine Article, with Author's Name Given

⁸Susan Renner–Smith, "Satellite-to-You TV," <u>Popular Science</u>, March 1978, p. 69.

[General-circulation magazines, as opposed to specialized professional or technical journals, are identified by date. The abbreviation for *page* or *pages* is used.]

Magazine Article, with No Author's Name Given

⁹"The New American Farmer," <u>Time</u>, 6 Nov. 1978, p. 92.

[Note that the date precedes the month, and no comma is used between the month and the year.]

Newspaper Article

¹⁰John H. Allan, "Fixed–Income Securities Ease," <u>New York Times</u>, Late City Ed., 15 June 1979, Sec. D, p. 7.

Encyclopedia Article

> [11]"Electricity." <u>Encyclopaedia Britannica</u>. 14th ed.

[Because encyclopedia articles are arranged alphabetically, page and volume numbers are unnecessary. If the encyclopedia article is signed, begin the footnote with the author's firat and last names.]

Report

> [12]Parker Evans, <u>The Erosion of Buried Cables</u> (Dayton, Ohio: Ohio Bell Telephone Company, 1970), p. 27.

Pamphlet or Booklet

> [13]U.S. Bureau of the Census, <u>Our Cities and Suburbs</u> (Washington, D.C.: Government Printing Office, 1973), p. 14.

Personal Interview

> [14]Personal interview with Virgil Denlinger, Assistant Chief of Police, Milwaukee, Wisconsin, 15 March 1979.

Second-and-later references. Second-and-later footnote references to a source are usually shorter than first references, since it is not necessary to repeat all the data furnished in the first footnote. In second-and-later references, it is ordinarily sufficient to give the author's last name and the appropriate page number or numbers. Keep in mind that a second footnote reference to a particular source may have a different page number—as long as the author, title, and other publication data are the same, it is still considered a second reference.

Ibid., p. 65. or

> [15]Evans, p. 32.

If you have footnoted more than one work by an author, second-and-later references should include the author's last name, a shortened version of the title of the work, and the page number or numbers.

> [16]Evans, <u>Erosion</u>, p. 41.   *If more than 2 works by author, title is needed*

For a second-and-later reference to a work that has more than one author, give the last name of each author and the appropriate page number.

> [17]Woodson and Conovers, p. 128.

To credit a work that appears in the immediately preceding footnote as well, simply repeat the information, inserting the new page number, or repeating the number if the page number is the same.

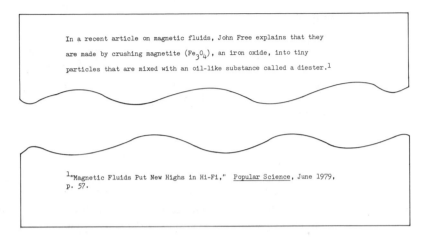

In a recent article on magnetic fluids, John Free explains that they are made by crushing magnetite (Fe_3O_4), an iron oxide, into tiny particles that are mixed with an oil-like substance called a diester.[1]

[1]"Magnetic Fluids Put New Highs in Hi-Fi," Popular Science, June 1979, p. 57.

FIGURE 12-15. Footnote with author's name appearing in text.

[18]Gardels, p. 9.
[19]Gardels, p. 12.
[20]Gardels, p. 12.

The author's name is omitted from a footnote when his or her full name is given in the text near the reference to the work cited (see Figure 12-15).

References in scientific and technical writing. In scientific and technical writing, the form used to give credit to your information sources differs from the form used in other fields. Information sources are listed in a separate section called "References." The entries in the reference section frequently are arranged according to the order in which they are first referred to in the text. In this system, number 1 in parentheses (1) after a quotation or a reference to a book or an article refers the reader to the information in the first entry in the reference section; number 2 in parentheses (2) refers the reader to the second entry in the reference section, and so on. A second number in parentheses, separated from the first by a colon, indicates the page number in the report or book from which the information was taken—for example, the notation "(3:27)" in the text indicates that the material is found on page 27 of entry 3 in the reference section.

The reference section for relatively short reports appears at the end of the report. For reports with a number of major sections or chapters, the reference section appears at the end of the section or the chapter. See Chapter 13, page 279, for information on the placement of a reference section in a formal report.

The details of reference systems in the sciences vary widely from field to field. Although the following examples are common in scientific and technical publications, consult publications in your field for precise details.

Book

> 1. Ying, R. Introductory laboratory manual of soil
>   science. Iowa State University Press, Ames, ed. 2.
>   1977.

[Note that the last name appears first, followed by one or two initials. In the title of the work, only the first word and proper nouns are capitalized, and underlining is not used.]

Journal Article

> 2. Hirst, E. N., and Carney, J. Effects of federal
>   residential energy conservation programs in California
>   and Nevada. Science, 1978, 199: 845-851.

[Only the first word and proper nouns in the article title are capitalized, and no quotation marks are used. The journal name is not underlined.]

A final word about footnotes: Be alert to the forms used by your employer or the publication for which you are writing. Also, once you have adopted a form, be consistent.

Bibliography

A *bibliography* is a list of books or articles arranged alphabetically at the end of a report or research paper. The purpose of a bibliography is to present the sources of the writer's information in a convenient, standardized form that will be useful to a reader who would like to locate any of the research materials the writer has included.

A bibliography may consist of all the material used in the preparation of a research paper (a *full* bibliography), or it may list only the material specifically referred to in the text (a *selected* bibliography). An *annotated* bibliography includes a brief description, by the writer, of some or all of the works listed.

Use a full bibliography when you have conducted a comprehensive literature search of all pertinent information sources for your topic; otherwise, use a selected bibliography. Use an annotated bibliography if you want to provide your readers with a convenient means of determining which of your information sources are useful to their needs.

When typing a bibliography, single-space within an entry and double-space between entries. Indent the second and subsequent lines of an entry five spaces from the left margin, so that the author's name will stand out.

The details of bibliographic systems vary from one field of study to another, but all bibliographic entries, no matter how complex the work being credited, should contain the author or corporate author's name, the full title of the work, and the facts of publication.

Alphabetizing.   Since bibliographic entries are arranged alphabetically, give the author's last name first, followed by first name. For an entry that has more than one author, give the first author's name in reverse order and then list the other name or names in normal order. *Doe, Jane Q., and John R. Roe* is the form for a two-author work. The form for a work with three authors or more is *Doe, Jane Q., John R. Roe, and June P. Low.*

Alphabetize all works by the same author according to their titles. When listing multiple works by the same author, replace the author's name in all entries except the first with a line made by typing ten hyphens, followed by a period.

```
Grahm, Frank, Jr. Disaster by Default: Politics and Water
     Pollution. New York: M. Evans, 1966.
----------. Since Silent Spring. Boston: Houghton Mifflin,
     1970.
```

When a work lists no author, editor, or compiler, alphabetize the entry according to the first major word in the title.

```
The Encyclopedia of Associations. 9th ed. 3 vols. Detroit:
     Gale Research, 1975.
```
[Alphabetize under *E.*]

Bibliographic Forms

The following list shows the *MLA* preferred style for bibliographic entries for nonscientific works.

Book, One Author

```
Hanley, Wayne. Natural History in America. New York:
     Quadrangle Press/New York Times Books, 1977.
```

[Note that in a bibliographic entry, page numbers are not ordinarily given for books, because the researcher may have read and made note cards for a good deal of the book. *Inclusive* page numbers are given for articles from periodicals (that is, for the first and last pages of the article).]

Book, Two Authors

```
Jelley, Herbert M., and Robert O. Herrmann. The American
     Consumer: Issues and Decisions. New York: McGraw-Hill,
     1973.
```

Book, Three or More Authors

```
Young, Hugo, Bryan Silcock, and Peter Dunn. Journey to
     Tranquility. Garden City, N.Y.: Doubleday, 1970.
```

Book Edition, If Not the First

```
Woodson, Wesley E., and Donald W. Conover. Human Engi-
     neering: Guide for Equipment Designers. 2nd ed.
     Berkeley: Univ. of California Press, 1964.
```

Multivolume Work

Bartholemew, John, ed. <u>Times Atlas of the World</u>. London:
Times Publishing, 1955. Vol. I.

Corporate Author

Commission on Vocational Education. <u>Job Selection in the</u>
<u>1980's</u>. Washington, D.C.: American Vocational Insti-
tute, 1973.

Journal Article

Gardels, Keith D. "A Controlled Experiment to Assess
Centralized Word Processing." <u>Technical Communication</u>
24 (1977), 2–6.

[The number before the year is the volume number; the numbers following the year
are the *inclusive* page numbers.]

Magazine Article, with Author's Name Given

Renner–Smith, Susan. "Satellite–to–You TV." <u>Popular</u>
<u>Science</u>, March 1978, pp. 66–69.

Magazine Article, with No Author's Name Given

"The New American Farmer." <u>Time</u>, 6 Nov. 1978, pp. 92–102.

Newspaper Article

Allan, John H. "Fixed–Income Securities Ease." <u>The_ New</u>
<u>York Times</u>, Late City Ed., 15 June 1979, Sec. D, p. 7.

Encyclopedia Article

"Electricity." <u>Encyclopedia Britannica</u>. 14th ed.

[If the encyclopedia article is signed, begin the entry with the author's last name and
alphabetize by the name.]

Report

Evans, Parker. <u>The Erosion of Buried Cables</u>. Dayton, Ohio:
Ohio Bell Telephone Company, 1970.

Pamphlet or Booklet

U.S. Bureau of the Census. <u>Our Cities and Suburbs</u>. Washington, D.C.: Government Printing Office, 1973.

Personal Interview

Denlinger, Virgil. Assistant Chief of Police, Milwaukee,
Wisconsin. Personal Interview. 15 March 1979.

Sample Bibliography

The bibliography that follows is intended to serve as a guide for alphabetization and entry style. It is not intended, of course, to serve as the bibliography for any specific work.

```
                        BIBLIOGRAPHY
Allan, John H. "Fixed-Income Securities Ease." New York
     Times, Late City Ed., 15 June 1979, Sec. D, P. 7.

Bartholemew, John, ed. Times Atlas of the World. London:
     Times Publishing, 1955. Vol. I.

Commission on Vocational Education. Job Selection in the
     1980's. Washington, D.C.: American Vocational Insti-
     tute, 1973.

Denlinger, Virgil. Assistant Chief of Police, Milwaukee,
     Wisconsin. Personal interview. 15 March 1979.

"Electricity." Encyclopaedie Britannica. 14th ed.

Evans, Parker. The Erosion of Buried Cables. Dayton, Ohio:
     Ohio Bell Telephone Company, 1970.

Gardels, Keith D. "A Controlled Experiment to Assess Cen-
     tralized Word Processing." Technical Communication
     24 (1977), 2-6.

Grahm, Frank, Jr. Disaster by Default: Politics and Water
     Pollution. New York: M. Evans, 1966.

----------. Since Silent Spring. Boston: Houghton Mifflin,
     1970.

Hanley, Wayne. Natural History in America. New York:
     Quadrangle Press/New York Times Books, 1977.

Jelley, Herbert M., and Robert O. Herrmann. The American
     Consumer: Issues and Decisions. New York: McGraw-Hill,
     1973.

"The New American Farmer." Time, 6 Nov. 1978, pp. 92-102.

Renner-Smith, Susan. "Satellite-to-You TV." Popular
     Science, March 1978, pp. 66-69.

U.S. Bureau of the Census. Our Cities and Suburbs. Wash-
     ington, D.C.: Government Printing Office, 1973.

Woodson, Wesley E.,and Donald W. Conover. Human Engineer-
     ing: Guide for Equipment Designers. 2nd ed. Berkeley:
     Univ. of Calif. Press. 1964.

Young, Hugo, Bryan Silcock, and Peter Dunn. Journey to
     Tranquility. Garden City, N.Y.: Doubleday, 1970.
```

CHAPTER SUMMARY

Many information sources are available to you as you research job-related topics. Libraries provide the most complete, systematically arranged body of information. Other sources include the personal interview, the questionnaire, knowledge gained from personal experience, and materials available to you from private and governmental organizations.

The *library* provides the tools for you to find books, articles, reference works, and other materials for your research. Once you have located the materials available in the library, take careful notes and record the source of your information.

A personal interview with an expert can provide you with up-to-date information not readily available in printed material. Select the person to interview, and obtain some background information on the interviewee. Prepare a list of specific questions to ask; take brief, memory-jogging notes of the answers; and summarize the notes in writing after the interview.

A questionnaire permits you to obtain the views of a group of people without having to go to the time and expense necessary for numerous personal interviews. Take full advantage of the increased number of views a questionnaire provides and design the questionnaire to produce as much information as you will need without its being a burden to answer. Keep the number of questions brief and word each one carefully so that the answers marked can be summarized conveniently for your purposes. In a letter accompanying the questionnaire, inform the recipient of who you are, the purpose of the questionnaire, the use to which the answers will be put, and the date by which you would like the information returned.

Other sources of information include your own knowledge and experience, and the pamphlets, booklets, reports, and other materials provided by companies, professional or trade associations, public-interest groups, and various governmental agencies. To tap your own resources, jot down what you know about a topic and supplement this information with any materials you have available at home or at work. Organize your notes into a rough outline. Based on this outline, you can determine the areas of the topic that require additional information. You can also pinpoint other areas that need to be double-checked for accuracy. A reference librarian can help you identify the types of information available from private organizations and governmental agencies. Be as specific as possible when you write for this type of material and enclose any fees that may be required. Allow time for mail handling so that the information will arrive when you need it.

Give complete and accurate credit to all of your information sources. Failure to do so will make you guilty of *plagiarism*. Information you quote, paraphrase, or summarize in your text must be credited in footnotes that appear either at the foot of the text page or in a separate section at the end of a chapter or section. In scientific and technical writing, source notes are listed consecutively in a "Reference" section in the order in which they first appeared in the text.

To provide readers with a convenient place to review your information sources, arrange your sources alphabetically in a *bibliography*. A *full bibliography* lists all the information sources examined in your research; a *selected bibliography* lists only the material actually referred to in the text. An *annotated bibliography* includes a brief description of some or all of your information sources. The type of bibliography you provide will depend on how much information about your research would be useful to your reader.

EXERCISES

Note: The exercises in this chapter may be used as the basis for the preparation of a formal report according to the guidelines presented in Chapter 13.

1. Select a topic from your career field or other area of interest. Using the card catalog in your library, locate five books on your topic. Prepare a separate 3" × 5" bibliography card for each book. (If you prefer, you may use, instead of a note card, a sheet of paper ruled into 3" × 5" segments.) Follow the instructions on pages 236–237 for preparing a bibliography card for a book.

2. Using the periodical index or indexes in your library, locate five articles, from magazines, newspapers, or journals, on the topic you chose for exercise 1. Prepare a separate 3" × 5" bibliography card for each item (or use a ruled sheet of paper as described in exercise 1). Follow the instructions on page 237 for preparing a bibliography card for an article.

3. Write a *paraphrase* of each of the two following paragraphs on a 4" × 6" note card (or use a sheet of paper ruled into 4" × 6" segments). Then, on a separate note card, *summarize* the information from each paragraph. Identify each card with a "slug" line and indicate the source from which the information was obtained.

   a. To keep pipes from freezing, wrap the pipes in insulation made especially for water pipes, or in layers of old newspaper, lapping the ends and tying them around the pipes. Cover the newspapers with plastic to keep out moisture. When it is extremely cold and there is real danger of freezing, let the faucets drip a little. Although this wastes water, it may prevent freezing damage. Know where the valve for shutting off the water coming into the house or apartment is located. You may as a last resort have to shut off this main valve and drain all the pipes to keep them from freezing and bursting.[1]

[1] Department of Energy, *Winter Survival: A Consumer's Guide to Winter Preparedness* (Washington, D.C.: Government Printing Office, 1978), p. 3.

b.   The Federal Energy Administration (FEA) estimated in 1976 that annual energy use in the United States was about 75 quadrillion BTUs (or 75 quads), and that use by 1985 would be 98.9 quads. The agency also estimated that even under the most favorable conditions the U.S. cannot expect to gain more than 6 quads from emerging technology by 1990. A more realistic figure, it indicated, might be 2 quads.

The emerging technologies evaluated by FEA included solar, geothermal, and synthetic fuels, but evidently excluded forest biomass. Energy currently obtained from wood is estimated at 1.1 to 1.7 quads. Members of the task force are confident that wood use for energy is increasing greatly, but we have no way of knowing the extent.[2]

4. Using the topic you chose in exercise 1, complete one or both of the following assignments, depending on your instructor's requirements: (1) create a ten-item sample questionnaire that you could use to gather information on the subject, or (2) interview someone knowledgeable about the subject and submit your rewritten and organized notes of the interview to your instructor. Also submit one of the following with your assignment, as appropriate: a letter to accompany your questionnaire or a letter requesting an interview.

5. Prepare a footnote for each of the following reference items. Follow the guidelines for correct footnote form provided in Chapter 12.

   a. A magazine article on page 42 of the August 1979 issue of *Studio Photography,* by Lou Jones, entitled "The Key to Location Photography."
   b. The unsigned "New Products" column of the same issue of *Studio Photography.* The column appears on page 13.
   c. The fourth edition of a 1976 book entitled *Environmental Conservation,* by Raymond F. Dassmann. The book is published by John Wiley, in New York City. Your reference is on page 365.
   d. An article entitled "Ensuring Safer Stomach Suctioning with the Salem Sump Tube," by Edwina A. McConnell, that appears on page 56 of the September 1977 issue of the journal *Nursing.*
   e. An article in *The Washington Post* entitled "Futuristic Autos—Prize-Winning Canadians Get 60 Miles Per Gallon," by William M. Adler. The article appears on page 8 of Section A in the August 19, 1979, issue.
   f. A booklet entitled *Controlling Fleas,* by the United States Department of Agriculture and published in Washington, D.C., by the Government Printing Office in 1978. Your reference is on page 5.

---

[2] "Forest Biomass as an Energy Source: Study Report of a Task Force of the Society of American Foresters," *Journal of Forestry* 77 (1979), 3.

g. You interviewed the Vice President of Ridgeway Electronics of Leesburg, Virginia, on April 14, 1979. Her name is Josetta Jameson.

h. A book entitled *A Walk in the Forest: The Woodlands of North America* and written by Albert List, Jr., and Ilka List. The book was published in New York by Thomas Y. Crowell in 1977. Your reference is on page 11.

i. Hallie Black's book, *Dirt Cheap: The Evolution of Renewable Resources,* published by William Morrow in New York in 1979. Your reference is on page 91.

j. An article from the 1977 edition of the *McGraw-Hill Encyclopedia of Science and Technology,* entitled "Lubricant."

k. A report published by Environmental Technologies, Inc., of Philipstown, Nebraska, entitled *Progress in Industrial Water Pollution Control.* The author of the report is Sanford Bond. The report was published in 1976; your reference is on page 27.

6. Prepare a bibliography entry for each item given in exercise 5. Follow the guidelines for correct bibliography entries provided in Chapter 12. Inclusive page numbers for items a and d are pages 41–42 and pages 54–62, respectively.

7. Alphabetize the bibliography entries you prepared for exercise 6.

13

Formal Reports

Formal reports are the written accounts of major projects. Projects that are likely to generate a formal report include research into new developments in a field, explorations on the advisability of launching a new product or an expanded service, or an end-of-year developmental review. The scope and complexity of the project will determine how long and how complex the report will be. Most formal reports—certainly those that are long and complex—require a carefully planned structure that provides the reader with an easy-to-recognize guide to the material in the report. Such aids to the reader as a table of contents, lists of illustrations, and abstract (brief summary of the report) serve to make the information in the report accessible to the reader. Making a formal topic outline, which lists the major facts and ideas in the report and indicates their relationship to one another, should help you write a well-organized report.

Most formal reports are divided into three major parts—front matter, body, and back matter—each of which, in turn, contains a number of elements. Just how many elements are needed for a particular report depends on the subject, the length of the report, and the kinds of material contained in the report.

ORDER OF ELEMENTS IN
A FORMAL REPORT

The arrangement of the elements in a formal report may vary. Many companies and governmental and other institutions have a preferred style for formal reports and furnish guidelines that staff members must follow when they write such reports. If your employer has prepared a set of style guidelines, follow it; if not, use the format recommended in this chapter.

The following list includes all the elements a formal report might contain.

```
                  FRONT MATTER

       Title Page
       Abstract
       Table of Contents
       List of Figures
       List of Tables
       Preface
       Abbreviations and Symbols


          BODY

       Introduction
       Footnotes
       Heads
       References

       BACK MATTER

       Bibliography
       Appendix(es)
       Glossary
```

Front Matter

The front matter, which includes all the elements that precede the body of the report, serves several purposes: it gives the reader a general idea of what the report is about and of the author's purpose in writing it; it gives the reader a chance to determine whether the report contains the kind of information he or she is looking for; and it provides a listing of the location in the report of chapters, headings, and illustrations and tables. Not all formal reports require every element in this listing. The elements of the front matter are numbered with lower-case Roman numerals. Throughout the report, page numbers should be centered near the bottom of the page.

Title Page.   The title page, which is unnumbered and considered page i, should include the following information.

1. Full title of the report.
2. Writer, principal investigator, compiler, etc.
3. Date or dates of the report. For one-time reports, you should list the date the report is distributed. For periodical reports, which may be issued monthly or quarterly, list the time period that the present report covers, as well as the date the report is distributed.
4. Name of the organization for whom the writer works.

These categories are standard on most title pages. Some organizations may require additional information.

```
                    Card Uniqueness:  A Solution to the

                         Credit Card Problems

                             of Tomorrow



                           Jason T. Smiley



                             April 19--



                 Fidelity Financial Consultants, Inc.
```

Abstract.   The abstract, which concisely describes the content and the scope of the report, is an expanded table of contents in sentence form. It states, usually in two hundred words or less, the subject the report discusses and notes any findings, conclusions, or recommendations contained in the report. Abstracts start on a new page.

An abstract is particularly helpful to readers because it provides a review of the report's contents in abbreviated form. Going through the abstract gives the reader the opportunity to decide whether it will be worth his or her time to read the report in full.

```
                             Abstract


        This report discusses the advantages of the electronic funds transfer
    system (EFTS), explores the possibility of the improper application of the
    system, and examines a probable solution to criminal use of the system.
    As EFTS becomes widespread, a means to prevent its unlawful use must be
    found.  Prevention has focused on the distribution of EFTS cards with
    unique identification for specific users and on preventing the illegal
    reproduction of the cards.  A solution to the problem of illegal
    duplication has been found in the production of a card imprinted with
    diffraction gratings that can be optically read.
```

Table of Contents.   A table of contents lists all the headings or sections of the report in their order of appearance, along with their page numbers. It includes a listing of all front matter and back matter except the title page and the table of contents itself. The table of contents begins on a new page.

Along with the abstract, a table of contents permits the reader to preview the contents of a report and to assess its value. It also aids a reader who may want to look at only certain sections of the report. For this reason, the wording of chapter and section titles in the table of contents, and their page numbers, should be identical to those in the text.

TABLE OF CONTENTS

iv

List of Figures.   Figures include all drawings, photographs, maps, charts, and graphs contained in the report. When a report contains more than five figures, they should be listed, along with their page numbers, in a separate section immediately following the table of contents. The section should begin on a new page and be entitled "List of Figures." Figure numbers, captions, and page numbers should be identical to those in the text. Figures are numbered consecutively with Arabic numbers throughout most reports. For long reports, number figures by chapter or by section (see page 281).

For a full discussion on the preparation and use of figures, see Chapter 15.

List of Tables.   Tables arrange information in columns and rows, appropriately labeled. When a report contains more than five tables, they should be listed, along with their page numbers, in a separate section called "List of

Tables," immediately following a list of figures (if there is one). Table numbers, captions, and page numbers should be identical to those in the text. Tables are numbered consecutively with Arabic numbers throughout most reports. For long reports, number tables by chapter or by section (see page 281).

For a full discussion on the preparation and use of tables, see Chapter 15.

Preface.   The preface is a statement by the author or authors of the purpose, background, or scope of the report. It may contain acknowledgment of help received during the course of the project or in the preparation of the report or cite permission obtained for the use of copyrighted works.

The preface follows the table of contents (or list of figures or tables), beginning on a separate page entitled "Preface."

Abbreviations and Symbols.   When the abbreviations and symbols used in a report are numerous, and when there is a chance that the reader will not be able to interpret them, the front matter should include a list of all abbreviations and symbols, and what they stand for in the report. Such a list, which follows the preface, is particularly appropriate for technical reports whose audience is not restricted to technicians.

Body

 The first page of text is unnumbered and is considered page 1. If there is no introduction, begin the report with the first major text heading.

Introduction.   An introduction provides background information that the reader may need in order to get the most from the report. Not every report needs an introduction. Background information that can be stated briefly may appear in the preface instead.

Footnotes.   If it is necessary to explain further something that appears in the text, place a note at the foot of the page. Mark explanatory footnotes with a single or a double asterisk (*, **) or a single or a double dagger (†, ‡). For full information on footnote form, see Chapter 12.

Heads.   Heads (also called "headings") are titles or subtitles within the body of a report that serve as guideposts for the reader. They divide the work into manageable segments, call attention to the main topics, and signal changes of topic.

In long and complicated reports, you may need several levels of heads to indicate major divisions and subdivisions of the topic. There is no one "correct" format for heads, but the following system is widely used.

1. The first-level head is in all capital letters, typed flush with the left margin on a line by itself, with one line of space above it and one line of space below it.
2. The second-level head is in capital and lower-case letters (that is, the first letter of the first word and of every important word is capitalized; prepositions of five letters or more usually begin with a capital). The head is also typed flush with the left margin on a line by itself, with one line of space above it and one line of space below it.
3. The third-level head is in capital and lower-case letters, typed flush with the left margin. What distinguishes it from the first- and second-level heads is that it is on the same line as the first sentence of the material it introduces. Therefore, it is followed by a dash (two hyphens, with no space between) or a period to set it apart from the text that follows and it is underlined, to stand out clearly on the page. There is one full line of space above the head.

The three levels are arranged as follows:

```
FIRST LEVEL HEAD

Begin text here.

Second Level Head

Begin text here.

Third Level Head. Begin text here.
```

The following selection from a formal report shows first-level and second-level heads on one page (the ellipses indicate that some material has been omitted from the original report).

```
ADVANTAGES OF THE
ELECTRONIC FUNDS TRANSFER SYSTEM

In an effort to make the cashless and checkless society a
reality, the financial community is developing the
Electronic Funds Transfer System (EFTS). The EFTS will
nearly eliminate our current system's massive paperwork by
transferring funds with electrical impulses. . . .

Personal Benefits

Under EFTS, an employee will no longer receive a payroll
check; his or her salary will, instead, be placed in an
interest-bearing account. This arrangement eliminates the
need for employees to stop at a bank on payday to cash
and/or deposit earnings. A prior arrangement permits
automatic payment by the bank of utility bills, along with
house or rent payments. . . .
```

Retailer Benefits

Consumer credit card purchases to online retailers result in
an instant transfer of funds from the consumer's account to
the retailer's account. Thus the retailer is assured of
immediate payment. Since a computer handles the transaction,
the retailer can obtain, by supplying the bank with a small
amount of additional information, a running inventory,
accurate records, and data for forecasting coming needs.
Similar benefits apply to the wholesaler.

Banking Benefits

The greatest benefit to banks is the elimination of check
handling. Each check now written must be handled a minimum
of twenty-six times. . . .

As you write your report, keep in mind the following guidelines.

1. A new head should signal a shift to a new topic. Lower-level heads should signal shifts to new subtopics within a major topic.
2. Within a topic, all heads at one level should be parallel in their relationship to the topic. Note that the section in the example, "Advantages of the Electronic Funds Transfer System" (a first-level head), is followed by three parallel second-level heads, all bearing the same relationship to the first-level head.
3. Too many heads on too many levels can be as bad as too few.

References.   If, in your report, you refer to material in or quote directly from a published work or other research source, you must provide a list of references (footnotes or notes) in a separate section called "References." List and number the references consecutively in the order in which they appear in the text. If your employer has a preferred reference style, follow it; otherwise, use the guidelines provided in Chapter 12.

References

[1]"Beating the New Credit Cards," Business Week, 11 Aug. 1973, pp. 120-121.

[2]C. A. Frank, "New Jobs Ahead for Bank Cards," Banking, Sept. 1973, p. 115.

[3]Dennis W. Richardson, Electric Money (Cambridge, Mass.: MIT Press, 1973), pp. 112-121.

[4]Financial Systems Marketing Newsletter, 2 June 1975, NCR Corporation.

[5]Gerald M. Walker, "Electronic Funds Transfer System," Electronics, July 1975, pp. 13-19.

Detailed information on the preferred reference style of several professional fields can be found in the following selected list of style guides.

CBE Style Manual. 3rd ed. Washington, D.C.: American Institute of Biological Sciences, 1972.

MLA Handbook for Writers of Research Papers, Theses, and Dissertations. New York: Modern Language Association, 1977.

Style Book and Editorial Manual. 5th ed. Chicago: Scientific Publications Division, American Medical Association, 1971.

Style Manual for Guidance in the Preparation of Papers. 2nd ed. New York: American Institute of Physics, 1967.

For relatively short reports, the references should go at the end of the report. For reports with a number of sections or chapters, the reference section should fall at the end of each major section or chapter. In either case, *every* reference section should be labeled as such and should start on a new page. If a particular reference appears in more than one section or chapter, it should be repeated in full in each appropriate reference section. If a reference is repeated *within* a section or chapter, follow the style for second-and-later references in Chapter 12.

Back Matter

The back matter of a formal report is composed of *supplemental* information —material that is not absolutely necessary for your reader to know but that may shed some additional light on the topic.

Bibliography.   If you have quoted from or referred to any research sources, you must include, in your report, a bibliography as well as a reference section. The bibliography, which usually appears in the back matter, is the listing, in alphabetical order, of all the sources of information you refer to in the text. If your report requires such a list, follow the guidelines provided in Chapter 12 for the preparation of a bibliography. Like other elements in the front and back matter, the bibliography starts on a new page, and is labeled by name.

Appendix.   Material typically placed in an appendix includes long charts, graphs, or tables; copies of questionnaires, texts of interviews, pertinent correspondence, and other material used in gathering information; and explanations too long for explanatory footnotes but helpful to the reader seeking further assistance or clarification.

A report may have one or more appendixes; generally, each appendix contains one type of material.

Place the first appendix on a new page directly after the bibliography. Additional appendixes also begin on a new page. Identify each with a title and a heading. Appendixes are ordinarily labeled Appendix A, Appendix B, and so on.

Appendix A

Sample Questionnaire

Glossary.   A *glossary* is a list of selected terms, on a particular subject, that are defined and explained. Include a glossary only if your report contains many words and expressions that will be unfamiliar to your intended audience. Arrange the terms alphabetically, with each entry beginning on a new line. Definitions then follow each term, dictionary style.

The glossary, labeled as such, appears directly after the appendix (if any), beginning on a new page.

GRAPHIC AND TABULAR MATTER

Formal reports often contain illustrations and tables to clarify and support the text. The numbering and sequencing of illustrations and graphs may vary. The following guidelines show one conventional system for integrating such material smoothly into the text. For a full discussion on creating and using illustrations and tables, see Chapter 15.

Figures

Identify each figure with a title and a number, in Arabic numerals, below the figure. Number figures sequentially throughout the report. For long reports, number figures by chapter or by section; according to this system, the first figure in Chapter 1 would be Figure 1.1 (or Figure 1-1), the second figure would be Figure 1.2 (or Figure 1-2); in Chapter 2, the first figure would be Figure 2.1, and so on.

In the text refer to figures by number rather than by location ("Figure 2," rather than "the figure below").

Tables

Identify each table with a title and a number, centered above the table. Number the tables sequentially throughout the report. For long reports, number tables by chapter or by section according to the system described for figure numbering.

Refer to tables in the text by number rather than by location ("Table 4" rather than "the above table").

OUTLINING

Nearly everything you write requires some planning. For relatively short items, like memos and letters, you may need to jot down only a few notes to make sure that you haven't left any important information out and that you've arranged the information in the clearest order. Longer pieces of writing generally require more elaborate planning. Where such planning is necessary, the formal topic outline provides the best means.

A *topic outline* consists of phrases arranged according to the logical development of your subject. To create a topic outline, begin by dividing your topic into its major sections or parts. If *these* sections need to be broken down, divide them into their major units. All items in an outline are identified by a number or a letter according to the following system.

```
I. First-level head
   A. Second-level head
      1. Third-level head
         a. Fourth-level head
            (i) Fifth-level head
```

Your subject will seldom require so many levels of division, but the system allows for a highly detailed outline if one is necessary.

Follow these guidelines in preparing a topic outline.

1. Begin the outline with a statement, in sentence form, about the purpose of your report.
2. Write all heads at one level in parallel grammatical form. If you begin with noun phrases, for example, make all heads at that level noun phrases. (For a discussion of parallelism, see Chapter 6.)

```
NOT  A. Personal benefits
     B. To benefit retailers
BUT  A. Personal benefits
     B. Retailer benefits
```

3. Divide the topic logically. A head must be divided into at least two parts if it is to be divided at all.

```
NOT  A. Retailer benefit
        1. Permits direct transfer of purchase price to
           retailer's account
BUT  A. Retailer benefits
        1. Permits direct transfer of purchase price to
           retailer's account
        2. Provides daily printout of vital records
```

The complete topic outline on page 283 was used in the preparation of the sample formal report that appears, in part, on pages 278–279. Note that outline heads become headings in the final version of the report.

<u>Outline</u>

This report discusses the advantages of and the problems
involved in the manufacture and use of magnetic stripe
credit cards in an electronic funds transfer system and
their possible solution.

  I. Advantages of the Electronic Funds Transfer System
     (EFTS)
    A. Personal benefits
      1. Eliminates banking trips
      2. Allows automatic bill payment
      3. Permits credit card purchases
      4. Provides monthly statement of transactions
    B. Retailer benefits
      1. Permits direct transfer of purchase price to
        retailer's account
      2. Provides daily printout of vital records
        a. Furnishes running inventory
        b. Provides data for future planning
    C. Banking benefits
      1. Eliminates check handling
      2. Allows transfer of checking account funds to
        savings accounts
        a. Enables bank to increase investments
        b. Enables bank to earn more interest
 II. Potential Misuses of EFTS and Their Causes
    A. Theft of card
      1. Unlimited use of card by thief until the theft is
        reported
      2. Duplication of card and sale of copies by thief
    B. Causes of card misuse
      1. Electronic information on card stripe trans-
        ferable to other cards
      2. Card user's secret number either forgotten by
        user or discovered by thief
III. Potential Solutions to EFTS Misuses
    A. Identification of each card with easily remembered
      secret number
    B. Embedding of each card with a diffraction-grating
      metallic stripe that can be optically read
      1. Each card given unique identification
      2. Stripe nonduplicatable and nonremovable from the card
 IV. Summary

Sample outline

CHAPTER SUMMARY

Formal reports, which are the written accounts of major projects, normally contain three major parts: front matter, body, and back matter.

The *front matter* of a formal report may include a title page, an abstract, a table of contents, a list of figures, a list of tables, and a preface.

The *body* of a formal report includes the text of the report, complete with footnotes and references. Sometimes an introduction precedes the text.

The *back matter* of a formal report may include a bibliography, appendix(es), and a glossary.

In preparing a formal report, it is often necessary to make a *topic outline*. Such an outline enables you to plan the report by arranging the points you intend to make in the most logical order.

EXERCISES

1. Come to class prepared to discuss the following questions.

   a. Why should a formal report contain a *table of contents*?
   b. What is the function of a *preface* in a formal report?
   c. What is the function of *footnotes* in a formal report?
   d. What function do *heads* perform in a formal report?
   e. What determines when a new head is to be used?
   f. What is the difference between a *reference section* and a *bibliography*?
   g. What types of material should appear in an *appendix*?
   h. What is the function of a *glossary* in a formal report?

2. Write a formal report on a topic from your career field or other area of interest. You may want to use the topic you selected and the information you gathered in doing the exercises for Chapter 12. Prepare a topic outline for the report and submit it for your instructor's review. Include *at least* the following elements in the report (plus any additional elements your paper may require): *title page, abstract, table of contents, preface, introduction, heads, references,* and *bibliography.*

14

Other Kinds of On-the-Job Communication

Much on-the-job writing—for example, proposals, minutes of meetings, and job descriptions—cannot be classified as either correspondence or reports. Yet such types of communication can be just as important as the letters, memos, and reports that you write. Another kind of communication—the printed form—frequently requires only a minimum of writing and yet can in some circumstances be the most effective and efficient way to communicate. This chapter deals with several of the less-recognized kinds of on-the-job communication: proposals, minutes of meetings, job descriptions, and printed forms.

PROPOSALS

Two kinds of proposals are commonly used in the business world: internal and external.

An *internal proposal* usually recommends change or improvement within an organization. The recommendation might be to expand cafeteria service, to combine multiple manufacturing operations, to introduce new working procedures, to start a car-pool program, and so on. An internal proposal is ordinarily prepared by an employee or by a department and then sent to a higher-ranking person in the organization for approval.

An *external proposal* is a sales document: an offer by a company or other organization to provide a potential customer with a product or a service. An electrical contractor might offer to rewire a homeowner's basement, at a cost of a few hundred dollars; an aerospace manufacturer might present a bid to the Department of Defense for the design of a multimillion-dollar weapons system. Some external proposals run a page or two and are usually written by one person; other proposals take up several volumes and may be the product of a number of skilled people whose work is coordinated by a small committee of experts.

The Internal Proposal

The internal proposal may range from a suggestion that the shop floor be swept twice a day to a detailed plan for a management-reporting system. Regardless of complexity, however, an internal proposal must meet several requirements if it is to be successful.

First, you must establish the fact that a problem exists for which a solution is necessary. If the management of your firm or organization is not convinced that a change is necessary, your proposal may either go unnoticed or, if read, be dismissed out of hand. In making your case, be specific. Christine Thomas, in her memo recommending the purchase of an automated typewriter (Chapter 1), did not merely say, "We can save money"; she was specific: "Last year we paid $3,700 to the Wilson Secretarial Agency for temporary help. . . . we can purchase the automated typewriter for $1,495." Your familiarity with the details of the issue will tell your reader that you know what you are talking about—and make it more likely that your reader will listen to what you have to say. (A review of "Persuading Your Reader," Chapter 5, would be useful.)

Next, make practical recommendations to solve the problem. What is practical will depend upon the situation, of course. But if your recommendations stem directly from the case you have made for change, and if they appear workable, your proposal should get a fair hearing. Again, be specific. To recommend to a plant superintendent, for instance, that "safety measures be taken immediately" is too vague. Give guidance: suggest, instead, that "heavy wire mesh screens be mounted on the front of all tow motors." Whenever it is appropriate, your proposed solution should include information about any equipment or material that will be required, a breakdown of costs, or a schedule for the completion of the task. Details like these may be subject to change, but they will stimulate thought and action.

Finally, especially if your proposal is long or complicated, furnish your reader with a conclusion that ties everything together. The conclusion should be brief, no more than a few sentences or a short paragraph, and should convey a spirit of cooperation. Offer to set up a meeting, to provide further facts, or to be of assistance as the task gets underway.

The following internal proposal, which was submitted to the management of a firm that manufactures electrical equipment, states the problem clearly, provides numerous supporting details, and recommends specific actions to solve the problem.

MEMORANDUM

TO: Harold Clurman, Plant Superintendent

From: Fred Nelson, Safety Officer

Date: August 4, 19--

Subject: Safety Practices for Group 333

Many accidents and near-accidents have occurred in
Group 333 because of the hazardous working conditions in
this area. This memorandum identifies those hazardous
conditions and makes recommendations for their elimination.

Hazardous Conditions

Employees inside the factory must operate the walk-along
crane through aisles that are frequently congested with
scrap metal, discarded lumber, and other refuse from the
shearing area. Many surfaces in the area are oil coated.
    The containers for holding raw stock and scrap metal
are also unsafe. On many of the racks, the hooks are bent
inward so far that the crane cannot fit into them properly
unless it is banged and jiggled in a dangerous manner. To
add to the hazard, employees in the press group do not
always balance the load in the racks. As a result, the
danger of falling metal is great as the unbalanced racks
swing practically out of control overhead. These hazards
endanger employees in Group 333 and in the raw-stock and
shearing areas because the crane passes over these areas.
    Hazards also exist in the yard and in the chemical
building. The present method of dumping strip metal into the
scrap bins is the most dangerous practice of all. To dump
this metal, the tow motor operator picks up a rack, with
the rack straddling the tow motor forks, and raises it over
the edge of the scrap-metal bin. The operator then rotates
the forks to permit the scrap metal to fall from one end of
the rack. As the weight shifts, the upright frame at the
other end of the rack slams into one of the tow motor forks
(now raised 12 feet above the ground, inside the scrap tub).
This method of operation has resulted in two tow motor
tip-overs in the past month. In neither incident was the
driver injured, but the odds are great that someone will be
seriously harmed if the practice continues.
    Group 333 employees must also dump tubs full of scrap
metal from the tow motor into the 10-foot-high scrap bins.
In order to dump the metal on the tow-motor forks, the
operator must raise the tubs high above the head. Because of
the unpredictable way in which the metal falls from the tubs,

many facial cuts and body bruises have resulted. Employees
who work in the yard are also subject to danger in winter
weather: all employees have been cut and bruised in falls
that occurred as they were climbing up on scrap bins covered
with snow and ice to dump scrap from pallets that had not
been banded.
        Finally, nearly all Group 333 employees who must handle
the caustic chemicals in the chemical building report
damaged clothing and ruined shoes. Poor lighting in the
building (the lights are nearly 20 feet above the floor),
storage racks positioned less than two feet apart, and
container caps incorrectly fastened have made these
accidents impossible to prevent.

Recommendations

To eliminate these hazards as quickly as possible, I
recommend that the following actions be taken.
1. That Group 333 supervisors rigorously initiate and
   enforce a policy to free aisles of obstructions.
2. That all dangerous racks be repaired or replaced.
3. That the Engineering Group develop a safe rack dumper.
4. That heavy wire mesh screens be mounted on the front of
   all tow motors.
5. That Group 333 employees not accept scrap in containers
   that have not been properly banded.

        I would like to meet with you and the supervisor of
Group 333 before the end of the month, as your schedule
permits. You will have my complete cooperation in working
out all of the details of the proposed recommendations.

cc: Supervisor, Group 333

Internal proposal

The External Proposal

In an external proposal, a company or other organization offers to provide a
product or a service to a prospective customer at a specified price. Such proposals may range from a one-page letter to an elaborate offering that covers
hundreds of pages, depending on the size and complexity of the project.
External proposals are usually solicited, either publicly or privately. Large,
complex proposals generally follow rigid formats that are specified by the company or the government agency soliciting the proposal; such proposals are
often prepared by professional proposal writers. Shorter external proposals,
which you are more likely to write, frequently take the form either of a letter or
of a report accompanied by a cover letter.

The preparation of an external proposal requires careful planning. First, find out exactly what the potential customer wants. For a small project, you can talk directly to the customer, either in person or by phone. For a large project, you may receive *specifications*—that is, a detailed statement of what the customer wants. A close reading of the specifications should tell you precisely how the customer expects the project to be carried out. Before you submit the proposal, find out, if possible, who your competitors are. If you know who else is submitting proposals, you can compare your company's strengths with those of other companies submitting bids, determine where you have advantages over the competitors, and emphasize those advantages in your proposal. For example, a small software company bidding for an Air Force contract at a local base would very likely be quite familiar with its competitors. A proposal writer who believes that the company has better-qualified personnel than its competitors might include in the proposal the résumés of the key people who would be involved in the project (the résumés would list the job experience and education of each staff member).

The format of an external proposal may vary, but every such proposal must contain three major parts: an introduction, a body, and a conclusion; many also provide a list of supplementary materials.

The *introduction* should state the purpose and the scope of the proposal and should specify the total cost of the project. Indicate the date on which your firm can begin the project and the date on which you expect that the work will be completed.

The *body* of the proposal should itemize the products or services you will furnish. Include a precise breakdown of the costs and a listing of the dates of the expected completion of various phases of the project. And, if it is appropriate, include a discussion of the procedures you will follow in carrying out the work.

The *conclusion* of the proposal should contain the dates during which the proposal is to be considered a valid offer. You certainly wouldn't want a prospective customer to accept your proposal a year or more later, when the price you have specified may no longer be profitable. Use your conclusion, moreover, to review any advantages your firm may have over the competing bidders. Express your appreciation for the opportunity to submit the proposal and your confidence in your company's ability to do the job to the customer's satisfaction. You may add that you look forward to establishing a good working relationship with the customer, and close by offering to provide any additional information that may be needed.

If such supplemental material as blueprints, price sheets, or a catalog accompany the proposal, include a list of them at the end of the proposal. Make certain that all such material is factual information; do not include advertising.

The following external proposal was submitted by a nursery in response to bids sent to several local nurseries.

PROPOSAL
TO LANDSCAPE THE NEW CORPORATE HEADQUARTERS
OF THE
WATFORD VALVE CORPORATION

Submitted to: Ms. Tricia Olivera, Vice-President

Submitted by: Jerwalted Nursery, Inc.

Date Submitted: February 1, 19--

Introduction states purpose and scope of proposal, indicates when project can be started and completed.

Jerwalted Nursery, Inc., proposes to landscape the new corporate headquarters of the Watford Valve Corporation, on 1600 Swason Avenue, at a total cost of $8,000. The lot to be landscaped is approximately 600 feet wide and 700 feet deep. Landscaping will begin no later than April 30, 19-- and will be completed by May 31.

The following trees and plants will be planted, in the quantities and sizes given and at the prices specified.

4 maple trees (not less than 7 ft.) @ $40
    each--$160

41 birch trees (not less than 7 ft.) @ $65
    each--$2,665

2 spruce trees (not less than 7 ft.) @ $105
    each--$210

Body lists products to be provided, cost per item.

20 juniper plants (not less than 18 in.) @ $15
    each--$300

60 hedges (not less than 18 in.) @ $7
    each--$420

200 potted plants (various kinds) @ $2
    each--$400

Total Cost of Plants = $4,155
Labor = $3,845
Total Cost = $8,000

Conclusion specifies time limit of proposal, expresses confidence, and looks forward to working with prospective customer.

All trees and plants will be guaranteed against defect or disease for a period of 90 days, the warranty period to begin June 1, 19--.

The prices quoted in this proposal will be valid until June 30, 19--.

Thank you for the opportunity to submit this proposal. Jerwalted Nursery, Inc., has been in the landscaping and nursery business in the St. Louis area for thirty years, and our landscaping has won several awards and commendations,

<table>
<tr><td>

It emphasizes
a strength;
the writer
knows that
the com-
petitors are
new to the
area.
</td><td>

```
including a citation from the National Associa-
tion of Architects. We are eager to put our
skills and knowledge to work for you, and we are
confident that you will be pleased with our
work. If we can provide any additional informa-
tion or assistance, please call.
```
</td></tr>
</table>

MINUTES OF MEETINGS

Organizations and committees keep official records of their meetings; such records are known as *minutes*. If, in the course of your work, you attend many business-related meetings, you may be asked to serve as *recording secretary* at some of them. The duties of the secretary are to write down and distribute the minutes of a meeting. Usually, at each meeting the minutes of the previous meeting are read aloud if printed copies of the minutes were not distributed to the members beforehand; the group then votes to accept the minutes as prepared or to revise or clarify specific items.

The minutes of meetings should include the following information.

1. Name of the group or committee that is holding the meeting.
2. Place, time, and date of the meeting.
3. Kind of meeting being held (a regular meeting or a special meeting called to discuss a specific subject or problem).
4. Number of members present. If the committee or board is small (ten or fewer), members' names should be given.
5. A statement that the chairperson and the secretary were present, or the name of the substitute if either one was absent.
6. A statement that the minutes of the previous meeting were approved or revised, or a statement that the reading of the minutes was dispensed with.
7. A list of the reports that were read and approved. It is seldom necessary to give a detailed account of the substance of the reports submitted.
8. All the main motions that were made, with statements as to whether they were carried, defeated, or tabled (vote postponed). Do not include motions that were withdrawn. It is also customary to include the names of those who made and seconded the motions.
9. Resolutions that were adopted, written out in full. If a resolution was rejected, make a simple statement to that effect.
10. A record of all ballots, complete with the number of votes cast "for" and "against."
11. The time that the meeting was adjourned (officially ended) and the place, time, and date of the next meeting.
12. The recording secretary's signature (and typed name) and, if desired, the signature of the chairperson.

Since minutes are often used to settle disputes, they must be accurate, complete, and clear. When approved, minutes of meetings are official and can be used as evidence in legal proceedings.

Keep your minutes brief and to the point. Give complete information on each topic, but do not ramble—conclude the topic and go on to the next one. Following a set format will help you keep the minutes concise. You might, for example, use the heading TOPIC, followed by the subheadings *Discussion* and *Action Taken,* for each major point taken up.

```
                   NORTH TAMPA MEDICAL CENTER


              Minutes of the Regular Meeting of the
                    Medical Audit Committee

     DATE: July 26, 19--

     PRESENT: G. Miller (Chairperson), C. Bloom, J. Dades,
              K. Gilley, D. Ingoglia (Secretary), S. Ramirez,
              D. Rowan, C. Tsien, C. Voronski.

     ABSENT: R. Fautier, R. Wolf

     Dr. Gail Miller called the meeting to order at 12:45 p.m.
     Dr. David Ingoglia made a motion that the June 1, 19--,
     minutes be approved as distributed. Dr. Carole Tsien
     seconded the motion, which was passed.
          The committee discussed and took action on the
     following topics.


     (1) TOPIC: Meeting Time

          Discussion: A discussion was held on the most con-
     venient time for the committee to meet.
          Action: The committee decided to meet on the fourth
     Tuesday of every month, at 12:30 p.m.
```

Keep abstractions and generalities to a minimum and, most important, be specific. If you are referring to a nursing station on the second floor of a hospital, say, "the nursing station on the second floor" or "the second-floor nursing station," not "the second floor."

Keep in mind the possibility that the minutes you are preparing may be used, at some time in the future, by a lawyer, a judge, or a jury who probably won't be familiar with the situation you are describing—and that you may not be reachable to explain what you wrote (even if you are available, you may not remember any of the details of the situation). After all, the reason for taking minutes is to create a permanent record that will be available if it should be needed—at any time and for any reason.

Be specific, too, when you refer to people. Avoid using titles (the chief of the Word Processing Unit) in favor of names and titles (Ms. Florence Johnson, head of the Word Processing Unit). And be consistent in the way you refer to people. Do not call one person *Mr.* Jarrell and another *Janet* Wilson. It may be unintentional, but a lack of consistency in titles or names may reveal a deference to one person at the expense of another. Avoid adjectives and adverbs that suggest either good or bad qualities, as in "Mr. Sturgess's *capable* assistant read the *extremely comprehensive* report of the subcommittee." Minutes should always be objective and impartial.

If a member of the committee is to follow up on something and report back to the committee at its next meeting, state clearly the member's name and the responsibility he or she has accepted. There should be no uncertainty as to what task the member will be performing for the committee.

When you have been assigned to take the minutes at a meeting, go adequately prepared. Bring more than one pen and plenty of paper. If it is convenient, you may bring a tape recorder as backup to your notes. Have ready the minutes of the previous meeting and any other material that you may need. If you do not know shorthand, take memory-jogging notes during the meeting and then expand them with the appropriate details immediately after the meeting. Remember that minutes are primarily a record of specific actions taken, although you may sometimes need to summarize what was said or state the essential ideas in your own words.

Following is a sample set of minutes that uses a less rigid format than the last set of sample minutes.

```
                 WARETON MEDICAL CENTER
                 DEPARTMENT OF MEDICINE



             Minutes of the Regular Meeting of the
                   Credentials Committee


DATE: April 18, 19--

PRESENT: M. Valden (Chairperson), R. Baron, M. Frank,
         J. Guern, L. Kingson, L. Kinslow (Secretary),
         S. Perry, B. Roman, J. Sorder, F. Sugihana

Dr. Mary Valden called the meeting to order at 8:40 p.m.
The minutes of the previous meeting were unanimously
approved, with the following correction: the name of the
secretary of the Department of Medicine is to be changed
from Dr. Juanita Alvarez to Dr. Barbara Golden.
```

```
Old Business

None.


New Business

The request by Dr. Henry Russell for staff privileges in the
Department of Medicine was discussed. Dr. James Guern made
a motion that Dr. Russell be granted staff privileges.
Dr. Martin Frank seconded the motion, which was passed
unanimously.
     Similar requests by Dr. Ernest Hiram and Dr. Helen
Redlands were discussed. Dr. Fred Sugihana made a motion
that both physicians be granted all staff privileges except
respiratory-care privileges, because the two doctors had not
had a sufficient number of respiratory cases. Dr. Steven
Perry seconded the motion, which was passed unanimously.
     Dr. John Sorder and Dr. Barry Roman asked for a clari-
fication of general duties for active staff members with
respiratory-care privileges. Dr. Richard Baron stated that
he would present a clarification at the next scheduled staff
meeting, on May 15.
     Dr. Baron asked for a volunteer to fill the existing
vacancy for Emergency Room duty. Dr. Guern volunteered. He
and Dr. Baron will arrange a duty schedule.
     There being no further business, the meeting was
adjourned at 9:15 p.m. The next regular meeting is scheduled
for May 15, at 8:40 p.m.


Respectfully submitted,
```

Leslie Kinslow

```
Leslie Kinslow
Medical Staff Secretary
```

Mary Valden, MD

```
Mary Valden, MD
Chairperson
```

JOB DESCRIPTIONS

To ensure an efficiently functioning organization, most large companies and many small ones find it necessary to specify, in a formal *job description,* the duties of and requirements for many of the jobs in the firm. Job descriptions fill several important functions: they provide information on which equitable salary scales can be based; they help management determine whether all responsibilities within a company are adequately covered; they let both prospective and currently working employees know exactly what is expected of them; and, together, a firm's job descriptions present a picture of the organization's structure.

Sometimes plant or office supervisors are given the task of writing the job descriptions of the employees assigned to them. In many organizations, though, an employee may draft his or her own job description, which is then checked over and approved by the immediate superior.

Format for Writing Job Descriptions

Although job description formats vary from organization to organization, the following headings are typical.

Accountability.   This section identifies, by title, the person or persons to whom the employee reports.

Scope of responsibilities.   This section provides an overview of the primary and secondary functions of the job and states, if it is applicable, who reports to the employee.

Specific duties.   This section gives a detailed account of the specific duties of the job, as concisely as possible.

Personal requirements.   This section lists the education, training, experience, and licensing required or desired for the job.

Tips for Writing Job Descriptions

If you have been asked to prepare a job description for your position, the following guidelines should be of help to you.

1. Before attempting to write your job description, keep a list of all the different tasks you do in a week or a month. Otherwise, you will almost certainly leave out some of your duties.
2. Focus on content. Remember that you are writing a description of your job, not of yourself.
3. List your duties in decreasing order of importance. Knowing how your various duties rank in importance makes it easier to set valid job qualifications.
4. Begin each statement of a duty with a verb, and be specific about what the duty is. Write "Answer and route incoming telephone calls" rather than "Handle telephone calls."
5. Review existing job descriptions that you know have been successful.

The following job description, which is a typical one, never mentions the person holding the job described; it focuses, instead, on the job and on the qualifications any person must possess to fill the position.

```
JOB TITLE: Welding Supervisor

ACCOUNTABILITY: Reports directly to the Plant Manager

SCOPE OF RESPONSIBILITIES: Is responsible for supervising
    the work of fifteen welders, for preparing production
    reports, for maintaining and replacing equipment, and for
    carrying out such duties as the Plant Manager may specify.

SPECIFIC DUTIES:
Supervises the work of fifteen welders. Evaluates, every six
    months, the performance of the welders assigned to him or
    to her. Instructs new employees in safe working habits.
    Prepares a monthly attendance report. Periodically checks
    the quality of work by examining tubes and balls for weld
    splatters and by reviewing the inspector's quality
    reports.

Prepares production reports. Prepares a monthly memorandum
    itemizing production for the preceding month, including
    reasons for any failure to meet the production schedule.

Maintains and replaces equipment. Maintains accurate logs
    for each machine. Makes sure that all equipment is in good
    operating condition and ready for the start of the next
    shift. Makes sure that all safety devices function
    properly.

Carries out such duties as the Plant Manager may specify.
    Meets each week with the Plant Manager and attends
    special meetings as requested. Attends in-service training
    programs and keeps up to date on the latest welding
    techniques.

PERSONAL REQUIREMENTS: Trade or technical college certifi-
    cation or degree in welding. Six years welding experience.
    Ability to interact well with employees and management.
    Desire to stay up to date in the field.
```

CREATING BUSINESS FORMS

Because they provide a time-saving, efficient, and uniform way to record data, *business forms* are used for countless purposes in almost all occupations. It is easier and quicker to supply information by filling out a well-designed form than by writing a detailed memorandum, letter, or report. Another advantage the form has over other types of written communication is that on *every copy* of a form each particular piece of information appears in the same place—a fact that is especially important when many people are furnishing similar information. If each person providing information sent in an individually written letter, every sheet of paper submitted would be different and require time-consuming reading and interpretation. When the information is supplied on a form, on the other hand, the person filling out the form will have spent less time and effort in furnishing the data, and the person using the information from the form will have a much easier task retrieving and evaluating the data.

Preparing the Form

To be effective, a form should make it easy for one person to supply information and for another person to retrieve and interpret the information. Ideally, a form should be self-explanatory, even to a person who has never seen it before. If you are preparing a form, plan it carefully first. Determine what kind of information you will be seeking and arrange the requests for information in a logical order—logical from the point of view of both the person supplying the data and the person receiving it.

It's a good idea to make a draft of the form, putting in all the requests for information you've decided to include, in the order you consider the most logical. If any co-workers will be using the form, show the draft to them— you'll be rewarded for the extra time this step takes by the helpful criticism and suggestions you are likely to receive. Once you're satisfied with the draft, you can then prepare a final copy of the form.

Instructions and captions.   To make certain that information will be easy to enter on your form, be sure that you give the proper instructions in the proper place. You've probably had the experience, at some time or another, of starting to fill out a form only to realize too late that you've put your name on the line intended for your street address. When the instructions are clear and properly placed, the person filling out the form will not be confused about which information goes where.

Instructions, which are used primarily for long, complicated forms, should go at the beginning of the form; they are often preceded by a heading designed to attract the reader's attention.

```
          INSTRUCTIONS FOR COMPLETING THIS FORM

    1. Complete the applicable blue shaded portions on the
       front of pages 1, 2, and 3.
    2. Mail page 1 to the Securi-Med Insurance Company at the
       address shown above.
    3. Give page 2 to your doctor.
    4. If services are rendered in a hospital, give page 3 to
       the hospital.
    5. Use the back of page 1 to itemize bills that are to go
       toward your major medical deduction.
```

Instructions for distributing the various copies of multiple-copy forms are normally placed at the bottom of the form. The instructions are repeated on every copy of the form.

On the form itself, requests for information are normally worded as captions. Keep captions brief and to the point; avoid unnecessary repetition by combining requests for related pieces of information under an explanatory heading.

CHANGE   `What make of car do you drive?` _____

               `What year was it manufactured?` _____

               `What model is it?` _____

               `What is the body style?` _____

TO   `Vehicle Information`

        `Make` _____   `Year` _____

        `Model` _____   `Body Style` _____

Planning for responses.   In preparing a form it is important to provide questions that can be answered simply and briefly. The best responses are check marks, circles, or underlining; next best are numbers, single words, or brief phrases. Sentence responses are the least effective, since they take the most time to write and to read.

Make captions as specific as possible. For example, if a requested date is other than the date on which the form is being filled out, make the caption read, "Effective date," "Date issued," or whatever it may be, rather than simply "Date." As in all job-related writing, put yourself in your reader's place and try to imagine what sort of requests would be clear to you.

Sequencing of data.   In designing a form, try to arrange your requests for information in an order that will be most helpful to the person filling out the form. At the top of the form, include *preliminary information,* such as the name of your organization, the title of your form, and any file number or reference number. In the *main portion* of the form, include the entries you need in order to obtain the necessary data. At the *end* of the form, include space for the signature of the person filling out the form and the date.

Within the main portion of your form, the arrangement of the entries should depend upon several factors. First, the subject matter of the entries will frequently determine the most logical order. A form requesting reimbursement for travel expenses, for instance, would logically begin with the first day of the week (or month) and end with the last day of the appropriate period. Second, if the response to one item is based upon the response to another item, be sure that the items appear in the correct order. Third, whenever possible, group requests for related information together. Fourth, if a form is to move from one individual or one department to another, to be partly filled out by each in turn, put the data to be supplied by the first individual or department at the top of the form, the data to be supplied by the second next, and so on (and each section of the form should state clearly who is responsible for its completion). Finally, entries should, in general, be arranged on the form from left to right and from top to bottom, since that is the way we are accustomed to reading.

In many cases, you'll want to title your form. The title of the form should describe its use and application. A title should be no more than a few words long and should normally be positioned at the top center of your form. If space is critical, the title can be placed at the top left-hand corner of the form.

Designing Forms

When you sit down to prepare the final version of a form, you should pay particular attention to details of design—the arrangement, on the page, of the entry lines (where the responses will be filled in), and the amount of space provided for the responses.

Entry lines.   The form can be laid out so that the person filling out the form supplies information on a writing line, in a writing block, or in square boxes. The *writing line* is simply a caption.

(Name)	(Telephone)

(Street Address)

(City)	(State)	(Zip Code)

(Age)	(Weight)	(Height)	(Sex)

The *writing block* is essentially the same except that each entry is enclosed in a ruled block, making it impossible for the person filling out the form to associate a caption with the wrong line.

Name		Telephone
Street Address		
City	State	Zip Code
Age	Weight	Height	Sex

On some forms, captions are set horizontally.

Destination	Source	Supplier	Method of Shipment

On other forms, they are set vertically.

Destination	
Source	
Supplier	
Method of Shipment	

When all the possible responses to any one question can be anticipated, you can save the person filling out the form time and effort by writing the question on the form, supplying a labeled *square box* for each possible answer, and instructing the person filling out the form to put an X in the box that corresponds to the correct answer. Such a plan will save you time and effort in retrieving the data as well. Be sure that your questions are both simple and specific.

EXAMPLE   Would you buy another Whapo? ☐ Yes   ☐ No

The boxes may either precede or follow the question. Be sure, however, that the boxes and their labels are close enough together that they will be unmistakably associated.

REVISE   red ☐   blue ☐   green ☐   yellow ☐

TO   red ☐   blue ☐   green ☐   yellow ☐

Spacing.   Be sure to provide enough space for the person filling out the form to enter the data. Everyone has filled out a form on which the address, signature, or other item could not possibly fit in the space allowed for it. Insufficient writing space or uneven lines are guaranteed to irritate the person filling out the form and make the information supplied hard to read. In a long form that is poorly designed, errors occur with increasing frequency as the person filling out the form becomes more and more frustrated. And if you have trouble reading responses that are too tightly spaced or that snake around the side of the form, you may introduce additional errors as you retrieve the data.

Forms may be filled out either in longhand or on a typewriter. Always allow sufficient space to accommodate both typewritten and handwritten responses. If you think that at least some people filling it out will use longhand, provide adequate space for a relatively large handwriting. And if you expect that some will reply by typewriter, take their needs into account as well. It is especially important to plan for typewritten responses if you intend to have your form *typeset* (composed on a machine that sets copy for books, newspapers, and other materials). If you do not inform the typesetter that the printed form must be easy to use on a typewriter, those who use a typewriter

---

Annual Reappointment Form   July 1, 19__ to June 30, 19__

CHILDREN'S MEDICAL CENTER

1735 Chapel Street

Dayton, Ohio 45404

NAME:

List appointments or offices held, teaching positions, independent studies in medical or dental societies or other medical organizations, and any other professional recognitions you would like to have included in your file:

_____

_____

_____

_____

_____

_____

_____

Do you wish a change in your privileges? If so, specify:_____

_____

Have there been any changes in your board specialties?   Yes [   ]   No [   ]

        If yes: Date_____

                 Specialty Board_____

Signature_____

Date_____

                              Return to: Chairman
                                          Credentials & Nominating Comm.

Business form I

CHILDREN'S MEDICAL CENTER

PHYSICIAN:	DEPARTMENT:
OFFICE ADDRESS:	SECTION:
OFFICE PHONE:	OHIO LICENSE NO:
STAFF STATUS:	BIRTHDATE:

****

1978-79		1979-80		1980-81		1981-82	
Satisfactory Health Status		Satisfactory Health Status		Satisfactory Health Status		Satisfactory Health Status	
Satisfactory Meeting Attendance		Satisfactory Meeting Attendance		Satisfactory Meeting Attendance		Satisfactory Meeting Attendance	
Satisfactory Medical Record Completion		Satisfactory Medical Record Completion		Satisfactory Medical Record Completion		Satisfactory Medical Record Completion	
No Disciplinary Action		No Disciplinary Action		No Disciplinary Action		No Disciplinary Action	
COMMITTEE APPOINTMENTS		COMMITTEE APPOINTMENTS		COMMITTEE APPOINTMENTS		COMMITTEE APPOINTMENTS	
APPROVED	DATE	APPROVED	DATE	APPROVED	DATE	APPROVED	DATE
Chairman, Cre- dentials Comm.		Chairman, Cre- dentials Comm.		Chairman, Cre- dentials Comm.		Chairman, Cre- dentials Comm.	
Chief of Staff		Chief of Staff		Chief of Staff		Chief of Staff	
Secretary, Board of Trustees		Secretary, Board of Trustees		Secretary, Board of Trustees		Secretary, Board of Trustees	

Business form II

may have difficulty aligning the form vertically in their machines. The reason is simple: on a typewriter, there are 6 lines to the inch, but on typesetting equipment there are 6.0386 lines to the inch—there's a hairline less space between typeset lines than between typewritten lines—and any typewriter will be off the writing line by the time it nears the bottom of a page-long form. Be sure, then, to remind the typesetter to set *exactly* 6 lines to the inch. And if the form will contain more than one response per line, align the column entries vertically whenever possible, so that the person filling out the form can set tabs on the typewriter (when the tab is pressed, the platen, or roller, automatically moves to a previously set point along the line). As for horizontal spacing, there are two kinds of typewriters: the *elite,* which has twelve characters (both letters and spaces) to the inch, and the *pica,* which has ten characters to the inch. Allow adequate space for responses typed on a pica typewriter.

CHAPTER SUMMARY

Proposals, job descriptions, and minutes of meetings—although not required as frequently as letters, memos, and reports—are nonetheless very important kinds of on-the-job writing. The use of well-designed forms is another form of communication which can sometimes, under the right circumstances, be more effective and efficient than writing.

Two kinds of proposals are commonly written in the business world: internal and external. An *internal proposal,* which is written to someone higher in the management structure of an organization, recommends a change or an improvement within an organization. An *external proposal* is a sales document that offers to provide a potential customer with a product or service, or both, at a specific price within a specified period of time.

Minutes are the official records of business meetings. Written by the designated secretary of the committee or group, they are used to settle disputes, and sometimes even as evidence in lawsuits.

Job descriptions specify the duties and requirements for specific jobs. They help management establish equitable salary scales and determine whether all responsibilities within a company are adequately covered. They help employees know exactly what is expected of them in their jobs.

Well-designed *business forms* provide a time-saving, efficient, and uniform way to record routine data that is quicker and easier than writing detailed letters or reports.

EXERCISES

1. Write a *proposal* in which you recommend change in a procedure. The procedure should be one with which you are familiar, either at school or at work. The proposal should state the nature of the problem and explain how the new procedure would be put into effect. Give at least three reasons for the change and support your reasons with facts that show the advantages of your proposal. Address the proposal to a dean or other school official (if the proposal is school-related) or to your immediate supervisor (if the proposal is work-related).

2. Attend a meeting of an organization of which you are a member. Go to the meeting prepared to take careful, complete notes of the proceedings of the

meeting. From the notes you have taken, write up the *minutes of the meeting.*

3. Interview someone who holds a job in a field that interests you. Based on the information you obtain about the job from the interview, prepare a *job description* of the position.

4. Prepare a weekly time card for factory employees at United Agricultural Products. Employees work Mondays through Fridays, 8 a.m. to noon, 12:30 to 3:30 p.m., and have a half hour for lunch. Include on the time card a column listing the days of the week (vertical column) and columns labeled "Time In," "Time Out" (morning), "Lunch," "Time In," "Time Out" (afternoon), and "Overtime" (horizontal columns). Supervisors are to fill in the time that employees actually arrive at work and leave for the day and the time of their lunch breaks. They are also to fill in the number of hours (if any) of overtime employees work each day. Include columns for the total hours worked each day and a final box or space for total hours worked for the week. Be sure to leave space for the dates the time card covers and for the signatures of both the employee and the supervisor.

15

Creating Tables and Illustrations

The primary purpose of including tables and illustrations in your writing is to increase your reader's understanding of what you are saying. Tables, graphs, drawings, charts, and maps—often collectively called *visuals* or *visual aids*—can often express ideas or convey information in ways that words alone cannot. Tables allow easy comparison between large numbers of statistics that would be difficult to understand if they appeared in sentence form. Graphs make trends and mathematical relationships immediately evident to the reader. And drawings and maps can frequently indicate shapes and relationships in space more concisely and efficiently than text can.

Make tables and illustrations functional parts of your writing. If they will not contribute directly to your reader's understanding, do not use them. And when they are necessary, consider your purpose and your reader carefully. For example, the drawing of an x-ray machine for a high school science class would be different from the illustration provided for the technician who repairs such machines.

Many of the qualities of good writing—simplicity, clarity, conciseness, directness—are just as important in the creation and use of tables and illustrations.

Tips for Creating Tables and Illustrations

The following general guidelines apply to most visual materials. Detailed guidelines for specific kinds of illustrations are given in the discussion of each type.

1. Keep the information the illustration is presenting as brief and as simple as possible.

2. Try to present only one type of information in each illustration.
3. Label or caption each illustration clearly.
4. When necessary, include a key that identifies any symbols and abbreviations you use in the illustration.
5. When appropriate, specify the proportions used, or include a scale of relative distances.
6. To make the illustration easier to read, whenever possible use lettering that goes from left to right rather than from top to bottom.
7. Keep terminology consistent. Do not, for instance, refer to something as a "proportion" in the text and as a "percentage" in the illustration.
8. Leave enough space around and within the illustration for easy viewing.
9. Position the illustration as close as possible to the text that refers to it; an illustration should never appear ahead of the first text reference to it, however.
10. Be certain that the significance of each illustration is clear from the text.
11. If several tables or illustrations are used, number the illustrations or tables consecutively. Number tables separately from illustrations.
12. In a formal report, if more than five tables or illustrations appear, list them, together with figure and page numbers, under a separate heading following the table of contents, labeled "List of Figures" or "List of Tables."

Presented with clarity and consistency, visuals can help your reader focus on key portions of your report. Be aware, though, that even the best illustration only supplements, or supports, the text. Your writing must carry the burden of providing context for the illustration and pointing out its significance.

A discussion of tables and illustrations commonly used in on-the-job writing follows. Your topic will ordinarily determine the best type or types of visual material to use when your text needs illustration.

TABLES

A table is useful for showing large numbers of specific, related data in a brief space. Because a table displays its information in rows and columns, the reader can easily compare data in one column with data in another; if such data were presented in the text, the reader would have to go through passages of figures.

Guidelines for Creating Tables

Table number. If you are using several tables, assign each a number; center the number and title above the table. Table numerals are usually Arabic,

Table number ——————————— Table 1

Boxhead

Title ——— Monthly Average Solar Energy*

Column headings

Month	Solar energy available, Btu/ft^2-mo (a)	Solar energy collectible, Btu/ft^2-mo (b)
January	53,500	5,307
February	57,000	6,139
March	71,500	14,054
April	71,000	14,314
May	70,000	17,115
June	70,000	18,635
July	72,000	21,468
August	71,200	18,231
September	66,500	16,971
October	62,000	12,595
November	51,000	8,823
December	47,200	6,012

Stub

Rule

Source —— SOURCE: NASA Langley Research Center.

*Latitude 37° N, Hampton, Virginia

Footnotes —— [a]Maximum values at 35° collector tilt angle on a clear day.

[b]Average value where percentage of cloud cover, collector efficiency, and so forth are taken into consideration.

Sample table and its parts

and they should be assigned sequentially to the tables throughout the text. Tables should be referred to in the text by table number rather than by location ("Table 4" rather than "the above table"). If your report or paper has more than five tables, list table titles, table numbers, and page numbers on a separate page immediately after the Table of Contents, labeled "List of Tables."

Table title. The title, which is placed just above the table, should describe concisely what the table represents.

Boxhead. The boxhead carries the column headings. Headings should be kept brief but descriptive. Units of measurement, where necessary, should be specified either as part of the heading or enclosed in parentheses beneath the heading. Standard abbreviations are acceptable. Avoid vertical lettering whenever possible.

Stub. The left-hand vertical column of a table is the stub. It lists the items about which information is given in the body of the table.

Body. The body comprises the data below the boxhead and to the right of the stub. Within the body, columns should be arranged so that the terms to be compared appear in adjacent rows and columns. Where no information exists for a specific item, substitute a row of dots or a dash to acknowledge the gap.

Rules. These are the lines that separate the table into its various parts. Horizontal rules are placed below the title, below the body of the table, and between the column headings and the body of the table. They should not be closed at the sides. The columns within the table may be separated by vertical rules if such lines aid clarity.

Source line. The source line, which identifies where the data were obtained, appears below the table (when a source line is appropriate).

Footnotes. Footnotes are used for explanations of individual items in the table. Symbols (*, #) or lower-case letters (sometimes in parentheses), rather than numbers, are ordinarily used to key table footnotes because numbers might be mistaken for the data in a numerical table.

Continuing tables. When a table must be divided so that it can be continued on another page, repeat the boxhead and give the table number at the head of each new page with a "continued" label ("Table 3, continued").

GRAPHS

Graphs, like tables, present numerical data in visual form. Graphs have several advantages over tables. Trends, movements, distributions, and cycles are more readily apparent in graphs than they are in tables. By providing a means for ready comparisons, a graph often shows a significance in the data not otherwise immediately evident. Be aware, however, that although graphs present statistics in a more interesting and comprehensible form than tables do, they are less accurate. For this reason, they are often accompanied by tables that give exact figures. There are many different kinds of graphs, most notably line graphs, bar graphs, pie graphs, and picture graphs.

Line Graphs

The line graph, which is the most widely used of all graphs, shows the relationship between two sets of figures. The graph is composed of a vertical axis and a horizontal axis that intersect at right angles. Each axis represents one set of figures. The relationship between the two sets is indicated by points plotted along appropriate intersections of the two axes. Once plotted, the points are connected to one another to form a continuous line, and the relationship between the two sets of data becomes readily visible.

The line graph's vertical axis usually represents amounts (the vertical axis in Figure 15-1 represents numbers of children), and its horizontal axis

usually represents increments of time (the horizontal axis in Figure 15-1 represents ten-year increases).

Line graphs with more than one plotted line are common because they
allow for comparisons between two sets of statistics. In creating such graphs,
be certain to identify each plotted line with a label or a legend, as shown in
Figure 15-2. You can emphasize the difference between the two lines by shading the space that separates them.

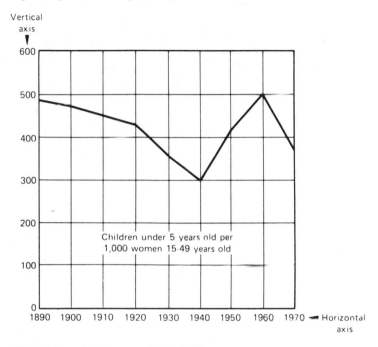

FIGURE 15-1. Fertility ratio: 1890–1970
SOURCE: U.S. Bureau of the Census

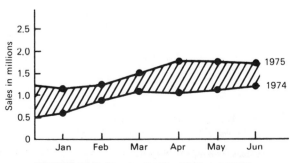

FIGURE 15-2. Truck sales for 1974 and 1975

Tips on Preparing Line Graphs

1. Give the graph a title that describes the data clearly and concisely.
2. If your report includes several illustrations, assign a figure number to each one.
3. Indicate the *zero point* of the graph (the point where the two axes meet). If the range of data shown makes it inconvenient to begin at zero, insert a break in the scale, as in Figure 15-3.
4. Divide the vertical axis into equal portions from the least amount at the bottom to the greatest amount at the top. Ordinarily, the caption for this scale is placed at the upper left. Lengthy captions can be placed vertically along the vertical axis, as in Figure 15-2.
5. Divide the horizontal axis into equal units from left to right. If a caption is necessary, center it directly beneath the scale.
6. The angle at which the curved line rises and falls is determined by the scales of the two axes—that is, by the units into which each axis is divided. It's important, therefore, to divide the vertical and horizontal scales so that they give an accurate visual impression of the data. The curve can be kept free of distortion if the ratio between the scales is kept constant. See Figures 15-4 and 15-5.
7. Hold grid lines to a minimum so that the curved lines stand out. Since precise values are usually shown in a table of data accompanying a graph, detailed grid lines are unnecessary. Note the increasing clarity of the three graphs in Figures 15-6, 15-7, and 15-8.
8. Include a key (which lists and explains symbols) when necessary, as in Figure 15-7. Sometimes a label will do just as well, as in Figure 15-8.

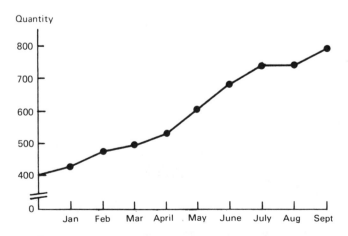

FIGURE 15-3. Widget sales for January–September 1979

9. If the information comes from another source, include a source line just under the graph at the lower left, as in Figure 15-1.
10. Place explanatory footnotes directly below the figure number. See Figure 15-11.
11. Make all lettering read horizontally if possible.

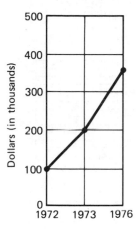

FIGURE 15-4. Sales growth, *Distorted curve*

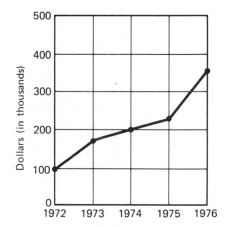

FIGURE 15-5. Sales growth, *Distortion-free curve*

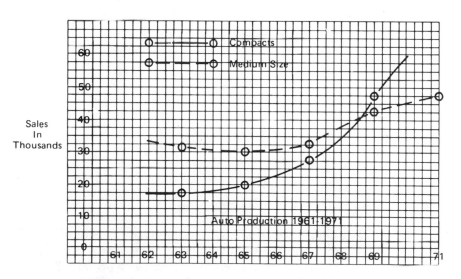

FIGURE 15-6. Production

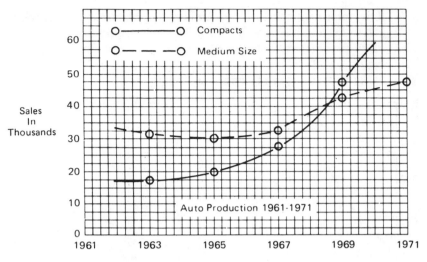

FIGURE 15-7. Auto production

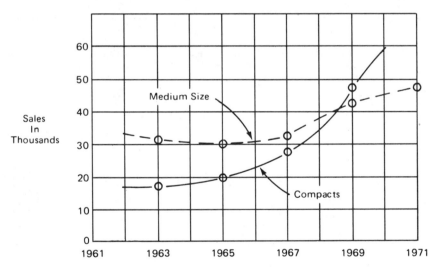

FIGURE 15-8. Auto production, 1961–1971

Bar Graphs

Bar graphs consist of horizontal or vertical bars of equal width but scaled in length to represent some quantity. They are commonly used to show (1) quantities of the same item for different time periods, (2) quantities of different items for the same time period, or (3) quantities of the different parts of an item that make up the whole.

Figure 15-9 is an example of a bar graph that shows varying quantities of the same item for the same time period. Each bar, which represents specific population figures, begins at the left scale. The left scale provides additional information in the form of the percentage of the whole population each bar (and therefore each state) represents.

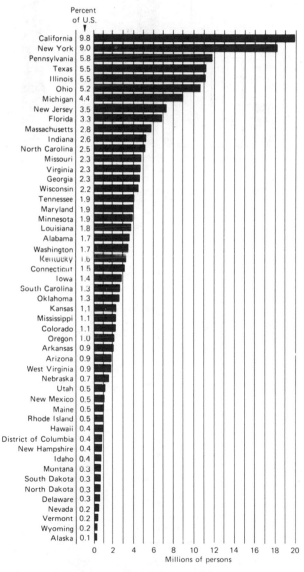

FIGURE 15-9. States ranked by total population, 1970
SOURCE: U.S. Bureau of the Census

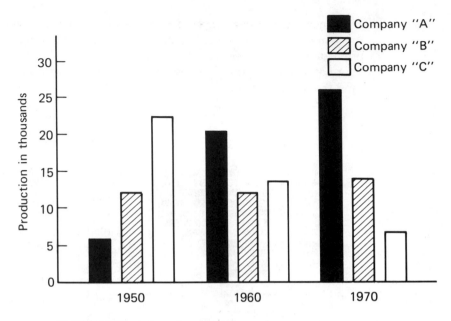

FIGURE 15-10. Auto parts production

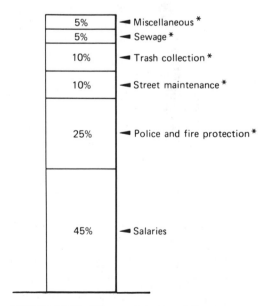

FIGURE 15-11. Your municipal tax dollar
* These figures do not include salaries.

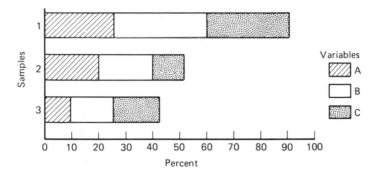

FIGURE 15-12. Example of 100 percent bar graph showing proportions of three variables in three samples

Some bar graphs show the quantities of different items for the same period of time. See Figure 15-10. (A bar graph with vertical bars is also called a *column graph.*) If the bar is not labeled, as in Figures 15-10 and 15-12, the different portions of the bar must be clearly indicated by shading, cross-hatching, or other devices. Include a key that represents the various subdivisions.

Bar graphs can also indicate what proportion of a whole the various component parts represent. In such a graph the bar, which is theoretically equivalent to 100 percent, is divided according to the proportion of the whole that each item sampled represents (see Figure 15-11). In some bar graphs the completed bar does not represent 100 percent, because all the parts of the whole have not been included in the sample (see Figure 15-12).

Pie Graphs

A pie graph presents data as wedge-shaped sections of a circle. The circle equals 100 percent, or the whole, of some quantity (a tax dollar, a bus fare, the hours of a working day), with the wedges representing the various parts into which the whole can be divided. In Figure 15-13, for example, the circle stands for a city tax dollar and is divided into units equivalent to the percentage of the tax dollar spent on various city services.

The relationships among the various statistics presented in a pie graph are easy to grasp, but the information is often rather general; for this reason, a pie graph is often accompanied by a table that presents the actual figures on which the percentages in the graph are based.

When you construct a pie graph, keep the following points in mind.

1. The complete, 360° circle is equivalent to 100 percent; therefore, each percentage point is equivalent to 3.6°.
2. To make the relative percentages as clear as possible, begin at the 12 o'clock position and sequence the wedges clockwise, from largest to smallest.

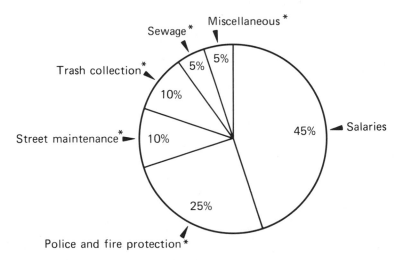

FIGURE 15-13. Your municipal tax dollar
* These figures do not include salaries.

3. If you shade the wedges, do so clockwise and from light to dark.
4. Keep all labels horizontal and, most important, give the percentage values of each wedge.
5. Finally, check to see that all wedges, as well as the percentage values given for them, add up to 100 percent.

Although pie graphs have strong visual impact, they also have drawbacks. If more than five or six items of information are presented, the graph looks cluttered. And, unless percentages are labeled on each section, the reader cannot compare the values of the sections as accurately as on a bar graph.

Picture Graphs

Picture graphs are modified bar graphs that use picture symbols to represent the item for which data are presented. Each symbol corresponds to a specified quantity of the item. See Figure 15-14. Note that precise figures are also included, since the picture symbol can indicate only approximate figures.

Tips on Preparing Picture Graphs

1. Make the symbol self-explanatory.
2. Have each symbol represent a single item.
3. Show larger quantities by increasing the number of symbols rather than by creating a larger symbol because it is difficult to judge relative size accurately.

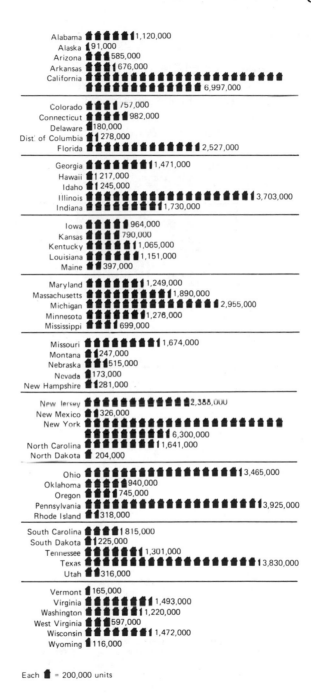

Alabama 🏠🏠🏠🏠🏠🏠 1,120,000
Alaska 🏠 91,000
Arizona 🏠🏠🏠 585,000
Arkansas 🏠🏠🏠🏠 676,000
California 🏠🏠🏠🏠🏠🏠🏠🏠🏠🏠🏠🏠🏠🏠🏠🏠🏠🏠🏠🏠🏠🏠🏠🏠🏠🏠🏠🏠🏠🏠🏠🏠🏠🏠 6,997,000

Colorado 🏠🏠🏠🏠 757,000
Connecticut 🏠🏠🏠🏠🏠 982,000
Delaware 🏠 180,000
Dist. of Columbia 🏠🏠 278,000
Florida 🏠🏠🏠🏠🏠🏠🏠🏠🏠🏠🏠🏠🏠 2,527,000

Georgia 🏠🏠🏠🏠🏠🏠🏠 1,471,000
Hawaii 🏠🏠 217,000
Idaho 🏠🏠 245,000
Illinois 🏠🏠🏠🏠🏠🏠🏠🏠🏠🏠🏠🏠🏠🏠🏠🏠🏠🏠🏠 3,703,000
Indiana 🏠🏠🏠🏠🏠🏠🏠🏠🏠 1,730,000

Iowa 🏠🏠🏠🏠🏠 964,000
Kansas 🏠🏠🏠🏠 790,000
Kentucky 🏠🏠🏠🏠🏠🏠 1,065,000
Louisiana 🏠🏠🏠🏠🏠🏠 1,151,000
Maine 🏠🏠 397,000

Maryland 🏠🏠🏠🏠🏠🏠🏠 1,249,000
Massachusetts 🏠🏠🏠🏠🏠🏠🏠🏠🏠 1,890,000
Michigan 🏠🏠🏠🏠🏠🏠🏠🏠🏠🏠🏠🏠🏠🏠🏠 2,955,000
Minnesota 🏠🏠🏠🏠🏠🏠 1,276,000
Mississippi 🏠🏠🏠🏠 699,000

Missouri 🏠🏠🏠🏠🏠🏠🏠🏠 1,674,000
Montana 🏠🏠 247,000
Nebraska 🏠🏠🏠 515,000
Nevada 🏠 173,000
New Hampshire 🏠🏠 281,000

New Jersey 🏠🏠🏠🏠🏠🏠🏠🏠🏠🏠🏠🏠 2,388,000
New Mexico 🏠🏠 326,000
New York 🏠🏠🏠🏠🏠🏠🏠🏠🏠🏠🏠🏠🏠🏠🏠🏠🏠🏠🏠🏠🏠🏠🏠🏠🏠🏠🏠🏠🏠🏠🏠 6,300,000
North Carolina 🏠🏠🏠🏠🏠🏠🏠🏠 1,641,000
North Dakota 🏠 204,000

Ohio 🏠🏠🏠🏠🏠🏠🏠🏠🏠🏠🏠🏠🏠🏠🏠🏠🏠🏠 3,465,000
Oklahoma 🏠🏠🏠🏠🏠 940,000
Oregon 🏠🏠🏠🏠 745,000
Pennsylvania 🏠🏠🏠🏠🏠🏠🏠🏠🏠🏠🏠🏠🏠🏠🏠🏠🏠🏠🏠🏠 3,925,000
Rhode Island 🏠🏠 318,000

South Carolina 🏠🏠🏠🏠 815,000
South Dakota 🏠🏠 225,000
Tennessee 🏠🏠🏠🏠🏠🏠🏠 1,301,000
Texas 🏠🏠🏠🏠🏠🏠🏠🏠🏠🏠🏠🏠🏠🏠🏠🏠🏠🏠🏠🏠 3,830,000
Utah 🏠🏠 316,000

Vermont 🏠 165,000
Virginia 🏠🏠🏠🏠🏠🏠🏠 1,493,000
Washington 🏠🏠🏠🏠🏠🏠 1,220,000
West Virginia 🏠🏠🏠 597,000
Wisconsin 🏠🏠🏠🏠🏠🏠🏠 1,472,000
Wyoming 🏠 116,000

Each 🏠 = 200,000 units

FIGURE 15-14. Number of housing units, by states, 1970
SOURCE: U.S. Bureau of the Census

DRAWINGS

A drawing is useful when you wish to focus on details or relationships that a photograph cannot capture (see Figure 15-15). A drawing can emphasize the significant piece of a mechanism, or its function, and omit what is not significant. However, if the precise details of the actual appearance of an object are necessary to your report or document, a photograph is essential.

When it is necessary to show the internal parts of a piece of equipment in such a way that their relationship to the device as a whole is clear, a *cutaway drawing* is necessary. See Figure 15-16.

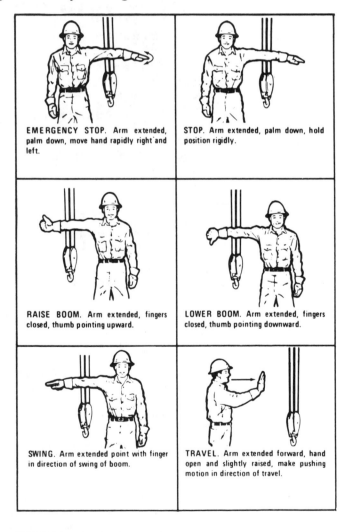

FIGURE 15-15. Hand signals for crane operation
SOURCE: Harnischfeger Corporation

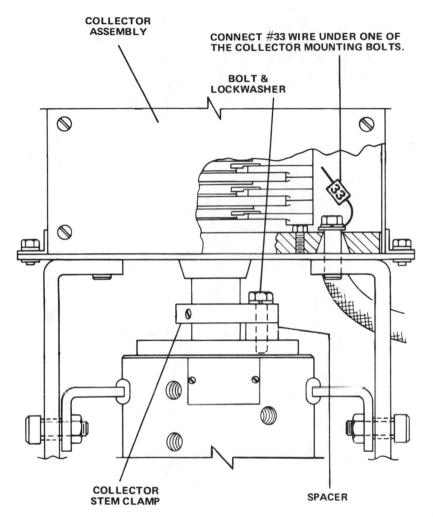

COLLECTOR
ASSEMBLY

CONNECT #33 WIRE UNDER ONE OF
THE COLLECTOR MOUNTING BOLTS.

BOLT &
LOCKWASHER

COLLECTOR
STEM CLAMP

SPACER

FIGURE 15-16. Detail view—collector
SOURCE: Harnischfeger Corporation

To show the proper sequence in which parts fit together, or when it is essential to show the details of each individual part, use an *exploded-view drawing.* See Figure 15-17.

Tips for Creating and Using Drawings

Many organizations have their own format specifications. In the absence of such specifications, the following tips will be helpful.

1. Give the drawing a clear title and a figure number, both of which should be centered below the drawing.

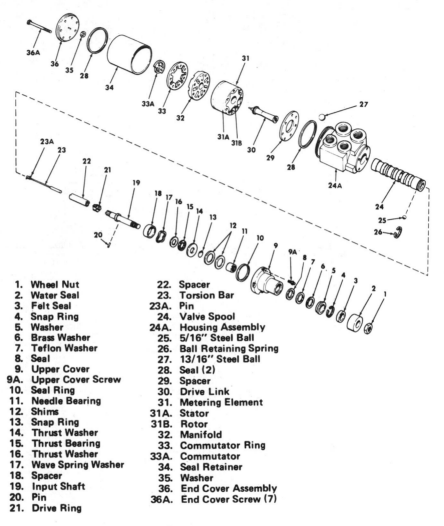

1. Wheel Nut
2. Water Seal
3. Felt Seal
4. Snap Ring
5. Washer
6. Brass Washer
7. Teflon Washer
8. Seal
9. Upper Cover
9A. Upper Cover Screw
10. Seal Ring
11. Needle Bearing
12. Shims
13. Snap Ring
14. Thrust Washer
15. Thrust Bearing
16. Thrust Washer
17. Wave Spring Washer
18. Spacer
19. Input Shaft
20. Pin
21. Drive Ring

22. Spacer
23. Torsion Bar
23A. Pin
24. Valve Spool
24A. Housing Assembly
25. 5/16" Steel Ball
26. Ball Retaining Spring
27. 13/16" Steel Ball
28. Seal (2)
29. Spacer
30. Drive Link
31. Metering Element
31A. Stator
31B. Rotor
32. Manifold
33. Commutator Ring
33A. Commutator
34. Seal Retainer
35. Washer
36. End Cover Assembly
36A. End Cover Screw (7)

FIGURE 15-17. Power steering valve
SOURCE: Harnischfeger Corporation

2. Place the source line, if there is one, aligned beneath the title.
3. Show the equipment from the point of view of the person who will use it.
4. When illustrating a subsystem, show its relationship to the larger system of which it is a part.
5. Draw the different parts of an object in proportion to one another, unless you indicate that certain parts are enlarged.
6. Where a sequence of drawings is used to illustrate a process, arrange them from left to right and from top to bottom.

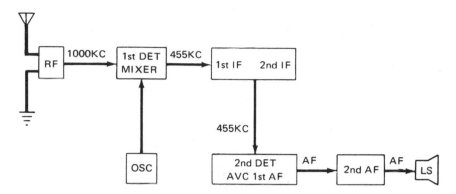

FIGURE 15-18. Flowchart of standard radio receiver showing stages of the process

7. Label parts in the drawing so that text references to them are clear.
8. Depending on the complexity of what is shown, labels may be placed on the parts themselves, or the parts may be given letter or number symbols, with an accompanying key. See Figure 15-17.

FLOWCHARTS

A flowchart is the diagram of a process that involves stages, with the sequence of stages shown from beginning to end. Figure 15 18 illustrates the stages by which electromagnetic waves are intercepted and modified in a radio receiver. When creating a flowchart, consider the following points.

1. Title the flowchart clearly. Position the title below the chart.
2. Assign a figure number if your report contains several illustrations.
3. Use arrows to show the direction of flow.
4. Label each step in the process, or identify it with a conventional symbol. Steps may also be represented pictorially or in captioned blocks.
5. Include a key if the flowchart contains any symbols your reader may not understand.
6. Leave adequate space on the page. Do not crowd the steps and directional arrows closely together.
7. As with all illustrations, place the flowchart as close as possible to that portion of the text which refers to it.

ORGANIZATIONAL CHARTS

An organizational chart shows how the various components of an organization are related to one another. Such an illustration is useful when you want to give

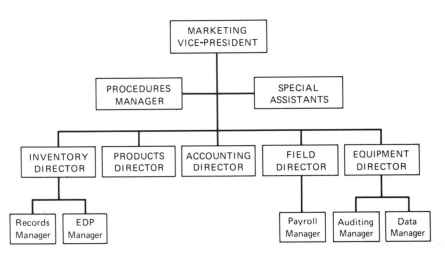

FIGURE 15-19. Cramer, Inc., field marketing organization

readers an overview of an organization or indicate the lines of authority within the organization. See Figure 15-19.

The title of each organizational component (office, section, division) is placed in a separate box. These boxes are then linked to a central authority. If your readers need the information, include the name of the person occupying the position identified in each box.

As with all illustrations, place the organizational chart as close as possible to the text that refers to it.

MAPS

Maps can be used to show the specific geographic features of the area represented (roads, mountains, rivers, etc.) or to show information according to geographic distribution (population, housing, manufacturing centers, etc.).

Bear these points in mind as you create maps for use with your text. See Figure 15-20.

1. Label the map clearly.
2. Assign the map a figure number if you are using enough illustrations to justify use of figure numbers.
3. Make sure all boundaries within the map are clearly identified. Eliminate unnecessary boundaries.
4. Eliminate unnecessary information from your map. For example, if population is important, do not include mountains, roads, rivers, etc.

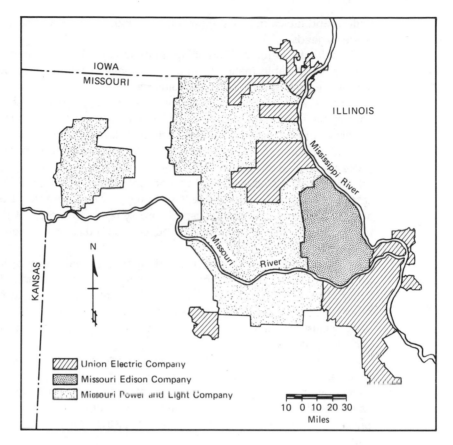

FIGURE 15-20. Location of service area of three utilities
SOURCE: U.S. Nuclear Regulatory Commission

5. Include a scale of miles or feet to give your reader an indication of the map's proportions.
6. Indicate which direction is north.
7. Emphasize key features by using shading, dots, crosshatching, or appropriate symbols.
8. Include a key telling what the different colors, shadings, or symbols represent.
9. Place maps as close as possible to the portion of the text that refers to them.

CHAPTER SUMMARY

Tables and illustrations—graphs, drawings, charts, and maps—can increase the reader's understanding of what you are saying; they can express ideas or convey information in ways that words alone cannot. To be effective, illustrations and tables must be appropriate to your purpose and suitable to your reader's needs.

A *table* is useful for listing large numbers of specific, related figures in a brief space. A table makes comparisons between figures easy because the figures are arranged in rows and columns.

There are several kinds of graphs. *Line graphs* are used to show the relationship between two or more sets of figures. *Bar graphs* are used to show the quantities of one item at different periods of time, the quantities of different items at the same period of time, or the quantities of different parts of an item (or of a whole). The circle of a *pie graph* equals 100 percent, or the whole, of an element. The wedge-shaped sections into which the circle is divided indicate the percentage of the whole that each division represents. *Picture graphs* are modified bar graphs that use picture symbols to represent the item for which information is given; each symbol corresponds to a specified quantity of the item.

Drawings are invaluable for depicting details of an object or for the relationship between objects. Frequently, a drawing is of the outside of an object. When, however, it is necessary to reveal the internal parts of a machine or other object, a *cutaway drawing* is appropriate. An *exploded-view drawing* is used to illustrate the way in which parts fit together or to present the details of each separate part.

When you want to present a visual depiction of various stages of a process, choose a *flowchart*. When, on the other hand, your purpose is to show how the various jobs in an organization relate to each other, or to indicate lines of authority within an organization, an *organizational chart* is appropriate. Material on geographical location or distribution can be displayed on a *map*.

EXERCISES

1. Create a table that shows the features of a seasonal maintenance task that you perform over the period of a year. Lawn and automobile care are among the kinds of tasks you may perform on a routine schedule.

2. Create a line graph that shows what percentages of the population of the United States owned homes for the periods discussed in the following passage.

> For a growing army of people, realizing the American dream of the good life is closely associated with owning a home. Of 63.4 million occupied housing units counted in the 1970 census, nearly 63 percent (about 40 million) were lived in by their owners. More than 7 million home-owners were added to the U.S. total between 1960 and 1970.
>
> The proportion of owner-occupied homes was 62 percent in 1960 and 55 percent in 1950. In 1940, the first complete housing census found that the owner-occupied proportion was less than 44 percent.[1]

[1] U.S. Bureau of the Census.

3. Prepare a pie graph showing 1979 ownership of commercial forest land in the United States. Ownership percentages by group are as follows: state and community, 6 percent; forest industries, 13 percent; federal lands, 21 percent; farms, 34 percent; other private ownership, 26 percent.

4. Prepare a bar graph showing how you budget your present income for a typical month.

5. Create a bar graph that plots student enrollments over the past twenty years at the school you are presently attending. Present the same information in a table.

6. Create a graph that compares sales in thousands of dollars among the various truck parts divisions of the ABC Corporation for 1974, 1978, and 1979. Sales for each division are as follows: axles—1979 ($225), 1978 ($200), 1974 ($75); universal joints—1979 ($125), 1978 ($100), 1974 ($35); frames—1979 ($125), 1978 ($100), 1974 ($50); transmissions—1979 ($75), 1978 ($65), 1974 ($50); clutches—1979 ($35), 1978 ($30), 1974 ($15); and gaskets and seals—1979 ($28), 1978 ($25), 1974 ($20).

7. Modify the following graph so that it can be understood more easily than it can in its present form.

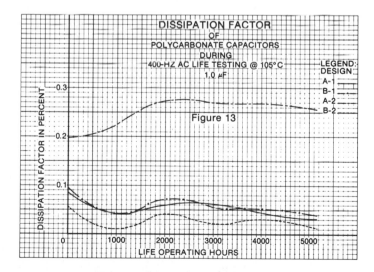

8. Select five drawings from reports, articles, or textbooks. Explain whether or not you think the illustrations make the text more meaningful or easier to follow. Take into consideration how well the illustrations support the ideas presented in the text and whether the illustrations have been correctly placed in relation to the text.

9. Explain whether a photograph or a line drawing would better illustrate features of the following subjects: a dry cell battery (for an article in a general encyclopedia); a flower arrangement (in a florist's brochure); an electrical outlet box (in a wiring instructions booklet); an automobile accident (for an insurance claims adjuster); the procedure for wrapping a sprained ankle (for a first aid handbook); and a tick (in a backpacker's handbook).

10. Draw a flowchart that traces the path you followed in locating and obtaining books from your library as outlined in Chapter 12.

11. Create an organizational chart of a club or group to which you belong.

16

Making an Oral Presentation

Nearly everyone must, at one time or another, make an oral presentation on the job. You may be asked, for example, to report orally on what you learned at a workshop you attended, on the progress of a special project, or on the results of an evaluation program. You may need to present a product or service to potential customers or give cost estimates to a committee. Or a part of your job may be to demonstrate devices to co-workers, give patients instructions for using medical equipment, or show customers how to operate machinery safely. Regardless of the type of job you have, you will very likely need to know how to make an effective oral presentation.

PREPARING AN ORAL PRESENTATION

Preparing an oral presentation is much like preparing to write. You must analyze your audience, determine your objective, and then organize your topic and prepare an outline.

Your Listeners

You cannot hope to communicate with your listeners effectively unless you know who they are. Are they co-workers, customers, clients, management, or fellow members of a professional organization? The answer to this question will help you determine how much knowledge of your subject your listeners already possess. If you are speaking to those in your own occupational field, you know that they understand the terminology of that field—so you can use it freely. If you are speaking to those outside your field, on the other hand, you should carefully define any special terms.

Knowing who your audience is will also help you recognize other factors that might improve your communication with your listeners. An audience composed of management is likely to be interested in the practical aspects of the material you are presenting: costs, scheduling, staff needs, and so on. If you are speaking to fellow technicians, on the other hand, they are likely to be concerned with the technical details of your presentation.

In preparing an oral presentation, you must pay particular attention to the size of your audience. Facial expressions and gestures that would be effective if you were speaking to half a dozen people sitting around a conference table, for example, would be lost on an audience of a hundred workers watching you demonstrate cardiopulmonary resuscitation. You probably could not rely at all on facial expressions to convey an idea; and instead of pointing with your finger at a chart, you'd have to use a pointer. The size of your audience can also influence the approach you take to your presentation. For a small group of listeners, for instance, you might plan a presentation that is mainly discussion, composed of a short talk and a long question-and-answer period. For a large audience, on the other hand, you would be more likely to prepare a longer, more formally organized presentation with only a brief question-and-answer period.

Your Objective

Determine the purpose of your presentation by asking, "What do I want my listeners to know, to be able to do, or to believe after I am finished?" Without a clear purpose, you will not know what to include in your presentation to make it effective, and you will either confuse your listeners or lose their interest.

One way to ensure that you have a specific, clear purpose is to write out a statement of your objective before you develop your presentation. Suppose, for example, that you are the assistant manager of the supply room at Westdale Medical Center. You must present an overview of how the supply room sterilizers, called "autoclaves," work. Your audience will be the new professional employees of the medical center. You might use the following statement of objective for your presentation: "To explain the purpose and operation of the autoclave so that new hospital employees understand and appreciate its value to the hospital's overall operation." After preparing such an objective, your next step is to develop an outline.

Your Outline

Speaking requires an approach to the development of your subject that differs slightly from the preparation a written report requires. Any audience has a limited attention span. A presentation crammed with difficult ideas or numerous statistics is sure either to confuse your listeners or to put them to sleep.

Cite facts and figures sparingly, and insert them in such a way that they directly support the major points you wish to make. Put your most important ideas into your opening and closing, where your listeners are more likely to remember them. Unless your presentation is short (under ten minutes), your conclusion should summarize the information presented in the rest of the talk.

There are as many ways to develop a topic in speaking as there are in writing. Several methods are especially good for oral presentations. The particular method of development you choose is less important than the fact that your subject is logically developed.

- *Increasing order of importance* develops your topic from the least important point to the most important point. This leaves the audience with the most important points fresh in their minds at the end.
- *The problem–solution pattern* first describes and analyzes the problem, then presents the criteria for evaluating possible solutions, and finally explains the advantages and disadvantages of each possible solution. Make sure, however, that you define the problem clearly and that you present the recommended solution clearly.
- *Cause-and-effect,* by stressing the connection between a result and a preceding event, explains why something happened or why you predict that something will happen. This approach can be used effectively in a speech because it holds the interest of the audience much as a detective story does.
- *Specific-to-general* begins with such specific details as statistics, expert opinion, and examples and then goes on to make a general statement that stems logically from the details.
- *General-to-specific* presents a general statement and then follows it with supporting details—statistics, expert opinion, and examples.

When you have determined the best method of development for your subject, create an outline for your presentation. The following example is based on the presentation by the assistant manager of the supply room to new employees. For a discussion of outlining, see Chapter 13.

```
                        OUTLINE
            Background  Information  About  the
                   Autoclave  (Sterilizer)

 I. Opening
    A. I am Steve Philisandro, Assistant Manager of the
       Supply Department.
    B. Ms. Cynthia Lipanski has given you an overview of
       the department--now I would like to give you some
       background about our autoclave sterilizer units.
    C. The points I will cover are explained in greater
       detail in our department manual, which each of our
       employees uses.
```

II. <u>Definitions</u>
    A. Sterilizing kills all living organisms, unlike dis-
       infecting, which merely inhibits the growth of
       organisms (especially pathogens).
    B. Sterilization kills multiplying organisms (including
       spores) with steam, under high temperature and
       pressure, or with gases.
    C. Briefly explain differences between steam autoclaves
       and ethylene oxide sterilizer (<u>point to units</u>).

III. <u>Materials</u>
    A. Materials that are sterilized include cloth, metal,
       glass, liquid, rubber, and plastic.
    B. Items that are sensitive to steam must be sterilized
       with the ethylene oxide unit: rubber goods, electric
       cords, telescopic lenses, and delicate instruments,
       for example.
    C. The materials, other than liquids, are wrapped in
       muslin or placed in <u>peel</u> packages and heat sealed
       (<u>show instrument and "peel" packages</u>).
    D. Liquids, such as saline, are placed in pyrex bottles
       with closures that allow steam to penetrate.
    E. Each type of material requires precise settings for
       time, pressure, and temperature (<u>show operators'</u>
       <u>manual</u>).

IV. <u>Procedure</u>
    A. Operator checks that items are properly wrapped and
       spaced on the sterilizer cart (<u>point to cart</u>).
    B. Chemical indicators are placed inside the packages
       and heat sensitive tape is used on the outsides.
    C. The operator loads the cart (cooled to prevent con-
       densation) into the sterilizer units.
    D. Although settings are usually pre-set, the operator
       checks time, temperature, and pressure (<u>show</u>
       <u>gauges</u>).
    E. The operator closes the door, then pushes the "lock"
       button; the operation proceeds automatically from
       that point.
    F. Lights on the front of door will indicate the com-
       pletion of cycle.
    G. The operator removes the sterilizer cart, using
       asbestos gloves.
    H. The packages are allowed to cool before they are
       placed on the storage shelves in the next room.
    I. Westdale's process is more automated than those at
       smaller hospitals.

V. <u>Closing</u>
    A. I hope I've given you some idea of how our sterilizer
       units work.
    B. Are there any questions?
    C. Thank you!
    D. Mrs. Sanches will now demonstrate Unit #2.

The amount of detail you should include in such an outline will depend upon both your confidence in front of a group and your familiarity with the subject. Obviously, the more confident and familiar with the subject you are, the less detail you will need. However, you may need to write out and read verbatim those portions that you feel need precise wording, such as important policy statements.

You will also need to decide what physical form of the outline you wish to use as notes for your presentation. Some speakers find that placing the outline in a three-ring binder keeps the pages in order. Other speakers prefer using 4" × 6" note cards because they are compact. Whatever form you find most convenient, use it.

Be careful not to cram the cards with too many notes. You should be able to grasp the information on a card at a glance so that you can maintain eye contact with your listeners. Number the cards so you don't get lost during your presentation.

Using Visual Aids

An important decision to make as you prepare your oral presentation is whether to use visual aids and, if so, what kind. You can choose graphs, drawings, tables, photographs, or models; you can present them by means of chalkboards, posters, flip charts, or overhead or slide projectors. Well-planned visual aids can add interest and emphasis to your presentation. They can also clarify and simplify your message by reinforcing its key points.

Visual aids can be overdone, of course. Do not attempt to use visual aids to flesh out a skimpy presentation or to form the focal point of a disorganized one. Use aids only if they clarify a point or make your presentation more vivid and concise. If they are necessary, be certain to check the physical arrangement and facilities of the room where you will speak. Does it have a chalkboard? a projector screen? a flip chart? Will a slide or overhead projector be available? Also consider room size. If you plan to use a chalkboard, will the writing be visible to those seated in the back? Everything you use must be tailored to scale. Check to see that nothing obstructs the view of any member of your audience. Keep in mind the following points as you prepare and use your visual aid:

1. Keep the amount of information on each visual aid to a minimum. It is usually a good idea to present only one point on each visual aid. Keep figures and equations to a minimum.
2. Do not write out sentences; use only words and phrases.
3. During your presentation emphasize a visual aid by pointing to it— with a physical gesture *and* with your text.
4. As you discuss the material on the visual aid, be sure that you don't block it with your body.
5. Be careful to talk to your listeners, not to the visual aid.

6. Do not simply read from the visual aid; after all, your audience can read. It is sometimes helpful, though, to list major points (usually in key words) on the visual aid to help your listeners keep them in mind as you discuss each in turn.

A complete range of visual aids is available. Each has advantages based on the size of the audience and the flexibility that your subject requires.

- A *chalkboard* is easy to use and easy to control; it gives you complete flexibility because you decide what goes on, what comes off, and when. It adds animation to your presentation because you must physically put the information on the board. If your information is too long to put on the board conveniently while you speak, put part or all of your message on ahead of time. A disadvantage of the chalkboard is that it slows you down if you must interrupt your presentation to write on the board as your listeners watch. Chalkboards are good with small and medium-size audiences (up to 40 people).
- A *poster* is good if it is large enough for your audience to see. Posters can be used for medium-size and large audiences (40 to 100 people). A common poster size is $2' \times 3'$. Prepare the poster ahead of time, and make your lettering large enough to be seen comfortably from the back of the room (check it yourself, ahead of time). Felt-tip markers are good writing instruments for posters. Put the poster on the easel only when you are ready to use it; otherwise, it will be distracting to your audience. A disadvantage of posters is that the material on them cannot easily be changed.
- A *flip chart* provides you with good control of what you want the audience to see—you flip it over only when you need it. You can draw your illustration ahead of time with light pencil lines and fill the lines in with the bold lines of a felt-tip pen during your presentation (sketching it during the presentation helps hold the audience's attention). Flip charts are good for the same size audiences as chalkboards.
- *Slide* and *overhead projectors* can be easy to use if you take the time to learn how to handle them. Do not put a slide or transparency on the screen until you need it. As you prepare your presentation, decide which slides you will use and where each one will go. Have them made up far enough in advance to be able to rehearse with them. Slides and transparencies may be used for audiences of various sizes (for large audiences, a larger screen is necessary).

DELIVERING AN ORAL PRESENTATION

Your oral presentation is most likely to be on a job-related topic. Therefore, you should be able to speak with knowledge and conviction about your subject. This is important because your listeners will have greater confidence in what you say if you speak with conviction.

The key to delivering your presentation well is to practice. Rehearse with your outline until you know exactly how you want to move from one idea to another. If you practice, you will have no problem with the words you want to use; they will come naturally, and you will have the confidence you need to face your listeners.

Generating Confidence and Enthusiasm

Speaking is like selling. If you believe in your topic, you will be enthusiastic about it, and your audience will find themselves thinking, "Hey, I didn't know that!" or nodding their heads in agreement as if to say, "I know exactly what you mean!"

You can expect to be nervous. But if you know what you are going to say and how you are going to say it—as you will if you have developed your subject and created a good outline—you can simply relax and talk. Your nervousness won't cause an all-out attack of stage fright. You can strengthen your confidence by being well prepared, by rehearsing, and by speaking in a strong and clear voice. A neat appearance can also add to your self-confidence.

You will have an advantage in delivering your presentation if you can project an image of friendliness; most people react favorably to a friendly approach. Friendliness cannot be faked; it must be honest to be effective. If you are naturally friendly, however, you can make that quality work to your advantage.

Another aspect of the image you project to your audience is your posture. Stand poised and erect, but not stiff. A slouching posture can harm your credibility with your listeners because they may assume that you don't care how you look or how you come across to others.

Getting and Holding Your Audience

The opening of a presentation can be crucial. It should arouse interest, stimulate curiosity, or impress your listeners with the importance of your subject. You can begin your presentation in a number of ways that will catch the attention of your listeners.

Stating a problem.   One way to catch the attention of your listeners is to describe a problem that directly affects them and then suggest a solution to it.

> For the past three months the accident rate in the Press Room has increased by 37 percent. We've experienced a number of minor accidents and half-a-dozen serious ones. I've done a thorough investigation of the press area, along with members of Security, and realize that we must set up some new procedures . . .

Definition.   Although the definition of a word can make a catchy opening, such a beginning should never be contrived—it should be used only if it provides insight into what follows.

> *Diastrophism* comes from the Greek word *diastrophe,* meaning "distortion," and it is applied to the distortion of the earth's crust that created oceans and mountains. It is not surprising, therefore, that geologists regard . . .

Interesting fact.   Often an interesting bit of information can be used to stimulate the attention of your listeners.

> A recent survey among retailers in our area revealed that the best way to sell a product is to *give it away.* Does that sound ridiculous? It isn't! And here's why . . .

You may also be able to use an interesting statistic as an opening.

> Approximately 15,000 requisitions, each containing from one to fourteen separate items, are processed each year by the Purchasing Department. Every item or service that is purchased . . .

Background information.   The background or history of a subject may be quite interesting and even put the topic in perspective for your listeners.

> The Chinese used bamboo poles to drill for oil; certainly today's giant rigs drilling in a hundred feet of water represent an immense technical advance in the search for oil. But whether four thousand years ago or today, in ancient China or in a modern city, in twenty fathoms of water or on top of a mountain, the object of drilling is and has always been the same—to manufacture a hole in the ground, inch by inch. The hole may be either for a development well . . .

This type of opening can easily be overdone. Use it only if the background information is of some value to your listeners. Never use it just to get started.

Quotations.   Occasionally, you can use a quotation to stimulate interest in your subject. To be effective, however, the quotation must be pertinent—not just a loosely related remark taken from a book of quotations simply because the item was listed under the subject heading of your topic. Often an effective quotation is one from a respected authority that points to a new trend or development.

> Richard Smith, president of the P. R. Smith Corporation, recently said, "I believe that the Photon projector will revolutionize our industry." His statement represents a growing feeling among corporate . . .

Objective. In reporting on a project or an activity of some kind, you may wish to open with a statement about the objective of the project. Such an opening gives your listeners a basis for judging the actual results of the project as you present them.

> Measuring heat transfer has been a costly, time-consuming, and all-too-often inexact procedure. The primary objective of this project was to develop new techniques for measuring heat transfer in a three-phase system. Our first step was to investigate . . .

Forecast. Sometimes you can use the forecast of a new development or trend to arouse the interest of your listeners.

> In the very near future, we may be able to call our local library and have a video tape of *Hamlet* or of last year's Super Bowl replayed on our wall television. This project and others are now being developed at Wincom Industries . . .

Delivery Techniques

When you stand up to speak, do not rush your opening. Begin by taking a good look at your listeners, and let them take a good look at you. Then begin your planned opening firmly and authoritatively. Never apologize for inconvenient conditions or tell your listeners how nervous you are (your audience probably won't notice your nervousness—so why call attention to it?).

Try to talk to your listeners about your subject just as you would talk to a friend about it. Be sure to maintain eye contact with most of your listeners, not with just one person. In addition to establishing a directness of communication with them, eye contact can provide you with feedback from your audience: if you are looking at your listeners, you will probably be able to notice if they begin to look puzzled or confused; the information can serve as a cue that you need to clarify the point you are making.

Be careful not to talk too fast. If you are even a little nervous, speaking too quickly is a real danger. Do not talk in a monotone; if you do, it will bore and finally lose your listeners. Enunciate carefully; say "going" instead of "gonna," and "don't you think?" instead of "dontchathink?" Try to eliminate sounds like "ah," "like," "okay?" and "yaknow?" Although they are so common that it may be impossible to eliminate them altogether, make a serious effort to do so. Also, learn to suppress nervous mannerisms, such as adjusting your clothing or smoothing your hair.

To emphasize a point, say it—then pause to let its significance register with your listeners—and then repeat the point. You can also achieve emphasis by varying the pitch of your voice, by varying the volume of your voice, and by varying the pace of your presentation. Gestures too can create emphasis. A closed fist, for example, can stress an idea dramatically. You can highlight a plea with a palms-up gesture, or indicate division by motioning first with one hand and then with the other hand. Be sure, though, to use gestures only when they come naturally; in other words, use the same gestures you would in ordinary conversation.

Refer to your notes openly, whether they are on 4" × 6" cards or 8½" × 11" paper. When you need to look at your notes, do so. Your listeners won't be impatient; they are human too. They won't expect you to be a spellbinding speaker, but they will expect you to be knowledgeable, prepared, and organized.

Rehearse your presentation until you can do it comfortably, in the allotted time, and with no major hesitations. Once you are ready, relax and don't worry about forgetting something. At this point you are not likely to forget a major point, and the sky won't fall if you overlook a minor point.

Concluding

When you are finished, conclude promptly but not abruptly. Don't end as though you were beating a hasty retreat. Plan the ending of your presentation the way you planned your opening. It's your last chance to get your message across, so don't waste it. You may find that it is most effective to conclude with a summary of your main points—so that your listeners will be more likely to remember them. Or, depending on your topic, you might end by making a recommendation, by asking a question, or by using any of the other techniques suggested on pages 24–26.

Question-and-Answer Period

Depending upon the occasion and your subject, you may want to provide for a question-and-answer session at the end of your presentation. If so, answer questions as completely as time allows or as the question deserves. Be sure that your answers are accurate. Don't be afraid to respond with "I don't know." Be polite and objective in responding to a hostile question, but be prepared to go on to the next question if it becomes evident that the questioner simply wants to argue. Don't play for laughs at a questioner's expense. You'll offend not only the questioner but the rest of your listeners as well.

EFFECTIVE LISTENING

Although you may spend only a small part of your time on the job making oral presentations, you probably spend a great deal of your time listening to others. You may receive oral instructions, attend workshops sponsored by your employer, or take courses as a part of your continuing education. Whatever the activity may be, it is important to develop effective listening skills.

Tips for Becoming an Effective Listener

You must be motivated to listen—either by an interest in the subject or by a desire to succeed on the job. The following guidelines may help you improve your listening skills.

- Develop a positive attitude toward the speaker. Good listeners assume, for example, that even though the subject may sound dull, the speaker is likely to say something that they can use.
- Do not be distracted by a speaker's personality or speaking style; rather, respond thoughtfully to the speaker's words and avoid making judgments too quickly.
- Be prepared. On the job, think and talk about the subject of a meeting or a workshop ahead of time. Preparation should enable you to understand the material better and to remember it more easily.
- Analyze the speaker's words and ideas while you are listening, but don't become so engrossed with your own analysis that you miss important points. Try to spot inconsistencies between the facts and the ideas that you hear. Listen "between the lines." Is the speaker using emotionally charged words? If so, are they appropriate? Can you think of other points that support or reject what the speaker is advocating? Do your own attitudes match those of the speaker? Analyzing a speaker's words and ideas not only helps you probe the meaning of the subject but also helps you remember key points
- Take notes. Being a good listener sometimes means being a good note taker. You may wish to record your own thoughts and questions as you are listening, so that you will remember to verify or ask them after the speaker is finished. The best note takers record only key words and phrases while they are listening, so that they won't miss anything that is being said.

You may not have time or need to follow all these guidelines—if you don't, use the technique or techniques that best help *you* absorb and remember. You may also find that some of these techniques work better when you are listening to formal oral presentations and others work better when you are listening to one or two people in conversations.

CHAPTER SUMMARY

Oral presentations are in many ways like written presentations.

First, you must analyze your audience. Who are they? Are they co-workers? Are they customers? Are they management? Whoever they are, you must gear your presentation specifically to them.

Then determine your objective: is it to inform? to persuade? to arouse your audience to action? Key your objective to the occasion and the audience, and fix it firmly in mind.

Then gather and organize your information as you would for any communication. Put your outline together using the most suitable method of development: increasing order of importance, problem-solution, specific-to-general, general-to-specific, and so on.

Prepare visual aids if they will help you achieve your objective. Remember to keep them simple (one idea per visual) and legible. They must be readable by every member of the audience.

Once you have put your material together, rehearse your presentation until you have all the ideas and their order engraved on your mind. Practice with your visuals so that they become a part of your talk, not simply add-ons. Adequate rehearsal gives you the confidence you need to present your material effectively.

The easiest part comes last—the actual presentation. Look at your audience for a moment before you start, then begin talking to them. Watch the people in the audience as you speak—they'll give you the cues you need to adjust your delivery. Speak slowly and distinctly.

Refer to your notes when you need to; the audience expects it. Gesture when it is appropriate. If you have practiced sufficiently, these things will come naturally.

And, finally, conclude your presentation, don't just end it. Summarize your main points or make a firm recommendation.

Much of your time is spent listening to others. Listening is an acquired skill, just as writing and speaking are skills.

Barriers to effective listening are attitudes and beliefs toward a subject, a tendency to assume that certain types of speakers (especially teachers and supervisors) will say what you expect them to say, personal feelings toward a speaker, noise and visual distractions, and poor posture and lack of eye contact with the speaker.

Ways to increase your effectiveness as a listener are to be motivated to listen (by interest in the subject or by a desire to succeed), to develop a positive attitude toward the presentation, not to be distracted by the speaker's personality or speaking style, to be prepared to receive the information being given you, and to develop an active mind that anticipates and analyzes the information being received.

EXERCISES

1. Come to class prepared to discuss in detail the differences between writing a report and presenting one orally.

2. Deliver a 5- to 10-minute oral report on a local matter with which you are familiar. Such topics might include neighborhood organizations or clubs, noisy neighbors, undisciplined pets, parking regulations, trash collection, and crime or vandalism.

3. Deliver a 5- to 10-minute talk on a school policy of which you disapprove. State the reasons for your disapproval and offer reasons why the policy should be changed or abolished.

4. Deliver a 5- to 10-minute talk explaining the purpose and function of a tool or piece of equipment typically used in your field. If possible, choose a device unfamiliar to someone outside your field. If the item is not too large, bring it to class; otherwise, rely on visual aids to clarify your explanation.

5. Deliver a 5- to 10-minute talk that describes a service that someone in your field provides to a customer, client, or patient. Ask a friend to play the role of the person being served, if such a role would aid the presentation.

6. Prepare a 10- to 15-minute talk that argues for or against a controversial issue in your career field. Typical topics would include training or accreditation practices, employment practices, professional or union affiliations, or any legislation current or pending that will affect your field.

17

Finding a Job

Before you begin your search for a job, do some serious thinking about your future. Decide first what you would most like to be doing in the immediate future. Then think about the kind of work you'd like to be doing two years from now *and* five years from now. Once you have established your goals, you can begin your job hunt with greater confidence because you'll have a better idea of what kind of job you are looking for and in what companies or other organizations you are most likely to find that job.

The search for a job can be logically divided into five steps: (1) locating the job you want, (2) preparing an effective résumé, (3) writing an effective letter of application, (4) conducting a successful interview, and (5) sending follow-up letters.

LOCATING THE JOB YOU WANT

A number of sources are available to help you locate the job you want: classified ads, letters of inquiry, trade and professional journals, school placement services, employment agencies, and the advice of friends and acquaintances.

Advertisements in Newspapers

Many employers advertise in the classified sections of newspapers. For the widest selection, look in the Sunday editions of local and big-city newspapers. Although reading dozens of want ads can be tedious, an item-by-item check is necessary if you are to do a thorough job search. The job you are looking for might be listed in the classified ads under any number of titles. A clinical medical technologist seeking a job, for example, might find the specialty listed under "Medical Technician," "Clinical Medical Technician," or "Laboratory Technician." Depending on a hospital's or a pathologist's needs, the listing could be more specific yet, such as "Blood Bank Technician," "Hematology Technician," or "Clinical Chemistry Technician." So play it safe—read *all* the ads. Occasionally, newspapers print special employment supplements that provide valuable information on many facets of the job market. Watch for these.

As you read the ads, take notes on such things as salary ranges, job locations, job duties and responsibilities, and even the terminology used in the ads to describe the work (a knowledge of the words and expressions that are generally used to describe a particular type of work can be helpful when you pre-prepare your résumé and letters of application).

Letters of Inquiry

If you would like to work for a particular firm, write and ask if it has an opening for someone with your qualifications. Normally, you should send the letter either to the director of personnel or to the specific department head; for a small firm, however, you can write to the head of the firm. Your letter should present a general summary of your employment background or training. It should be brief and to the point, expressing interest in such a job but leaving everything else to your résumé, which you enclose with the letter.

Trade and Professional Journals

Many occupations have associations that publish periodicals of general interest to members. Such periodicals often contain a listing of current job opportunities. If you were seeking a job in forestry, for example, you could check the job listings in the *Journal of Forestry,* published by the Society of American Foresters. To learn about the trade or professional associations for your occupation, consult the following reference books at a convenient library.

> *Encyclopedia of Associations*
> *Encyclopedia of Business Information Sources*
> *National Directory of Employment Services*

School Placement Services

Check with the career counselors in your school's job-placement office. Government, business, and industry recruiters often visit job-placement offices to interview prospective employees; the recruiters also keep college placement offices aware of their company's current employment needs. While you are in the placement office, ask to see a current issue of the *College Placement Annual*. This publication lists the occupational requirements and addresses of over a thousand industry, business, and government employers.

State Employment Agencies

Most states operate free employment agencies that are in business specifically to match applicants and jobs. If your state has one, register with the local employment office. It may have just the job you want; if not, it will keep your résumé on file and call you if such a job comes along.

Private Employment Agencies

Private employment agencies are profit-making organizations that are in business to help people find jobs—for a fee. Choose a private employment agency carefully. Some are well established and quite reputable, but others have questionable reputations. Check with your local Better Business Bureau as well as with friends and acquaintances before signing an agreement with a private employment agency.

Reputable private employment agencies provide you with job leads and help in organizing your campaign for the job you want. They may also provide useful information on the companies doing the hiring.

Who pays the fee if you are offered and accept a job through a private agency? Sometimes the employer will pay the agency's fee. Otherwise, you must pay either a set fee or a percentage of your first month's salary on the new job. Before signing a contract, be sure you understand who is paying the fee and, if *you* are, how much you are agreeing to pay. As with any written agreement, read the fine print carefully.

Friends and Acquaintances

Consult with people you know whose judgment you respect. It's especially useful to speak to people who are already working in your chosen field. Family, friends, neighbors, teachers, members of the clergy—any one might provide exactly the job lead you need.

Other Sources

Local, state, and federal government agencies offer many employment opportunities. Local government agencies are listed in the white pages of your telephone directory under the name of your city, county, or state. For information about jobs with the federal government, contact the U.S. Civil Service Commission and the Federal Personnel and Management Office, both of which have branches in most major cities. They are listed in the white pages of the telephone book under "U.S. Government."

If you are a veteran, local and campus Veterans' Administration offices can provide material on special placement programs for veterans. Such agencies can supply you with the necessary information about the particular requirements or entrance tests for your occupation.

PREPARING AN EFFECTIVE RÉSUMÉ

A *résumé,* the key element in a job hunt, is a summary of your qualifications. It tells a prospective employer about your job objectives, your training and education, your work experience, and your personal data. It itemizes, in one or two pages, the qualifications you can mention only briefly in a letter of application. Based on the information the résumé supplies, prospective employers can decide whether to ask you to come in for a personal interview. If you do have an interview, the interviewer can base specific questions on the data the résumé contains. For all these reasons, the résumé is vital.

In preparing to write the résumé, determine what kind of job you are seeking. Then ask yourself what information about you and your background would be most important to a prospective employer in the field you have chosen. On the basis of your answers to this question, decide what sort of details you should include in your résumé and how you can most effectively present your qualifications. Analyze yourself and your background. What jobs have you held? What were your principal duties in each of them? What experience did you gain that would be of value in the kind of job you are seeking? When and how long were you on each job? Consider your education. List the college or colleges you attended, the dates you attended each one, the degree you received, your major field of study, and any academic honors you achieved. The significant details of your education or training and of any job experience you may have had—along with personal data (your name and address, date of birth, and so on)—are what make up a résumé.

A number of different formats can be effectively used. The most important thing is to make sure that your résumé is attractive, well organized, easy to read, and free of errors. A common format uses the following heads:

Heading
Personal Data
Employment Objective
Education
Employment Experience
References

Underline or capitalize the heads to make them stand out on the page. Whether you list education or experience first depends on which is stronger in your background. If you are a recent graduate, list education first; if you have one or more years of related job experience, list experience first. In both cases, list the most recent education or job experience first, the next most recent experience second, and so on.

The Heading

Place the title, "résumé," centered at the top of the page. Start with your name, address, and telephone number. These are usually centered on the page. Do not include a date in the heading; if you do, you'll have to keep changing it.

RÉSUMÉ

Victoria T. Fromme
2107 Wyoming Street
Atlanta, Georgia 30307
Telephone: (404) 256-6320

Date of Birth

Personal Data

Include your date of birth, your Social Security number, and your marital status (it's better to give your date of birth than your age, so your résumé won't become out of date on your next birthday).
No

Employment Objective   optional

State not only your immediate employment objective but the direction you hope your career will take.

EMPLOYMENT OBJECTIVE

A responsible position in an engineering department in which I may use my training in computer sciences to solve engineering-related problems.

Education

List the college or colleges you attended, the dates you attended each one, the degree or degrees you received, your major field of study, and any academic honors you earned. Then give the name of the high school you attended, its location, and the dates you attended.

```
EDUCATION

Georgia Institute of Technology, Atlanta; September 19--
    to present.
Expect to receive a Bachelor of Science degree in
    Engineering in June 19--.
Major Courses: Calculus I, II, III, IV; Differential
    Equations; Methods of Digital Computations; Advanced
    Computer Techniques; Software Utilization; Special
    Computer Techniques; Graphic Display.
Activities and honors:
  Phi Chi Epsilon--Honor Society for Women in Business and
    Engineering
  Society of Women Engineers--Secretary-Treasurer during
    Junior Year
  American Institute of Industrial Engineers--Secretary
    during Senior Year
  Engineering Science Club
  Received Doris Harlow Scholarship two consecutive years
  Grade average: 3.46/4.00
  Dean's List during 6 of 8 semesters

Butler County Community College, Butler, Pennsylvania;
    September 19-- to May 19--

Knoch High School, Saxonburg, Pennsylvania; September 19--
    to June 19--
```

optional
(put separately)

Employment Experience

List all your full-time jobs, starting with the most recent and working backward. If you have had little full-time work experience, list part-time and temporary jobs too. Give the details of your employment, including the job title, dates of employment, and the name and address of the employer. Provide a concise description of your duties only for those jobs whose duties are similar to those of the job you are seeking; otherwise, give only a job title and a brief description. Specify any promotions or pay increases you received. If you have been with one company a number of years, highlight your accomplishments during those years. List military service as a job: give the dates you served, your duty specialty, and your rank at discharge. Discuss the duties only if they relate to the job you are applying for.

```
EMPLOYMENT EXPERIENCE

September 19-- to Present
Participating in the Professional Training Program at
Computer Systems International, Atlanta, Georgia.
Assigned to Design Department, as Production Trainee;
to Word Processing Department, as Clerical Assistant;
to Engineering Department, as Programer Trainee.

April 19-- to September 19--
Lifeguard at Vacationland Amusement Park, Hillsdown,
   Pennsylvania.
Chief lifeguard at end of summer, supervising three other
   lifeguards.
```

References

You can include references as part of the résumé or provide a statement on the résumé that references will be furnished upon request. Either way, do not give anyone as a reference without first obtaining his or her permission to do so.

```
REFERENCES

Furnished upon request.
```

Some résumés are arranged not in reverse order of time but according to duties, starting with the job most closely related in function to the job you seek. Since this type of résumé relies heavily on experience, it is not one that a recent graduate would normally use.

Do not list your present salary in your résumé. If it is too high, you may automatically price yourself out of a job for which you are applying. If it is too low, any offer you receive might well be less than it might have been otherwise.

As you write your résumé, use action verbs and state ideas concisely. There is no reason to avoid *I* altogether, but it is best not to overuse it.

```
NOT          I was promoted to shop foreman in June 19--.
BUT          Promoted to shop foreman in June 19--.
```

Be truthful in your résumé. If you give false data and are found out, the consequences could be serious. At the very least, you will have seriously damaged your credibility with your employer.

Make your résumé flawless before mailing it. If you are not a skilled typist, you may want to have it professionally typed. Printing usually produces more professional-looking copies than does photocopying. This is no time for economy.

Following are two sample résumés: one by a recent community-college graduate and one by an applicant who has been employed for many years. The writer of the first résumé has had only limited work experience and therefore puts the education section first and gives more than minimum information about his college work—including a note that he plans to enroll in a night-school bachelor's degree program.

RÉSUMÉ

David B. Edwards
6819 Locustview Drive
Topeka, Kansas 66614
(913) 233-1552

PERSONAL DATA

Date of birth: August 17, 1960; Social Security number:
  472-11-0068; unmarried.

EMPLOYMENT OBJECTIVE

Employment as a mechanical engineering technician, with the
  ultimate goal of becoming a mechanical engineer.

EDUCATION

19--. Graduated from Fairview Community College, Topeka,
  Kansas, with an Associate Degree in Mechanical Engineering. Grade average: 3.5/4.0 (Dean's List for six
  quarters). Future plans: Intend to study for bachelor's
  degree in mechanical engineering at a local university
  offering a night-school program.

19--. Graduated from Central High School, Topeka, Kansas.

EMPLOYMENT EXPERIENCE

June 19-- to Present. Handyman Home Center, part-time salesman while attending Fairview Community College.

REFERENCES

Furnished upon request.

Sample résumé I

The second sample résumé puts work experience first because the applicant has had nine years of significant employment—a fact that is much more important to a prospective employer than the applicant's educational data.

RÉSUMÉ

Alfred Mandillo
7761 Shalamar Drive
Dayton, Ohio 45424
(513) 233-4137 (Home)
(513) 255-3730 (Business)

PERSONAL DATA

Date of birth: January 31, 1951; Social Security number:
   341-72-9107; married, four children.

EMPLOYMENT OBJECTIVE

Position of greater responsibility and growth potential in
   the field of technical exhibit design.

EMPLOYMENT EXPERIENCE

June 19-- to Present. Manager, Engineering Drafting
   Department.
   Air Force Orientation Group, Wright-Patterson Air Force
   Base, Ohio (official exhibit design, construction, and
   display agency for the U.S. Air Force).

Duties: Responsible for the management of the Engineering
   Drafting Department; supervise staff of seventeen drafting
   mechanics. Support engineering design staff, exercising
   judgment in the selection of materials and equipment for
   the design and construction of exhibits. Write specifications, deal with vendors, and initiate procurement
   procedures.

April 19-- to June 19--. Supervisor, Graphic Illustrators.
   Henderson Advertising Agency, Cincinnati, Ohio.
   Advanced from Illustrator to Graphic Technician, and then
   promoted to supervisor of five illustrators and four
   drafting mechanics. Monitored and approved work orders
   and analyzed requirements. Selected appropriate media and
   techniques for orders. Rendered illustrations in pencil or
   ink.

EDUCATION

September 19-- to June 19--
   Edison State College, Wooster, Ohio.
   Graduated with an Associate Degree in Mechanical Engineer-
   ing Technology, June 19--.

September 1963 to June 1967
   Walter Davis High School, Columbus, Ohio.

Sample résumé II

WRITING AN EFFECTIVE
LETTER OF APPLICATION

The letter of application is essentially a sales letter. In it, you are trying to sell your services and, in most cases, will be competing with other applicants. Your immediate objective is to have your letter read by someone in the organization who has authority to screen job applicants; your ultimate goal is to obtain an interview. Therefore, your letter must do three things: catch your reader's attention favorably, convince your reader that you are qualified for the position, and request an interview. Try to accomplish the three objectives in a one-page letter.

Your reader should be able to learn immediately what the purpose of your letter is—you should not waste his or her time with inappropriate formalities or unnecessary details. You should state clearly that you are looking for a job with the organization. It may be a specific job that was advertised or that you learned about from another source, or you may have heard that the company has the kind of position you seek and are writing to inquire whether it has any openings for a candidate with your background. Be sure to tell your reader why you feel you are qualified for the job and that you will be available for an interview. The following is a list of the information you should provide in your letter of application:

1. If you are applying for a specific job, identify the job by title and state how you heard about it. If you are not applying for a specific job, explain that you are seeking a particular kind of job and are writing to inquire whether the organization has any openings for such a job.
2. List your qualifications for the job in summary form. If you are still a student or are a recent graduate and have had little work experience, stress your education; if you have been employed in a related field, emphasize your work background. Then refer the reader to the résumé for other important details.
3. State where you can be reached and when you will be available for an interview.

Send the letter of application to the organization to which you are applying. Include in the letter any information that is pertinent to the particular job you are applying for—details that you cannot include in the résumé because it is not written for a specific job.

The start of a letter of application is crucial in catching your reader's attention. One way to begin your letter is to state your employment objective and your interest in fulfilling your goal within the organization to which you are writing.

```
I am looking for a responsible position in an engineering
department in which I may use my training in computer
```

```
sciences to solve engineering-related problems. I would be
interested in exploring the possibility of obtaining such
a position within your firm.
```

Or you could begin the letter of application by naming someone you have met from the organization who has told you about a job (you may have met such a person at a conference or convention, through a friend, and so on). This kind of approach has the advantage of establishing the fact that an employee evidently feels that you may be qualified for the job. Then in the next paragraph of your letter of application you can give a summary of your qualifications.

```
During the recent NOMAD convention in Washington, a
member of your sales staff, Mr. Dale Jarrett, informed me
of a possible opening for a manager in your Dealer Sales
Division. My extensive background in the office machine
industry, I believe, makes me highly qualified for the
position.
```

Once you have opened, your aim is to convince your reader that you are a highly qualified candidate for the position. Expand upon the qualifications you mentioned in the opening and present any additional qualifications that might be particularly appropriate for the specific job. Think carefully about the requirements of the job and then stress those aspects of your background that would interest a prospective employer most. Highlight any related experience listed in your résumé that is especially pertinent to the job you are applying for. If you are applying for a sales job, for example, indicate that other jobs you have held have taught you how to present a product line effectively. If you are applying for a job as an office manager, indicate any supervisory experience you have had.

Close your letter with a direct request for an interview. If the prospective employer is located near you, you can request the recipient of your letter either to send you a note or to call you to set up an appointment. If considerable expense would be required for an interview, let the prospective employer bring up the subject of the interview.

Be sure to type the letter, and make it error-free and attractive.

Following are three sample letters of application. One is by a recent college graduate; the second is by a university student who is about to graduate; and the third is by someone who has had many years of work experience.

The opening paragraph of the first letter states that the applicant read in a local newspaper about the company's plan to build a new plant. Since the writer is not applying for a specific job opening, he explains what sort of position he is looking for. The second paragraph contains a brief description of the writer's qualifications for the job. In the last paragraph, he indicates where he can be reached to arrange for an interview.

4 Washington Boulevard
Detroit, MI 48214
June 14, 19--

Personnel Manager
Loudons, Inc.
4619 Drove Lane
Gary, IN 46409

Dear Sir or Madam:

The <u>Detroit Free Press</u> recently reported that Loudons is
constructing a new assembly plant near Gary. I would like to
apply for a position as a foreman in the new plant.

I am a recent graduate of Midlands Community College in
Detroit, with an Associate Degree in Industrial Engineering.
In addition, I have worked for the past three years, on a
part-time basis while attending Midlands and now on a full-
time schedule, at Michigan Industries, Inc., as a special-
assignment worker. My duties required me to work closely
with plant foremen, general foremen, and plant supervisors
and gave me extensive exposure to quality-control techniques
and manufacturing processes. Details of my education and
work experience are contained in the enclosed résumé.

I will be happy to meet with you at your convenience and
provide any additional information you may need. You can
reach me either at my home address or at (313) 233-6312
during regular business hours.

Sincerely,

James L. Nardinski

James L. Nardinski

Letter of application I

In the second sample letter of application, the writer does not specify
where she learned of the opening because she does not know whether a position is actually available. Instead, because she is about to graduate, she uses
the first paragraph to summarize her educational qualifications. She includes a
description, in paragraph 2, of related work experience. In the last paragraph
she indicates where she can be reached to set up an interview.

The third sample letter opens with an indication of where the writer
learned of the job vacancy. The second paragraph summarizes the candidate's qualifications for the job. The final paragraph asks for an interview and
specifies where the writer can be reached.

2701 Wyoming Street
Atlanta, Georgia 30307
May 29, 19——

Ms. Laura Goldman
Chief Engineer
Acton, Inc.
80 Roseville Road
St. Louis, Missouri 63130

Dear Ms. Goldman:

I am looking for a responsible position in an engineering
department in which I may use my training in computer
sciences to solve engineering problems. I would be
interested in exploring the possibility of obtaining such
a position within your firm.

I expect to receive a Bachelor of Science degree in Engineering from Georgia Institute of Technology in June, when I
will have completed the Computer Systems Engineering program
of the Engineering Department. Since September 19—— I have
been participating, through the university, in the Professional Training Program at Computer Systems International,
in Atlanta. In the program I was assigned, on a rotating
basis, to several staff sections in apprentice positions.
Most recently I have been assigned as Programmer Trainee in
the Engineering Department and have gained a great deal of
experience in computer applications. Details of the academic
courses I have taken are contained in the enclosed résumé.

I look forward to hearing from you soon. I can be contacted
at my office phone (415) 866-7000, ext. 312, or at my home
(415) 256-6320.

Sincerely yours,

Victoria J. Fromme

Victoria T. Fromme

Letter of application II

522 Beethoven Drive
Roanoke, Virginia 24017
November 15, 19--

Miss Cecilia Smathers
Vice-President, Dealer Sales
Hamilton Office Machines, Inc.
6194 Main Street
Hampton, Virginia 23661

Dear Miss Smathers:

During the recent NOMAD convention in Washington, a member
of your sales staff, Mr. Dale Jarrett, informed me of a
possible opening for a Manager in your Dealer Sales
Division. My extensive background in the office machine
industry, I believe, makes me highly qualified for the
position.

I was with the Technology, Inc., Dealer Division from its
formation in 1969 to its phase-out last year. During this
period, I was involved in all areas of dealer sales, both
within Technology, Inc., and through personal contact with a
number of independent dealers. Between 1967 and 1969 I
served as Assistant to the Dealer Sales Manager as a Special
Representative. My education and work experience are
contained in the enclosed résumé.

May I have an appointment for an interview with you to
discuss my qualifications in detail? Please write to me at
my home or telephone me at (703) 449-6743 any weekday.

                              Sincerely,

                              Gregory Mindukakis

                              Gregory Mindukakis

Enclosure: Résumé

Sample letter of application III

THE INTERVIEW

A job interview may last for thirty minutes, or it may take several hours; you may be interviewed by one person or by several, either at one time or in a series of interviews. The job interview is too important to walk into unprepared.

Before the Interview

Learn everything you can about the potential employer before the interview. What kind of business is it? Is the company locally owned? Is it a nonprofit organization? If it is public employment, at what level of government is it? Does it provide a service, and, if so, what kind? How large is the business? Is the owner self-employed? Is it a subsidiary of a larger operation? Is it expanding? Where will you fit in? This kind of information can be obtained from current employees, from such company literature as employee publications, or from the business section of back issues of local newspapers (available in the local library). You may be able to learn the company's size, sales volume, products, credit rating, the location of its plants, its subsidiary companies, new products, building programs, and such information from its annual reports, from *Moody's Industrials, Dunn and Bradstreet, Standard and Poor's, Thomas' Register,* and from other business reference sources a librarian might suggest. What you cannot find through your research, ask your interviewer.

Try to anticipate the questions your interviewer might ask, and prepare your answers in advance. The following list includes some of the questions that interviewers typically ask.

- What are your short-term and long-term occupational goals?
- What are your major strengths and weaknesses?
- Do you work better with others or alone?
- Why do you want to work for this employer?
- How do you spend your time?

Some of these questions are difficult. Give them careful thought.

During the Interview

Promptness is important. Be sure that you arrive for your interview at the appointed time. It's usually a good idea, in fact, to arrive ahead of time, since you may be asked to fill out an application before you meet your interviewer. Take a copy of your résumé and a pen with you. The résumé will be helpful because it contains much of the same information the application asks for: personal data, work experience, education. Read the form carefully before beginning to fill it out. The application form provides the company with a record for its files—it also gives the company an opportunity to see how closely you follow directions, how thoroughly you complete a task, and how neat you are. Therefore, fill the form out carefully, and proofread it when you are finished. Why risk a careless mistake now?

The interview will actually begin before you are seated. What you wear and how you act will be closely observed. The way you dress matters. The rule of thumb is to dress conservatively, avoiding extremes. Be well-groomed. For men, a recent haircut and a clean shave are essential; if you wear a beard, have a barber trim it. For women, basic clothes with simple jewelry look most businesslike. Avoid heavy perfume and gaudy lipstick and nail polish.

Remain standing until you are offered a seat. Then sit up straight (good posture suggests self-assurance), look at the interviewer, and try to appear relaxed and confident. Never chew gum. Don't smoke unless the interviewer does or offers you a cigarette. During the interview, you will be a little nervous. This is a natural reaction, and the interviewer expects it. Use this nervous energy to your advantage by channeling it into alertness. Listen carefully and record important information in your memory. Do not attempt to take extensive notes during the interview, although it is acceptable to jot down a few facts and figures.

When answering questions, don't ramble or stray away from the subject. Say only what you must in order to answer each question properly and then stop, but avoid giving just "yes" and "no" answers, which usually don't permit the interviewer to learn enough about you. Some interviewers allow a silence to fall just to see how you will react. The burden of conducting the interview is the interviewer's, not yours—and he or she may interpret it as a sign of insecurity if you rush in to fill a void in the conversation. If such a silence would make you uncomfortable, be ready to ask an intelligent question about the company.

Highlight your qualifications for the job you are seeking, but admit obvious limitations as well. Remember also that the job, the company, and the location must be right for you. Ask about such factors as opportunity for advancement, fringe benefits (but don't create the impression that your primary interest is security), educational opportunity and assistance, and recreational and cultural activities in the community (if accepting the job would require you to relocate).

If the interviewer overlooks important points, bring them up. But, if possible, let the interviewer mention salary first. If you are forced to bring up the subject, put it into a straightforward question. If you have taken the trouble to learn the prevailing salaries in your field, you will be better prepared to discuss salary. It is usually unwise to attempt to bargain, especially if you are a recent graduate. Many companies have inflexible starting salaries for beginners.

Interviewers look for a degree of self-confidence and an understanding, on the part of the candidate, of the field in which he or she is applying for a job. Less is expected of a beginner, but even a newcomer must show some command of the subject. One way to impress your interviewer is to ask questions about the company that are related to your line of work. Interviewers also respond favorably to outgoing applicants. They look for people who can communicate, who can present themselves well. Jobs today require inter-action of all kinds: person-to-person, department-to-department, division-to-division. Candidates who cannot look the interviewer in the eye or explain why they are applying for the job are not likely to do well in a work situation either.

At the conclusion of the interview, thank your interviewer for his or her time. Indicate that you are interested in the job (if true), and try to get an idea of when you can expect to hear from the company (but don't press too hard).

SENDING FOLLOW-UP LETTERS

When you leave, jot down the pertinent information you learned during the interview (this information will be especially helpful in comparing job offers). A day or two later, send the interviewer a brief note of thanks, saying that you find the job attractive and feel you can fill it well.

```
                                        2647 Sitwell Road
                                        Charlotte, NC 28210
                                        March 17, 19--


Mr. F. E. Vallone
Personnel Manager
Calcutex Industries, Inc.
3275 Commercial Park Drive
Raleigh, NC 27609

Dear Mr. Vallone:

I want to express my appreciation for the informative and
pleasant interview we had last Wednesday and to request that
you extend my thanks to Mr. Wilson of the Servocontrol Group
as well. I came away from our meeting most favorably
impressed with Calcutex Industries. I find the position
you are filling to be an attractive one and feel confident
that my qualifications would enable me to perform the duties
to everyone's advantage.

                                        Sincerely yours,

                                        Philip Ming

                                        Philip Ming
```

Follow-up letter I

If you are offered a job you want, write a brief letter of acceptance as soon as possible—certainly within a week. The format for such a letter is simple: begin by accepting the job you have been offered. Identify the job by title and state the exact salary, so that there will be no confusion on these two important points. The second paragraph might go into detail about moving dates and reporting for work. The details will vary, depending on the nature of the job offer. Conclude the letter with a statement that you are looking forward to working for your new employer. The following is a typical letter of acceptance.

2647 Peters Road
Glen Oaks, NJ 07448
March 26, 19--

Mr. F. E. Vallone
Personnel Manager
Calcutex Industries, Inc.
3275 Commercial Park Drive
Westerville, MA 02160

Dear Mr. Vallone:

I am pleased to accept your offer of $865 per month as a junior design draftsman in the Calcutex Group.

After graduation on August 30, I plan to leave Glen Oaks on Tuesday, September 2. I should be able to find suitable living accommodations within a few days and be ready to report for work on the following Monday, September 8. Please let me know if this date is satisfactory to you.

I look forward to what I am sure will be a rewarding future with Calcutex.

Very truly yours,

Philip Ming

Philip Ming

Follow-up letter II

Since, in your job search, you may have applied to more than one organization (it is certainly legitimate to do so) and may receive more than one job offer, you may at some time need to write a letter of refusal. Be especially tactful and courteous because the employer you are refusing has spent time and effort interviewing you and may have counted on your accepting the job. The following is an example of a job refusal letter. It acknowledges the consideration given the applicant, offers a logical reason for his refusal of the offer, and closes on a pleasant note.

2647 Peters Road
Glen Oaks, NJ 07448
March 26, 19--

Mr. F. E. Vallone
Personnel Manager
Calcutex Industries, Inc.
3275 Commercial Park Drive
Westerville, MA 02160

Dear Mr. Vallone:

I enjoyed talking with you about your opening for a junior
design draftsman, and I was gratified to receive your offer.
Although I have given the offer serious thought, I have
decided to accept a position with a commercial drafting
agency. The job I have chosen will provide me with a greater
variety of duties, which I feel will develop my skills more
fully in the long run.

I appreciate your consideration and I am sure I would have
enjoyed working for your company.

Sincerely,

Philip Ming

Philip Ming

Letter of refusal

CHAPTER SUMMARY

The search for a job consists of five steps: (1) locating the job you want, (2) preparing an effective résumé, (3) writing an effective letter of application, (4) conducting a successful interview, and (5) sending follow-up letters.

Classified advertisements in newspapers; letters of inquiry; advertisements in trade and professional journals; school placement services; state and private employment agencies; the advice of friends and acquaintances; and local, state, and federal agencies are all sources you can use in locating a job.

Before writing your résumé, determine the exact job you are seeking and who the prospective employers are. Then ask yourself what information about you and your background would be most important to that job and those employers. On the basis of your answer to this question, determine what details should be included in your résumé and how you can most effectively present your qualifications. Then prepare your résumé accordingly.

A letter of application must catch your reader's attention, create a desire for your services, and request an interview. Be sure that it includes the specific job for which you are applying, a brief summary of your qualifications for the job, and when and where you can be reached to set up an interview.

Before going to the interview, learn everything you can about your prospective employer. Arrive for the interview promptly. During the interview, highlight your strengths for the job you are applying for, demonstrate your knowledge of your field, and demonstrate self-confidence. After the interview, make notes of important information you learned during the interview. A day or two later, send the interviewer a brief note of thanks.

If you are offered a job that you plan to accept, send a letter of acceptance to the employer within a few days of receiving the offer. If you have decided to refuse the offer, send a letter as soon as possible, expressing your appreciation for the company's time and effort in considering you for the job.

EXERCISES

1. Write a one-page version of your résumé as it will read either at the end of the present semester or when you graduate. Type the error- and blemish-free résumé on high-quality white bond paper.

2. Write a letter to a past or a present teacher or employer (or other appropriate person) asking permission to use him or her as a job reference. Be prepared to explain in class why you think this person is especially well qualified to comment on your job qualifications.

3. Write a letter to an actual firm for which you would like to work, asking if there is a position available for someone with the qualifications you expect to have either at the end of the present semester or when you graduate.

4. Write a letter of application in response to an advertisement for a job for which you will be qualified upon graduation. Type your letter on the same kind of paper you used for exercise 1.

5. Assume that you have been interviewed for the job in exercise 4. Write a follow-up letter expressing thanks for the interview.

6. To prepare for an interview with a prospective employer, list three questions you think the interviewer may ask you, exclusive of the questions given in the text. Then list six questions you would like to ask the interviewer. Arrange both lists from most important to least important. Come to class prepared to discuss both lists.

Handbook

The first section of this handbook surveys the parts of speech—the functions performed by separate words or groups of words within sentences. The second section treats phrases, clauses, sentences, and paragraphs, the larger structures which words build. The final section reviews punctuation, the system of symbols that clarifies the structural relationships among words and parts of sentences. Since the parts of speech, the larger structural elements, and the system of punctuation work together, you can use the entries in this handbook as separate items for quick reference or as interrelated sections for a more thorough review of English grammar and the conventions of usage.

PARTS OF SPEECH

Part of speech is a term used to describe the class of words to which a particular word belongs, according to its function in a sentence. Each function in a sentence (naming, asserting, describing or modifying, joining, exclaiming) is performed by a word belonging to a certain part of speech.

If a word's function is to name something, it is a noun or pronoun. If a word's function is to make an assertion about something, it is a verb. If its function is to describe or modify something, the word is an adjective or an adverb. If its function is to join or link one element of the sentence to another, it is a conjunction or a preposition. If its function is to express an exclamation, it is an interjection.

NOUNS

A noun names a person, place, thing, concept, action, or quality.

Types of Nouns

The two basic types of nouns are proper nouns and common nouns.

Proper nouns.   Proper nouns name specific persons, places, things, concepts, actions, or qualities. They are usually capitalized.

EXAMPLES   New York, Abraham Lincoln, U.S. Army, Nobel Prize, Montana, Independence Day, Amazon River, Butler County, Magna Carta, June, Colby College

Common nouns.   Common nouns name general classes or categories of persons, places, things, concepts, actions, or qualities. The term *common noun* includes all types of nouns except proper nouns, although some nouns (turkey/Turkey) may be common and proper.

EXAMPLES   human, college, knife, bolt, string, faith, copper

Concrete nouns identify those things that can be detected by the five senses: by seeing, hearing, tasting, touching, or smelling.

EXAMPLES   house, carrot, ice, tar, straw, grease

Abstract nouns refer to things that cannot be detected by the five senses.

EXAMPLES   love, loyalty, pride, valor, peace, devotion, harmony

Collective nouns indicate groups or collections of persons, places, things, concepts, actions, or qualities. They are plural in meaning but singular in form when they refer to groups as units.

EXAMPLES   audience, jury, brigade, staff, committee

Functions of Nouns

Nouns may function as subjects of verbs, as objects of verbs and prepositions, as complements, or as appositives.

EXAMPLES   The *metal* bent as *pressure* was applied to it. (subject of a verb, naming the thing about which the verb makes an assertion)

The bricklayer cemented the *blocks* efficiently. (direct object of a verb, naming the thing acted on by the verb)

The company awarded our *department* a plaque for safety. (indirect object of a verb, naming the recipient of the direct object)

The *event* occurred within the *year.* (object of a preposition, naming the thing linked by the preposition to the rest of the sentence)

An equestrian is a *horseman.* (subjective complement, renaming the subject of the sentence)

We elected the sales manager *chairman.* (objective complement, renaming the direct object)

George Thomas, the *treasurer,* gave his report last. (appositive, amplifying the noun that precedes it)

Forms of Nouns

Nouns can show number (singular or plural) and possession.

Singular and plural nouns.   The singular form of a noun refers to one thing, the plural to more than one. Most nouns form the plural by adding s.

EXAMPLE   *Dolphins* are capable of communication with humans.

Nouns ending in s, z, x, ch, and sh form the plural by adding *es.*

EXAMPLES   How many size *sixes* did we produce last month?
              The letter was sent to all the *churches.*
              Our company supplies cafeterias with *dishes* and *glasses.*

Those ending in a consonant plus y form the plural by changing the y to *ies.*

EXAMPLE   The store advertises prompt delivery but limits the number of *deliveries* scheduled on a single day.

Some nouns ending in o add *es* to form the plural, and others add only s.

EXAMPLES   One tomato plant produced thirty *tomatoes.*
              We installed two *dynamos* in the plant.

Some nouns ending in f or fe add s to form the plural; others change the f or fe to *ves.*

EXAMPLES   cliff/cliffs, fife/fifes, leaf/leaves, knife/knives

Some nouns require an internal change to form the plural.

EXAMPLES   woman/women, man/men, mouse/mice, goose/geese

Some nouns do not change in the plural form.

EXAMPLE   *Fish* swam lazily in the clear brook while a few wild *deer* mingled with the *sheep* in a nearby meadow.

Most compound nouns joined by hyphens form the plural in the first noun. (This rule is reversed only if the main word is last.)

EXAMPLE   He provided jobs for his two *sons-in-law.*

If you are in doubt about the plural form of a word, look up the word in a good dictionary. Most dictionaries give the plural form if it is made in any way other than by adding *s* or *es.*

Possessive nouns.   Nouns most often form the possessive case, indicating ownership, by adding *'s.*

EXAMPLES   The *chairman's* statement was forceful.
The *table's* mahogany finish was scratched.
The installation of the plumbing is finished except in the *men's* room.

Singular nouns ending in *s* may form the possessive by adding either an apostrophe alone or *'s.*

EXAMPLES   a waitress' uniform or a waitress's uniform
an actress' career or an actress's career

Plural nouns ending in *s* add only an apostrophe to form the possessive.

EXAMPLE   The architects' design manual contains many illustrations.

With word groups and compound nouns, add the *'s* to the last noun.

EXAMPLES   The *chairman of the board's* report was distributed.
My *son-in-law's address* was on the envelope.

To show individual possession with a pair of nouns, use the possessive with both.

EXAMPLES   Both the *Senate's* and *House's* galleries were packed for the hearings.
Mary's and *John's* presentations were the most effective.

To show joint possession with a pair of nouns, use the possessive with only the last.

EXAMPLES   The *Senate and House's* joint committee worked out a compromise.
Mary and John's presentation was the most effective.

PRONOUNS

A pronoun is a word that is used as a substitute for a noun. The noun which a pronoun replaces is called its antecedent.

Types of Pronouns

Pronouns fall into several different categories: personal, demonstrative, relative, interrogative, indefinite, reflexive, intensive, and reciprocal.

Personal pronouns.   The personal pronouns refer to the person or persons speaking (*I, me, my, mine; we, us, our, ours*); the person or persons spoken to (*you, your, yours*); or the person or thing (or persons or things) spoken of (*he, him, his; she, her, hers; it, its; they, them, their, theirs*).

EXAMPLES   *I* wish *you* had told *me* that *she* was coming with *us*.

If *their* figures are correct, *ours* must be in error.

Demonstrative pronouns.   The demonstrative pronouns (*this, these, that, those*) indicate or point out the thing being referred to.

EXAMPLES   *This* is my desk.

These are my co-workers.

That will be a difficult job.

Those are incorrect figures.

Relative pronouns.   The relative pronouns (*who, whom, which, whose,* and *that*) perform two functions. They substitute for nouns or preceding ideas, and they connect and establish the relationships between parts of sentences. (Refer to the second section of the *Handbook* for a discussion of dependent and independent clauses.)

EXAMPLES   The personnel manager told the applicants *who* would be hired.

The supervisor, *whose* office is next door, keeps those records.

Interrogative pronouns.   Interrogative pronouns (*who, whom, which, whose,* and *what*) ask questions. They differ from relative pronouns in two ways. Although relative pronouns connect or show relationship and introduce dependent clauses, interrogative pronouns only ask questions and may introduce independent sentences that ask questions.

EXAMPLES   *Who* went to the meeting in Detroit?

Which copier does two-sided copying?

Indefinite pronouns.   Indefinite pronouns specify a class or group of persons or things rather than a particular person or thing. *All, another, any, anyone, anything, both, each, either, everybody, few, many, most, much, neither, nobody, none, several, some,* and *such* are indefinite pronouns.

EXAMPLE   Not *everyone* liked the new procedures; *some* even refused to follow them.

Reflexive pronouns.   The reflexive and intensive pronouns (*myself, your-self, himself, herself, itself, oneself, ourselves, yourselves,* and *themselves*) always end with the suffix *-self* or *-selves.*

EXAMPLE   I asked *myself* the same question.

Intensive pronouns.   The intensive pronouns are identical in form with the reflexive pronouns (*see* just above), but they perform a different function. They emphasize or intensify their antecedents.

EXAMPLE   I *myself* asked the same question.

Reciprocal pronouns.   The reciprocal pronouns (*one another* and *each other*) indicate relationships among people or things. Use *each other* when referring to two persons or things and *one another* when referring to more than two.

EXAMPLES   Sam and Ruth work well with *each other.*

              The crew members work well with *one another.*

Grammatical Properties of Pronouns

Person.   *Person* refers to the forms of a personal pronoun that indicate whether the pronoun represents the speaker, the person spoken to, or the person (or thing) spoken about. If the pronoun represents the speaker, the pronoun is in the first person.

EXAMPLE   *I* followed the directions in the manual.

If the pronoun represents the person or persons spoken to, the pronoun is in the second person.

EXAMPLE   *You* should report to Ms. Cooper before noon.

If the pronoun represents the person or persons spoken about, the pronoun is in the third person.

EXAMPLE   *They* followed the procedure that *he* had outlined.

Person	Singular	Plural
First	I, me, my	we, ours, us
Second	you, your	you, your
Third	he, him, his	they, them, their
	she, her, hers	
	it, its	

Identifying pronouns by person helps you avoid illogical shifts from one person to another. A very common error is to shift from the third person to the second person.

REVISE   *Employees* must sign the guard's logbook whenever *you* enter a restricted area.

TO   *Employees* must sign the guard's logbook whenever *they* enter a restricted area.

OR   *You* must sign the guard's logbook whenever *you* enter a restricted area.

Gender.   *Gender* refers to forms of words that designate sex. English recognizes three genders: masculine, feminine, and neuter (to designate objects considered neither masculine nor feminine). The gender of most words can be identified only by the choice of the appropriate pronoun (*he, she,* or *it*). Only these pronouns and a few nouns (such as *actor* and *actress*) reflect gender.

Gender is important to writers because they must be sure that nouns and pronouns within a grammatical construction agree in gender. A pronoun, for example, must agree with its antecedent noun in gender. A woman is *she* or *her,* not *it;* a man is *he* or *him,* not *it;* a barn is *it,* not *he* or *she.*

EXAMPLE   Because Wanda Martin supervised *her* sales staff as effectively as Frank Martinez supervised *his,* the company doubled *its* profits.

Number.   *Number* signifies how many things a word refers to. A singular pronoun substitutes for a noun that names one thing; a plural pronoun replaces a noun that names two or more things.

EXAMPLE   The manager took *her* break after the employees took *their* breaks.

All singular pronouns (I, he, she, it) change form in the plural (we, they) except *you.*

EXAMPLE   Since *he* organizes efficiently and *she* supervises effectively, *they* are both valuable employees.

Number is a frequent problem with only a few indefinite pronouns (*each, either, neither,* and those ending with *-body* or *-one,* such as *anybody, anyone, everybody, nobody, no one, somebody, someone*). Since these pronouns are normally singular, they require singular verbs and are referred to by singular pronouns.

EXAMPLE   As *everyone* arrives for the meeting and takes *his* seat, please hand *him* a copy of the confidential report. *No one* should leave without returning *his* copy before *he* goes.

Case.   Pronouns have forms to show the subjective, objective, and possessive cases. A pronoun is in the *subjective case* when it is used as the subject of
a clause or sentence, representing the person or thing acting or existing. The
subjective case is also used when the pronoun follows a linking verb, such as
to be. (A linking verb connects the pronoun with the subject it renames.)

EXAMPLES   *He* is my boss.
                    My boss is *he.*

A pronoun is in the *objective case* when it indicates the person or thing receiving the action of a verb or when it follows a preposition.

EXAMPLES   Mr. Davis hired Tom and *me.* (not I)
                    Between *you* and *me,* his facts are questionable.

To test whether a pronoun is in the subjective case or the objective case, try it
with a transitive verb (one that requires a direct object, a person or thing to
receive the action expressed by the verb). *Hit* and *resembled* are useful verbs
for this test. If the form of the pronoun can precede the verb, it is in the subjective case. If it must follow the verb, it is in the objective case.

EXAMPLES   *She* hit the baseball. (subjective case)
                    The baseball hit *her.* (objective case)
                    They resembled their cousins. (subjective case)
                    Their cousins resembled *them.* (objective case)

A pronoun in the *possessive case* expresses ownership.

EXAMPLE   He took *his* notes with him on the business trip.

Subjective	Objective	Possessive
I	me	my, mine
we	us	our, ours
you	you	your, yours
he	him	his
she	her	her, hers
it	it	its
they	them	their, theirs
who	whom	whose

   You may have trouble deciding which case to use in certain types of sentences. To test for the proper case when a pronoun modifies a noun, try the
sentence without the noun.

EXAMPLES   (*We/Us*) pilots fly our own planes.

We fly our own planes. (You would not write, "*Us* fly our own planes.")

He addressed his remarks directly to (*we/us*) technicians.

He addressed his remarks directly to *us*. (You would not write, "He addressed his remarks directly to *we*.")

If compound pronouns cause problems in determining case, try testing each separately.

EXAMPLES   In his letter, John mentioned *you* and *me*.

In his letter, John mentioned *you*.

In his letter, John mentioned *me*.

To determine the case of a pronoun that follows *as* or *than*, try mentally adding the words that are normally omitted.

EXAMPLES   The director does not have as much formal education as *he* [does]. (You would not write, "Him does.")

His friend was taller than *he* [was tall]. (You would not write, "Him was tall.")

An appositive is a noun or noun phrase that follows and amplifies another noun or noun phrase. A pronoun appositive takes the case of its antecedent.

EXAMPLES   Two systems analysts, Joe and *I*, were selected to represent the company. (*Joe and I* is in apposition to the subject, *systems analysts*, and therefore must be in the subjective case.)

The systems analysts selected two members of our department —Joe and *me*. (*Joe and me* is in apposition to *two members*, which is the object of the verb *selected*, and therefore must be in the objective case.)

Usage of Pronouns

Pronouns must agree with and clearly refer to their antecedents.

Pronoun–antecedent agreement. The noun for which a pronoun substitutes is called its antecedent. A personal pronoun in the first or second person does not normally require a stated antecedent.

EXAMPLES   *I* like my job.

You were there at the time.

We all worked hard on the project.

A personal pronoun in the third person usually has a stated antecedent.

EXAMPLE   John presented the report to the directors. *He* (John) first read *it* (the report) to *them* (the directors) and then asked for *their* (the directors') questions.

Agreement, grammatically, means the correspondence in form between different elements of a sentence. A pronoun must agree with its antecedent in person, gender, and number. (See the preceding pages of the Handbook for additional information about these properties of pronouns.)

A pronoun must agree with its antecedent in *person.*

REVISE   If *laboratory technicians* do not update *their* records every day, *you* will not have accurate data.

TO   If *laboratory technicians* do not update *their* records every day, *they* will not have accurate data.

OR   If *you* do not update *your* records every day, *you* will not have accurate data.

A pronoun must agree with its antecedent in *gender.*

EXAMPLE   *Isabel* was already wearing *her* identification badge, but *Tom* had to clip on *his* badge before they could pass the security guard.

Traditionally, a masculine, singular pronoun has been used to agree with antecedents that include both sexes, such as *anyone, everybody, nobody, one, person, someone,* or *student.*

EXAMPLE   *Anyone* who meets this production goal will double *his* bonus.

Many people are now sensitive to an implied sexual bias in such usage. When graceful alternatives are available, use them. One solution is to use *he or she* instead of *he* alone or *his or her* instead of *his* alone. Another possibility is to omit the pronoun completely if it isn't essential to the meaning of the sentence.

REVISE   *Everybody* completed *his* report on time.

TO   *Everybody* completed *his or her* report on time.

OR   *Everybody* completed a report on time.

The best solution often is to rewrite the sentence in the plural. Do not, however, attempt to avoid expressing gender by resorting to a plural pronoun when the antecedent is singular.

REVISE   *Everybody* completed *their* report on time.

TO   The *employees* completed *their* reports on time.

A pronoun must agree with its antecedent in *number.*

REVISE	Because the *copier* has been used so much, *they* have been overheating.
TO	Because the *copier* has been used so much, *it* has been over-heating.

Use a singular pronoun with an antecedent like *anyone, each, everybody,* or *everyone* unless to do so would be illogical because the meaning is obviously plural.

EXAMPLES	*Everyone* returned to *his or her* department.
	Everyone applauded when I demonstrated our new product for *them*.

Collective nouns may be singular or plural, depending on meaning.

EXAMPLES	The *staff* prepared *its* annual report.
	The *staff* returned to *their* offices after the meeting.

A compound antecedent joined by *or* or *nor* is singular if both elements are singular and plural if both are plural.

EXAMPLES	Either the *supervisor* or the *foreman* should present *his* report on the accident.
	Neither the *stockholders* nor the *executive officers* wanted *their* company to be taken over by Coast International.

When one of the antecedents connected by *or* or *nor* is singular and the other plural, the pronoun agrees with the nearest antecedent.

EXAMPLES	Either the *receptionist* or the *typists* should go on *their* lunch breaks.
	Either the *typists* or the *receptionist* should go on *her* lunch break.

A compound antecedent with its elements joined by *and* requires a plural pronoun.

EXAMPLE	The *architect* and the *designer* prepared *their* plans.

If the two elements refer to the same person, however, use the singular pronoun.

EXAMPLE	The *architect and designer* prepared *his* plan.

Pronoun reference.   The noun to which a pronoun refers must be un-mistakably clear. Pronoun references may be unclear if they are general, hidden, or ambiguous.

A *general (or broad) reference,* or one that has no real antecedent, may confuse your reader.

REVISE   He sold plumbing supplies in Iowa for eight years; *this* has helped him in his present job as sales manager.

TO   His eight years selling plumbing supplies in Iowa have helped him in his present job as sales manager.

A *hidden reference,* or one that has only an implied antecedent, is another problem.

REVISE   Electronics technicians must continue to study because *it* is a dynamic science.

TO   Electronics technicians must continue to study *electronics* because *it* is a dynamic science.

REVISE   A high-lipid, low-carbohydrate diet is called "ketogenic" because it favors *their* formation.

TO   A high-lipid, low-carbohydrate diet is called "ketogenic" because it favors the formation of ketone bodies.

The third basic problem is an *ambiguous reference,* or one that can be interpreted in more than one way.

REVISE   Susan worked with Jeanette on the presentation, but *she* prepared most of the slides. (Who prepared most of the slides, Susan or Jeanette?)

TO   Susan worked with Jeanette on the presentation, but Jeanette prepared most of the slides.

Ambiguous references frequently occur with the pronouns *it* and *they.*

REVISE   The fire marshal examined the stairway and inspected the basement storage room; *it* had suffered extensive smoke damage.

TO   The fire marshal examined the stairway, which had suffered extensive smoke damage, and inspected the basement storage room.

REVISE   The inspector checked the scales and the time clocks; *they* needed to be leveled again.

TO   The inspector checked the scales and the time clocks; the scales needed to be leveled again.

Do not repeat an antecedent in parentheses following the pronoun. If you feel that you must identify the pronoun's antecedent in this way, you need to rewrite the sentence.

REVISE   The specialist met the patient's mother as soon as she (the specialist) arrived at the hospital emergency room.

TO   As soon as the specialist arrived at the hospital emergency room, she met the patient's mother.

ADJECTIVES

An adjective modifies or describes a noun or pronoun.

Types of Adjectives

An adjective makes the meaning of a noun or pronoun more exact by pointing out one of its qualities (descriptive adjective) or by imposing boundaries upon it (limiting adjective).

EXAMPLES   a *hot* iron (descriptive)

He is *cold.* (descriptive)

ten automobiles (limiting)

his desk (limiting)

Limiting adjectives include some common and important categories:
Articles (a, an, the)
Numeral Adjectives (one, two, first, second)
Indefinite Adjectives (all, any, each, no, some)
Demonstrative Adjectives (this, that, these, those)
Possessive Adjectives (my, his, her, its, your, our, their)
Interrogative and Relative Adjectives (whose, which, what)
Of these, the forms of the demonstrative, possessive, and interrogative and relative adjectives derive from pronouns and are sometimes called pronominal adjectives.

Comparison of Adjectives

Most adjectives add the suffix -*er* to show comparison with one other item and the suffix -*est* to show comparison with two or more other items. The three degrees of comparison are called the positive, the comparative, and the superlative.

EXAMPLES   The first ingot is *bright.* (positive form)

The second ingot is *brighter.* (comparative form)

The third ingot is *brightest.* (superlative form)

Many two-syllable adjectives and most three-syllable adjectives, however, are preceded by *more* or *most* to form the comparative or the superlative.

EXAMPLES   The new facility is *more impressive* than the old one.

The new facility is the *most impressive* in the city.

A few adjectives have irregular forms of comparison (*much, more, most; little, less, least*).

Absolute words (such as round, unique, perfect, exact, and infinite) are not logically subject to comparison. After all, something either is or is not round; it isn't rounder or roundest. Language, however, is not always logical, so these words are sometimes used comparatively.

EXAMPLE   Phase-locked loop circuits make FM tuner performance *more exact* by decreasing tuner distortion.

Placement of Adjectives

When limiting and descriptive adjectives appear together, the limiting adjectives precede the descriptive adjectives, with the articles usually in the first position.

EXAMPLE   *the ten gray* cars (article, limiting adjective, descriptive adjective)

Within a sentence, an adjective can precede its noun or follow its noun.

EXAMPLES   The *small* jobs are given priority.

Priority is given when a job is *small*.

In a larger, more complex construction, an adjective may shift from preceding its noun to following it.

EXAMPLES   We passed a *big* budget.

We negotiated a contract *bigger than our competitor's*.

An adjective is called a predicate adjective when it follows a linking verb, such as *to be*. By completing the meaning of a linking verb, a predicate adjective describes or limits the subject of the verb.

EXAMPLES   The job is *easy*.

The manager was very *demanding*.

An adjective also can follow a transitive verb and modify its direct object (the person or thing that receives the action of the verb).

EXAMPLES   The lack of lubricant rendered the bearing *useless*.

They painted the office *white*.

Usage of Adjectives

Nouns can sometimes function as adjectives, especially when precise qualification is necessary.

EXAMPLE   The *test* conclusions led to a redesign of the system.

Frequently, business and technical writing is weakened by too many nouns strung together to form unit modifiers. Therefore, exercise caution when you use nouns as adjectives.

REVISE   The test control group meeting was held last Wednesday.
TO   The meeting of the test control group was held last Wednesday.
OR   The test control group met last Wednesday.

Furthermore, you should avoid general adjectives (*nice, fine, good*) and trite or overused adjectives (a *fond* farewell). In fact, it is good practice to question the need for most adjectives in your writing. Often, your writing not only will read as well without an adjective but may be even better without it. If you need to use an adjective, select one that expresses your meaning as exactly as possible.

VERBS

A verb is a word, or a group of words, that describes an action or affirms a condition or a state of existence.

EXAMPLES   The antelope *bolted* at the sight of the hunters.
She *was saddened* by the death of her friend.
He *is* a wealthy man now.

A verb is an essential part of a sentence since the verb makes an assertion about the action or existence of its subject, the someone or something that is its topic. Within a sentence, a verb alone is called a simple predicate; a verb with its modifiers and complements forms a complete predicate. When a subject and a predicate convey a complete thought, they form a sentence (or independent clause). When a subject and a predicate do not convey a complete thought, they form a dependent clause. In contrast to a clause, a phrase is a group of words without the subject-predicate combination.

Types of Verbs

Verbs may be described as either transitive or intransitive; the intransitive verbs include linking verbs.

Transitive verbs.   A transitive verb requires a *direct object* to complete its meaning. The direct object normally answers the question *whom* or *what* by naming the person or thing that receives the action of the verb.

EXAMPLE   They *laid* the *foundation* on October 24. (*Foundation* is the direct object of the transitive verb *laid.*)

Some transitive verbs (such as *give, wish, cause,* and *tell*) may be followed by an *indirect object* as well as a direct object. The indirect object is usually a person and answers the question "to whom or what?" or "for whom or what?" The indirect object precedes the direct object.

EXAMPLE   Georgiana Anderson *gave* the *treasurer* a *letter.* (*Treasurer* is the indirect object and *letter* is the direct object of the transitive verb *gave.*)

Intransitive verbs.   An intransitive verb is a verb that does not require an object to complete its meaning. It makes a full assertion about the subject without assistance (although it may have modifiers).

EXAMPLES   The water *boiled.*
             The water *boiled* rapidly.
             The engine *ran.*
             The engine *ran* smoothly and quietly.

Linking verbs.   Although intransitive verbs do not have objects, certain intransitive verbs may take complements. These verbs are called linking verbs because they link the subject of a sentence to words following the verb. When this subjective complement is a noun (or pronoun), it refers to the same person or thing as the noun (or pronoun) that is the subject.

EXAMPLES   The conference table *is* an antique.
             Maria *should be* the director.

When the complement is an adjective, it modifies the subject.

EXAMPLES   The study *was* thorough.
             The report *seems* complete.

Such intransitive verbs as *be, become, seem,* and *appear* are almost always linking verbs. Others, such as *look, sound, taste, smell,* and *feel,* may function either as linking verbs or as simple intransitive verbs.

EXAMPLES   Their antennae *feel* delicately. (simple intransitive verb meaning that they have a delicate sense of touch)
             Their antennae *feel* delicate. (linking verb meaning that they seem fragile to the touch)

Forms of Verbs

By form, verbs may be described as either finite or nonfinite.

Finite verbs. A finite verb is the main verb of a clause or sentence. It makes an assertion about its subject, and it can serve as the only verb in its clause or sentence. Finite verbs may be either transitive or intransitive (including linking) verbs. They change form to reflect person (I *see*, he *sees*), tense (I *go*, I *went*), and number (he *writes*, they *write*).

EXAMPLES   The telephone *rang,* and the secretary *answered* it.

When the telephones *ring,* you *answer* them.

A *helping verb* (sometimes called an *auxiliary verb*) is a verb that is added to a finite or main verb to help indicate mood (I ran, had I run), tense (I was, I am, I will), and voice (I hit, I was hit). Together, the helping verb and the main verb form a verb phrase.

EXAMPLES   The work *had* (helping verb) begun.

I *am* going.

I *was* going.

I *will* go.

I *should have* gone.

I *must* go.

The most commonly used helping verbs are the various forms of *have* (*has, had*), *be* (*am, is, are, was, were*), *do* (*did, does*), and *can, may, might, must, shall, will, would, should,* and *could.* Phrases that function as helping verbs often include *to,* the sign of the infinitive: for example, *am going to* and *is about to* (compare *will*), *has to* (compare *must*), and *ought to* (compare *should*).

EXAMPLES   I *am going to* quit.

I *will* quit.

She *has to* get a raise.

She *must* get a raise.

The helping verb always precedes the main verb, although other words may come between them.

EXAMPLE   Machines *will* (helping verb) never completely *replace* (main verb) people.

Nonfinite verbs or verbals. Nonfinite verbs are the verbals (gerunds, infinitives, and participles) which, although they are derived from verbs, actually function as nouns, adjectives, or adverbs.

When the *-ing* form of a verb functions as a noun, it is called a *gerund.*

EXAMPLE   *Seeing* is *believing.*

An *infinitive,* which is the root form of a verb, can function as a noun, an adverb, or an adjective. Because the word *to* usually precedes an infinitive, it is considered the sign of an infinitive.

EXAMPLES   He hates *to complain.* (noun, direct object of the verb *hates*)

The valve closes *to stop* the flow. (adverb, modifies the verb *closes*)

This is the proposal *to select.* (adjective, modifies the noun *proposal*)

A *participle* is a verb form that functions as an adjective. The present participle ends in *-ing.*

EXAMPLE   *Declining* sales forced us to close the branch office.

The past participle may end in *ed, t, en, n,* or *d.*

EXAMPLES   What are the *estimated* costs?

Repair the *bent* lever.

Here is the *broken* calculator.

What are the *known* properties of this metal?

The story, *told* many times before, was still interesting.

The perfect participle is formed with the present participle of *have* and the past participle of the main verb.

EXAMPLE   *Having gotten* (perfect participle) a large raise, the *smiling* (present participle), *contented* (past participle) employee worked harder than ever.

Grammatical Properties of Verbs

Verbs can show person, number, mood, voice, and tense.

Person.   Like personal pronouns, verbs change form to indicate first person (the speaker), second person (the person spoken to), and third person (the person or thing spoken about). Verbs change form to agree (or correspond grammatically) with their subjects.

EXAMPLES   I *see* (first person) a yellow tint, but he *sees* (third person) a yellow-green hue.

I *am* (first person) convinced, and you *are* (second person) convinced; unfortunately, he *is* (third person) not convinced.

Number.   *Number* refers to the forms of a verb that can indicate whether the subject of a verb is singular (signifying one thing) or plural (signifying more than one). In the present tense, indicative mood, most verbs show the third person singular (he, she, or it) by adding an s or es to the form used to agree with the third person plural (they).

EXAMPLES   She *works* every day. (singular)

They *work* every day. (plural)

The verb *to be,* however, normally changes form to indicate the plural.

EXAMPLES   I *am* (He *is*) ready to begin work. (singular)

We *are* ready to begin work. (plural)

Mood.   *Mood* refers to the functions of verbs: making statements or asking questions (indicative mood), giving commands (imperative mood), or expressing hypothetical possibilities (subjunctive mood).

The *indicative* mood refers to an action or a state that is conceived as fact.

EXAMPLES   *Is* the setting correct?

The setting *is* correct.

The *imperative* mood expresses a command, suggestion, request, or entreaty.

EXAMPLES   *Install* the wiring today.

Please *let* me know if I can help.

The *subjunctive* mood expresses something that is contrary to fact, conditional, or hypothetical; it can also express a wish, a doubt, or a possibility. The verb *be* is the only one in English that preserves many changes in form to show the subjunctive mood.

EXAMPLES   The senior partner insisted that he (I, you, we, they) *be* in charge of the project.

If the salesman (I, you, we, they) *were* to close the sale today, we would meet our monthly quota.

Most verbs other than *be* do not change form for the subjunctive. Instead, helping verbs show the subjunctive function.

EXAMPLE   *Had I known* that you were here, I would have come earlier.

The advantage of the subjunctive mood is that it enables you to express clearly whether or not you consider a condition contrary to fact. If so, use the subjunctive; if not, use the indicative.

EXAMPLES   If I *were* president of the firm, I would change several personnel policies. (subjunctive mood)

I *am* president of the firm, but I don't feel that I control every aspect of its policies. (indicative mood)

Be careful not to shift haphazardly from one mood to another within a sentence; to do so makes the sentence unbalanced as well as ungrammatical.

REVISE   Put the clutch in first (imperative); then you should put the truck in gear (indicative).

TO   Put the clutch in first (imperative); then put the truck in gear (imperative).

OR   You should put the clutch in first (indicative); then you should put the truck in gear (indicative).

Voice.   The grammatical term *voice* refers to whether the subject of a sentence or clause acts or receives the action. The sentence is in the active voice if the subject acts, in the passive voice if the subject is acted upon. The passive voice consists of a form of the verb *to be* and a past participle of the main verb.

EXAMPLES   The aerosol bomb *propels* the liquid as a mist. (active)

            The liquid *is propelled* as a mist by the aerosol bomb. (passive)

In your writing, the active voice provides force and momentum, but the passive voice lacks these qualities. The reason is not difficult to find. In the active voice, the verb identifies what the subject is doing, thus emphasizing the subject and the action. On the other hand, the passive voice emphasizes what is being done to the subject, rather than the subject or the action. As a rule, use the active voice unless you have good reason not to.

EXAMPLES   The report *was written* by Joe Albright in only two hours. (passive voice) (*Report* takes precedence over Joe and the writing.)

            Joe Albright *wrote* the report in only two hours. (active voice) (Here the writer and writing receive the emphasis.)

            Things *are seen* by the normal human eye in three dimensions: length, width, and depth. (passive voice) (*Things* takes precedence over the eye's function.)

            The normal human eye *sees* things in three dimensions: length, width, and depth. (active voice) (Here the eye's function—which is what the sentence is about—receives the emphasis.)

Sentences in the passive voice may state the actor, but they place the actor in a secondary position as the object of a preposition ("*by* the normal human eye").

The passive voice has its advantages, however; when the doer of the action is not known or is not important, use the passive voice.

EXAMPLE   The firm *was established* in 1929.

When the doer of the action is less important than the receiver of the action, use the passive voice.

EXAMPLE   Bill Bryant *was presented* the award by President Colby.

Be careful about shifting voice within a sentence.

REVISE   We *worked* late last night, and all the tests *were* finally *completed.*

TO   We *worked* late last night, and finally we *completed* all the tests.

Tense.   *Tense* is the grammatical term for verb forms that indicate time distinctions. The six basic tenses in English are past, past perfect, present, present perfect, future, and future perfect. Each of these has a corresponding progressive form that shows action in progress and is created by combining the helping verb *be,* in the appropriate tense, with the present participle (*-ing*) form of the main verb.

Basic	Progressive
I began (past)	I was beginning (past)
I had begun (past perfect)	I had been beginning (past perfect)
I begin (present)	I am beginning (present)
I have begun (present perfect)	I have been beginning (present perfect)
I will begin (future)	I will be beginning (future)
I will have begun (future perfect)	I will have been beginning (future perfect)

The simple *past tense* indicates that an action took place in its entirety in the past. The past tense is usually formed by adding *-d* or *-ed* to the root form of the verb.

EXAMPLE   We *closed* the office early yesterday.

The *past perfect tense* indicates that one past event preceded another. It is formed by combining the helping verb *had* with the past participle of the main verb.

EXAMPLE   He *had finished* by the time I arrived.

The simple *present tense* represents action occurring in the present, without any indication of time duration.

EXAMPLE   I *use* the breaker.

A general truth is always expressed in the present tense.

EXAMPLE   He learned the truth of the saying "time *heals* all wounds."

The present tense can be used to present actions or conditions that have no time restrictions.

EXAMPLE   Water *boils* at 212° F.

The present tense can be used to indicate habitual action.

EXAMPLE   I *pass* the paint shop on the way to the office every day.

The present tense can be used as the *historical present* to make things that occurred in the past more vivid.

EXAMPLE   It is 1865, and the founder of our company is pushing his cart through Philadelphia, delivering fish to his customers. He *works* hard, *expands* his business, and *builds* the firm that still bears his name.

The *present perfect tense* describes something from the recent past that has a bearing on the present—a period of time before the present but after the simple past. The present perfect tense is formed by combining a form of the helping verb *have* with the past participle of the main verb.

EXAMPLES   He *has retired,* but he visits the office frequently.

We *have finished* the draft and are ready to begin revising it.

The simple *future tense* indicates a time that will occur after the present. It uses the helping verb *will* (or *shall*) plus the main verb.

EXAMPLE   I *will finish* the job tomorrow.

The *future perfect tense* indicates action that will have been completed at a future time. It is formed by linking the helping verbs *will have* to the past participle of the main verb.

EXAMPLE   He *will have driven* the test car 40 miles by the time he returns.

Conjugation of Verbs

The conjugation of a verb arranges all forms of the verb so that the differences caused by changing tense, number, person, and voice are readily apparent. Following is a conjugation of the verb *drive*. Its principal parts, used to construct its various forms, are *drive* (infinitive and present tense), *drove* (past tense), *driven* (past participle), and *driving* (present participle).

Tense	Number	Person	Active voice	Passive voice
Present		1st	I drive	I am driven
	Singular	2nd	You drive	You are driven
		3rd	He drives	He is driven
		1st	We drive	We are driven
	Plural	2nd	You drive	You are driven
		3rd	They drive	They are driven
Progressive Present		1st	I am driving	I am being driven
	Singular	2nd	You are driving	You are being driven
		3rd	He is driving	He is being driven

Tense	Number	Person	Active voice	Passive voice
Progressive Present				
	Plural	1st	We are driving	We are being driven
		2nd	You are driving	You are being driven
		3rd	They are driving	They are being driven
	Singular	1st	I drove	I was driven
		2nd	You drove	You were driven
		3rd	He drove	He was driven
Past				
	Plural	1st	We drove	We were driven
		2nd	You drove	You were driven
		3rd	They drove	They were driven
	Singular	1st	I was driving	I was being driven
		2nd	You were driving	You were being driven
		3rd	He was driving	He was being driven
Progressive Past				
	Plural	1st	We were driving	We were being driven
		2nd	You were driving	You were being driven
		3rd	They were driving	They were being driven
	Singular	1st	I will drive	I will be driven
		2nd	You will drive	You will be driven
		3rd	He will drive	He will be driven
Future				
	Plural	1st	We will drive	We will be driven
		2nd	You will drive	You will be driven
		3rd	They will drive	They will be driven
	Singular	1st	I will be driving	I will have been driven
		2nd	You will be driving	You will have been driven
		3rd	He will be driving	He will have been driven
Progressive Future				
	Plural	1st	We will be driving	We will have been driven
		2nd	You will be driving	You will have been driven
		3rd	They will be driving	They will have been driven
	Singular	1st	I have driven	I have been driven
		2nd	You have driven	You have been driven
		3rd	He has driven	He has been driven
Present Perfect				
	Plural	1st	We have driven	We have been driven
		2nd	You have driven	You have been driven
		3rd	They have driven	They have been driven
	Singular	1st	I had driven	I had been driven
		2nd	You had driven	You had been driven
		3rd	He had driven	He had been driven

Tense	Number	Person	Active voice	Passive voice
Past Perfect	Plural	1st	We had driven	We had been driven
		2nd	You had driven	You had been driven
		3rd	They had driven	They had been driven
	Singular	1st	I will have driven	I will have been driven
		2nd	You will have driven	You will have been driven
		3rd	He will have driven	He will have been driven
Future Perfect	Plural	1st	We will have driven	We will have been driven
		2nd	You will have driven	You will have been driven
		3rd	They will have driven	They will have been driven

Usage of Verbs

Subject-verb agreement. Agreement, grammatically, means the correspondence in form between different elements of a sentence. Just as a pronoun must agree with its antecedent in person, gender, and number, so a verb must agree with its subject in person and number.

EXAMPLES   *I am* going to approve his promotion. (The singular, first person subject, *I,* requires the singular, first person form of the verb, *am.*)

His *colleagues are* envious. (The plural, third person subject, *colleagues,* requires the plural, third person form of the verb, *are*).

Do not let phrases and clauses that fall between the subject and the verb mislead you.

EXAMPLES   *Teaching* proper oral hygiene to children, even when they are excited about learning, *requires* patience. (The verb *requires* must agree with the singular subject of the sentence, *teaching,* rather than the plural subject of the preceding clause, *they.*)

Be careful to avoid making the verb agree with the noun immediately before it if that noun is not its subject. This problem is especially likely to occur when a modifying phrase containing a plural noun falls between a singular subject and its verb.

EXAMPLES   *Each* of the engineers *is* experienced. (The subject of the verb is *each,* not *engineers.*)

Only *Bob,* of all the district managers, *has doubled* his sales this year. (The subject of the verb is *Bob,* not *managers.*)

Proper *cleaning* of the machines and tools *takes* time. (The subject of the verb is *cleaning,* not *machines and tools.*)

Words like *type, part, series,* and *portion* take singular verbs even when such words precede a phrase containing a plural noun.

EXAMPLES   A *series* of directions *was given* to each branch manager.

A large *portion* of most employee handbooks *is* devoted to the responsibilities of the worker.

Subjects expressing measurement, weight, mass, or total often take singular verbs even though the subject word is plural in form. Such subjects are treated as a unit.

EXAMPLES   *Ten pounds is* the shipping weight.

Fifty dollars is her commission for each unit she sells.

When such subjects refer to the individuals that make up the unit, however, a plural verb is required.

EXAMPLE   If you need to make change, *fifty dollars are* in the office.

Similarly, collective subjects take singular verbs when the group is thought of as a unit, and plural verbs when the individuals are thought of separately.

EXAMPLES   The *jury is* reaching its decision. (*Jury* is thought of as a unit.)

The *jury are* returning to their hotel rooms for the night. (*Jury* is thought of as separate individuals.)

A book with a plural title requires a singular verb.

EXAMPLE   *Monetary Theories is* a useful source.

Some abstract nouns are singular in meaning though plural in form: *mathematics, news, physics,* and *economics.*

EXAMPLES   *News* of the merger *is* on page four of the *Chronicle.*

Textiles is an industry in need of import quotas.

Some words are always plural, such as *trousers* and *scissors.*

EXAMPLE   His *trousers were* torn by the machine.

The *scissors were* on the table.

BUT   A *pair* of trousers *is* on order.

A *pair* of scissors *was* on the table.

Indefinite pronouns such as *some, none, all, more,* and *most* may be singular if they are used with mass nouns or plural if they are used with count nouns. Mass nouns identify things that comprise a mass and cannot be separated into countable units (such as electricity, water, wood, and oil); count nouns identify things that can be separated into countable units (such as desks, engines, pencils, and drivers).

EXAMPLES *Most* of the oil *has* been used.

Most of the drivers *know* why they are here.

Some of the water *has* leaked.

Some of the pencils *have* been used.

One and *each* are normally singular.

EXAMPLES *One* of the brake drums *is* still scored.

Each of the original founders *is* scheduled to speak at the dedication ceremony.

Following a relative pronoun such as *why, which,* or *that,* a verb agrees in number with the noun to which the pronoun refers (its antecedent).

EXAMPLES Steel is one of those *industries* that *are* hardest hit by high energy costs. (*That* refers to *industries.*)

She is an *employee* who *is* rarely absent. (*Who* refers to *employee.*)

She is one of those *employees* who *are* rarely absent. (*Who* refers to *employees.*)

A subjective complement is a noun or adjective in the predicate of a sentence, following a linking verb. The number of a subjective complement does not affect the number of the verb—the verb must always agree with the subject.

EXAMPLE The *topic* of his report *was* rivers. (The subject of the sentence is *topic,* not *rivers.*)

Sentences with inverted word order can cause problems with agreement between subject and verb.

EXAMPLE From this work *have come* several important *improvements.* (The subject of the verb is *improvements,* not *work.*)

A compound subject is one that is composed of two or more elements joined by a conjunction such as *and, or, nor, either . . . or,* or *neither . . . nor.* Usually, when the elements are connected by *and,* the subject is plural and requires a plural verb.

EXAMPLE *Education* and *experience are* valuable assets.

There is one exception to the *and* rule. Sometimes the elements connected by *and* form a unit or refer to the same person. In this case, the subject is regarded as singular and takes a singular verb.

EXAMPLES *Ice cream and cake is* his favorite dessert.

His *lawyer and business partner* prepares the tax forms. (His lawyer is also his business partner.)

A compound subject joined by *or* or *nor* requires a singular verb with two singular elements and a plural verb with two plural elements.

EXAMPLES   Neither the *doctor* nor the *nurse is* on duty.

Either the *doctors* or the *nurses are* on duty.

A compound subject with a singular element and a plural element joined by *or* or *nor* requires that the verb agree with the element nearest to it.

EXAMPLES   Neither the doctor nor the *nurses are* on duty.

Neither the doctors nor the *nurse is* on duty.

ADVERBS

An adverb modifies the action or condition expressed by a verb.

EXAMPLE   The recording head hit the surface of the disk *hard*. (The adverb tells *how* the recording head hit the disk.)

An adverb may also modify an adjective, another adverb, or a clause.

EXAMPLES   The graphics department used *extremely* bright colors. (modifying an adjective)

The redesigned brake pad lasted *much* longer than the original model. (modifying another adverb)

Surprisingly, the machine failed. (modifying a clause)

Functions of Adverbs

An adverb answers one of the following questions.
Where?

EXAMPLE   Move the throttle *forward* slightly.

When?

EXAMPLE   Replace the thermostat *immediately*.

How?

EXAMPLE   Add the solvent *cautiously*.

How much?

EXAMPLE   The *nearly* completed report was lost in the move.

These questions can be answered by typical adverbs such as *almost, seldom, down, also, now, ever, always, once,* and *twice.*

EXAMPLES   I *rarely* work on the weekend.

I have worked overtime *twice* this week.

Some adverbs (such as *however, therefore, nonetheless, nevertheless, consequently, accordingly,* and *then*) can join two independent clauses, each of which could otherwise stand alone as a sentence.

EXAMPLE   I rarely work on the weekend; *nevertheless,* this weekend will be an exception.

Other adverbs, such as *where, when, why,* and *how,* ask questions.

EXAMPLE   *How* many hours did you work last week?

Comparison of Adverbs

Adverbs, like adjectives, show three degrees of comparison: the positive (the basic form of the adverb), the comparative (showing comparison with one other item), and the superlative (showing comparison with two or more other items). Adverbs normally are compared by adding *-er* or *-est* to them or by inserting *more* or *most* in front of them. One-syllable adverbs use the comparative ending *-er* and the superlative ending *-est.*

EXAMPLES   This copier works *faster* than the old one.
This copier works *fastest* of the three tested.

Most adverbs with two or more syllables end in *-ly,* and most adverbs ending in *-ly* are compared by inserting the comparative *more* or the superlative *most* in front of them.

EXAMPLES   He moved *more quickly* than the other company's salesman.
Of all the salesmen, he moved *most quickly.*

Less and *least* are antonyms, or opposites, of *more* and *most.*

EXAMPLES   He moved *less quickly* than the other company's salesman.
Of all the salesmen, he moved *least quickly.*

A few irregular adverbs require a change in form to indicate comparison.

EXAMPLES   Our training program functions *well.*
Our training program functions *better* than most others in the industry.
Our training program functions the *best* in the industry.

Adverbs Made From Adjectives

Many adverbs are simply adjectives with *-ly* added, such as *dashingly* and *richly.* Sometimes, the adverb form is identical to the adjective form: *early,* *hard, right,* and *fast.* Resist the temptation to drop the *-ly* ending from such adverbs as *surely, differently, seriously, considerably, badly,* and *really.*

REVISE   The breakdown of the air conditioning equipment damaged the computer system *considerable.*

TO   The breakdown of the air conditioning equipment damaged the computer system *considerably.*

On the other hand, resist the temptation to coin awkward adverbs by adding *-ly* to adjectives (*firstly, muchly*).

REVISE   He slumped *tiredly* into the chair.

TO   *Tired,* he slumped into the chair.

Placement of Adverbs

An adverb may appear almost anywhere in a sentence, but its position may affect the meaning of the sentence. Avoid placing an adverb between two verb forms where it will be ambiguous because it can be read as modifying either.

REVISE   The supplier remembered *quickly* to thank the purchasing agent for the order. (Did the supplier remember quickly or did he thank the agent quickly?)

TO   The supplier *quickly* remembered to thank the purchasing agent for the order.

The adverb is commonly placed in front of the verb it modifies.

EXAMPLE   The accountant *meticulously* checked the figures.

An adverb may, however, follow the verb (or the verb and its object) that it modifies.

EXAMPLES   The gauge dipped *suddenly.*
They repaired the computer *quickly.*

The adverb may be placed between a helping verb and a main verb.

EXAMPLE   He will *surely* call.

If an adverb modifies only the main verb, and not any accompanying helping verbs, place the adverb immediately before the main verb.

EXAMPLE   The alternative proposal has been *effectively* presented.

An adverb phrase, however, should not separate the parts of a verb.

REVISE   This suggestion has *time and time again* been rejected.

TO   This suggestion has been rejected *time and time again.*

To emphasize an adverb that introduces an entire sentence, you can put the adverb before the subject of the sentence.

EXAMPLES   *Clearly,* he was ready for the promotion when it came.

Unfortunately, fuel rationing has been necessary.

In writing, such adverbs as *nearly, only, almost, just,* and *hardly* are placed immediately before the words they limit. A speaker can place these words earlier and avoid ambiguity by stressing the word to be limited; a writer, however, can ensure clarity only through correct placement of the adverb.

REVISE   The punch press *almost* costs $47,000.

TO   The punch press costs *almost* $47,000.

CONJUNCTIONS

A conjunction connects words, phrases, or clauses. A conjunction can also indicate the relationship between the two elements it connects. (For example, *and* joins together, but *or* selects and separates.)

Types of Conjunctions

Conjunctions may be coordinating, correlative, or subordinating. In addition, certain adverbs act as conjunctions.

Coordinating conjunctions.   A coordinating conjunction is a word that joins two sentence elements that have identical functions. The coordinating conjunctions are *and, but, for, nor, or, so,* and *yet.*

EXAMPLES   Bill *and* John work at the Los Angeles office. (joining two proper nouns)

To hear *and* to obey are two different things. (joining two phrases)

He would like to include the test results, *but* that would make the report too long. (joining two clauses)

Correlative conjunctions.   Correlative conjunctions are coordinating conjunctions that are used in pairs. The correlative conjunctions are *either . . . or, neither . . . nor, not only . . . but also, both . . . and,* and *whether . . . or.* To ensure not only symmetry but also logic in your writing, follow correlative conjunctions with parallel sentence elements that are alike in function and in construction.

EXAMPLE   Bill will arrive *either* on Wednesday *or* on Thursday.

Subordinating conjunctions.   A subordinating conjunction connects sentence elements of different weights, normally independent clauses that can stand alone as sentences and dependent clauses that cannot. The most frequently used are *so, although, after, because, if, where, than, since, as, unless, before, that, though, when,* and *whereas.*

EXAMPLE   He left the office *after* he had finished writing the report.

Conjunctive adverbs.   A conjunctive adverb is an adverb that has the force of a conjunction because it is used to join two independent clauses. The most common conjunctive adverbs are *however, moreover, therefore, further, then, consequently, besides, accordingly, also, too.*

EXAMPLE   The engine performed well in the laboratory; *moreover,* it surpassed all expectations during its road test.

Usage of Conjunctions

Beginning a sentence with a coordinating conjunction.   There is no rule against beginning a sentence with a coordinating conjunction; in fact, coordinating conjunctions can be strong transitional words and at times can provide emphasis.

EXAMPLE   I realize that the project was more difficult than expected and that you have also encountered personnel problems. *But* we must meet our deadline.

Starting sentences with conjunctions is acceptable in even the most formal English. But, like any other writing device, this one should be used sparingly lest it become ineffective and even annoying.

PREPOSITIONS

A preposition is a word that links a noun or pronoun (its object) to another sentence element.

Functions of Prepositions

Prepositions express such relationships as direction (*to, into, across, toward*), location (*at, in, on, under, over, beside, among, by, between, through*), time (*before, after, during, until, since*), or figurative location (*for, against, with*). Although only about seventy prepositions exist in the English language, they are used frequently. Together, the preposition, its object, and the object's modifiers form a prepositional phrase, which acts as a modifier.

Many words that function as prepositions also function as adverbs. If the word takes an object and functions as a connective, it is a preposition; if it has no object and functions as a modifier, it is an adverb.

EXAMPLES   The manager sat *behind* the desk in his office. (preposition)

The customer lagged *behind;* then she came in and sat down. (adverb)

Usage of Prepositions

Do not use unnecessary prepositions, such as "off *of,*" "inside *of,*" and "at about."

REVISE   The client arrived *at about* four o'clock.

TO   The client arrived *at* four o'clock. (to be exact)

OR   The client arrived *about* four o'clock. (to be approximate)

Avoid adding the preposition *up* to verbs unnecessarily.

REVISE   Call *up* and *see* if he is in his office.

TO   Call and *see* if he is in his office.

Do not omit needed prepositions.

REVISE   He was oblivious and not distracted by the view from his office window.

TO   He was oblivious *to* and not distracted *by* the view from his office window.

If a preposition falls naturally at the end of a sentence, leave it there.

EXAMPLE   I don't remember which file I put it *in.*

Be aware, however, that a preposition at the end of a sentence can indicate that the sentence is awkwardly constructed.

REVISE   Corn was the crop in the field that the wheat was planted *by.*

TO   The wheat was planted next to the corn field.

The object of a preposition, the word or phrase following the preposition, is always in the objective case. Despite this rule, a construction such as "between you and *me*" frequently and incorrectly appears as "between you and *I.*"

REVISE   The whole department has suffered because of the quarrel between *he* and Bob.

TO   The whole department has suffered because of the quarrel between *him* and Bob.

Certain verbs (and verb forms), adverbs, and adjectives are used with certain prepositions. For example, we say "interested *in,*" "aware *of,*" "devoted *to,*" "equated *with,*" "abstain *from,*" "adhere *to,*" "conform *to,*" "capable *of,*" "comply *with,*" "object *to,*" "find fault *with,*" "inconsistent *with,*" "independent *of,*" "infer *from,*" and "interfere *with.*"

INTERJECTIONS

An interjection is a word or phrase of exclamation that is used independently to express emotion or surprise or to summon attention. *Hey! Ouch! Wow!* are strong interjections. *Oh, well,* and *indeed* are mild ones. An interjection functions much as *yes* or *no,* in that it has no grammatical connection with the rest of the sentence in which it appears. When an interjection expresses a sudden or strong emotion, punctuate it with an exclamation mark.

EXAMPLE   His only reaction was a resounding, *"Wow!"*

Punctuate a mild interjection with a comma (or a pair of commas).

EXAMPLES   Well, that's done.
Oh, well, that's done.

Because they get their main expressive force from sound, interjections are more common in speech than in writing. They are rarely appropriate to business or technical writing.

PHRASES, CLAUSES, SENTENCES, AND PARAGRAPHS

Good written communication relies upon the writer's ability to put words together so that they convey a message to a reader in the most effective and efficient way. The writer can use a number of tools to help communicate ideas to a reader; among them are phrases, clauses, sentences, and paragraphs.

PHRASES

Although a phrase is the most basic meaningful group of words, it does not make a full statement. Unlike a clause, it does not contain both a subject (words which name someone or something) and a predicate (words which make an assertion about the subject). Instead, a phrase is based on a noun, a verbal, or a verb without a subject.

EXAMPLES   I can finish the project *by August fifth.*
Operating the machine is difficult.
She *has been working* hard this summer.

A phrase may function as an adjective, an adverb, a noun, or a verb.

EXAMPLES   The subjects *on the agenda* were all discussed. (adjective)
We discussed the project *with great enthusiasm.* (adverb)

> *Hard work* is her way of life. (noun)
>
> The chief engineer *should have been notified*. (verb)

Even though phrases function as adjectives, adverbs, nouns, or verbs, normally they are named for the kind of word around which they are constructed —preposition, verb, noun, or the three verbals (participle, infinitive, and gerund). For definitions of the parts of speech, refer to the first section of the Handbook.

Prepositional Phrases

A preposition is a word that shows the relationship between the noun or pronoun that is its object and another sentence element. Prepositions express relationships such as direction, location, and time. A preposition, its object, and the object's modifiers form a prepositional phrase, which acts as a modifier.

EXAMPLE   After the meeting, the regional managers adjourned *to the executive dining room.*

Verb Phrases

A verb phrase consists of a main verb preceded by one or more helping verbs.

EXAMPLES   Company officials discovered that a computer *was emitting* more data than it *had been asked* for.

He *will file* his tax forms on time this year.

Noun Phrases

A noun phrase consists of a noun and its modifiers.

EXAMPLES   *Many large companies* use computers.

Have *the two new employees* fill out *these forms.*

Participial Phrases

A participial phrase consists of a participle plus its object and any modifiers. A participial phrase functions as an adjective, so it must modify a noun or pronoun and must be placed so that this relationship is clear.

EXAMPLE   *Looking very pleased with himself,* the sales manager reported on the success of the policies he had introduced.

Infinitive Phrases

An infinitive is the root form of a verb (go, run, talk), one of the principal parts that are used to construct the various forms of a verb. An infinitive generally follows the word *to,* called the sign of the infinitive. An infinitive phrase consists of the word *to* plus an infinitive and any objects or modifiers.

EXAMPLE   *To succeed in this field,* you must be willing *to assume responsibility.*

Gerund Phrases

When the *-ing* form of a verb functions as a noun, it is called a gerund. A gerund phrase, which also must function as a noun, consists of a gerund plus any objects or modifiers.

EXAMPLES   *Preparing an annual report* is a difficult task.

She liked *running the department.*

CLAUSES

A clause is a part of a sentence that contains both a subject (the word or group of words that name someone or something as a topic) and a predicate (the main verb and its modifiers and complements that make an assertion about the subject).

Every subject-predicate word group in a sentence is a clause. Unlike a phrase, a clause can make a complete statement because it contains a finite verb (as opposed to a nonfinite verb or verbal) as well as a subject. Every sentence must consist of at least one clause. A clause that conveys a complete thought and thus could stand alone as a sentence is an independent clause.

EXAMPLE   *The scaffolding fell* when the rope broke.

A clause that could not stand alone without the rest of its sentence is a dependent or subordinate clause.

EXAMPLE   I was at the St. Louis branch *when the decision was made.*

A dependent clause may function as a noun, an adjective, or an adverb in a larger sentence; an independent clause may be modified by one or more dependent clauses.

EXAMPLE   While I was in college, I studied differential equations. (*While I was in college* is a dependent clause functioning as an adverb; it modifies the independent clause *I studied differential equations.*)

A clause may be connected with the rest of its sentence by a coordinating conjunction, a subordinating conjunction, a relative pronoun, or a conjunctive adverb. (Refer to the first section of the Handbook for discussions of pronouns and conjunctions.)

EXAMPLES   Peregrine falcons are about the size of a large crow, *and* they have a wingspread of three to four feet. (coordinating conjunction)

Mission control will have to be alert *because* the space laboratory will contain a highly flammable fuel at launch. (subordinating conjunction)

It was Robert M. Fano *who* designed and developed the earliest "Multiple Access Computer" system at M.I.T. (relative pronoun)

It was dark when we arrived; *nevertheless,* we began to tour the factory. (conjunctive adverb)

Independent Clauses

Unlike a dependent clause, an independent clause is complete in itself. Although it might be part of a larger sentence, it always can stand alone as a separate sentence.

EXAMPLE   *We abandoned the project* because the cost was excessive.

Dependent Clauses

A dependent (or subordinate) clause is a group of words that has a subject and a predicate but requires a main clause to complete its meaning. A dependent clause can function in a sentence as a noun, an adjective, or an adverb.

As nouns, dependent clauses may function in sentences as subjects, objects, or complements.

EXAMPLES   *That human beings can learn to control their glands and internal organs by direct or indirect means* is now an established fact. (subject)

The trouble is *that we cannot finish the project by May.* (subjective complement)

I learned *that drugs ordered by brand name can cost several times as much as drugs ordered by generic name.* (direct object)

As adjectives, dependent clauses can modify nouns or pronouns. Dependent clauses are often introduced by relative pronouns and relative adjectives (*who, whom, whose, which, what, that*).

EXAMPLE   The man *who called earlier* is here. (modifying *man*)

As adverbs, dependent clauses may express relationships of time, cause, result, or degree.

EXAMPLES   You are making an investment *when you buy a house.* (time)

A title search was necessary *because the bank would not otherwise grant a loan.* (cause)

Consult an attorney *so that you will be aware of your rights and obligations.* (result)

Monthly mortgage payments should not be much more *than the buyer earns in one week.* (degree)

Dependent clauses clarify the relationships between thoughts. As a result, dependent clauses can present ideas more precisely than simple sentences or compound sentences (which combine two independent clauses).

REVISE   The sewage plant is located between Millville and Darrtown. Both villages use it. (two thoughts of approximately equal importance)

TO   The sewage plant, *which is located between Millville and Darrtown,* is used by both villages. (one thought, the plant's location, subordinated to the other, its service area)

REVISE   He arrived at his office early, and he was able to finish the report without any interruptions. (two thoughts of approximately equal importance)

TO   Since he arrived at his office early, he was able to finish the report without interruptions. (one thought, his early arrival, subordinated to the other, his completion of the report)

Subordinate clauses effectively express thoughts that describe or explain another statement. They can state where, when, how, or why an event occurred, thus supplying logical connections that may not be obvious from the context. Too much subordination, however, may be worse than none at all. A string of dependent clauses, like a string of simple sentences, may obscure the important ideas.

REVISE   He had selected classes *that* had a slant *that* was specifically directed toward students *who* intended to go into business. (three dependent clauses of approximately equal importance)

TO   He had selected classes *that* were specifically directed to business students. (one dependent clause emphasizing the most important of the three points)

SENTENCES

A sentence is a sequence of words that contains a subject and a predicate and conveys a complete thought. A sentence normally has at least two words: a subject (something or someone) and a predicate (an assertion about the action or state of existence of the subject).

EXAMPLE   Sales (subject) declined (assertion about the subject).

To the basic sentence can be added modifiers—words, phrases, and clauses that expand, limit, or make more exact the meanings of other sentence elements.

EXAMPLE   *Computer* sales declined *during the month of August.*

In most sentences, the subject is a noun phrase rather than a single word, and the predicate is a verb or verb phrase with appropriate modifiers, objects, or complements.

EXAMPLE   A good personnel department (subject) screens job applicants carefully. (predicate)

Sentences may be classified according to *structure* (simple, compound, complex) and *intention* (declarative, interrogative, imperative, exclamatory).

Structure

Simple sentences.   A simple sentence has one clause. In its most basic form, the simple sentence contains only a subject and a predicate.

EXAMPLES   Profits rose.
              The strike ended.

Both the subject and the predicate may be compounded to include several items without changing the basic structure of the simple sentence.

EXAMPLES   *Bulldozers and road graders* have blades. (compound subject)
              Bulldozers *strip, ditch, and backfill.* (compound predicate)

Likewise, although modifiers may lengthen a simple sentence, they do not change its basic structure.

EXAMPLE   *The recently introduced* procedure works *very well.*

Compound sentences.   A compound sentence combines two or more related independent clauses that are of equal importance.

EXAMPLE   Drilling is the only way to collect samples of the layers of sediment below the ocean floor, *but* it is by no means the only way to gather information about these strata.[1]

The independent clauses of a compound sentence may be joined by a

[1] Bruce C. Heezen and Ian D. MacGregor, "The Evolution of the Pacific," *Scientific American* (November 1973), p. 103.

comma and a coordinating conjunction, by a semicolon, or by a conjunctive adverb preceded by a semicolon and followed by a comma.

EXAMPLES   The plan was sound, *and* the staff was eager to begin. (comma and coordinating conjunction)

The plan was sound; the staff was eager to begin. (semicolon)

The plan was sound; *therefore,* the staff was eager to begin. (conjunctive adverb)

Complex sentences.   A complex sentence contains one independent clause and at least one dependent clause.

EXAMPLE   We lost some of our efficiency (independent clause) when we moved (dependent clause).

A dependent clause may occur before, after, or within the independent clause. The dependent clause can function within a sentence as a subject, an object, or a modifier.

EXAMPLES   *What he proposed* is irrelevant. (subject)

We know *where it is supposed to be.* (object)

Fingerprints, *which were used for personal identification in 200 B.C.,* were not used for criminal identification until about 1800. (modifier)

Because complex sentences offer more variety than simple ones, changing a compound sentence into a complex sentence can produce a more precise statement. When one independent clause becomes subordinate to another, the relationship between the two is more clearly established.

EXAMPLES   We moved, *and* we lost some of our efficiency. (compound sentence with coordinating conjunction)

When we moved, we lost some of our efficiency. (complex sentence with subordinating conjunction)

A complex sentence indicates the relative importance of two clauses and expresses the relationship between their ideas. Normally, the independent clause states the main point, and the dependent clause a related, but subordinate, point.

EXAMPLE   Although the warehouse was damaged by the fire, all the employees escaped safely from the building.

Intention

By intention, a sentence may be declarative, interrogative, imperative, or exclamatory.

A *declarative sentence* conveys information or makes a factual statement.

EXAMPLE   This motor powers the conveyor belt.

An *interrogative sentence* asks a direct question.

EXAMPLE   Does the conveyor belt run constantly?

An *imperative sentence* issues a command.

EXAMPLE   Start the generator.

An *exclamatory sentence* is an emphatic expression of feeling, fact, or opinion. It is a declarative sentence that is stated with great force.

EXAMPLE   The heater exploded!

Construction

Parts of sentences.   Within a sentence, every word or word group functions as a sentence element. A *subject* names (and perhaps includes words that describe) the person or thing that is the topic of the sentence.

EXAMPLE   *The new machine* ran.

A *verb* describes an action or affirms the condition or state of existence of its subject.

EXAMPLE   The new machine *ran*.

A *complement* is used in the predicate (with the verb) to complete the meaning of a sentence. There are four kinds of complements. The first, the *direct object,* names the person or thing on which a transitive verb acts. The direct object normally answers the question *what* or *whom.*

EXAMPLES   He wrote *a letter.*
            I admire *the boss.*

The second, the *indirect object,* names the recipient of the direct object, the person or thing something is done to or for.

EXAMPLE   He wrote *the company* a letter.

The third, the *objective complement,* describes or renames a direct object.

EXAMPLE   I like my coffee *hot.*

The last, the *subjective complement,* describes or renames the subject of a sentence.

EXAMPLE   The director seems *confident.*

A *modifier* expands, limits, or makes more exact the meaning of other sentence elements.

EXAMPLE   *Automobile* production decreased *rapidly.*

A connective ties together or indicates subordination or coordination of parts of sentences.

EXAMPLE   I work hard each week, *but* I relax *when* I play racquetball.

An *appositive* is a noun or noun phrase that follows and amplifies another noun or noun phrase.

EXAMPLE   Bob, *the personnel director,* just interviewed another engineer.

An *absolute* is a participial or infinitive phrase that modifies a statement as a whole and is not linked to it by a subordinate conjunction or preposition.

EXAMPLE   *To speak bluntly,* the proposal is unacceptable.

An *expletive* is a word such as *it* or *there* that fills the position of other words.

EXAMPLE   *It* is certain that he will go.

Sentence patterns.   Subjects, verbs, and complements are the main elements of the sentence. Everything else is subordinate to them in one way or another. The following are the basic sentence patterns with which a writer works.

EXAMPLES   The cable snapped. (subject—verb)

Generators produce electricity. (subject—verb—direct object)

The test results gave us confidence. (subject—verb—indirect object—direct object)

Repairs made the equipment operational. (subject—verb—indirect object—objective complement)

The metal was aluminum. (subject—linking verb—subjective complement)

Most sentences follow the subject—verb—complement pattern. In "The company dismissed Joe," for example, you recognize the subject and the object by their positions before and after the verb. In fact, readers interpret what they read more easily because they expect this sentence order. As a result, departures from it can be effective, if used sparingly for emphasis and variety, but annoying if overdone.

An inverted sentence places the elements in other than normal order.

EXAMPLES   A better job I never had. (direct object—subject—verb)

More optimistic I have never been. (subjective complement—subject—linking verb)

Inverted sentence order can be used in questions and exclamations; it can also be used for emphasis.

EXAMPLES   Have you a pencil? (verb—subject—complement)

How heavy your book feels! (complement—subject—verb)

In sentences introduced by expletives (*there, it*), the subject comes after its verb because the expletive occupies the subject's normal location before the verb.

EXAMPLES   *There* (expletive) *are* (verb) certain *principles* (subject) of drafting that must not be ignored. (Compare: "Certain principles of drafting there are [that is, "exist"] that must not be ignored.")

It (expletive) *is* (verb) difficult (complement) *to work* (subject) in a noisy office. (Compare: "To work in a noisy office is difficult.")

Unusual sentence order, however, cannot be used often without tiring or puzzling the reader. Instead, a sentence that moves quickly from subject to verb to complement is clear and easy to understand. The writer's problem is to preserve the clarity and directness of this pattern but to write sentences that use more complicated forms to present more information. A skillful writer depends on subordination, the relative weighing of ideas, to make sentences more dense. As the following example shows, a sentence can be rewritten in several ways by subordinating the less important ideas to the more important ideas.

REVISE   The city manager's report was carefully illustrated, and it covered five typed pages.

TO   The city manager's report, *which covered five typed pages,* was carefully illustrated. (adjectival clause)

OR   The city manager's report, *covering five typed pages,* was carefully illustrated. (participial phrase)

OR   The *carefully illustrated* report of the city manager covered five typed pages. (participial phrase)

OR   The *five-page* report of the city manager was carefully illustrated. (single modifier)

OR   The city manager's report, *five typed pages,* was carefully illustrated. (appositive phrase)

The effective subordination of words, phrases, and clauses produces varied, concise, and emphatic sentences.

Common Sentence Problems

The most common sentence problems are faulty subordination, run-on sentences, sentence fragments, and dangling and misplaced modifiers.

Faulty subordination.   Faulty subordination occurs (1) when a grammatically subordinate element, such as a dependent clause, actually contains the main idea of the sentence or (2) when a subordinate element is so long or detailed that it overpowers the main idea. You can avoid the first problem, expressing the main idea in a subordinate element, by deciding which idea is the main idea. Both of the following sentences, for example, appear logical, but each emphasizes a different point.

EXAMPLES   Although the new filing system saves money, many of the staff are unhappy with it.

The new filing system saves money, although many of the staff are unhappy with it.

In this example, if the writer's main point is that *the new filing system saves money,* the second sentence is better. If the main point is that *many of the staff are unhappy,* then the first sentence is better.

The other major problem with subordination is putting so much detail into a subordinate element that it overpowers the main point by its sheer size and weight.

REVISE   If company personnel do not fully understand what the new contract that was drawn up at the annual meeting of the district managers this past month in New Orleans requires of them, they should call or write the Vice-President for Finance.

TO   If company personnel do not fully understand what the new contract requires of them, they should call or write the Vice-President for Finance.

Run-on sentences.   A run-on sentence, sometimes called a fused sentence, is made up of two or more sentences without punctuation to separate them. The term sometimes includes pairs of independent clauses separated by only a comma, although these are usually called comma faults or comma splices. Run-on sentences can be corrected by (1) making two sentences, (2) joining the two clauses with a semicolon (if they are closely related), (3) joining the two clauses with a comma and a coordinating conjunction, or (4) subordinating one clause to the other.

REVISE   The training division will offer three new courses interested employees should sign up by Wednesday. (run-on sentence)

OR   The training division will offer three new courses, interested employees should sign up by Wednesday. (comma fault or comma splice)

TO   The training division will offer three new courses. Interested employees should sign up by Wednesday. (period)

OR   The training division will offer three new courses; interested employees should sign up by Wednesday. (semicolon)

OR   The training division will offer three new courses, so interested employees should sign up by Wednesday. (comma plus coordinating conjunction)

OR   Since the training division will offer three new courses, inter-
                 ested employees should sign up by Wednesday. (one clause
                 subordinated to the other)

Sentence fragments and minor sentences. A sentence that is missing an essential part (subject or predicate) is called a sentence fragment.

EXAMPLES   She changed jobs. (sentence)

                 And earned more money. (fragment)

But having a subject and a predicate does not automatically turn a clause into
a sentence. The clause must also make an independent statement. "I work" is
a sentence; "If I work" is a fragment because the subordinating conjunction *if*
makes the statement a dependent clause.

    Sentence fragments are often introduced by relative pronouns (*who,
whom, whose, which, that*) or subordinating conjunctions (such as *after, although, because, if, when* and *while*). When you use these introductory
words, you can anticipate combining the dependent clause that follows with a
main clause to form a complete sentence.

REVISE   The accounting department received several new calculators.
                 After its order was processed.

TO   The accounting department received several new calculators
                 after its order was processed.

    A sentence must contain a main or finite verb; verbals (gerunds, parti-
ciples, and infinitives) will not do the job. The following examples are sentence fragments because they lack main verbs. Their verbals (*working, to skip,
expecting*) cannot function as finite verbs.

EXAMPLES   *Working* overtime every night during tax season.

                 To skip the meeting.

                 The manager *expecting* to place an order.

    Fragments may reflect incomplete or confused thinking. The most com-
mon type of fragment is the careless addition of an afterthought.

REVISE   These are the branch tellers. *A dedicated group of employees.*

TO   These are the branch tellers, a dedicated group of employees.

The following examples illustrate common types of sentence fragments.

REVISE   Health insurance rates have gone up. *Because medical ex-
                 penses have increased.* (adverbial clause)

TO   Health insurance rates have gone up because medical expenses
                 have increased.

REVISE   The engineers tested the model. *Outside the laboratory.* (prepo-
                 sitional phrase)

TO   The engineers tested the model outside the laboratory.

REVISE	*Having finished the job.* We submitted our bill. (participial phrase)
TO	Having finished the job, we submitted our bill.
REVISE	We met with Jim Rodgers. *Former head of the sales division.* (appositive)
TO	We met with Jim Rodgers, former head of the sales division.
REVISE	We have one major goal this month. *To increase the strength of the alloy without reducing its flexibility.* (infinitive phrase in apposition with *goal*)
TO	We have one major goal this month: to increase the strength of the alloy without reducing its flexibility.

Occasionally, a writer intentionally uses an incomplete sentence. This kind of deliberate fragment, called a *minor sentence,* makes sense, in its context, because the missing element is clearly implied by the preceding sentence or clearly understood without being stated.

EXAMPLES	In view of these facts, is new equipment really necessary? *Or economical?*
	You can use the one-minute long-distance rates any time between eleven at night and eight in the morning. *Any night of the week.*

Minor sentences are elliptical expressions that are equivalent to complete sentences because the missing words are obvious to a reader from the context.

EXAMPLES	Why not?
	How much?
	Ten dollars.
	At last!
	This way, please.
	So much for that idea.

Although they are common in advertising copy and fictional dialogue, minor sentences are not normally appropriate to business or technical writing.

Dangling and misplaced modifiers.   A *dangling modifier* is a word or phrase that has no clear word or subject to modify. Most dangling modifiers are phrases with verbals (gerunds, participles, and infinitives). Correct this problem by adding the appropriate noun or pronoun for the phrase to modify or by making the phrase into a clause.

REVISE	After finishing the negotiations, dinner was relaxing.
TO	After finishing the negotiations, we relaxed at dinner.
REVISE	Entering the gate, the administration building is visible.
TO	As you enter the gate, the administration building is visible.

A *misplaced modifier* refers, or appears to refer, to the wrong word or phrase. The misplaced element can be a word, a phrase, or a clause.

REVISE	Our copier was used to duplicate materials for other departments that needed to be reduced.
TO	Our copier was used to duplicate materials that needed to be reduced for other departments.

You can avoid this problem by placing modifiers as close as possible to the words they modify. Position each modifier carefully so that it says what you mean.

EXAMPLES	We *just* bought the property for expansion.
	We bought *just* the property for expansion.

A *squinting modifier* is ambiguous because it is located between two sentence elements and might refer to either one. To correct the problem, move the modifier or revise the sentence.

REVISE	The union agreed during the next week to return to work.
TO	During the next week, the union agreed to return to work.
OR	The union agreed to return to work during the next week.

Other sentence faults.   The assertion made by the predicate of a sentence about its subject must be logical.

REVISE	Mr. Wilson's *job* is a salesman.
TO	*Mr. Wilson* is a salesman.
REVISE	Jim's *height* is six feet tall.
TO	*Jim* is six feet tall.

Do not omit a required verb.

REVISE	The floor is swept and the lights out.
TO	The floor is swept, and the lights *are* out.
REVISE	I never have and probably never will write the annual report.
TO	I never have *written* and probably never will write the annual report.

Do not omit a subject.

REVISE	Although he regarded price-fixing as wrong, he engaged in it until abolished by law.
TO	Although he regarded price-fixing as wrong, he engaged in it until *it was* abolished by law.

Avoid compound sentences containing clauses with little or no logical relationship to each other.

| REVISE | My department is responsible for all company publications, and the staff includes twenty writers, three artists, and four typists. |
| TO | My department is responsible for all company publications. The staff includes twenty writers, three artists, and four typists. |

Effective Sentences

Effective sentences guide and engage a reader's attention. They can alert a reader to ideas weighted equally (through parallel structure) or differently (through subordination). In addition, carefully constructed and revised sentences clarify ideas for the reader. Besides alerting a reader to especially significant information, sentences can be varied in length, pattern, and style to avoid boring a reader. Most writers wait until they are revising to concentrate on effective sentences. Then, they can try to eliminate confusion and monotony by building clear, precise, and varied sentences.

Sentence parallelism.   Express coordinate ideas in similar form. The very construction of a sentence with parallel elements helps the reader to grasp the similarity of its parts.

| EXAMPLE | Similarly, atoms come and go in a molecule, but the molecule remains; molecules come and go in a cell, but the cell remains; cells come and go in a body, but the body remains; persons come and go in an organization, but the organization remains.[2] |

Emphatic sentences.   Subordinate your minor ideas to emphasize your more important ideas.

| REVISE | We had all arrived, and we began the meeting early. |
| TO | Since we had all arrived, we began the meeting early. |

The most emphatic positions within a sentence are the beginning and the end. Do not waste them by burying the main idea in the middle of the sentence between less important points or by tacking on phrases and clauses almost as afterthoughts. For example, consider the following original and revised versions of a statement written for a company's annual report to its stockholders.

| REVISE | Sales declined by 3 percent in 1975, but nevertheless the company had the most profitable year in its history, thanks to cost savings that resulted from design improvements in several of our major products; and we expect 1976 to be even better, since further design improvements are being made. (The sentence begins with the bad news, buries the good news, and trails off at the end.) |

[2] Kenneth Boulding, *Beyond Economics* (Ann Arbor: University of Michigan Press, 1968), p. 131.

TO   .   Cost savings from design improvements in several major products not only offset a 3-percent sales decline but made 1975 the most profitable year in the company's history. Further design improvements now in progress promise to make 1976 even more profitable. (The sentence beginnings emphasize *cost savings* and *design improvements;* the ends stress profits. The middle of the first sentence buries *sales decline.*)

Reversing the normal word order is also used to achieve emphasis.

EXAMPLES   I will never agree to that.

That I will never agree to.

Never will I agree to that.

Clear sentences.   Uncomplicated sentences most clearly state complex ideas. If readers must unravel a complicated sentence in addition to a complex idea, they are likely to become confused.

REVISE   Burning fuel and air in the production chamber causes an expansion of the gases formed by combustion, which in turn pushes the piston down in its cylinder so that the crankshaft rotates and turns the flywheel, which then transmits to the clutch the power developed by the engine.

TO   Burning fuel and air in the production chamber causes an expansion of the gases formed by combustion. These gases push the piston down in its cylinder so that the crankshaft rotates. Then the flywheel on the end of the crankshaft transmits to the clutch the power developed by the engine.

Just as simpler sentences can make complex ideas easier to understand, so more complex sentences can make groups of simple ideas easier to read.

REVISE   The industrial park was designed carefully. A team of architects and landscape designers planned it. It has become a local landmark.

TO   The carefully designed industrial park, planned by a team of architects and landscape designers, has become a local landmark.

Sentence length.   Varying sentence length makes writing more interesting to the reader because many sentences of the same length become monotonous.

Short sentences often can be combined effectively by converting verbs to adjectives.

REVISE   The steeplejack was *exhausted.* He collapsed on the scaffolding.

TO   The *exhausted* steeplejack collapsed on the scaffolding.

Sentences that string together short, independent clauses may be just as tedious as a series of short sentences. Either connect such clauses with subordinating connectives, thereby making some dependent, or turn some clauses into separate sentences.

REVISE   This river is 60 miles long, *and* it averages 50 yards in width, *and* its depth averages 8 feet.

TO   This river, *which* is 60 miles long and averages 50 yards in width, has an average depth of 8 feet.

OR   This river is 60 miles long. It averages 50 yards in width and 8 feet in depth.

Although too many short sentences make your writing sound choppy and immature, a short sentence can be effective at the end of a passage of long ones.

EXAMPLE   I believe that man is about to learn that the most practical life is the moral life and that the moral life is the only road to survival. He is beginning to learn that he will either share part of his material wealth or lose all of it; that he will respect and learn to live with other political ideologies if he wants civilization to go on. This is the kind of argument that man's actual experience equips him to understand and accept. *This is the low road to morality. There is no other.*[3]

In general, short sentences are good for emphatic statements. Long sentences are good for detailed explanations and support. Nothing is wrong with a long sentence, or even with a complicated one, as long as its meaning is clear and direct. Either a noticeably short or long sentence can be used to good effect because its length will draw the reader's attention. When varied for emphasis or contrast, sentence length becomes an element of style.

Word order.   When successive sentences all begin in exactly the same way, the result is likely to be monotonous. You can make your sentences more interesting by occasionally starting with a modifying word, phrase, or clause. This could be a single adjective, adverb, participle, or infinitive; it could be a prepositional phrase, a participial phrase, or an infinitive phrase; or it could be a subordinate clause.

EXAMPLES   *Fatigued,* the project director slumped into a chair. (adjective)
                Lately, our division has been very productive. (adverb)
                Smiling, he extended his hand to the irate customer. (participle)
                To learn, you must observe and ask questions. (infinitive)
                Work having already begun, there was little we could do. (absolute construction)

[3] Saul Alinsky, *Rules for Radicals* (New York: Random House, 1971), p. 25.

In the morning, we will finish the report. (prepositional phrase)

Following the manual, she located and repaired the faulty parts. (participial phrase)

To reach the top job, she introduced constructive alternatives to unsuccessful policies. (infinitive phrase)

Because we now know the results of the survey, we may proceed with certainty. (adverb clause)

Overdoing this technique can also be monotonous; use it with moderation.

Be careful in your sentences to avoid confusing separations of subjects and verbs, prepositions and objects, and the parts of verb phrases. Your reader expects these patterns and reads more quickly and easily when they are clear.

REVISE   The manager worked closely with, despite personality differences, the head engineer. (preposition and object separated)

TO   Despite personality differences, the manager worked closely with the head engineer.

This is not to say, however, that subject and verb never should be separated by a modifying phrase or clause.

EXAMPLE   John Stoddard, who founded the firm in 1943, is still an active partner.

Vary the position of modifiers in your sentences to achieve variety as well as different emphases or meanings. The following examples illustrate four different ways the same sentence could be written by varying the position of its modifiers.

EXAMPLES   Gently, with the square end up, slip the blasting cap down over the time fuse.

With the square end up, gently slip the blasting cap down over the time fuse.

With the square end up, slip the blasting cap gently down over the time fuse.

With the square end up, slip the blasting cap down over the time fuse gently.

Loose and periodic sentences.   A loose sentence makes its major point at the beginning and then adds subordinate phrases and clauses that develop the major point. You express yourself most naturally and easily in this pattern. A loose sentence could end at one or more points before it actually ends, as the periods in parentheses illustrate in the following example.

EXAMPLES   It went up (.), a great ball of fire about a mile in diameter(.), an elemental force freed from its bonds(.) after being chained for billions of years.[4]

A compound sentence is generally classed as loose since it could end after its first independent clause.

EXAMPLE   Copernicus is frequently called the first modern astronomer; he was the first to develop a complete astronomical system based on the motion of the earth.

Complex sentences are loose if their subordinate clauses follow their main clauses.

EXAMPLE   The installation will not be completed on schedule(.) because heavy spring rains delayed construction.

A periodic sentence delays its main idea until the end by presenting subordinate ideas or modifiers first. Skillfully handled, a periodic sentence lends force, or emphasis, to the main point by arousing the reader's anticipation and then presenting the main point as a climax.

EXAMPLE   During the last decade or so, the attitude of the American citizen toward automation has undergone a profound change.

Do not use periodic sentences too frequently, however, for overuse may irritate a reader who tires of waiting for your point. Likewise, avoid the sing-song monotony of a long series of loose sentences, particularly a series containing coordinate clauses joined by conjunctions. Instead, experiment in your writing, especially during revision, with shifts from loose sentences to periodic sentences.

PARAGRAPHS

A paragraph is a group of sentences that supports and develops a single idea; like an essay in miniature, it expands upon the central idea stated in its topic sentence (*italicized*).

> *The arithmetic of searching for oil is stark.* For all his scientific methods of detection, the only way the oilman can actually know for sure that there is oil in the ground is to drill a well. The average cost of drilling an oil well is over $100,000, and drilling a single well may cost over $1,000,000! And once the well is drilled, the odds against its containing any oil at all are 8 to 1![5]

Paragraphs perform three essential functions: (1) they develop the central ideas stated in their topic sentences; (2) they break material into logical units;

[4] William L. Laurence
[5] *The Baker World,* Baker Oil Tools, Inc.

and (3) they create physical breaks on the page, which visually assist the reader.

Topic Sentences

A topic sentence states the central idea of a paragraph; the rest of the paragraph then supports and develops that statement with pertinent details.

The topic sentence is most often the first sentence of the paragraph. It is effective in this position because it lets the reader know immediately what subject the paragraph will develop.

> *The fundamental conception of statistics is that of an infinitely large series of measurements, or population.* Since all observable data is subject to influence by uncontrollable and variable change factors, the values recorded in a series of measurements exhibit corresponding variations. If the mean value is calculated the individual values will be seen to be more or less closely distributed around it. Since the chance factors operate equally in a positive or negative fashion, the distribution is symmetrical. The larger the number of measurements the closer will mean value approach the "true" value of the measured object. Only with an infinite number of measurements, however, will it be identical with the "true" value.[6]

On rare occasions, the topic sentence logically falls in the middle of a paragraph.

> It is perhaps natural that psychologists should awaken only slowly to the possibility that behavioral processes may be directly observed, or that they should only gradually put the older statistical and theoretical techniques in their proper perspective. But it is time to insist that science does not progress by carefully designed steps called "experiments," each of which has a well-defined beginning and end. *Science is a continuous and often a disorderly and accidental process.* We shall not do the young psychologist any favor if we agree to reconstruct our practices to fit the pattern demanded by current scientific methodology. What the statistician means by the design of experiments is design which yields the kind of data to which *his* techniques are applicable. He does not mean the behavior of the scientist in his laboratory devising research for his own immediate and possibly inscrutable purposes.[7]

Although the topic sentence is usually most effective early in the paragraph, a paragraph can lead up to the topic sentence to achieve emphasis. When a topic sentence ends a paragraph, it also can serve as a summary or conclusion, based on the details that were designed to lead up to it.

[6] *Documenta Geigy,* 5th ed. (Ardsley, N.Y.: Geigy Pharmaceuticals, 1956), p. 31.
[7] B. F. Skinner, "A Case History in Scientific Method," *The American Psychologist,* 2 (May 1956), 232.

Energy does far more than simply make our daily lives more comfortable and convenient. Suppose you wanted to stop—and reverse—the economic progress of this nation. What would be the surest and quickest way to do it? Find a way to cut off the nation's oil resources! Industrial plants would shut down; public utilities would stand idle; all forms of transportation would halt. The country would be paralyzed, and our economy would plummet into the abyss of national economic ruin. *Our economy, in short, is energy-based.*[8]

Because several paragraphs are sometimes necessary to develop different aspects of an idea, not all paragraphs have topic sentences. In this situation, transition between paragraphs is especially important so the reader knows that the same idea is being developed through several paragraphs.

To conserve valuable memory space, a large portion of the software package remains on disk; only the most frequently used portion resides in internal memory all of the time. The disk-resident software is organized into small modules that are called into memory as needed to perform specific functions.

Transition

The disk-resident portion of the operating system contains routines that are used less frequently in system operation, such as the peripheral-related software routines that are used for correcting errors encountered on the various units, and the log and display routines that record unusual operating conditions in the system log. The disk-resident portion of the operating system also contains Monitor, the software program that supervised the loading of utility routines and the user's programs.

Transition

The memory-resident portion of the operating system maintains strict control of processing. It consists of routines, subroutines, lists, and tables that are used to perform common program functions, such as processing input/output operations, calling other software routines from disk as needed, and processing errors.[9]

In this example, the idea expressed in the topic sentence is developed in three paragraphs, rather than one, so that the reader can more easily assimilate the two separate parts of the main idea.

Paragraph Coherence and Unity

A good paragraph has unity and coherence. Unity means singleness of purpose, based on a topic sentence that states the central idea of the paragraph. When every sentence in the paragraph contributes to the central idea, the paragraph has unity. Coherence means being logically consistent throughout the paragraph so that all parts naturally connect with one another. Coherence is advanced by carefully chosen transitional words that tie together ideas as they are developed.

[8] *The Baker World,* Baker Oil Tools, Inc.
[9] *NCR Century Operating Systems Manual,* NCR Corporation.

Any company which operates internationally today faces a host of difficulties. Inflation is worldwide. Most countries are struggling with *other* economic problems *as well. In addition,* there are many monetary uncertainties and growing economic nationalism directed against multinational companies. *Yet* there is ample business available in most developed countries if you have the right products, services, and marketing organization. To maintain the growth NCR has achieved overseas, we recently restructured our international operations into four major trading areas. *This* will improve the services and support which the Corporation can provide to its subsidiaries around the world. *At the same time* it established firm management control, insuring consistent policies around the world. *So* you might say the problems of doing business abroad will be more difficult this year but we are better organized to meet those problems.[10]

Good paragraphs often use details from the previous paragraph, thereby preserving and advancing the thought being developed. Appropriate conjunctions and the repetition of key words and phrases can help to provide unity and coherence among, as well as within, paragraphs.

Six high power thyristors connected in a three-phase bridge configuration form the basic armature module. When necessary, the modules are paralleled to meet higher power requirements. The basic armature module is constructed as a convenient *pull-out tray.* All *armature trays* are interchangeable.

For optimum shovel performance it is also desirable to use thyristors in the control of motor fields. These smaller thyristors are also arranged in a *pull-out tray* arrangement called a *field tray.*

Should a fault *ever* occur in a tray, an *indicator tray* is provided, which by means of pilot lights indicates which tray is the source of the trouble. Through the *pull-out* tray concept, the mine electrician can quickly replace the faulty tray and need not troubleshoot.[11]

PUNCTUATION

Punctuation is a system of symbols that help the reader understand the structural relationships within (and the intention of) a sentence. Marks of punctuation may link, separate, enclose, terminate, classify, and indicate omissions from sentences. Most of the thirteen punctuation marks can perform more than one function. The use of punctuation is determined by grammatical conventions and the writer's intention. Misuse of punctuation can cause your reader to misunderstand your meaning. The following are the thirteen marks of punctuation.

[10] *1974 Annual Report,* NCR Corporation.
[11] Harnischfeger Corporation

apostrophe	,
brackets	[ ]
colon	:
comma	,
dash	—
exclamation mark	!
hyphen	-
parentheses	( )
period	. (including ellipses and leaders)
question mark	?
quotation marks	" " (including ditto marks)
semicolon	;
slash	/

COMMAS

The comma is used more often than any other mark of punctuation because it has such a wide variety of uses: it can link, enclose, separate, and show omissions. Effective use of the comma depends upon your understanding of how ideas fit together. Used with care, the comma can add clarity and emphasis to your writing; used carelessly, it can cause confusion.

To Link

Coordinating conjunctions (*and, but, for, or, so, nor, yet*) require a comma immediately preceding them when they are used to connect independent clauses.

EXAMPLE   Human beings have always prided themselves on their unique capacity to create and manipulate symbols, but today computers are manipulating symbols.

Independent clauses that are short and have single subjects and single predicates sometimes are exceptions to this rule. Although such a sentence does not require a comma preceding the coordinating conjunction, it usually includes a comma.

EXAMPLE   The cable snapped and the power failed.

OR   The cable snapped, and the power failed.

To Enclose

Commas are used to enclose nonrestrictive and parenthetical sentence elements. Nonrestrictive elements provide additional, nonessential information about the things they modify; parenthetical elements insert extra information into the sentence. Each is set off by commas to show its loose relationship with the rest of the sentence.

EXAMPLES   Our new Detroit factory, *which began operations last month,* should add 25 percent to total output. (nonrestrictive clause)

We can, *of course,* expect their lawyer to call us. (parenthetical element)

Similarly, commas enclose nonrestrictive participial phrases.

EXAMPLE   The lathe operator, *working quickly and efficiently,* finished early.

Phrases in apposition (which follow and amplify another expression) are enclosed in commas.

EXAMPLE   Our company, *the Blaylok Precision Company,* is doing well this year.

A direct address should be enclosed in commas.

EXAMPLE   You will note, *Mark,* that the surface of the brake shoe complies with the specifications.

To Separate

Commas are used to separate introductory elements from the rest of the sentence, to separate items from each other, to separate subordinate clauses from main clauses, and to separate certain elements for clarity or emphasis.

To separate introductory elements.   In general, use a comma after an introductory clause or phrase unless it is very short. This helps indicate to a reader where the main part of the sentence begins.

EXAMPLE   *Since many rare fossils never occur free from their matrix,* it is wise to scan every slab with a hand lens.

When long modifying phrases precede the main clause, they should always be followed by a comma.

EXAMPLE   *During the first field-performance tests last year at our Colorado proving ground,* the new motor failed to meet our expectations.

When an introductory phrase is short and closely related to the main clause, the comma may be omitted.

EXAMPLE   *In two seconds* a 20° temperature is created in the test tube.

Certain types of introductory words must be followed by a comma. One such is a noun used in direct address.

EXAMPLE   *Bill,* here is the statement you asked me to audit.

A mild introductory interjection (such as *oh, well, why, indeed, yes,* and *no*) must be followed by a comma.

EXAMPLES   *Yes,* I will make sure your request is approved.

                Indeed, I will be glad to send you further information.

An introductory adverb, like *moreover* or *furthermore,* must be followed by a comma.

EXAMPLE   *Moreover,* this policy will improve our balance of payments.

Occasionally, when adverbs are closely connected to the meaning of an entire sentence, they should not be followed by a comma. (Test such sentences by reading them aloud. If you pause after the adverb, use the comma.)

EXAMPLE   *Perhaps* we can still solve the environmental problem. *Certainly* we should try.

To separate items from each other.   Commas should be used to separate words in a series.

EXAMPLE   Basically, plants control the wind by *obstruction, guidance, deflection,* and *filtration.*

Phrases and clauses in coordinate series, like words, are punctuated with commas.

EXAMPLE   It is well known that plants absorb noxious gases, act as receptors of dust and dirt particles, and cleanse the air of other impurities.

   Although the comma before the last word in a series is sometimes omitted, it is generally clearer to include it. The following sentence illustrates the confusion that may result from omitting the comma.

EXAMPLE   Random House, Allyn and Bacon, Doubleday and Dell are publishing companies. (Is "Doubleday and Dell" one company or two? "Random House, Allyn and Bacon, Doubleday, and Dell" removes the doubt.)

When adjectives modifying the same noun can be reversed and make sense, or when they can be separated by *and* or *or,* they should be separated by commas.

EXAMPLE   The *dull, cracked* tools needed to be repaired.

When an adjective modifies a noun phrase, no comma is required.

EXAMPLE   He was wearing his *old cotton tennis hat.* (*old* modifies the noun phrase *cotton tennis hat; cotton* modifies the noun phrase *tennis hat.*)

Never separate a final adjective from its noun.

REVISE   He is a conscientious, honest, reliable, worker.

TO   He is a conscientious, honest, reliable worker.

Commas are conventionally used to separate distinct items. Use commas between the elements of an address written on the same line.

EXAMPLE   Walter James, 4119 Mill Road, Dayton, Ohio 45401

Use a comma to separate the elements of a date written on the same line. When the day is omitted, however, the comma is unnecessary.

EXAMPLES   July 2, 1949
                      July 1949

Use commas to separate the elements of Arabic numbers.

EXAMPLE   1,528,200

Use a comma after the salutation of a personal letter.

EXAMPLE   Dear John,

Use commas to separate the elements of geographical names.

EXAMPLE   Toronto, Ontario, Canada

Use a comma to separate names that are reversed.

EXAMPLE   Smith, Alvin

To separate subordinate clauses. Use a comma between the main clause and a subordinate clause when the subordinate clause comes first.

EXAMPLE   While the angry crowd outside the embassy waited, the ambassador drank cocktails.

Use a comma following an independent clause that is only loosely related to the dependent clause that follows it.

EXAMPLE   The plan should be finished by July, even though I lost time because of illness.

In all cases, use a comma following a long introductory dependent clause.

EXAMPLE   By artificially stimulating the electrochemical action of the brain, scientists have learned more about the brain in the past two decades than ever before.

To separate elements for clarity or emphasis. Two contrasting thoughts or ideas can be separated by commas for emphasis.

EXAMPLES   The project was finished on time, but not within the cost limits.

The specifications call for 100-ohm resistors, not 1000-ohm resistors.

It was Bill, not Matt, who suggested that the names be changed.

Use a comma to separate a direct quotation from its introduction.

EXAMPLE   Morton and Lucia White said, "Men live in cities but dream of the countryside."

Do not use a comma, however, when giving an indirect quotation.

EXAMPLE   Morton and Lucia White said that men dream of the countryside even though they live in cities.

Sometimes commas are used simply to make something clear that might otherwise be confusing.

REVISE   The year after Xerox and 3M outproduced all the competition.
TO   The year after, Xerox and 3M outproduced all the competition.

If you need a comma to separate the consecutive uses of the same word, rewrite the sentence.

REVISE   The assets we had, had surprised us.
TO   We were surprised at the assets we had.

To Show Omissions

In certain coordinate constructions, a comma can replace a missing, but implied, sentence element.

EXAMPLE   Some were punctual; *others, late.* (replaces *were*)

Conventional Use With Other Punctuation

A comma always goes inside quotation marks.

EXAMPLE   Although he called his presentation "adequate," the audience thought it was superb.

Except with abbreviations, a comma should not be used with a period, question mark, exclamation mark, or dash.

REVISE   "I have finished the project.," he said.
TO   "I have finished the project," he said. (omit the period)
REVISE   "Have you finished the project?," I asked.
TO   "Have you finished the project?" I asked. (omit the comma)

Comma Problems

The most frequent comma problems are the comma fault and the use of superfluous commas.

Comma faults. Do not attempt to join two independent clauses with only a comma; this is called a "comma splice" or "comma fault."

REVISE   The new medical plan was comprehensive, the union negotiator was pleased.

Such a comma fault could be corrected in several ways.
Substitute a semicolon.

TO   The new medical plan was comprehensive; the union negotiator was pleased.

Add a conjunctive adverb preceded by a semicolon and followed by a comma.

TO   The new medical plan was comprehensive; *therefore,* the union negotiator was pleased.

Add a conjunction following the comma.

TO   The new medical plan was comprehensive, *so* the union negotiator was pleased.

Create two sentences. (Be aware, however, that putting a period between two closely related and brief statements may result in two weak sentences.)

TO   The new medical plan was comprehensive. The union negotiator was pleased.

Subordinate one clause to the other.

TO   *Because* the new medical plan was comprehensive, the union negotiator was pleased.

Superfluous commas. A number of common writing errors involve placing commas where they do not belong. These errors often occur because writers assume that a pause in a sentence should be indicated by a comma. It is true that commas usually signal pauses, but it is not true that pauses *necessarily* call for commas.

Be careful not to place a comma between a subject and verb or between a verb and its object.

REVISE   The extremely wet weather throughout the country, makes spring planting difficult.

TO   The extremely wet weather throughout the country makes spring planting difficult.

REVISE   The advertising department employs, four writers, two artists, and one photographer.

TO   The advertising department employs four writers, two artists, and one photographer.

Do not use a comma between the elements of a compound subject or a compound predicate consisting of only two elements.

REVISE   The chairman of the board, and the president prepared the press release.

TO   The chairman of the board and the president prepared the press release.

REVISE   The production manager revised the work schedules, and improved morale.

TO   The production manager revised the work schedules and improved morale.

Placing a comma after a coordinating conjunction (such as *and* or *but*) is an especially common error.

REVISE   We doubled our sales, and, we reduced our costs.

TO   We doubled our sales, and we reduced our costs.

REVISE   We doubled our sales, but, we still did not dominate the market.

TO   We doubled our sales, but we still did not dominate the market.

Do not place a comma before the first item or after the last item of a series.

REVISE   We are purchasing new office furniture, including, desks, chairs, and tables.

TO   We are purchasing new office furniture, including desks, chairs, and tables.

REVISE   She was an efficient, reliable, worker.

TO   She was an efficient, reliable worker.

SEMICOLONS

The semicolon links independent clauses or other sentence elements of equal weight and grammatical rank. The semicolon indicates a greater pause between clauses than a comma would, but not so great a pause as a period would.

When the independent clauses of a compound sentence are not joined by a comma and a conjunction, they are linked by a semicolon.

EXAMPLE   No one applied for the position; the job was too difficult.

Make sure, however, that the relationship between the two statements is so clear that a reader will understand why they are linked without further explanation. Often, such clauses balance or contrast with each other.

EXAMPLE   Our last supervisor allowed only one long break each afternoon; our new supervisor allows two short ones.

Use a semicolon between two main clauses connected by a coordinating conjunction (*and, but, for, or, nor, yet*) if the clauses are long and contain other punctuation.

EXAMPLE   In most cases these individuals are corporate executives, bankers, Wall Street lawyers; but they do not, as the economic determinists seem to believe, simply push the button of their economic power to affect fields remote from economics.[12]

A semicolon should be used before conjunctive adverbs (such as *therefore, moreover, consequently, furthermore, indeed, in fact, however*) that connect independent clauses.

EXAMPLE   I won't finish today; moreover, I doubt that I will finish this week.

The semicolon in this example shows that *moreover* belongs to the second clause.

Do not use a semicolon between a dependent clause and its main clause. Remember that elements joined by semicolons must be of equal grammatical rank or weight.

REVISE   No one applied for the position; even though it was heavily advertised.

TO   No one applied for the position, even though it was heavily advertised.

A semicolon may also be used to separate items in a series when they contain commas within them.

EXAMPLE   Among those present were John Howard, president of the Omega Paper Company; Carol Martin, president of Alpha Corporation; and Larry Stanley, president of Stanley Papers.

COLONS

The colon is a mark of anticipation and introduction that alerts the reader to the close connection between the first statement and the one following.

[12] Robert Lubar, "The Prime Movers," *Fortune* (February 1960), p. 98.

A colon may be used to connect a clause, word, or phrase to the list or series that follows it.

EXAMPLE   We carry three brands of watches: Timex, Bulova, and Omega.

A colon may be used to introduce an indented or centered list.

EXAMPLE   The following corporations manufacture computers:
Univac   Control Data Corporation
NCR Corporation   IBM
Burroughs   Honeywell

Do not, however, place a colon between a verb and its objects.

REVISE   The three fluids for cleaning pipettes are: water, alcohol, and acetone.

TO   The three fluids for cleaning pipettes are water, alcohol, and acetone.

Do not use a colon between a preposition and its object.

REVISE   I would like to be transferred to: Tucson, Boston, or Miami.

TO   I would like to be transferred to Tucson, Boston, or Miami.

A colon may be used to link one statement to another that develops, explains, amplifies, or illustrates the first. A colon may be used in this way to link two independent clauses.

EXAMPLE   Any large organization must confront two separate, though related, information problems: it must maintain an effective internal communication system, and it must maintain an effective external communication system.

Occasionally, a colon may be used to link an appositive phrase to its related statement if special emphasis is needed.

EXAMPLE   Only one thing will satisfy Mr. Sturgess: our finished report.

Colons are used to link numbers in Biblical references and time designations.

EXAMPLES   Genesis 10:16 (chapter 10, verse 16)
9:30 a.m.

In a ratio, the colon indicates the proportion of one amount to another. (The colon replaces *to.*)

EXAMPLE   The cement is mixed with the water and sand at a ratio of 7:5:14.
7:3 = 14:x

A colon follows the salutation in business letters.

EXAMPLES   Dear Ms. Jeffers:

Dear Sir:

Dear George:

The first word after a colon may be capitalized if the statement following is a complete sentence, a formal resolution or question, or a direct quotation.

EXAMPLE   This year's conference attendance was low: We did not advertise widely enough.

If a subordinate element follows the colon, however, use a lower-case letter following the colon.

EXAMPLE   There is only one way to stay within our present budget: to reduce expenditures for research and development.

PERIODS

A period (also called a full stop or an end stop) usually indicates the end of a declarative sentence. Periods also link (when used as leaders) and indicate omissions (when used as ellipses).

Uses of Periods

Although their primary function is to end declarative sentences, periods also end imperative sentences that are not emphatic enough for an exclamation mark.

EXAMPLE   Send me any information you may have on the subject.

Periods may also end questions that are really polite requests and questions that assume an affirmative response.

EXAMPLE   Will you please send me the specifications.

Periods end incomplete or minor sentences. These sentences are common in advertising but are rarely appropriate to business or technical writing.

EXAMPLE   Bell and Howell's new Double-Feature Cassette Projector will change your mind about home movies. *Because if you can press a button, now you can show movies. Instantly. Easily.*

Do not use a period after a declarative sentence that is quoted within another sentence.

REVISE	"The project has every chance of success." she stated.
TO	"The project has every chance of success," she stated.

A period, by convention, is placed inside quotation marks.

EXAMPLES   He liked to think of himself as a "tycoon."
He stated clearly, "My vote is yes."

Use periods after initials in names.

EXAMPLES   W. T. Grant, J. P. Morgan

Use periods as decimal points with numbers.

EXAMPLES   109.2, $540.26, 6.9%

Use periods to indicate abbreviations.

EXAMPLES   Ms., Dr., Inc.

Use periods following the numbers in numbered lists.

EXAMPLE   1.
2.
3.

Periods as Ellipses

When you omit words from quoted material, use a series of three spaced periods—called ellipsis marks—to indicate the omission. Such an omission must not change the essential meaning of the passage.

EXAMPLE   "Technical material distributed for promotional use is sometimes charged for, particularly in high-volume distribution to educational institutions, although prices for these publications are not uniformly based on the costs of developing them." (without omission)

"Technical material distributed for promotional use is sometimes charged for . . . although prices for these publications are not uniformly based on the costs of developing them." (with omission)

When introducing a quotation that begins in the middle of a sentence rather than at the beginning, you do not need ellipsis marks; the lower-case letter with which you begin the quotation already indicates an omission.

EXAMPLE   "When the programmer has determined a system of runs, he must create a systems flowchart to trace the data flow through the system." (without omission)

The booklet states that the programmer "must create a systems flowchart to trace the data flow through the system." (with omission)

If an ellipsis follows the end of a sentence, retain the period at the end of the sentence and add the three ellipsis marks to show the omission.

EXAMPLES   "During the year, every department participated in the development of a centralized computer system. The basic plan was to use the computer to reduce costs. At the beginning of the year, each department received a booklet explaining the purpose of the system." (without omission)

"During the year, every department participated in the development of a centralized computer system. . . . At the beginning of the year, each department received a booklet explaining the purpose of the system." (with omission)

Periods as Leaders

When spaced periods are used in a table to connect one item to another, they are called leaders. The purpose of leaders is to help the reader align the data.

EXAMPLE

Weight	Pressure
150 lbs.	1.7 psi
175 lbs.	2.8 psi
200 lbs.	3.9 psi

Period Fault

The incorrect use of a period is sometimes called a period fault. When a period is inserted prematurely, the result is a sentence fragment.

REVISE   After a long day at the office during which we finished the report. We left hurriedly for home.

TO   After a long day at the office during which we finished the report, we left hurriedly for home.

When a period is left out, the result is an incorrect fused (or run-on) sentence.

REVISE   The work plan showed the utility lines they might interfere with construction.

TO   The work plan showed the utility lines. They might interfere with construction.

QUESTION MARKS

The question mark (?) indicates questions. Use a question mark to end a sentence that is a direct question.

EXAMPLE   Where did you put the specification?

Use a question mark to end any statement with an interrogative meaning (a statement that is declarative in form but asks a question).

EXAMPLE   The report is finished?

Use a question mark to end an interrogative clause within a declarative sentence.

EXAMPLE   It was not until July (or was it August?) that we submitted the report.

When used with quotations, the question mark may indicate whether the writer who is doing the quoting or the person being quoted is asking the question. When the writer doing the quoting asks the question, the question mark is outside the quotation marks.

EXAMPLE   Did she say, "I don't think the project should continue"?

On the other hand, if the quotation itself is a question, the question mark goes inside the quotation marks.

EXAMPLE   She asked, "When will we go?"

If the writer doing the quoting and the person being quoted both ask questions, use a single question mark inside the quotation marks.

EXAMPLE   Did she ask, "Will you go in my place?"

Question marks may follow each item in a series within an interrogative sentence.

EXAMPLE   Do you remember the date of the contract? its terms? whether you signed it?

A question mark should never be used at the end of an indirect question.

REVISE   He asked me whether sales had increased this year?
TO   He asked me whether sales had increased this year.

When a directive or command is phrased as a question, a question mark usually is not used, but a request (to a customer or a superior, for instance) would almost always require a question mark.

EXAMPLES   Will you please make sure that the machinery is operational by August 15.

Will you please telephone me collect if your entire shipment does not arrive by June 10?

EXCLAMATION MARKS

The exclamation mark (!) indicates an expression of strong feeling. It can signal surprise, fear, indignation, or excitement but should not be used for trivial emotions or mild surprise. Exclamation marks cannot make an argument more convincing, lend force to a weak statement, or call attention to an intended irony—no matter how many are stacked like fence posts at the end of a sentence.

The most common use of an exclamation mark is after an interjection, phrase, clause, or sentence to indicate strong emotion.

EXAMPLES   Ouch! Oh! Stop! Hurry!

The subject of this meeting—note it well!—is our budget deficit.

The gas line is leaking! Clear the building!

When used with quotation marks, the exclamation mark goes outside unless what is quoted is an exclamation.

EXAMPLE   The boss yelled, "Get in here!" Then Ben said, "No, sir"!

PARENTHESES

Parentheses ( ) are used to enclose words, phrases, or sentences. Parentheses can suggest intimacy, implying that something is shared between the writer and the reader. Parentheses de-emphasize (or play down) an inserted element. The material within parentheses can clarify a statement without changing its meaning. Such information may not be essential to a sentence, but it may be interesting or helpful to some readers.

EXAMPLE   Aluminum is extracted from its ore (called bauxite) in three stages.

Parenthetical material pertains to the word or phrase immediately preceding it.

EXAMPLE   The development of IBM (International Business Machines) is an American success story.

Parentheses may be used to enclose the figures or letters that mark items in a sequence or list. When they appear within a sentence, enclose the figures or letters with two parentheses rather than only one parenthesis.

EXAMPLE   The following sections deal with (1) preparation, (2) research, (3) organization, (4) writing, and (5) revision.

Parenthetical material does not change the punctuation of a sentence. A comma following a parenthetical word, phrase, or clause appears outside the closing parenthesis.

EXAMPLE   These oxygen-rich chemicals, including potassium permanganate (KM_nO_4) and potassium chromate ($KCrO_4$), were oxidizing agents.

If a parenthesis closes a sentence, the ending punctuation appears after the parenthesis. When a complete sentence within parentheses stands independently, however, the ending punctuation goes inside the final parenthesis.

EXAMPLES   The institute was founded by Harry Denman (1902 – 1972).

The project director outlined the challenges facing her staff. (This was her third report to the board.)

Use parentheses with care because they are easily overused. Avoid using parentheses where other marks of punctuation are more appropriate.

HYPHENS

The hyphen functions primarily as a spelling device. The most common use of the hyphen is to join compound words. Check your dictionary if you are uncertain about whether to hyphenate a word.

EXAMPLES   able-bodied, self-contained, carry-all, brother-in-law

A hyphen is used to form compound numbers and fractions when they are written out.

EXAMPLES   twenty-one, one-fifth

Two-word and three-word unit modifiers that express a single thought are frequently hyphenated when they precede a noun (a *clear-cut* decision). If each of the words could modify the noun without the aid of the other modifying word or words, however, do not use a hyphen (a *new digital* computer—no hyphen). If the first word is an adverb ending in *-ly,* do not use a hyphen (*hardly* used, *badly* needed). Finally, do not hyphenate such modifying phrases when they follow the nouns they modify.

EXAMPLES   Our office equipment is *out of date.*

Our *out-of-date* office equipment will be replaced next month.

A hyphen is always used as part of a letter or number modifier.

EXAMPLES   15-cent stamp, 9-inch ruler, H-bomb, T-square

When each item in a series of unit modifiers has the same term following the hyphen, this term need not be repeated throughout the series. For smoothness and brevity, add the term only to the last item in the sequence.

REVISE   The third-floor, fourth-floor, and fifth-floor rooms have been painted.

TO   The third-, fourth-, and fifth-floor rooms have been painted.

When a prefix precedes a proper noun, use a hyphen to connect the two.

EXAMPLES   pre-Sputnik, anti-Stalinist, post-Newtonian

A hyphen may (but not must) be used when the prefix ends and the root word begins with the same vowel. When the repeated vowel is *i,* a hyphen is almost always used.

EXAMPLES   re-elect, re-enter, anti-inflationary

A hyphen is used when ex- means "former."

EXAMPLES   ex-partners, ex-wife

The suffix *-elect* is connected to the word it follows with a hyphen.

EXAMPLES   president-elect, commissioner-elect

Hyphens identify prefixes, suffixes, or syllables written as such.

EXAMPLE   *Re-, -ism,* and *ex-* are word parts that cause spelling problems.

Hyphens should be used between letters showing how a word is spelled (or misspelled).

EXAMPLE   In his letter, he spelled "believed" b-e-l-e-i-v-e-d.

To avoid confusion, some words and modifiers should always be hyphenated. *Re-cover* does not mean the same thing as *recover,* for example; the same is true of *re-sent* and *resent, re-form* and *reform, re-sign* and *resign.*

A hyphen can stand for *to* or *through* between letters, numbers, and locations.

EXAMPLES   pp. 44-46
the Detroit-Toledo Expressway
A-L and M-Z

Finally, hyphens are used to divide words at the ends of typed or printed lines. Words are divided on the basis of their syllables, which can be determined with a dictionary. If you cannot check a word in a dictionary, pronounce the word to test whether each section is pronounceable. Never divide a word so near the end that only one or two letters remain to begin your next typed line. If a word is spelled with a hyphen, divide it only at the hyphen break unless this division would confuse the reader. In general, unless the length of your typed line will appear awkward, avoid dividing words.

QUOTATION MARKS

Quotation marks ("   ") are used to enclose direct repetition of spoken or written words. Under normal circumstances, they should not be used to show emphasis. Enclose in quotation marks anything that is quoted word for word (direct quotation) from speech.

EXAMPLE   She said clearly, "I want the progress report by three o'clock."

Do not enclose indirect quotations—usually introduced by *that*—in quotation marks. Indirect quotations paraphrase a speaker's words or ideas.

EXAMPLE   She said that she wanted the progress report by three o'clock.

Handle quotations from written material the same way: place direct quotations within quotation marks, but not indirect quotations.

EXAMPLES   The report stated, "During the last five years in Florida, our franchise has grown from 28 to 157 locations."
The report indicated that our franchise now has 157 locations in Florida.

When a quotation is longer than five typed lines, single-space and indent each line five spaces from the left margin. Do not enclose the quotation in quotation marks.

Use single quotation marks (the apostrophe key on a typewriter) to enclose a quotation that appears within another quotation.

EXAMPLE   John said, "Jane told me that she was going to 'hang in there' until the deadline is past."

Slang, colloquial expressions, and attempts at humor, although infrequent in business and technical writing in any case, seldom rate being set off by quotation marks.

REVISE   Our first six months in the new office amounted to little more than a "shakedown cruise" for what lay ahead.
TO   Our first six months in the new office amounted to little more than a shakedown cruise for what lay ahead.

Use quotation marks to point out that particular words or technical terms are used in context for a special purpose.

EXAMPLE   The "plumbers," a White House undercover organization, was set up to stop "leaks."

Use quotation marks to enclose titles of short stories, articles, essays, radio and television programs, short musical works, paintings, and other art works.

EXAMPLE   Did you see the article "No-Fault Insurance and Your Motor-cycle" in last Sunday's *Journal?*

Titles of books and periodicals are underlined (to be typeset in italics).

EXAMPLE   Articles in the <u>Business Education Forum</u> and <u>Scientific American</u> quoted the same passage.

Some titles, by convention, are neither set off by quotation marks nor under-lined, although they are capitalized.

EXAMPLES   the Bible, the Constitution, the Gettysburg Address

Commas and periods always go inside closing quotation marks.

EXAMPLE   "We hope," said Ms. Abrams, "that the merger will be an-nounced this week."

Semicolons and colons always go outside closing quotation marks.

EXAMPLES   He said, "I will pay the full amount"; this was a real surprise to us.

The following are his favorite "sports": eating and sleeping.

All other punctuation follows the logic of the context: if the punctuation is part of the material quoted, it goes inside the quotation marks; if the punctuation is not part of the material quoted, it goes outside the quotation marks.

Quotation marks may be used as ditto marks, instead of repeating a line of words or numbers directly beneath an identical set. In formal writing, this use is confined to tables and lists.

EXAMPLE   A is at a point equally distant from L and M.
B " " " "   "   "   " S and T.
C " " " "   "   "   " R and Q.

DASHES

The dash (—) is a versatile, yet limited, mark of punctuation. It is versatile be-cause it can perform all the functions of punctuation (to link, to separate, to enclose, and to show omission). It is limited because it is an especially em-phatic mark that is easily overused. Use the dash cautiously, therefore, to indi-cate more informality, emphasis, or abruptness than the conventional punc-tuation marks would show. In some situations, a dash is required; in others, a dash is a forceful substitute for other marks.

A dash can indicate a sharp turn in thought.

EXAMPLE   That is the end of the project—unless the company provides additional funds.

A dash can indicate an emphatic pause.

EXAMPLE   Consider the potential danger of a household item that contains mercury—a very toxic substance.

Sometimes, to emphasize contrast, a dash is also used with *but*.

EXAMPLE   We may have produced work more quickly—but our results have never been as impressive as these.

A dash can be used before a final summarizing statement or before repetition that has the effect of an afterthought.

EXAMPLE   It was hot near the ovens—steaming hot.

Such a thought may also complete the meaning of the sentence.

EXAMPLE   We try to speak as we write—or so we believe.

A dash can be used to set off an explanatory or appositive series.

EXAMPLE   Three of the applicants—John Evans, Mary Stevens, and Thomas Brown—seem well qualified for the job.

Dashes set off parenthetical elements more sharply and emphatically than do commas. Unlike dashes, parentheses tend to reduce the importance of what they enclose. Contrast the following sentences.

EXAMPLES   Only one person—the president—can authorize such activity.
Only one person, the president, can authorize such activity.
Only one person (the president) can authorize such activity.

Use dashes for clarity when commas appear within a parenthetical element; this avoids the confusion of too many commas.

EXAMPLE   Retinal images are patterns in the eye—made up of light and dark shapes, in addition to areas of color—but we do not see patterns: we see objects.

A dash can be used to show the omission of words or letters.

EXAMPLE   Mr. A— told me to be careful.

The first word after a dash is never capitalized unless it is a proper name. When typing, use two consecutive hyphens (--) to indicate a dash.

APOSTROPHES

The apostrophe (') is used to show possession, to mark the omission of letters, and to indicate the plural of Arabic numbers and letters.

Possession

An apostrophe is used with an *s* to form the possessive case of many nouns.

EXAMPLE   A recent scientific analysis of *New York City's* atmosphere con-
cluded that a New Yorker on the street inhaled toxic materials
equivalent to 38 cigarettes a day.

Singular nouns ending in *s* may form the possessive either by an apostrophe
alone or by *'s*.

EXAMPLES   a waitress' uniform, an actress' career
a waitress's uniform, an actress's career

Use only an apostrophe with plural nouns ending in *s*.

EXAMPLES   a managers' meeting, the technicians' handbook, a motorists'
rest stop

When a noun ends in multiple consecutive *s* sounds, form the possessive by
adding only an apostrophe.

EXAMPLES   Jesus' disciples, Moses' sojourn

With word groups and compound nouns, add the *'s* to the last noun.

EXAMPLE   My daughter-in-law's business has been thriving.

With a series of nouns, the last noun takes the possessive form to show joint
possession.

EXAMPLE   Michelson and *Morley's* famous experiment on the velocity of
light was made in 1887.

To show individual possession with a series of nouns, each noun should take
the possessive form.

EXAMPLE   *Bob's* and *Susan's* promotions will be announced Friday.

The apostrophe is not used with possessive pronouns. (*It's* is a contraction of
it is, not the possessive form of *it.*)

EXAMPLES   yours, its, his, ours, whose, theirs

In names of places and institutions, the apostrophe is usually omitted.

EXAMPLES   Harpers Ferry, Writers Book Club

Omission

An apostrophe is used to mark the omission of letters in a word or date.

EXAMPLES   can't, I'm, I'll

the class of '61

Plurals

Apostrophes are often used to indicate the plural forms of numbers.

EXAMPLES   5's, 30's, two 100's

An apostrophe and an *s* may be added to show the plural of a word as a word. (The word itself is underlined or italicized.)

EXAMPLE   There were five *and's* in his first sentence.

If a term consists entirely of capital letters or ends with a capital letter, however, the apostrophe is not required to form the plural.

EXAMPLES   The university awarded seven *Ph.D.s* in engineering last year.

He had included 43 *ADDs* in his computer program.

SLASHES

Although not always considered a mark of punctuation, the slash (/) performs punctuating functions by separating and showing omission. The slash is called various names: slant line, virgule, bar, shilling sign.

The slash is often used to separate parts of addresses in continuous writing.

EXAMPLE   The return address on the envelope was Ms. Rose Howard/62 W. Pacific Court/Claremont/California/91711.

The slash often indicates omitted words and letters.

EXAMPLES   miles/hour (for "miles per hour")

c/o (for "in care of")

w/o (for "without")

The slash separates the numerator from the denominator of a fraction.

EXAMPLES   2/3 (2 of 3 parts); 3/4 (3 of 4 parts); 27/32 (27 of 32 parts)

In informal writing, the slash is also used in dates to separate day from month and month from year.

EXAMPLE   2/29/79

The slash is sometimes used to indicate brackets when a typewriter has no bracket key.

EXAMPLE   The report stated that "the success of the affirmative action plan at the Westchester/New York/plant should be an inspiration for the industry."

BRACKETS

The primary use of brackets ([ ]) is to enclose a word or words inserted by an editor or writer into a quotation from another source.

EXAMPLE   He stated, "Wheat prices will continue to rise [no doubt because of the Russian wheat purchase] until next year."

Brackets are also used to set off a parenthetical item within parentheses.

EXAMPLE   We have all been inspired by the energy and creativity of our president, Roberta Jacobs (and her father, Frederick Jacobs [1910 – 1966]).

Index